studies in jazz

The Institute of Jazz Studies
Rutgers—The State University of New Jersey
General Editors: Dan Morgenstern and Edward Berger

Where the Dark and the Light Folks Meet

Race and the Mythology, Politics, and Business of Jazz

Studies in Jazz, No. 60

Randall Sandke

THE SCARECROW PRESS, INC.
Lanham • Toronto • Plymouth, UK
2010

Published by Scarecrow Press, Inc.
A wholly owned subsidiary of The Rowman & Littlefield Publishing Group, Inc.
4501 Forbes Boulevard, Suite 200, Lanham, Maryland 20706
http://www.scarecrowpress.com

Estover Road, Plymouth PL6 7PY, United Kingdom

British Library Cataloguing in Publication Information Available

Library of Congress Cataloging-in-Publication Data

Sandke, Randy.
  Where the dark and the light folks meet : race and the mythology, politics, and business of jazz / Randall Sandke.
     p. cm. — (Studies in jazz ; no. 60)
  Includes bibliographical references and index.
  ISBN 978-0-8108-6652-2 (cloth : alk. paper) — ISBN 978-0-8108-6990-5 (ebook)
  1. Jazz—History and criticism. 2. Jazz—Political aspects—United States. 3. Music and race—United States. I. Title.
  ML3508.S27 2010
  781.6509—dc22   2009037977

∞ ™ The paper used in this publication meets the minimum requirements of American National Standard for Information Sciences—Permanence of Paper for Printed Library Materials, ANSI/NISO Z39.48-1992.

Printed in the United States of America

This book is dedicated to the memory of those who were kind enough to let me interview them and who are no longer with us—musicians Harold Ashby, Johnny Blowers, Conte Candoli, Doc Cheatham, Buck Clayton, Art Farmer, Chris Griffin, Bob Haggart, Milt Hinton, Jay McShann, Flip Phillips, and Arvell Shaw, and jazz historian Richard B. Allen.

Basin Street
Is the street,
Where all the dark
And the light folks meet

—*"Basin Street Blues." Music by Spencer Williams,*
lyrics by Glenn Miller and Jack Teagarden

The critics and guys who write about jazz think they know more about what went on in New Orleans than the guys that were there. They don't know nothing. They're wrong most of the time.

—*George "Pops" Foster (1892–1969), bassist with King Oliver, Sidney*
Bechet, Louis Armstrong, et al. From Foster and Tom Stoddard, Pops
Foster: The Autobiography of a New Orleans Jazzman

Gary Giddins: You didn't think of jazz as—people didn't think of jazz as black music?

Buddy Tate (longtime saxophonist with the Count Basie Orchestra): No, I didn't; we didn't. And—oh no, we never did. I mean, if it was good, we listened to it and we copied off the records. You know what I mean?

—*Buddy Tate interview conducted in 1980 by Garry Giddins*
for the Smithsonian Jazz Oral History Project

Contents

Series Editor's Foreword

Ed Berger

I first met Randy Sandke when we were both freshmen at Indiana University in 1966. I was playing a Louis Armstrong record (not the most common sound echoing through a college dorm) and he stuck his head in and immediately identified the track. We've been friends ever since. His abilities as a trumpet player were evident then, as was his appreciation of the full spectrum of jazz history. In the ensuing decades, he has evolved both as an artist and as a theorist. He has also overcome obstacles, including a throat ailment that forced him to give up the trumpet for a decade early in his career.

Another obstacle, which he has not entirely overcome, is the typecasting and pigeonholing that still pervades the jazz world. When Sandke first arrived on the New York scene in the early 1980s, he quickly became associated with the new swing and repertory movements. While his knowledge of the Armstrong and Beiderbecke styles ideally suited him to these traditional settings, his equally deep assimilation of Clifford Brown, Freddie Hubbard, and the more experimental aspects of jazz composition rarely found a commercial outlet. As a result, Sandke has led an almost dual musical life. He supported himself by making a string of acclaimed "mainstream" recordings for Concord and other labels, playing with Benny Goodman, Buck Clayton, and other surviving swing giants, and being everyone's first call for historic recreations. At the same time he has steadfastly pursued his original music based on his "metatonal" theory, a system of expanding the harmonic vocabulary used in jazz (see his *Harmony for a New Millennium: An Introduction to Metatonal Music*, Second Floor Music, 2001). To fulfill his musical vision, Sandke has had to self-finance his more experimental recordings, which are largely unknown to his mainstream audience.

Sandke brings a unique combination of talents to bear on this study. His credentials as a musician are impeccable and he has experienced the "jazz life" firsthand. While not an academic, he is a serious thinker who has devoted his life to studying music—all music. The subject of this book—the intersection of jazz and race in America—is sure to draw fire from many quarters. Most other writers have shied away from dealing with this topic head on, which makes it all the more necessary to air it frankly and honestly. Mr. Sandke's position will certainly not please everyone, and it is sure to arouse controversy and harsh criticism, both informed and uninformed. I and my series coeditor Dan Morgenstern may not agree with all of Sandke's conclusions, but we applaud his courage in raising these sensitive issues, and hope this important work will lead to a constructive dialogue among open-minded people. At the very least, this book will force a reevaluation of many long-held and hitherto sacred assumptions prevalent within the jazz world.

1

~

Is Jazz About Music Anymore?

"It is only music that matters. But to talk of music is risky, and entails responsibility. Therefore some find it preferable to seize on side issues. It is easy, and enables you to pass as a deep thinker."

—Igor Stravinsky

The history of jazz has been told and retold ever since the 1930s, when a handful of amateur enthusiasts first attempted to solve the mysteries of its murky and largely undocumented past. In the ensuing years, jazz has become the subject of serious study at numerous colleges and universities, dissected in an ever-widening stream of literature, and examined in films and television documentaries. Yet despite all this attention, a fundamental question seems to go unanswered, or at least unresolved: does jazz represent the expression of a distinct and independent African-American culture, isolated by its long history of slavery, segregation, and discrimination? Or, even when produced by African-Americans (or anyone else for that matter), is it more properly understood as the juncture of a wide variety of influences under the broader umbrella of American and indeed world culture? For simplicity's sake we can refer to the first approach as exclusionary and the second as inclusionary.

This is a question that ultimately doesn't require an either/or answer, as there is truth in both positions. But the degree to which one accepts one or the other of these contrasting orientations can produce startlingly different results. From a handful of basic assumptions a torrent of corollaries flow, and these can have a direct impact on how the music is perceived.

It is my contention that the majority of jazz writers have overwhelmingly supported the exclusionary view. Stretching all the way back to the first generation of jazz writers and continuing up to the present day, jazz commentators and historians have tended to emphasize the differences between black and white culture, and categorize musicians according to race. This outlook is perhaps only natural, given that the music sprang from a black environment, and the overwhelming majority of its greatest exponents have been African-American. In addition, black and white musicians rarely performed together during the first thirty to forty years of the music's history.[1] Recorded evidence shows that stylistic differences according to race are often plainly discernable, especially in the early days of jazz.

But there is another reason why jazz writers have consistently emphasized the separateness and exceptionalism of the black experience. Going back to the beginnings of jazz scholarship and on through today there has been a marked tendency to combine the study of jazz with a desire to effect positive social change. Many jazz historians felt, and still feel, that it is their duty to use jazz as a tool to promote social and economic justice for African-Americans. Obviously, this goal is beyond reproach, and I support it wholeheartedly. In many ways jazz commentators, especially those of the prewar era, were remarkably effective in altering widely held notions of black cultural and intellectual inferiority. Their tireless championing of the many great African-American jazz artists provided a necessary antidote to prevailing and pejorative racial stereotypes. At a time when segregation was still legally sanctioned in many parts of the country, their efforts were not only controversial, but also courageous. I firmly believe these writers played a significant role in tipping the scales of public opinion, and paving the way for the groundbreaking civil rights legislation of the 1950s and 1960s. For this, any fair-minded American owes them a debt of gratitude.

But the willingness to combine history with a social or political agenda, no matter how noble and altruistic, presents a slippery slope. As we shall see, many writers were not above compromising historical accuracy in their zeal to promote social change. Some constructed elaborate theories out of the scantest evidence, if not whole cloth, and these in turn have been cited over and over throughout the jazz literature. Facts that did not fit prevailing ideologies were ignored, and mythology often trumped reality. Although myths have undoubtedly played a large and sometimes beneficial role in the popularization of jazz, they often bear little or no relation to reality.

Furthermore, the attempt to delineate the nature of jazz along racial lines has always been a tricky business, prone to false or misleading assumptions. It is indisputable that the origins of jazz lie in black culture: the "active ingredients," those musical elements that set jazz apart from other styles, are deeply rooted in two preexisting African-American musical genres, ragtime and blues (though of course, both styles contain culturally hybrid elements as well). But black culture has always been much more porous and open to outside influences than most commentators are likely to admit. Secondly, jazz found acceptance very early on within a cross-section of American society, where it took its place within the sphere of popular, and eventually art music. As jazz made its way through this wide-ranging cultural maze it absorbed other influences that extended well beyond any mythological notion of a hermetically sealed black culture. I would argue that jazz attained much of its richness and sophistication from the interaction of a wide variety of musical traditions and attitudes, and that African-American musicians from the very beginning of jazz have been much more worldly and well-rounded than most writers give them credit for.

Due to the law of unintended consequences many harmful side effects have arisen from the exclusionary viewpoint. A particular danger in racial essentialism is the stereotyping of musicians. In much of the literature jazz is represented as a kind of urban folk music, and blacks are typically depicted as natural and largely untutored musicians. This left a lot of creative and adventurous artists, such as Louis Armstrong and Duke Ellington, open to censure when they departed from ideological norms. These views also hurt African-American musicians wishing to express themselves in musical genres other than blues and jazz. Black artists found it nearly impossible to find acceptance in the concert and commercial studio fields until comparatively recently, and there's no doubt that an image of innate but culturally restricted talents helped reinforce discriminatory hiring practices. Even today, forward-looking African-American musicians can be criticized for deviating from norms advocated by certain black jazz authorities who feel that jazz should not stray too far from its "tradition" of incorporating blues and swing.

White musicians have been inversely stereotyped as inauthentic jazz players. They have been accused of "appropriating" a black style and at the same time criticized for not being able to master it. Though often victimized by the same shady business practices that plague black musicians, white musicians are widely presumed to be in a superior position to profit from jazz, mainly through proffering a watered-down version of the real thing. The African-American cultural critic Gerald Early wrote recently of the "frustration of being a white jazz musician in such a starkly racialized field, in some ways more repulsively racialized than in the 1920s or 1930s. . . . Even in this age of diversity we still seem to be bedeviled with the question of whether whites can play jazz, whether blacks are more gifted jazz players, whether whites have ever done anything truly innovative in jazz."[2]

A salient feature of exclusionist ideology is to regard black and white musicians as distinct categories. Typical of this approach is *Jazzmen* (1939), the first jazz history book published in the United States, with its separate chapters on African-American musicians (titled simply "New Orleans Music") and white musicians ("White New Orleans"). During the 1930s many jazz writers were alarmed by the ascendance of Tin Pan Alley and the popularity of well-disciplined big bands with written arrangements, and to counteract this trend they often over-romanticized the early days of jazz. Accordingly jazz was portrayed as arising from an insulated black environment, unsullied by commercial pressures. It represented the pure and authentic expression of a peasant population forced to rely solely on its own cultural resources due to a forced separation of the races.

Ironically, the exclusionist outlook was introduced precisely when jazz bands themselves were integrating, a trend largely supported by the public. As the African-American pianist Teddy Wilson, featured with the Benny Goodman trio and quartet, wrote in 1941: "Lots of people have asked me about mixed bands and the attitudes of audiences toward them. All I can say is that we never had any trouble, and that we were always treated with the utmost respect and consideration."[3] As the music brought people together across racial lines, many jazz authorities were policing racial boundaries; their work and influence will be discussed in the following chapter. Some took contradictory stands; John Hammond, for instance, produced interracial recording sessions while writing stinging attacks on white musicians in general, as well as certain black artists who didn't adhere to his populist principles.

Throughout the forties and fifties jazz continually grew more integrated. It also grew in complexity, developing at an ever-faster pace, and became heralded as America's greatest contribution to the arts. The GI Bill produced the most educated audiences America had ever known, and by and large they welcomed a dizzying pace of innovation that came to be known as bebop, cool, and progressive jazz. Yet this was also an era in which writers such as Rudi Blesh, Marshall Stearns, and a little later Gunther Schuller insisted that jazz was essentially an extension of traditional African music.

In the turbulent sixties, jazz came to be viewed as a musical component of the black liberation struggle. Leading the way was the African-American author and activist LeRoi Jones (now known as Amiri Baraka), who proclaimed jazz "black music." In 1969 the white jazz writer Ralph J. Gleason agreed by saying, "Jazz is black music and as such is part of black culture, which encompasses what is being called these days 'the black experience.' It represents a world other than that reflected in the organs of white society."[4] The African-American saxophonist and social activist Archie Shepp went further, stating, "Jazz is a music born out of oppression, born out of the enslavement of my people."[5] To such commentators, the music was an emblem of black suffering at the hands of a racist white establishment. The idea that jazz was a manifestation of joy rooted in freedom of expression, or an ideal marriage between democracy and meritocracy, seemed hopelessly naïve to these new voices. Jazz became widely viewed as the embodiment of "black soul," even as the vast majority of African-Americans were abandoning it in favor of more popular forms of dance-oriented music.

"Jazz as response to oppression" theories proliferated in the seventies, eighties, and nineties and filtered into mainstream conventional wisdom. These beliefs were taken up by a new generation of jazz scholars eager to display their liberal credentials at a time when the stereotype of black inferiority had been supplanted by the pervasive white-equals-racist paradigm. This was a period characterized by race-based initiatives and other forms of racial redress. For the first time in two hundred years of American history, simple exclusionary formulas were accepted, even extolled, by liberal intellectuals, who viewed them as a necessary price to pay for societal progress.

By the 1980s and 1990s, the supposed place of jazz in society had become less a forum for independent self-expression and more an emblem of black pride. Jazz musicians were expected to "celebrate" the jazz tradition rather than explore new creative territory. The original ethos of jazz, as far as promoting a unique and original vision, was largely discounted. And for the first time in the history of jazz, nonmusicians seemed to be guiding the music's direction more than the musicians themselves.

Business interests aligned with society's desire to expatiate for past racial sins by promoting young and unknown black jazz players. The stars of bygone years were in declining age and the major record companies decided to create overnight jazz sensations, and just as artificially as the pop stars they routinely mass-produced. This was advantageous from a bottom-line standpoint: young players could appeal to the all-important youth market, and potentially yield a long-term return on investment. They also often lacked the business savvy of more experienced musicians. Since many segments of the American public, as well as certain key overseas markets, associated authentic jazz with African-American players, it was only prudent business policy to concentrate on young black musicians. I don't mean to imply that these "young lions," as they came to be known, were devoid of talent, but most were awarded their enviable status before they had a chance to earn it. Once again the ethos of jazz had been subverted.

The exclusionary agenda may have reached its apotheosis in the ten-part, six-million dollar television series *Jazz*, produced for PBS by Ken Burns and aired in 2001.[6] Burns was quoted in *The New York Times* as saying, "Race is the soul of the country, and nowhere is it more evident than in jazz, where a music came out of the black community and with great generosity was shared with the country."[7] The Burns series, though touted as groundbreaking in its exposition of racial dynamics throughout jazz history, was in fact a rehash of stale ideas that had become reflexive conventional wisdom for a period of thirty years.

What's the upshot of all this social engineering in the name of jazz? Why is it misleading to characterize jazz as black music pure and simple? First of all, the concept of "black music" hardly provides a full and accurate picture of such a multifaceted cultural phenomenon as jazz. As art critic Robert Hughes states, "Surprises crackle, like electric arcs, between the interfaces of culture. . . . Separatism denies the value, even the possibility, of such a dialogue. It rejects exchange."[8] In an age of ethnocentrism and identity politics the tendency has been to ignore or severely downplay these interrelationships. "Because race-based politics and programs thrive on differences," wrote Alfred Appel Jr. in his provocative book *Jazz Modernism*, "academic multiculturalists would discourage the idea of jazz as multicultural."[9] Dan Morgenstern, probably the dean of jazz authorities for the last three decades, has spoken out against the "excess baggage of historicity, questionable aesthetics, and political correctness that seem to becloud much of our present-day perceptions of jazz."[10]

Even more significantly, exclusionist ideology has had a profound impact on the music itself. Extra-musical agendas have so overtaken the jazz world that I fear they threaten its very artistic survival. Any art must constantly renew itself by absorbing outside influences and fresh ideas. If such innovations are regarded with suspicion, as contaminating the purity of an already established art form, there is little room for creative growth. Not surprisingly, conservative musical trends have dominated the jazz world for the past quarter-century.

Moreover, in an era devoted to promoting group identity, the very notion of individuality has been called into question. It is impossible to imagine jazz divorced from the strong and singular personalities who created it. Nevertheless, pressures to conform to ideological norms have had the effect of stifling individual creativity. Already there are rumblings in Europe that America has ceded its lead in creating cutting-edge jazz, and many American musicians have suffered a significant drop in work as a result.[11] Without the European and Japanese market, jazz may cease to exist as a viable profession for American musicians.

Yet there is still more bitter fruit that exclusionist ideology has produced. The integration that flourished within the jazz world from the mid-thirties onward became compromised with calls for black nationalism in the sixties. By the eighties, the tendency was for jazz groups to self-segregate, a trend that hasn't entirely disappeared today.

Through the dark days of legalized segregation and on into the civil rights era, jazz shone as a beacon for achieving interracial respect and understanding. It seemed as if the dream of a color-blind society was within reach in the jazz world, where musicians were judged on merit and not skin color. Status in the jazz world was conferred on the basis of real achievement and not some artificial standard of rank or pedigree, and the music itself was infused with honesty and integrity.

Many older players have told me of the respect and affection permeating the jazz world they knew. Tenor saxophonist Flip Phillips (born Joseph Filipelli in 1915) thought it only natural to seek out African-American mentors: "I was only a kid but Coleman Hawkins and Lester Young encouraged me. Before that Pete Brown. I played with Frankie Newton and he gave me plenty of encouragement. I was twenty-two or -three and we opened at Kelly's Stable. Nat King Cole was the relief trio and Art Tatum played the off night. We all used to hang out together. There was no racial thing at all—none whatsoever. I used to go up to Harlem to Monroe's and I'd get home at eight in the morning. I met Charlie Christian there, and Jimmy Blanton there. There was plenty of encouragement. It was just beautiful. Everybody was happy. You're *supposed* to be happy playing."[12]

The West Coast-based trumpeter Conte Candoli told me, "Most of the guys I know like Sweets [Edison], Clark Terry and Dizzy: you would never know there was any kind of racial scene because they were just glorious—great people. Even Charlie Parker."[13] And Louis Armstrong himself once said of his audiences and legions of white fans, "I have always loved my white folks, and they have always proved that they loved me and my music. I have never had anything to be depressed about in that respect, only respect and admiration."[14]

"We were miles ahead of everybody else," stated the African-American bass player Milt Hinton. "Musicians have been integrating way before society decided to do that."[15] But as jazz scholar Ted Gioia recently noted, "Jazz stood out, at least for many decades, as one of the few arenas where some of us (maybe even most of us) could throw away our racial baggage that simmered through the rest of society and deal with each other through the unmediated channel of artistic collaboration. Somehow we lost that thread. Instead of leading the rest of society we have fallen far behind. The clamor of racial politics now resounds loudly in the jazz world."[16]

Having once been in the vanguard, jazz has fallen prey to the same racial divisions that have plagued the rest of American society. The overwhelming racialization of jazz has not only denied outside musical influences, stifled creativity, and pitted group against group: it has also overlooked the crucial role that white audiences and presenters have played in disseminating and promoting the music. Business interests have indeed frequently exploited black musicians, but they have helped enrich many as well.

This complex subject is typically reduced to simplistic clichés. In his book *Rhythm and Business*, Norman Kelley repeats a familiar refrain: "The history of black music has been a continuous replay of the uncontested and lucrative exploitation of black cultural forms by whites."[17] Harold Cruse, in his influential 1967 book *The Crisis of the Negro Intellectual*, noted a "whole history of organized duplicity and exploitation of the Negro jazz artist—the complicated tie-in between booking agencies, the musicians' union, the recording companies, the music publishers, the managers, the agents, the theater owners, the night-club owners, the crooks, shysters, and racketeers."[18] While I don't dispute many of these claims, I think they should be examined dispassionately before drawing the standard sweeping generalizations.

Jazz simply could not have made it from the cabaret and dance hall to the concert hall without the intercession of businessmen. For one thing, the music would never (or barely) have been recorded. Untold opportunities for African-Americans would not have existed if not for the efforts of white promoters. Certainly their motives were often not altruistic, but by opening doors, they enabled many artists to prosper. And there have always been those on the business side whose involvement with jazz is solely a labor of love.

Since the dawn of the new millennium there have been many hopeful signs that exclusionary ideology—certainly in its more extreme forms—is receding, not only in the jazz world but in society as a whole. Barack Obama in now the first African-American president of the United States, and his message of racial transcendence has found deep resonance throughout the country.

Yet jazz remains encumbered by the socio-political baggage that has clung to it since its story was first told. Allow me to show you what I mean. Following are two alternative histories of jazz. The first is a standard politically correct version as taught in many colleges across the land:

Blacks were the most lowly and despised class in New Orleans. Discrimination shut them out of the wider world and they had to devise their own cultural practices. When Jim Crow laws swept through the South after Reconstruction, the proud French-speaking Creoles were consigned to the same lowest rung of society inhabited by blacks. The melding of a sophisticated Creole tradition with the crude but heartfelt music of darker-skinned descendants of slaves produced jazz.

Jazz initially received little attention from whites, with the exception of a few white musicians who produced a pale imitation of it. But the white public came to embrace jazz once it had been watered down to suit their tastes. As these young white musicians sought fame and fortune, the real authentic black jazz players were making much less money playing for their own people. Following the Great Migration, black areas in the North were just as shut in by racism and discrimination as the neighborhoods where jazz grew up in New Orleans.

Jazz finally reached the masses in the 1930s, but only when white swing bands appropriated the styles of black bands playing in Harlem and Kansas City. Black musicians became so frustrated with this turn of events that they developed a new music they hoped white musicians couldn't steal: bebop.

White musicians responded by devising "cool jazz," yet another watered-down pseudo-style, and its popularity forced black musicians to create funky hard bop. Eventually, this was whitened too as funk turned into fusion, making even more white players rich. Black musicians also created avant-garde jazz, which sometimes went by the name "New Black Music." Finally, Wynton Marsalis arrived on the scene to take jazz back to its roots and celebrate its past traditions.

Now let's consider another encapsulated history that I believe is much truer to the historical record:

The white public developed a taste for the music of African-Americans as far back as colonial times. Meanwhile, blacks were increasingly acculturated to European-derived musical styles. The broad acceptance found by minstrel companies (both white and black), gospel choirs (such as the Fisk Jubilee Singers), and later ragtime, attests to a widespread, cross-cultural interest in African-American music. Though African-American music has maintained many distinctive qualities, it has always absorbed many hybrid elements.

When syncopated dances swept the country in the 1890s black bands were preferred across the land, especially by the white upper class. In New Orleans all bands played roughly the same repertoire, though in differing ways. There, too, the new syncopated styles made black bands more popular than white bands. Many white musicians took to these new styles, which could be heard throughout the city. These musicians had to adapt to remain competitive. Soon many played jazz exclusively, as indicated by the abundance of non-reading professional white musicians in turn-of-the-century New Orleans.

When black and white bands from New Orleans took to the road and spread jazz up north, many observers pointed to the interracial character of the music. But Prohibition would segregate jazz musicians almost as much as the Jim Crow laws of the South. Prohibition was rarely enforced in the emerging black belts, so organized crime moved in and established a new form of nightclub that took the country by storm: the black-and-tan. Black-and-tans were not limited to a few upscale establishments, such as the famed Cotton Club, but were a vast nationwide phenomenon. African-American bands were hired to "jazz it up" for whites eager to trade their disposable cash for sin, at least as far as imbibing illegal alcohol.

The power and excitement of the "wild" and hot music they performed became a major attraction in itself. The stereotype of blacks as jazz players would both help and hinder black musicians, but the image became fixed in the public mind.

Then . . . but that's the subject of this book, and what follows will fill in many of the gaps of this storyline and refute much of the conventional wisdom found in standard jazz texts. The point is that one view of history paints jazz as restricted, limited, conditioned by the evils of segregation—a cultural expression so ingrained in the black experience that whites can barely fathom its true meaning. The other view, the one presented in this book, places jazz squarely within the mainstream of American culture, even though it was created and in large part creatively driven by blacks. As a living art form, jazz is open to anyone with something personal and unique to contribute. The jazz ethos is again free to live and flourish.

I can personally attest to the many obstacles facing musicians today as a result of the "de-musicalizing" of jazz. Creating the music is the easy part—getting anyone to listen objectively through the white noise generated by politics and business is much more difficult. For as long as I've been a professional musician I have attempted to present an alternative way of improvising and composing. This style, which I call "metatonal" music, offers a third approach to jazz, other than traditional harmonically based methods and free jazz. To date, not one article has been written about metatonal music, even though I have recorded several examples since 1985 and written a book on the subject.[19] Many other musicians active today are also eager to contribute new ideas, yet too often find their efforts greeted only by deaf ears and closed minds. All of this confirms my belief that jazz and music parted company long ago.

I have responded by doing what artists have done since time immemorial: namely, continuing to create while managing the necessities of life as best I can. I used to think that art of high quality and originality would eventually be recognized, especially within the jazz world. I must say I don't believe that anymore.

I am well aware that by merely raising many of these issues I will be accused of pursuing my own selfish agenda. This I won't deny and wish to state it explicitly: I want to see music judged on its own terms, free of external considerations. Of course jazz is an immense subject that touches on many other areas of human experience. But I feel strongly that any examination of jazz must be grounded in a knowledge of—and hopefully love and respect for—jazz as music first and foremost.

This book begins by looking at the major jazz writers from the 1930s up to the present, and examining their work in relation to the historical record. Then we'll return to the 1960s to see how radical and unpopular ideas evolved into mainstream conventional wisdom. I'll show how these ideas, along with attempts to achieve racial redress, have dominated the jazz world since the 1980s. We'll next examine the business side of jazz to see how much the familiar scenario of artistic exploitation—and especially black artistic exploitation—fits the reality. Finally, I'll look at the issue of race itself, and conclude by considering the present state of jazz and what the future may hold.

My book does not purport to be a full accounting of jazz history, but rather an examination of interracial contact—where the dark and the light folks meet—as it applies to the music. Plenty of jazz history is intraracial: of and between African-American musicians, or, to a lesser extent, white musicians. But I feel that this history, particularly as regards black contributions to jazz, is already well documented. Some may accuse me of overstating the importance of cross-racial influences on jazz. However, I am not trying to place any strict quantitative value on my findings, but simply presenting them so others can draw their own conclusions.

I am all too aware of the pitfalls of frankly discussing racial issues in present-day America. Race has been called the wound that won't heal. Almost any position on it will be regarded unfavorably by someone. The African-American sociologist Yehudi O. Webster sums up these difficulties: "Any remark about the black experience may be considered controversial, or objectionable. For example: 'blacks have their own culture.' One response could be: 'It is racist to suggest that blacks, despite almost four centuries of residency, are not fully Americanized.' If the contrary is voiced—'blacks do not have their own culture'— the reaction could be: 'to deny the uniqueness of the black experience is racist.'"[20]

A friend in academia asked why on earth I wanted to kick this "hornet's nest" around. The answer is: I don't, but I feel someone has to. I would prefer it not be me, but having accepted the challenge I also accept the inevitable consequences. For the record, I am an integrationist—a believer in Martin Luther King Jr.'s vision that everyone should be treated with dignity and respect, and granted equal protection under the law, regardless of skin color. If that makes me an old-fashioned fuddy-duddy, or even a racist in the jaundiced eyes of some, so be it. Deep in my heart of hearts I am secure in the knowledge that I am not.

I should make it clear that nowhere in this book do I question the existence of black culture. Nor would I fail to acknowledge the tremendous impact it has had on American culture as a whole. However it's often impossible to determine precisely where one begins and the other ends. I also do not dispute the fact that jazz was created by African-Americans, nor that the vast majority of its greatest exponents have been black. This amazing profusion of world-class talent has no historical parallel, except perhaps the Italian Renaissance. I would not argue that these artists have received too much attention; if anything they have not received enough.

The point I wish to make is that the leading figures of jazz, regardless of race, have created music that can stand on its own terms next to the best art of any epoch. Their work doesn't need to be propped up with the aid of socio-political theorizing. And any true understanding of jazz music requires a wider lens than a narrow "black culture" perspective provides.

This book may raise more questions than it answers. It should not be taken as the last word on anything, but rather, as a call to further research. Where I criticize certain conclusions by well-known and widely accepted writers and pundits I don't mean to suggest that their work should be condemned outright. On the contrary, I have the greatest respect and sympathy for most of them, especially that first generation of jazz writers who strove to create a coherent history out of a stack of old records and a few stray interviews. I merely ask that we take a fresh look at the many smug assumptions hovering all around us like pestering gnats.

In the chapter on jazz mythology ("Good Intentions and Bad History"), the reader will notice that I do not address the question of whether or not jazz originated in New Orleans. Though some writers, notably Charles Edward Smith and more recently Francis Davis, have disputed this notion, I do not. Undoubtedly, similar musical developments were taking place in other parts of the country, but nowhere did they reach the level of maturity and sophistication achieved in New Orleans. Numerous citations—in newspapers and eyewitness accounts stretching from New York to California—affirm that early New Orleans musicians were perceived as distinctive, even revolutionary, when they performed outside their hometown.

Before we begin, I'd like to introduce two highly influential personages, largely unknown to the jazz community, who nevertheless did much to inform the evolving racial debate of the twentieth century. Their work became the theoretical backbone for many of the activist jazz writers from the 1930s up to the present day. They are Franz Boas, the founder of cultural anthropology, and his student, Melville Herskovits, a key pioneer of cultural relativism.

Both believed their work as scientists needed to serve a higher social purpose. "It is one of the duties of science, too often neglected, to combat prejudice," wrote Boas in 1939.[21] His face bore scars from duels with anti-Semitic classmates in his native Germany. When Boas emigrated to America in 1883, the fledgling disciplines of anthropology and sociology were dominated by white supremacists searching for a scientific basis to explain the perceived inferiority of non-Aryan races. Boas succeeded in turning these ideas on their head. In an 1894 speech, he declared that current anthropology was nothing more than a political tool for suppressing the American Negro. He demonstrated that every claim of black inferiority was either false or dependent on the Negro's history of privation. The plight of the American Negro was the product of racism, he maintained, not the cause of it.

Over the next half-century these views gained wide acceptance as they were spread and developed by a host of Boas's influential students. Among them were Margaret Mead, Ruth Benedict, Zora Neale Hurston, Kenneth Clark (who, in addition to being the first African-American president of the American Psychological Association, provided key testimony in the 1954 Supreme Court decision that struck down school segregation), and Melville Herskovits.

Like Boas, Herskovits was Jewish and a victim of discrimination. When Margaret Mead went off to Samoa she attempted to sublet her New York apartment to Herskovits but management refused him access. Herskovits was to take Boas's egalitarian notions a step further. Whereas Boas believed in the primacy of the individual, Herskovits stressed the importance of the group and the equality of all cultures. "Cultural relativism," he wrote in 1955, "is a philosophy that recognizes the values set up by every society to guide its own life, and that understands their worth to those who live by them, though they may differ from one's own. Instead of underscoring differences from absolute norms that, however objectively arrived at, are nonetheless a product of a given time and place, the relativistic point of view brings into relief the validity of every set of norms for the people who have them."[22]

These ideas opened the floodgates to radical new ways of thinking, which provided the intellectual underpinning for a new academic orthodoxy. Taking these views to their logical conclusion, one is obliged to infer that any mode of human conduct is as valid as any other. Individuals are to be viewed primarily as members of a group. No group can rightfully judge another. Any notion of universal truth must be scuttled. Art is to be judged primarily for its cultural relevance. The idea of merit is an elitist fiction.

We are now ready to proceed.

NOTES

1. There was, however, much more interracial "sitting in" than is often thought. Earl Hines, speaking of Chicago in the 1920s, said, "I don't know how many different [white] musicians came to sit in and jam with us. Whatever section they wanted to sit in, why a musician would step out of his chair. We all got a kick listening to each other, and we all tried to learn." Dance, *The World of Earl Hines*, 49.

2. Ward and Burns, *Jazz*, 324–331.

3. Teddy Wilson, "Audiences Warmer in the South Than in New York," *Music and Rhythm*, April 1941, 34. Although Billie Holiday famously described her unhappy experiences with white bands and white audiences, she also had problems

with black bands due to her heroin addiction and difficult personality. As Buck Clayton told me in an interview, Holiday's attitude was consistently "on the pessimistic side."

4. Gleason, *Celebrating The Duke*, 21.

5. Backus, *Fire Music: A Political History of Jazz*, 86.

6. Peter Watrous, "Telling America's Story Through America's Music," *New York Times*, October 1, 2000.

7. Watrous, "Telling America's Story Through America's Music."

8. Hughes, *Culture of Complaint*, 124.

9. Appel, *Jazz Modernism*, 42.

10. Morgenstern, *Living With Jazz*, 293.

11. See Stuart Nicholson's *Is Jazz Dead? (Or Has It Moved To A New Address)*, (New York: Routledge, 2005). I think Nicholson overstates his case, but the book raises many important and provocative issues.

12. Taped interview with Flip Phillips, 1990.

13. Taped interview with Conte Candoli, 1999.

14. Armstrong, *Satchmo*, 195.

15. Taped interview with Milt Hinton, 1990.

16. Taylor, ed., *The Future of Jazz*, 31.

17. Norman Kelley, *Rhythm and Business*, 12.

18. Cruse, *The Crisis of the Negro Intellectual*, 110.

19. That is, no article has appeared in America. The only one I'm aware of was written by Leon Lhoëst for the Dutch Journal *Muziekmozaïek*.

20. Webster, *The Racialization of America*, 191.

21. Franz Boas, "Franz Boas on Intellectual Freedom," *New Masses*, February 14, 1939.

22. Herskovits, *Cultural Anthropology*, 364.

2

~

The Activist Jazz Writers

"I do think that you failed to give colored musicians a break; and that
is why I exaggerated the other extreme, since the public is inclined to
believe you and musicians of your opinion."

—Jazz historian Marshall Stearns, in a letter dated January 11, 1937,
to Nick LaRocca, cornetist of the Original Dixieland Jazz Band

The attempt to shackle jazz to the procrustean bed of ideology goes
back to the very beginnings of jazz criticism. The first generation of
jazz writers, those active in the 1930s, laid the foundation for the study of
jazz history as we know it today. But the tumultuous times they lived in
did much to inform their work. The country was in the grip of the Great
Depression and many felt that capitalism itself was in its death throes.
Fascism was on the rise in Europe and the ensuing bloodbath was not far
off. Back home, segregation prevailed in many parts of the country, and
everywhere African-Americans were routinely victimized by repressive
attitudes and customs. Bloody confrontations between labor and management were rife as unions struggled to establish themselves. In the musical
sphere, commercial big bands with written arrangements were the order
of the day, and the music business was dominated by powerful booking
agencies, managers, press agents, and newly formed entertainment conglomerates whose tentacles stretched into radio, recording, and motion
pictures.

It's a small wonder that a great many jazz writers of the time found
solace in left-wing aspirations, and were eager to combine their love of
jazz with a zeal to promote social change. Thus the jazz writer as activist

15

was born. Though these writers hardly saw eye-to-eye on every issue, they shared remarkably similar backgrounds: most were born into privilege, Ivy League educated, and closely affiliated with the Popular Front of the 1930s.

The Popular Front was an international movement that arose in response to the Great Depression and the threat of fascism. In the United States, the movement centered around union advocacy, various antifascist causes, and the fight for racial equality. For a variety of social issues, the "old left" was indeed a vanguard for positive and necessary change in America. Many of their once-radical views have since become enshrined in law, taking the country several steps closer to its founding principles.

I have no quarrel with the ideals, or even the motives, of this generation of writers—at least as far as improving equality of opportunity in America. My concern is rather to determine whether they bent the truth in order to further their social agenda. To what extent did ideology prevail over accurate and impartial history? To answer that question we first need to review the background and milieu of the writers themselves.

"The Popular Front jazz subculture . . . created a network of aficionados, critics, promoters, and collectors who organized concerts, nightclubs, record stores, magazines, and recording companies, and fought for an end to the color line in the music industry and the recognition of African-American musics," writes Michael Denning in his book *The Cultural Front*:

> Though there were heated debates over jazz in the left press and some left-wing critics criticized contemporary jazz, virtually all of the major jazz critics of the period were on the left. The revival and recovery of traditional New Orleans jazz was largely the work of Charles Edward Smith and Frederic Ramsey Jr., who together edited the pioneering collection *Jazzmen*. . . . Alan Lomax recorded Jelly Roll Morton's music and memories for the Library of Congress in 1939: he later used the recordings in writing Morton's "autobiography," *Mister Jelly Roll* (1950). Charles Edward Smith reviewed jazz for the *Daily Worker*, B. H. Haggin wrote for *The Nation*, and Otis Ferguson wrote for *The New Republic*."[1]

Many got their start writing for the *Daily Worker* and *New Masses*, media organs affiliated with the American Communist party. Also within the Popular Front orbit were writer and producer John Hammond; author Ralph Ellison; poet Langston Hughes; Milt Gabler, owner of the Commodore Music Shop and Commodore Records (the first record label solely devoted to jazz); Eric Bernay, business manager for *New Masses* and founder of the jazz and folk label Keynote Records; Norman Granz, the jazz impresario and founder of several labels including Clef, Norgran, and Verve; and nightclub owners Barney Josephson and Max Gordon.

The communist party had taken an interest in jazz as early as 1928. In that year, the Sixth Congress of the Comintern, held in Moscow, hammered out a proposal to establish an independent "Black Republic of the South" stretching from Virginia to Texas. As S. Frederick Starr notes in his book *Red and Hot*, "This flabbergasting proposition was the brainchild of Marxist sociologists in Moscow who had been no closer to America than the Lenin Library. None of the four American Negroes who attended the Congress had any knowledge of the South, while the New York-based American Communist party would have been powerless to reverse the policy, even if it had tried to do so."[2]

Stalin personally participated in the formulation of the "Colonial Theses," which sought to prove, among other things, that southern blacks represented a distinct nationality whose culture should be distinguished not only from the white population but also from northern and middle-class blacks. Jazz was to be defined as a proletarian music indigenous to the southern black belt, and its obvious urban connection would be denied. "How could jazz be considered a proletarian music?" asks Starr.

> The answer revisionist critics proposed was disarmingly simple: there existed not one but two forms of jazz, one proletarian and the other bourgeois. The proletarian variant was rooted in Negro folk life and bore the scars of past oppression. The bourgeois variant derived not from folk blues but from the vulgar commercialism of Tin Pan Alley. Bourgeois jazz was popular culture "from above," devised by capitalist exploiters to lull the masses to sleep and stifle their growing class consciousness. . . . The distinctive feature of their position was that they assigned far more importance to the sociological context of jazz than to its musical identity."[3]

These critics were hardly all ardent Stalinists, but Stalinist directives do represent an extreme that colored even mainstream liberal ideology of that time. In two important respects, the vast majority of first-generation jazz writers concurred with the communist party line as applied to jazz. First of all, they sought to distinguish commercial jazz (exemplified by Paul Whiteman in the twenties and many swing bands in the thirties) from "real" jazz. The term "jazz" would refer exclusively to that variety of "hot" music characterized by improvisation. Many subsequent jazz commentators have stumbled over the conundrum that Whiteman and others did not "co-opt" a black style so much as these writers co-opted the term jazz. Up to that time, "jazz" had a broad generic meaning referring to any type of syncopated dance music. This new cadre of authorities imposed their own narrow definition, which has stuck to the music up to the present day. Secondly, these writers all agreed that jazz was fundamentally African-American in origin and nature, with white players largely consigned to the role of imitators at best or exploiters at worst. They also sought to portray jazz as authentic Negro "folk music" that should resist contamination from other sources, such as Tin Pan Alley, classical music, or the new swing big bands, with their commercial tendency to "over-orchestrate." Of the early writers on jazz, Michael Gold (editor and music columnist for the *Daily Worker*), Charles Edward Smith (contributor to several influential jazz books and music critic for the *Daily Worker*), Frederic Ramsey Jr. (a contributor to *Jazzmen* and recipient of grants from the National Endowment for the Humanities, the Guggenheim Foundation, and the Ford Foundation), Winthrop Sargeant (author of *Jazz, Hot and Hybrid*), and Wilder Hobson (author of *American Jazz Music*) all argued that jazz was essentially Negro folk music. In Smith's view, the musical family of spirituals, the blues, and hot jazz "has its roots in the denial of the American negro of the 'right to self-determination'," while American popular music is "brought out to hoodwink the masses and divert them from revolutionary class struggles."[4] In other words, jazz is the innate musical expression of an unlettered and oppressed people.

Such a view may strike many today as an example of "liberal racism"; that is, it was meant to show understanding and respect for blacks but was in fact limiting and patronizing. This paternalistic outlook, as it became more widely accepted, would produce restrictive stereotypes for both black and white musicians. Blacks were hindered in finding acceptance in the concert, studio, and mainstream pop fields, and whites were negatively typecast within the jazz world.

The criticisms this group heaped on Louis Armstrong show the pitfalls of assigning such narrow definitions to creative jazz artists. In the late 1920s, as Armstrong's popularity soared, especially among whites, he was encouraged to record popular songs with big band accompaniment. His sales for a single record sometimes reached the 100,000 mark at a time when the record business was in an unprecedented slump. The historical verdict on these remarkable recordings is well summed up by record producer and historian George Avakian: "What might have been a disastrous managerial move was turned into a one-man show of warmth, inventiveness and sheer personality such as the record business had never seen before."[5] Despite sloppy section work and trite arrangements, Armstrong's singing and virtuoso trumpet playing are showcased as never before on these recordings. But rather than hail this achievement—the first of its kind for an African-American musician in terms of sales and widespread appeal—most of the early jazz writers were scornful and dismissive. Charles Edward Smith sniffed that Armstrong's music "succumbs more and more to the white man's notion of Harlem jazz."[6] John Hammond proclaimed that Armstrong's "deterioration began when he chose to think of himself as a soloist, as a performer, rather than as an ensemble musician."[7] Ironically, when Armstrong abandoned his big band and returned to traditional jazz in the mid-forties, a later generation of critics condemned him for not keeping up with the times.

Hammond was even more damning of Duke Ellington, who dared to present himself as an urbane sophisticate and serious composer. In *Metronome* in 1935, Hammond wrote "The Tragedy of Duke Ellington," a withering review of Ellington's extended piece "Reminiscing in Tempo":

> His music is losing the distinctive flavor it once had, both because of the fact that he has added slick, un-Negroid musicians to his band and because he himself is aping Tin Pan Alley composers for commercial reasons. . . . But the real trouble with Duke's music is the fact that he has purposely kept himself from any contact with his people. . . . He consciously keeps himself from thinking about such problems as those of the Southern share croppers, the Scottsboro boys, intolerable working and relief conditions in the North and South. . . . He has never shown any desire of aligning himself with forces that are seeking to remove the causes of these disgraceful conditions. Consequently Ellington's music has become vapid and without the slightest semblance of guts."[8]

This condemnation of Ellington for "aping Tin Pan Alley composers for commercial reasons" is ironic, as Hammond himself was a key figure responsible for the marriage of Tin Pan Alley with jazz. By the mid-thirties the jukebox had become a major promotional tool for record sales, and Hammond persuaded executives of the Brunswick label to make black covers of white popular songs for "juke joints" in black neighborhoods. He produced nearly two dozen sessions featuring Billie Holiday with the Teddy Wilson Orchestra reprising tunes made popular by such mainstream figures as Bing Crosby and Fred Astaire.

A scion of the Vanderbilts, Hammond grew up with a "household staff of sixteen servants [that] included a butler and footman, governesses and maids, a cook and kitchen help, not to mention the two chauffeurs and various day workers."[9] He described himself as "an inheritor of the guilt before the obligations of wealth." After graduating from Hotchkiss preparatory school and spending a year at Yale, Hammond inherited the "ample certainly, but not princely sum" of $12,000 a year.[10] From that point on he was free to do as he pleased, which meant producing jazz recordings and contributing articles to left-wing and music journals.

"I write best when I am angry, when protesting injustice, criticizing bad music or uncaring musicians,"[11] Hammond stated. It was not in his nature to doubt his motives or the basic truth of his strong opinions. But sometimes his ideology served as a rationalization for his business interests. In his *Down Beat* article "Did Bessie Smith Bleed to Death While Waiting for Medical Aid?" Hammond claimed the singer's death was "but another example of disgraceful conditions in a certain section of our country already responsible for the killing and maiming of legitimate union organizers."[12] Having heard an unfounded rumor, Hammond maintained that Smith's death was the result of being refused admittance to a white hospital after her car crashed into a truck outside Clarksdale, Mississippi. In reality, Smith was treated at the scene by a white doctor and taken directly to a black hospital. Though Hammond never tired of railing against "commercialism," he ended his article with: "Be that as it may, the UHCA [United Hot Clubs of America, a record label Hammond was associated with] is busy sponsoring a special Bessie Smith memorial album. . . . Take it from one who cherished all the records [in the album] that this will be the best buy of the year in music."

Hammond's version of events would eventually pass into American folklore. In 1960 Edward Albee's play *The Death of Bessie Smith* perpetuated the myth. In 1972 Stanley Crouch published his first work of fiction, titled *Ain't No Ambulances for No Nigguhs Tonight*. The story took on a life of its own and continues to haunt people's imaginations. As Chris Albertson writes in his biography of the great blues singer, "Bessie Smith became better known for the way in which she had allegedly died than for what she had done in life."[13]

There are endless examples of Hammond's skewed thinking and hypocrisy, despite his claim that "financial independence does bolster one's integrity." In his 1936 article "Sold—For Less Than a Song" (written for *New Masses* under the pseudonym Henry Johnson), he excoriated Ellington's manager Irving Mills, calling him a "vulture" and the "leading exponent" of exploiting black composers by buying their works outright instead of paying royalties. "It is significant to note that Irving Mills, who is credited with the writing of hundreds of tunes, cannot read a note of music."[14] Other writers have accused Mills of taking advantage of Duke Ellington, even as he did everything within his power to boost the bandleader's career. All of this is fair game for criticism, except for the fact that Hammond accepted a job from Mills in 1934. In his autobiography, Hammond said this job "could not have come at a more opportune time." He also offered a much more flattering portrait of the music publisher: "I still have affection for Irving Mills. He was a man who saved black talent in the 1930s, when there was no one else who cared whether it worked or not."[15]

Hammond saw the specter of racial prejudice everywhere. Regarding the decline of bandleader Fletcher Henderson's career from the late twenties on, Hammond felt that "the color bar crippled his ambition and made him cynical of the intentions of all white people."[16] Moreover, Henderson exhibited a "lassitude born of years of exploitation, so that when opportunities came to help himself he was unprepared to take advantage of them."[17] But Henderson's wife told a very different story: "He was never the same after he had that automobile accident down in Kentucky [in 1928]. Everything would seem comical to him and he never achieved to go higher than he was. He never had much business sense but after that accident, he had even less."[18]

Hammond fancied himself "the reformer, the impatient protestor, the sometimes-intolerant champion of tolerance."[19] But others saw him differently. In a profile on Hammond in the September 1938 issue of *HRS Society Rag*, Otis Ferguson wrote,

> He is known as the Critic, Little Father, the Guardian Angel, and the Big Bringdown . . . every place he goes he presently spies the taint of commercialism in art or the sordid hand of capitalism clutching workers. He burns. He speaks out. . . . As a working critic, John Hammond suffers mainly from a complete lack of temperance and caution. He hasn't established for himself the intervening marks on the scale of achievement between "it's terrific" and "it stinks." As Dean of the Swing Critics, accustomed to deference and not having his word disputed, he has developed a habit of knowing the answers and what's more giving them to you—it doesn't matter whether you asked . . . John won't compromise on anything because he never learned to and he never learned to because he never had to.[20]

Hammond viewed the public's rising acceptance of white jazz musicians with alarm. (He had a long and close but stormy relationship with Benny Goodman, who married Hammond's sister Alice in 1942.) "When he goes around saying 'white musician' the way you'd use the term 'greaseball,'" wrote Ferguson, "he not only confuses his readers and upsets his own standards but starts the Jim Crow car all over again, in reverse. Some will tell you that you're not doing much to eliminate a color line by drawing it all over the place yourself, and certainly something ought to be done among those of Mother Hammond's Chickens who have been led into believing that criticism consists in saying: Which is better, black or white? And raising all that hell."[21]

More and more, a chorus of influential writers seemed to feel that the best way to champion blacks was to discredit white musicians. Paul Eduard Miller, a regular contributor to jazz magazines of the thirties and forties, concluded that "Negroes are superior. As regards technique, emotional expression, originality of phrasing, and rhythmic impulse they are supreme, and any argument to the contrary is mere sophistry, the philosophy of a misled neophyte." According to Miller, black superiority sprang from a "tradition" based on an innate familiarity with unspecified "essential requirements of swing" that white musicians had to "laboriously" acquire. As a result, "The important landmarks in the process of [jazz] evolution are curiously though definitely all very dark in color."[22] Here we should remind ourselves that these comments were written at a time when it was daring to suggest that African-Americans were superior to whites in any type of human endeavor. Even music magazines of the time rarely featured pictures of African-Americans on their covers. I'm not gainsaying Miller's motives, but rather pointing out the inherent dangers and consequences of this line of argument. Are we to conclude that African-Americans cannot produce first-rate novels because they lack the "tradition" of fiction writing? Or that they could never excel in ballet or grand opera?

Likewise Rudi Blesh, in his book *Shining Trumpets*, stated that jazz poses "difficulties almost insurmountable for the white player." He also wrote of a "deep-seated jealousy on the part of white musicians and consumers toward their Negro fellow-citizens, who alone can practice the style with integrity and understand it as a language." Blesh, an interior decorator and furniture designer by trade, joined a long line of self-appointed white arbiters determined to dictate the parameters of, in his words, "the pure Negroid influence" in music.[23] Like Hammond, Blesh believed that Duke Ellington suffered the ill effects of over-sophistication. "As for jazz," he wrote, "the Duke has never played it." He saw bop as an attempt by black musicians to "disavow their heritage." Blesh yearned for the "primitive, exciting goodness" of earlier jazz, and claimed jazz had reached its pinnacle in 1926![24]

Equally extreme views had already arrived from overseas. Among the first jazz books to appear in America were two by the French jazz critic Hugues Panassié: *Le Jazz Hot*, from 1934 (published in the U.S. as *Hot Jazz* in 1936), and *The Real Jazz*, from 1942. Like many jazz writers, Panassié was a child of privilege. His family, which descended from French nobility and possessed a lavish apartment in Paris plus a chateau in the South of France, provided him with an independent income.

Le Jazz Hot was a relatively balanced appraisal of jazz based on recordings Panassié had acquired in France. But in his second book, the difference between "real" and "fake" jazz was as clear as black and white. "Since jazz is a music created by the black race, it is very difficult, almost impossible for a white man to get to the heart of it at first shot," wrote the reformed Panassié. "While the Negro masses among themselves have an instinctive feeling for this music, white people approach it with resistance and adopt it very slowly." Although he had not yet visited America, Panassié stated that "as a consequence of the ostracism to which, in the United States, the whites had subjected the colored people, the Negroes lived apart, among themselves, and did not participate in the prevailing cultural stream, but formed a primitive intellectual society of their own." Sometimes his opinions recapitulate noble savage mythology, as when he says, "The Negro, who had originally been purer and closer to nature than the whites, was continually perverted by them."[25]

What accounted for this radical change in Panassié's thinking? Increasingly he had fallen under the spell of the sometime musician and full-time marijuana peddler Milton "Mezz" Mezzrow. In 1929 Mezzrow arrived in Paris, where he earned some much-needed cash by giving clarinet lessons to Panassié. The critic expressed his gratitude for Mezzrow's guidance in a letter, which said in part, "Dear Milton, if you had not come to France and taught me so many things I would never have been able to write this book." In another missive he gushed, "I don't think there was ever a white man who is able to play the right kind of jazz (before all, the blues) with such sincerity and inspiration as you do."[26] As George Avakian maintains, "Mezzrow was regarded here as an amateur but in France he was looked upon as a jazz god."[27]

As a teenager Mezzrow spent time in reform school for stealing a car, and in 1941 he served an 18-month sentence for selling marijuana. By that time he was living in Harlem and married to an African-American woman. He was the epitome of what Norman Mailer famously described as the "white Negro," and at times believed his skin was actually turning black. He even listed himself as "Negro" on his draft registration card. Mezzrow's autobiography, *Really the Blues*, was cowritten with Bernard Wolfe, a Marxist and former personal secretary to Leon Trotsky. In it Mezzrow claimed, "Nobody could ever touch the Negro race, nobody could ever play as good as them, it had to be born in you." Despite his questionable musical ability, Mezzrow felt no qualms about voicing his strong and divisive opinions. As Chicago pianist Art Hodes once remarked, "Mezz had enough ego for three people."[28]

This criticism leveled at white jazz players from across the Atlantic led the guitarist and bandleader Eddie Condon to comment, "I don't tell a Frenchman how to jump on a grape." Condon, a white musician who matured in Chicago in the 1920s and continued playing traditional jazz into the early 1970s, had to contend with scorn from many sides. In the 1940s, his often racially mixed circle was chastised by Leonard Feather and Barry Ulanov, the most outspoken critic-champions of bop, for being "outdated survivals of a bygone era." Meanwhile, Frederic Ramsey Jr. and William Russell (another contributor to *Jazzmen*) resurrected the careers of elderly New Orleans figures such as Bunk Johnson and George Lewis to show what authentic classic jazz, unsullied by the taint of later influences (or white impurity), was supposed to sound like. (Ironically, Bunk Johnson often chafed at the repertoire and musicians they paired him with; given his choice he preferred playing pop tunes of the day, such as "Out of Nowhere" and "Maria Elena.")

Leonard Feather, an early disciple of John Hammond, was actually one of the most magnanimous critics when it came to matters of race. He noted that a "very large proportion" of the greatest jazz musicians have been black, but attributed this to a lack of wider professional opportunities for African-Americans. He believed that increased integration was leading to a "breaking down of stylistic lines" according to race. In "Jazz in American Society," an article published in the 1960 edition of his *Encyclopedia of Jazz*, Feather spoke out against reverse discrimination: "The hostility toward white musicians is part of a syndrome that has developed as the Negro jazzman, becoming more acutely conscious of his own role in the music and his esthetic potential, developed a concomitant awareness of the discrimination to which he had been subjected. . . . He uses the Crow Jim theory as a psychological crutch, and clings desperately to an art he feels he can still call his own in a society that has tried so often to steal from him and suppress him." Feather goes on to quote pianist Billy Taylor: "Jazz is no longer the exclusive medium of expression of the Negro. . . . In each stage of its development jazz has become more and more the medium of expression of all types of Americans and, to a surprising degree, musicians from other lands and other cultures."[29] Feather's 1949 book, *Inside Be-bop*—the first book entirely devoted to the new style—lists nearly as many whites as blacks in the biographical index of representative musicians. Today bebop is almost exclusively associated with black artists in the minds of most contemporary jazz historians.

Feather also consistently denounced discriminatory practices facing black musicians. His article "How Have Jim Crow Tactics Affected Your Career?" in the September 1944 issue of *Esquire* was based on a symposium he conducted with several prominent African-American sidemen and leaders. That same year, in the same magazine, Feather instituted a critics' poll, an openly acknowledged effort to give more attention to black musicians at a time when popular polls largely favored whites. In the first poll, twenty African-American artists, as opposed to just six whites, were voted in. In later years, *Down Beat*, *Metronome*, and many other magazines followed Feather's lead by featuring annual critics' polls.

Unlike Hammond, however, Feather was not independently wealthy and had to make a living by producing jazz records, recording his own compositions, doing public relations work for bands, and writing books, articles, and liner notes. He couldn't afford the ideological "purity" that Hammond espoused, and perhaps as a result, could be all over the ideological map: sometimes open-minded and generous, and at other times partisan and contentious. Whereas Hammond was called "the big bringdown," Feather was known in some circles as "the empty suit."

Occasionally Feather engaged in racial missteps of his own, but it is hard to tell if this was the result of good intentions gone bad or a desire to garner sensational headlines. One example stands out simply because it received so much attention. In a 1951 *Down Beat* piece "No More White Bands for Me, Says Little Jazz," Feather quoted trumpeter Roy "Little

Jazz" Eldridge saying, "It's not worth the glory, not worth the money, not worth anything . . . Never again!"[30] One reason for the notoriety of this account is that it was reprinted in Nat Hentoff and Nat Shapiro's book *Hear Me Talkin' To Ya,* and in Feather's own *Encyclopedia of Jazz* and *The Book of Jazz.* But according to Eldridge's biographer John Chilton, "Roy felt aggrieved at the way Feather had slanted his story, and he remained angry over the article for many years. In 1982 Eldridge told Dan Morgenstern, 'They thought I was putting the white race down and it didn't have nothing to do with that.'"[31] The truer nature of Eldridge's feelings was revealed when he accepted engagements with Charlie Barnet, Gene Krupa and Benny Goodman after supposedly saying he'd never work in white bands again.

Nevertheless, Feather deserves much credit for speaking out on a host of important and controversial issues, and for fiercely holding on to his egalitarian views. "As soon as the rigid segregation under which [black jazz musicians] had lived began to relax," he wrote in 1960, "it became clear that given a freer interchange of ideas anyone could play jazz, according to his environment, his ability and his value as an individual, not as white or Negro."[32] He also opined, "Jazz, originally the music of the American Negro and the American white, will become more than ever the music of the human being."[33] But Feather's inclusionary voice would become an increasingly lonely and isolated one in the coming decades.

Marshall Stearns, a Harvard-educated professor of English literature, is best known for his 1956 book *The Story of Jazz.* The book had its genesis in a series of articles Stearns wrote for *Down Beat,* which appeared from June 1936 to April 1938 under the title "A Short History of Swing." This series represents the first time an American author endeavored to present a coherent history of jazz.

In the mid-to-late 1930s there was much disagreement on the origins of jazz, and Stearns chose to tackle this thorny subject head-on. (In 1938 a public dispute arose between Jelly Roll Morton and W. C. Handy after Handy was introduced on Robert Ripley's *Believe It Or Not* radio show as "the originator of jazz and blues"; Morton fired off letters to *Down Beat* and the *Baltimore Afro-American* stating that he had invented jazz in 1902.) Stearns's articles didn't attribute jazz to any single source, but essentially ignored any white participation in early New Orleans jazz. (The role of white musicians in the formative years of jazz will be discussed in chapter four.) Nick LaRocca, cornetist with the Original Dixieland Jazz Band, was enraged and in a letter to *Down Beat* claimed that he and his band were the true originators of jazz. In a personal letter to LaRocca, quoted at the outset of this chapter, Stearns admitted he "exaggerated the other extreme" because he felt the public was too apt to associate jazz with white musicians at the height of the swing era.

Within the two decades that separate "A Short History of Swing" and *The Story of Jazz*, Stearns became obsessed with the idea of direct parallels between African culture and jazz. Nearly half his book is devoted to speculation on the origins of jazz, which he views as rooted in traditional African sources.

Stearns was profoundly influenced by the work of sociologist Melville Herskovits, who is cited eleven times in the footnotes to *The Story of Jazz*. Herskovits, like Stearns, wished to delineate a "Negro past" in order to help achieve a brighter future for African Americans. His highly influential book *The Myth of the Negro Past*—which is frequently listed in the bibliographies of jazz books throughout the forties, fifties, and sixties—argues in favor of a strong and direct connection between African and African-American culture. In the preface to the 1958 edition Herskovits explicitly characterizes his book as "an attempt to lay bare assumptions underlying interracial conflict, and thus to help place programs of action on a foundation of fact rather than of presupposition." In combining history with social activism, he hoped "the American Negro, in discovering that he has a past, has added assurance that he will have a future."[34]

This call was taken up by Nat Hentoff, who has been described as an "all purpose heretic." In his book *The Jazz Life*, he describes how as a young man, "My night school in jazz was the Savoy Café in Boston. . . . From the bouncers, waiters, and musicians I heard through the years an anthology of Jim Crow in America."[35] A strong, early influence on him was the African-American trumpeter Frankie Newton, one of the very few jazz musicians to openly embrace communism. Hentoff made no bones about combining his love of jazz with deeper social concerns, including the fight for civil rights and the defense of civil liberties under the banner of the First Amendment. This has led him to take unpopular and sometime extreme positions on social issues, such as backing black separatists in their quest for "community control" in the sixties (which in practice meant firing all white schoolteachers in black neighborhoods).

At the same time, Hentoff has championed many white players and spoken out against Crow Jim—a term writer Barry Ulanov introduced to describe reverse racism in the jazz world. Nevertheless, such characteristic magnanimity has not prevented Hentoff from occasionally veering off into divisive and controversial territory. He was the first jazz writer to suggest that black "soul jazz" was a reaction against the primarily white West Coast school, which he described as "low in soul and high in pretensions."[36] Hentoff's eastern chauvinism met up with his racial activism when he wrote, "Here were these white guys [in California] appropriating black music, stripping it of its soul, and making much more money than the deep swingers in the jazz capital of the world [New York]."[37] Pit-ting groups of musicians against each other, especially along racial lines, would remain a favorite pastime of the new jazz intelligentsia.

Martin Williams, born Martin Tudor Hansfield Williams in 1924, came from a family that had, in his words, "delusions of aristocracy."[38] Though not especially well off, they managed to send Martin to the St. Christopher Episcopal Preparatory School and the University of Virginia. Like Hammond, Williams seems to have suffered guilt pangs from this privileged background. Also like Hammond, he was in constant conflict with parents who disdained his fascination with black culture. "I'm a southern kid. I've still got all the latent stuff in me [about race] that I haven't dealt with," he candidly admitted.[39] John Gennari, in his book on the history of jazz criticism, writes that Williams was "famous for his imperious manner and donnish conceits, yet he was also obsessed with his limitations as a jazz writer." In another revealing admission Williams wrote, "I've often considered writing a column dedicated to the proposition that musicians are the only qualified critics."[40]

Williams's work often betrays a patronizing attitude toward white jazz musicians. In his influential book *The Jazz Tradition*, only one chapter of twenty devoted to individual musicians profiles a white player, Bix Beiderbecke.[41] Though Williams praises Beiderbecke, his prejudices are implicit, as when he accuses the cornetist of having "rhythmic problems" without offering any specific examples. (I strongly believe there are none to be found.) Williams rhetorically asks, "Why is it really enlightened or unprejudiced to assume that Negroes could not have something called 'natural rhythm?' . . . It seems to me perfectly valid to say (whether the basis is racial, ethnic, environmental, or whatever) that black jazzmen in general have had fewer rhythmic problems than white jazzmen."[42] I'll examine this statement in a later chapter, but suffice it to say that Williams's lone profile of a white jazz musician serves to underline the white race's inability to master the jazz idiom. The chapter also bears the unfortunate title "The White Man's Burden" (taken from a Rudyard Kipling poem of 1899), conjuring up associations with colonialism and white supremacy.

In 1970 Williams became director of a jazz program at the Smithsonian Institution. There he produced *The Smithsonian Collection of Classic Jazz*, a seven-LP box set that was meant to reflect a cross-section of the music. This collection has been widely used as a teaching tool in university jazz courses ever since its release. Out of eighty-six selections, only three were by white artists, and even for this tiny sampling he was apologetic. In his notes Williams suggests that the inclusion of two cuts by Beiderbecke might be a bit excessive. Once again he singles out a white musician, the great and seminal jazz guitarist Eddie Lang, for having a faulty sense of rhythm. Obviously Williams's lack of musical literacy didn't prevent him from making sweeping pronouncements about the abilities of musicians.

A later, enlarged edition of *The Smithsonian Collection*, prepared for CD release, includes more tracks by white artists, but these were added only at the urging of coproducer Dan Morgenstern.

Williams wasn't an ideologue as such. He sometimes wrote admiringly about white jazz musicians, as in his 1991 book *Jazz Changes*, which includes entries devoted to Bob Brookmeyer, Gerry Mulligan, Steve Kuhn, Jimmy Giuffre, Scott LaFaro, Steve Swallow, Gary Peacock, Art Pepper and George Shearing. But looking at the totality of his work, Williams displays an overwhelming tendency to downplay the contributions of white jazz musicians and damn them with faint praise.

Gary Giddins, a Williams protégé, seems to share many of the same biases. Again, it would be unfair to call Giddins an out-and-out ideologue. But throughout his books, one is struck by the sheer number of prominent white players from all over the jazz spectrum who are merely mentioned in passing, if not omitted entirely. A prime example is Michael Brecker, who is widely regarded as the most influential saxophonist of his generation. In his 1981 book *Riding On a Blue Note*, Giddins describes Brecker as a "journeyman musician."[43] Brecker is also given short shrift in Giddins's 1986 book *Rhythm-A-Ning*, which tells us that the saxophonist "searches sonically for Albert Ayler without quite finding him."[44] Brecker is nowhere to be found in Giddins's *Visions of Jazz: The First Century* from 1998, nor is his highly acclaimed brother, the trumpeter and composer Randy Brecker.

Likewise, stellar saxophonist Chris Potter, the 2000 winner of the prestigious Danish Jazzpar Prize, is totally ignored by Giddins. Ken Peplowski, one of the most fluent jazz clarinetists ever, is treated with perpetual scorn. So many musicians I respect and admire are given little if any space by Giddins, whose aesthetic criteria are perplexing. I once asked the veteran and thoroughly individual pianist John Bunch if Giddins had ever written about him. "I don't think he even knows who I am," replied Bunch. Giddins has the distinction of being one of the first jazz journalists with a regular byline (he wrote a feature column *Weather Bird* in *The Village Voice* from 1973 to 2003) to simply banish whole categories of full-time working jazz musicians from his myopic field of vision.

Giddins also employs a double standard, exempting himself from a criticism he heaps on musicians. Many musicians, myself included, would prefer to devote themselves entirely to their own music but are often obliged to perform historic jazz styles in order to make a living. Giddins has often held our feet to the fire for this, and has even questioned our musical sincerity and fundamental ability to express a personal message.

Martin Williams championed the work of several African-American jazz writers, including LeRoi Jones (Amiri Baraka), A. B. Spellman, Albert Murray, and Stanley Crouch. Like Panassié, Jones radicalized over time in his assessment of whites and their ability to play jazz. In his 1963 book *Blues People*, Jones was willing to accept that Bix Beiderbecke, "as a mature musician, was even an innovator." Nevertheless he believed that for whites jazz was a "learned art," while for blacks it was an indigenous cultural expression. "White is then not 'right,' as the old blues had it, but a liability since the culture of white precludes the possession of the Negro 'soul.'"[45] Whites just were not, and never could be, "blues people." For Jones, and many subsequent writers, the words "white" and "appropriation" would be inextricably linked.

Jones also accused white critics of failing to understand the wider social implications of jazz. He was quite successful in appropriating the word "blues," much as the first-generation jazz critics appropriated the word "jazz." To Jones, who drew heavily on the work of Herskovits, the blues was not so much a musical form as the manifestation of a worldview conditioned by slavery and discrimination. In "Jazz and the White Critic," an essay published in *Down Beat* in 1963, Jones wrote, "Negro music is essentially the expression of an attitude, or a collection of attitudes, about the world, and only secondarily an attitude about the way music is made."[46] In other words, jazz was more a state of being than a type of music. Not all black intellectuals of the time were convinced by this approach. Ralph Ellison, in a review of *Blues People* for the *New York Review of Books*, wrote: "The tremendous burden of sociology which Jones would place upon this body of music is enough to give even the blues the blues."[47] As we've seen already, this "tremendous burden of sociology" had been a part of jazz writing from the very start.

By 1967, when Jones published his collection *Black Music*, he was railing against black musicians who sought "formal training," accusing them of "doctrinaire whitening." His writing had metamorphosed into quasi-poetic rants: "White boys, in lieu of the initial passion . . . which be their constant minstrel need, the derogation of the real . . . Stealing Music . . . stealing energy (lives): with their own concerns and lives finally, making it White Music. . . . Actually the more intelligent the white, the more the realization he has to steal from niggers," and so on.[48] His growing extremism led Leonard Feather to write, "The myth of race, a curious distortion of Hitler's theories, almost disappeared in jazz until the stirring of a chauvinistic theory that Negroes are the only real 'blues people' caused an alarming new rift."[49]

LeRoi Jones's other main concern was promoting avant-garde jazz, which he preferred to call "New Black Music." In 1968, Jones, along with activist Larry Neal, founded the Black Arts Movement, described by Neal as the "aesthetic and spiritual sister of the Black Power concept." According to Jones, this aesthetic was based on the principles that, "Black art has to be collective, it has to be functional, it has to be committed and that actually, if it's not stemming from conscious nationalism, then at this time it's invalid. When I say collective, that it comes from the collective experience of black people, when I say committed, it has to be committed to change, revolutionary change. When I say functional, it has to have a function to the lives of black people."[50] He castigated members of the black avant-garde who collaborated with white musicians and fell out with many as a result.

Jones moved from the bohemian and integrated Lower East Side to Harlem in order to translate his ideas into action. It was then that Jones converted to Islam and adopted the name Amiri Baraka, which signifies a divine presence possessing charisma and wisdom. But by 1974 his attempts to found a cultural movement unraveled, as he and his followers were increasingly divided by bitter internal disputes. Baraka was by that time an avowed Marxist with increasingly extreme views. As the black jazz writer A. B. Spellman points out, "The reality is that it was Greenwich Village which heard the evolution of the New, not Harlem. The man standing in line for the Otis Redding show at the Apollo almost certainly never heard of tenor saxophonist Albert Ayler, and wouldn't have the fuzziest idea what he was doing if he did hear him."[51] At an outdoor avant-garde concert that Baraka produced in Harlem, local residents actually pelted the performers with eggs. Following this rejection by the "blues people" themselves, Jones sought sanctuary in the academic world, accepting teaching positions at Yale, George Washington University, and the State University of New York in Stony Brook, Long Island, where he served as professor of Africana Studies and is now professor emeritus.

The idea of a "blues aesthetic" was also taken up by the African-American cultural critic Albert Murray. In his first book, *The Omni-Americans* (1970), Murray explains that the blues idiom developed as "a survival technique, esthetic equipment for living, and a central element in the dynamics of U.S. Negro life style." He refers to white jazz musicians as "white 'jazz musicians,'" and writes,

> *White Americans do not take the privileged status of white people for granted. They work at it. . . .* In other words, beneath the ever so carefully structured surface of solipsistic complacency and seemingly thoughtless condescension, there is almost always the anxiety of a people who live in unrelieved anticipation of disaster. For, people who really feel secure in their status just simply do not expend all of the time and energy, not to mention the ingenuity, that white colonialists have always been convinced is necessary to "keep Negroes in their place" . . . the vaguest hint of black hostility is more than enough to throw the most arrogant white Americans into a frenzy of trigger-happy paranoia.[52]

In his 1976 book *Stomping the Blues*, Murray acknowledges that the blues form, in musical terms, "is a synthesis of African and European elements, the product of an Afro-American sensibility in an American mainland situation." But Murray's "blues aesthetic" is much less ecumenical, to the extent that it can be clearly formulated at all. The book, which Stanley Crouch called the "only poetics of jazz," and Martin Williams said was "by far the most stimulating interpretation of the meaning of jazz in African-American life," insinuates more than it states. One is left wondering why, if the blues are so fundamental to jazz, Robert Johnson or B. B. King aren't considered the greatest of all jazz players. (And why do critics and the public in general have more difficulty accepting white jazz musicians than white blues artists such as Eric Clapton or Stevie Ray Vaughan?) Murray's answer is that though "there is much to be said" for the "authentic earthiness of Blind Lemon Jefferson and Leadbelly . . . there is a good deal more to be said for the no less authentic extensions and refinements" from the "consecrated professionals" of jazz. "The point is that unless the idiom is not only robust and earthy enough but also refined enough with a range comprehensive enough to reflect the subtleties and complexities of contemporary experience, it is not likely to be a very effective counteragent of the blues or any other demons, devils or dragons."[53]

In *Stomping the Blues* white musicians are almost entirely consigned to a few footnotes. In one footnote, Murray excoriates white critics for promoting a "redefinition of blues music that will legitimize the idiomatic authenticity of certain white musicians, whose very accents indicate that they are not native to the idiom but who nonetheless enjoy reputations (and earnings) as great performers." He also objects to "these same writers" who "forever intrud[e] the name of Bix Beiderbecke into discussions about such seminal blues-idiom trumpet players as Buddy Bolden, Bunk Johnson, Freddie Keppard, King Oliver, and Louis Armstrong."[54]

Murray's aesthetic theories are perhaps a little more clearly spelled out in his book *The Hero and the Blues*, though they are also buried in lengthy discussions of Greek tragedy, Marx, Freud, Herman Melville, Hemingway, Trotsky, Thomas Mann, André Malraux, James Joyce and William Faulkner. The blues, according to Murray, display a "pronounced emphasis on stylization," which is defined as the African-American's ability to transform raw experience into "the actual texture of all human existence not only in the United States or even the contemporary world at large, but also in all places throughout the ages." The blues tradition accepts "adversity as an inescapable condition of human existence," but heroically "displays an affirmative disposition toward all obstacles." Improvisation becomes the "ultimate human (i.e., *heroic*) endowment," and "swing" is seen as the ability to "perform with grace under pressure."[55]

Evidently white musicians do not share in the same "heroic" outlook toward adversity, and their music—whether conceived in aesthetic or merely functional terms—cannot be the all-encompassing expression of heroic survival that music is to black people. In the blues aesthetic, Murray sees hope for the survival of all mankind, if only the rest of the world would learn its lessons. In contrast to Baraka, Murray argues that jazz should not be relegated to an independent black culture; rather, it should take center stage as *the* leading voice of American culture. There is more than a little tension between Murray's messianic views and his desire to emphasize the exclusive racial provenance of jazz.

This unresolved dichotomy is also evident in the writings of Murray's disciple Stanley Crouch. Here I must step in and say that I know Stanley and find him quite likable in many ways. I admire the way he's risen from a very humble background to become a formidable critic of society and the arts. I also appreciate that he's always been willing to debate me and many others who don't necessarily share his views (though he's a much better talker than listener). Nevertheless, I find many of his beliefs extreme and often tendentious.

Like Murray, Crouch is extremely inconsistent on the question of to what degree jazz represents a black aesthetic that is essentially foreign to white players and critics. His put-downs of white musicians extend back to the sixties, when he recorded an album consisting of a "rap on cultural repression," in which he laments the fame of Dave Brubeck as opposed to trombonist Joe "Tricky Sam" Nanton, Janis Joplin as opposed to Howlin' Wolf, and Gerry Mulligan as opposed to alto saxophonist "Black Arthur" Blythe.[56] Later attacks would be waged against arranger Gil Evans—whose output, in Crouch's opinion, amounted to nothing more than "high-level television music"—and Bill Evans, who "didn't understand jazz rhythms; wasn't playing in the tradition."[57]

More recently Crouch has targeted other leading white musicians in a series of articles for *JazzTimes* magazine. In "The Place of the Bass," he states that Scott LaFaro, who is often credited with liberating the bass from its role as timekeeper, "conceives of rhythm-section counterpoint in the obvious way it would function had jazz been invented in Europe. That is not as profound, for this music, as when we hear [African-American musicians] Paul Chambers, Ray Brown, etc. to cite just a few examples."[58] In another article, "Putting the White Man in Charge," Crouch writes, "White musicians who *can* play are too frequently elevated far beyond their abilities in order to allow white writers to make themselves feel more comfortable about being in the role of evaluating an art from which they feel substantially alienated." This diatribe was specifically aimed at jazz critic Francis Davis and trumpeter Dave Douglas. Crouch accuses Davis of "lift[ing] up . . . Dave Douglas as an antidote to too much authority from the dark side of the tracks." He also opines that the African-American musicians Don Byron and Mark Turner "accept an imposed aesthetic of 'pushing the envelope' in ways that have nothing to do with blues and swing."[59]

Crouch's political views have undergone profound changes since his formative years in East Los Angeles during the days of the Watts riots, the Black Panthers, and student unrest. He is often viewed as a conservative on social issues regarding blacks, though he is better described as an ideological maverick. His musical views, on the other hand, have gone through a complete about-face. Crouch arrived in New York in 1975 as the drummer for, and roommate of, avant-garde saxophonist David Murray. From 1979 to 1988, when Crouch was a staff writer for *The Village Voice*, he was quick to use this pulpit to preach the virtues of new jazz in general and David Murray in particular (revealing a penchant for conflict of interest á la Hammond and Feather). But in the early 1980s he switched his allegiance to Wynton Marsalis and became a staunch advocate of more traditional forms of jazz, specifically those that exhibit "the blues" and "swing." It's more than a little ironic that an ex-avant-garde drummer has appointed himself the ultimate arbiter of who swings and who does not.

What hasn't changed in all these years is Crouch's condescending attitude towards white jazz musicians. Constantly lurking beneath his often genial exterior is the unreconstructed black radical ideologue of the sixties. One often gets the feeling from his writings that, like Baraka, he believes "if it's white it ain't right" as far as jazz is concerned.

Since 1987 Crouch has been an artistic consultant for Jazz at Lincoln Center; he is also now a columnist for the *New York Daily News*. This increasing public visibility—along with his desire to promote jazz as a message that speaks to all the world—has led him to adapt his more strident views to accommodate a broader audience. Crouch has evolved into something of a master of the mixed message. In one of his *JazzTimes* pieces, entitled "Come In—The Negro Aesthetic of Jazz," he begins by recounting a story told to him by Martin Williams: "There used to be a group of white jazz musicians who would say, when there were only white guys around, 'Louis Armstrong and those other people had a nice little primitive thing going, but we really didn't have what we now call jazz until Jack Teagarden, Bix, [Frank] Trumbauer and their gang gave it some sophistication. Bix is the one who introduced introspection to jazz. Without him you would have no Lester Young or no Miles Davis."[60] Thus a discussion purportedly about the inclusiveness of the black aesthetic begins with a second-hand account from a guilt-ridden, white southern jazz critic showing how white jazz musicians (who are never identified) can be racist. Crouch goes on to say, "Negroes in America, through extraordinary imagination and new instrumental techniques, provided a worldwide forum for the expression of the woes and the wonders of human life. Look like what you look like, come from wherever you come from, be either sex and any religion, but understand that blues and that swing are there for you too—if you want to play jazz." In other words, if a musician adopts the primacy of blues and swing, he or she can play jazz, but with the caveat that blues and swing are not just musical styles but ways of life rooted in the black experience. Just as in Orwell's *Animal Farm*, everybody is equal but some are more equal than others.

By insisting that the blues and swing are not merely musical phenomena, and that jazz cannot be separated from a monolithic black culture, Baraka, Murray, Crouch, and other writers have succeeded in placing jazz criticism out of the realm of music and firmly under the thrall of social concerns. With the "blues aesthetic" as a criterion for evaluating musicians, jazz criticism becomes an entirely subjective affair. Such theories advocating black exceptionalism rarely hold up well under scrutiny, and similar ones advancing white exceptionalism would immediately be denounced as racist. But unfortunately a great many current writers, and especially those within academic circles, take these views as a given. And they, like most of their predecessors throughout the history of jazz writing, see it as their duty to use jazz as a tool to fight perceived social injustice.

John Gennari, assistant professor of English at the University of Vermont and author of *Blowin' Hot and Cold: Jazz and Its Critics*, writes that jazz is a music "born of slavery and segregation" and refers to the "jazz world's overt racism." In addition he detects the ongoing "power of systematic, institutional racism in a culture founded on white supremacy."[61]

Scott DeVeaux, music professor at the University of Virginia and author of *The Birth of Bebop: A Social and Musical History*, writes, "Jazz is strongly identified with African-American culture, both in the narrow sense that its particular techniques ultimately derive from black American folk traditions, and in the broader sense that it is expressive of, and uniquely rooted in, the experience of black Americans." Moreover: "My courses in jazz history are designed to inculcate a feeling of pride in a racially mixed university for an African-American musical tradition that manages, against all odds, to triumph over obstacles of racism and indifference."[62]

At Harvard, Ingrid Monson is the Quincy Jones Professor of African-American Music. "I want people to listen to music and take a step back, to think about activism," she said in a recent interview.[63]

I don't mean to denigrate these three scholars, whose work is in many respects important and exemplary. But I do wish to emphasize some of the basic, underlying beliefs and values that inevitably inform their writing.

Much has changed in American racial affairs over the last seventy years, but little seems to have changed in the minds of many jazz pundits.

The mythology of jazz is alive as ever, as is the desire to force the music into an ideological mold. Jazz has become increasingly racialized, to the point that, even in the twenty-first century, race continues to be a barrier to self-expression within the jazz world. Let's now take a look at some of the more creative history that jazz writers have devised to advance their theories.

NOTES

1. Denning, *The Cultural Front*, 335–337.
2. Starr, *Red & Hot*, 102.
3. Starr, 97–98.
4. Starr, 99.
5. George Avakian, liner notes to *The Louis Armstrong Story*, vol. 4, Columbia CL 854.
6. Charles Edward Smith, "Class Content of Jazz Music," *The Daily Worker*, October 21, 1933.
7. Hammond and Townsend, *John Hammond On Record*, 107.
8. Tucker, ed., *The Duke Ellington Reader*, 118–120.
9. Hammond and Townsend, 25.
10. Hammond and Townsend, 67. To be fair, the $12,000 yearly sum was all Hammond received from his family and, though perfectly adequate in the Depression, it never rose in later years. Hammond died nearly broke, while his mother managed to squander away the family fortune.
11. Hammond and Townsend, 51.
12. John Hammond, "Did Bessie Smith Bleed to Death While Waiting for Medical Aid?" *Down Beat*, November 1937, 3.
13. Albertson, *Bessie*, 215–226.
14. Henry Johnson (John Hammond), "Sold—For Less Than a Song," *New Masses*, July 7, 1936, 29.
15. Hammond and Townsend, 132.
16. Firestone, *Swing, Swing, Swing*, 114.
17. Hammond and Townsend, 116.
18. Shapiro and Hentoff, *Hear Me Talkin' To Ya*, 222.
19. Hammond and Townsend, 404.
20. Ferguson, *The Otis Ferguson Reader*, 98–103. HRS was the Hot Record Society, a record shop and eventually reissue label founded by Stephen Smith and his circle of jazz enthusiasts.
21. Ferguson, 102.
22. Stowe, *Swing Changes*, 78. Originally printed in *Down Beat*, October, 1936, 5.
23. Blesh, *Shining Trumpets*, 27.
24. Blesh, 9, 285, 356, 368.
25. Panassié, *The Real Jazz*, vii, 5, 8, 53.
26. Mezzrow and Wolfe, *Really the Blues*, 270, 330, 352.
27. Taped interview with George Avakian, 2003.

28. Hodes, *Hot Man*, 68.

29. Feather, *The New Edition of the Encyclopedia of Jazz*, 79–88.

30. Leonard Feather, "No More White Bands for Me, Says Little Jazz," *Down Beat*, May 18, 1951.

31. Chilton, *Roy Eldridge*, 187.

32. Feather, *The New Edition of the Encyclopedia of Jazz*, 23.

33. Feather, *The Book of Jazz*, 53. This quote only appears in later editions (1961 on), which included a revised version of his essay "Jazz and Race."

34. Herskovits, *The Myth of the Negro Past*, xxviii–xxix.

35. Hentoff, *The Jazz Life*, 16–17.

36. Gennari, 175.

37. Gennari, 175.

38. Gennari, 71.

39. Gennari, 73.

40. Gennari, 185.

41. For the second revised edition, a chapter on white pianist Bill Evans was included as well.

42. Williams, *The Jazz Tradition*, 65–74.

43. Giddins, *Riding on a Blue Note*, 173.

44. Giddins, *Rhythm-A-Ning*, 58.

45. LeRoi Jones, *Blues People*, 149, 153, 219.

46. Reprinted in LeRoi Jones, *Black Music*, 13.

47. Ralph Ellison, "The Blues," *The New York Review of Books*, February 6, 1964.

48. LeRoi Jones, *Black Music*, 205.

49. Gennari, 57.

50. Abiodun Jeyifous, "Black Critics and Black Theatre In America," *The Drama Review* 18, no. 3 (September 1974): 41. Originally in *Black Fire: An Anthology of Afro-American Writing*, eds. LeRoi Jones and Larry Neal (New York: William Morrow, 1968).

51. Gennari, 285.

52. Murray, *The Omni-Americans*, 45–46.

53. Murray, *Stomping the Blues*, 214.

54. Murray, *Stomping the Blues*, 50. One wonders if Murray ever listened to Keppard—whose ragtime feel shares more with LaRocca than Armstrong—or to Beiderbecke for that matter.

55. Murray, *The Hero and the Blues*, 83, 106.

56. Stanley Crouch, *Ain't No Ambulances for No Nigguhs Tonight*, Flying Dutchman FDS 105 (1969).

57. Lees, *Cats of Any Color*, 208–209.

58. Stanley Crouch, "The Place of the Bass," *JazzTimes*, April 2002, 28. Bassist Greg Cohen told me of an incident that took place at an Ornette Coleman rehearsal. Ornette invited Stanley to sit in on drums, which thrilled him to no end. Afterwards, however, Coleman began talking about how much he missed "Scotty" LaFaro, calling him the greatest bass player he ever worked with.

59. Stanley Crouch, "Putting the White Man in Charge," *JazzTimes*, April 2003, 28.

60. Stanley Crouch, "Come In—The Negro Aesthetic of Jazz," *JazzTimes*, October 2002, 18.

61. Gennari, 22, 129, 384.

62. DeVeaux, "Constructing the Jazz Tradition," in *The Jazz Cadence of American Culture*, ed. Robert O'Meally (New York: Columbia University Press, 1998), 486, 505. DeVeaux's ideology gets the better of him in his book *The Birth of Bebop* when he compares the careers of Woody Herman and Billy Eckstine to demonstrate endemic racism in the music business. He ignores the fact that Herman earned his success after a ten-year period of struggle; that he was forced to disband his orchestra in 1946; and that he was hounded by the IRS until the day he died. Eckstine's short-lived big band had serious disciplinary problems, including a sax section made up entirely of heroin abusers. More importantly, it was formed during the final days of the big band era, and Eckstine went on to a highly successful career as a solo artist.

63. Zoe M. Savitsky, "Ingrid Monson: A Portrait," *The Harvard Crimson*, February 23, 2006.

3

~~

Good Intentions
and Bad History

"If you're not a reality, whose myth are you?"

—Sun Ra

As we've just seen, several generations of jazz writers believed it was their duty to combat racism by depicting the music as an outgrowth of African culture; as the product of an insular black community; and as a reaction to segregation and discrimination. But how does the historical record actually compare with these assessments?

AFRICAN GENESIS

In his book *The Story of Jazz*, Marshall Stearns devotes an entire chapter to "Jazz and West African Music." In it he states, "An assortment of West African musical characteristics are preserved, more or less intact, in the United States."[1] Rudi Blesh, in his jazz history *Shining Trumpets*, states, "African music is the key that unlocks the secrets of jazz." He further opines, "Jazz . . . is a synthesis of African and European material so predominantly African in character and method that it might be more accurate to define it as an African art form."[2]

The use of polyrhythms in jazz is frequently cited as a direct retention from West African musical practices. But are the rhythmic approaches of jazz and West African music really the same? Or is jazz related to African music the way English is related to Indo-European; that is, as one of many offshoots that have evolved into separate and discrete languages?

Obviously, the musical traditions of West Africa are hardly uniform. But one underlying principle remains constant throughout the majority of styles, and is most evident in traditional drum ensembles. Here I must describe a non-Western musical phenomenon in Western musical terms because these are the only ones I have at my disposal. The easiest way to describe this principle is by saying that traditional West African music is characterized by the simultaneous use of two or more related but opposing meters. Nowhere else in the world has this level of rhythmic complexity been so highly developed.

As musicologist A. M. Jones writes: "Rhythm is to the African what harmony is to the Europeans, and it is in the complex interweaving of contrasting rhythmic patterns that he finds his greatest aesthetic satisfaction."[3] Likewise John Miller Chernoff says, "In African music there are always at least two rhythms going on. There seems to be no unifying or main beat."[4]

This device, which really defines traditional West African music, is still extremely rare not only in Western classical music, but in all the New World music of the African diaspora, including jazz. When the music of Africa was transplanted to shores ruled by Western colonizers it became compressed into a box of simple and regular meters common to Western European music: 2/4, 3/4, 4/4, and the like. This compression gave rise to new musical idioms characterized by syncopation, which can be described as a restless interaction between strong and weak beats. Since the concept of a single underlying meter, with its consequent emphasis on regularly repeated strong beats, is foreign to traditional African music, so is the concept of syncopation. You just can't snap your fingers on beats 2 and 4 to traditional West African music, or in most cases even discern where beat 1 is. In this way, the rhythmic basis of jazz differs markedly from its African predecessors. Regular meters continue to dominate the music of African-Americans, whether in the pop, religious, or jazz spheres. And to most listeners accustomed to regular meters, traditional African music still sounds alien.

The use of polyrhythms in jazz is frequently mentioned, but not the totally different way polyrhythms function in African music. In African music, opposing rhythmic groupings furnish an ongoing structure from which the entire performance derives its basic identity. In jazz, polyrhythms function by creating a feeling of momentary tension that ultimately resolves by reemphasizing the basic meter—much like the role dissonance plays in harmony.

As I've already indicated, examples of continuous polyrhythm in jazz are practically nonexistent. Much more common are passages like Louis Armstrong's wondrous scat vocal on "Hotter Than That." In the second half of this chorus, a syncopated rhythmic phrase in the space of three quarter notes (superimposed over the original 4/4 time) is repeated for a full nine bars before finally resolving. Pianist Mel Powell's arrangement of "Get Happy" for the Benny Goodman sextet features the rhythm section in 7 against the melody played in 4, but this does not continue past the melody chorus. Even the metric modulation practiced by the Miles Davis quintet of the 1960s adheres to the same principle of tension-and-release.[5] In Western classical music, Stravinsky supplies more consistent examples of continual opposing meters, such as the "Danse de la Terre" from *The Rite of Spring* (1913) and "The Soldier's March" in *L'histoire du soldat* (1918). But what all of these instances show is how fundamentally distinct they are from the metric practices of African music.

Despite all these obvious differences, jazz writers have often bent over backwards to demonstrate the African origins of jazz. At the same time many African-American musicians have been quick to deny any such direct link, insisting instead that jazz was created in America by African-Americans.

In his book *Early Jazz*, Gunther Schuller tries to demonstrate the link between jazz and African music in strictly musical terms. He takes an example of traditional African music, "Sovu Dance," and reorchestrates it for a 1920s-style jazz band. But in the process he is forced to omit rhythms from his African prototype that are "least likely to appear in jazz."[6] Thus his hybrid composition is stripped of its most characteristic African element, the opposing meters, and proves nothing.

Researchers who have traveled to West Africa and studied the music firsthand tend to be much more guarded in claiming direct parallels. The English blues historian Paul Oliver, for example, came away feeling that "in the jazz sense, West African drum orchestras do not 'swing.' The 'ride' of a New Orleans jazz band, and the 'slow and easy' slow-drag of a country blues band, have no counterpart in the forceful thrust of the multilineal drum rhythms. . . . Improvisation on a theme, which is fundamental to jazz, also appears to owe little to improvisation with tight rhythmic patterns on the [African] drums. . . . Whatever the links with African drumming, conceptually jazz music is very different."[7] The American jazz scholar Samuel Charters, who also conducted fieldwork in Africa, arrived at a similar conclusion: "Things in the blues had come from the tribal musicians of the old kingdom, but as a style the blues represented something else. It was essentially a new kind of song that had begun with the new life in the American South."[8]

Jazz has never taken hold in West Africa, and the only jazz musicians from the continent who have made reputations in the United States have been South Africans, such as Abdullah Ibrahim (Dollar Brand) and Hugh Masekela. In South Africa, European influences are widespread, and furthermore, a number of African-Americans emigrated there during the 1930s.

One of the few African-American musicians to show a passionate devotion to African music is pianist Randy Weston, who was exposed to it
through workshops conducted by Marshall Stearns at the Lenox (Massachusetts) School of Jazz in the mid-fifties. Weston has employed African
drummers in his groups, but even then the bulk of his performances rely
on a standard, westernized approach to rhythm. When Weston toured
Africa (usually Muslim North Africa) he would tell audiences, "This is
your music after it crossed the Atlantic, after it came into contact with
European civilization. Your music has changed in our hands, but the basic
traditions are still the same. This is what happened to your music."⁹ Some
of the "basic traditions" may have remained, but the underlying African
multi-metric approach had been fundamentally altered.

During the late fifties, when many African states were achieving independence from colonial rule, there was a brief vogue for traditional
African drumming in New York. A nightclub called the African Room
opened on Third Avenue, not far from the United Nations headquarters.
A Ghanaian native named Kofi Ghanaba performed there (using the stage
name of Guy Warren) and secured a recording contract with RCA Victor
through the efforts of Nat Hentoff. Around the same time John Hammond signed Babatunde Olatunji to Columbia. Olatunji was a Nigerian
who originally came to America to study political science. Both drummers recorded with jazz musicians: Warren with Lawrence Brown of the
Duke Ellington Orchestra, and Olatunji with Cannonball Adderley, Clark
Terry, Yusef Lateef, and Charles Lloyd. Olatunji's first record, *Drums of
Passion*, became something of a surprise hit, and he later played on Max
Roach and Oscar Brown Jr.'s *Freedom Now Suite*.

But the marriage between traditional African music and jazz never
really took off, for the simple reason that to do so would require a fundamental alteration of the basic character of one or the other. Jazz would
have to sacrifice its syncopations, or African music would have to give
up its multi-metrics. Jazz is replete with examples of rhythmic borrowing
from other musics of the African diaspora—Afro-Cuban jazz, Brazilian
samba and bossa nova, Puerto Rican salsa, and so on—but all of these folk
sources share the same metrical approach common to music of the West.

A musical union between traditional African music and jazz may yet take
place. I'm only saying that it hasn't happened yet, at least in terms of producing a new and identifiable style, despite the fact that many of the greatest jazz artists have tried. As Dizzy Gillespie recalled, "Charlie Parker and
I were closely connected with the African Academy of Arts and Research
from Nigeria, and we became closely acquainted with some of the Africans
that were studying in the United States. And we played benefits all over
New York, just with trumpet and the saxophone and African drums."¹⁰ But
significantly, Gillespie preferred working with Afro-Cuban drummers such

as Chano Pozo, whose style was, like Gillespie's, based on standard time signatures. As Gillespie succinctly stated, "Our music in the United States and the African concept of rhythm have one difference: the African music is polyrhythmic and we are basically monorhythmic."[11] John Coltrane gave financial support to Olatunji's Center for African Culture in Harlem, and played one of his final dates there, but never recorded with the drummer.

While many jazz writers continue to draw a direct parallel between the rhythmic styles of African music and jazz, many African-American musicians have been quite outspoken in emphasizing the differences. Pianist and arranger Mary Lou Williams distrusted the growing interest in all things African during the sixties. She referred to this movement as "Afro" and once wrote, "Afro has nothing to do with jazz. Jazz grew up on its own here in America . . . Black Americans don't have to go back to Africa to get their dignity. They've got it here."[12]

Kid Ory, trombonist on many seminal recordings with Louis Armstrong and Jelly Roll Morton, also questioned the African origins of jazz. "They haven't got it now," he said. "How could it come from there?"[13]

One of the most well-known refutations of a direct Africa-jazz connection came from drummer Art Blakey. He'd made several albums with African musicians, and maintained that he'd traveled to Africa in the late 1940s to study philosophy and religion (though some doubts have been raised on this point). "Jazz is known all over the world as an American musical art form and that's it. No America, no jazz," he stated. "This is our contribution to the world, though they want to ignore it and are always trying to connect it to someone else. It couldn't come from anyone but us. It couldn't come from the Africans. We made this music, whatever they want to call it . . . African music is entirely different, and the Africans are much more advanced than we are rhythmically, though we're more advanced harmonically."[14]

One contemporary jazz scholar, Ingrid Monson of Harvard, has disputed Blakey's intent in making this statement. She sees it as an example of an "interaction between subordinates and those who dominate, in this case predominantly white journalists."[15] But Blakey addressed his comments to fellow African-American drummer Art Taylor, who was openly soliciting candid, antiestablishment views from jazz musicians for his book *Notes and Tones*. To Monson, Blakey represents a "trickster figure," who "cleverly mediates between the understandings of the hegemonic and the subaltern." I think it's arrogant and condescending for Monson to doubt Blakey's sincerity. The drummer had firsthand experience working with traditional African drummers and was quite capable of expressing his opinions in clear and unequivocal language.

Folklorist Alan Lomax and New Orleans guitarist Danny Barker engaged in a heated and revealing exchange on this subject during a Jelly

Roll Morton symposium at Tulane University in 1982. The assembled audience listened to two Morton performances of "Maple Leaf Rag," recorded by Lomax for the Library of Congress. In the first recording Morton demonstrated the original ragtime style; in the second he showed how this style had evolved into jazz. After these recordings were played Lomax told the audience, "It seems to me that Jelly Roll here uses a great many of the resources of African style in making this marvelous jazz composition. . . . It's a great big, typical European compositional form which he treats in a totally African style. I think it is constantly amazing about Jelly Roll, how he's handling both the European heritage in an extremely skilled way, and giving up very little of the African background."

Danny Barker couldn't have disagreed more. "Now you see, what you have there with Jelly Roll's doing to the 'Maple Leaf Rag,' that's New Orleans," he said. "That's something that came out of New Orleans. It didn't come out of Africa. I've heard hundreds of records of, and from Africans. African is nothing like no New Orleans music . . . King Oliver, Kid Punch [Miller], Buddy Petit, [Henry] Kid Rena; they have nothing to do with Africa. It's New Orleans. Something came out of New Orleans. Just like oil come out of Oklahoma, jazz come out of New Orleans. That has nothing to do with Africa. You ain't gonna sell me Africa. I don't want to hear nothing about Africa."

Lomax attempted to get in the last word by saying, "You just made a beautiful African speech, Danny." An exasperated Barker shot back, "Man, listen to him."[16]

I agree with ethnomusicologist John Miller Chernoff, author of *African Rhythm and African Sensibility*, that African retentions in American music are generally those aspects of music that cannot be transcribed in Western notation. These retentions are numerous and significant, but often have more to do with musical attitude and nuance than any specific technique. When African performance practice gets applied to Western-oriented music, its influence clearly remains but in an altered state. Slides and variable pitches are heard in relation to Western scales and tonality, and the polymetrics of African rhythm become compressed in what's known in the West as "common time."

Jazz is a homegrown music, created by African-Americans. Let's just leave it at that.

CONGO SQUARE

Congo Square figures prominently in jazz histories as a kind of missing link: the place where African music survived intact and was passed on to the first generation of jazz musicians. *Jazzmen* (1939), the first book on jazz history published in America, opens with Congo Square: "That the Negroes had not forgotten their dances, even after years of repression and exile from their native Africa, is attested by descriptive accounts of the times."[17] The book also claims, "In New Orleans you could still hear the bamboula on Congo Square when Buddy Bolden cut his first chorus on cornet."[18] And: "The leader of the first great [jazz] orchestra, Buddy Bolden, was already in his teens before the Congo Square dances were discontinued." [19] *Jazzmen* provides no footnotes on sources, but does mention an article from the *New York World* that had been quoted at length in Herbert Asbury's colorful book on New Orleans, *The French Quarter* (1936). Neither book reveals the identity of the article's author, but it was none other than Lafcadio Hearn, writing in 1883. Hearn was a world traveler who became famous for chronicling exotic destinations and local folklore, and from 1877 to 1888 he lived in New Orleans.

In his book *Jazz: From the Congo to the Metropolitan* (published in America in 1944), Belgian writer Robert Goffin unearthed another, more extensive article on Congo Square, written in 1886 for *Century Magazine* by New Orleans novelist George Washington Cable. "This evidence," wrote Goffin, "leaves not the slightest doubt as to the survival of the African tradition."[20] Goffin's book also stressed a direct connection between African music and dance and the rise of early jazz.

Congo Square is cited a dozen times in the index to Rudi Blesh's jazz history, *Shining Trumpets*, published in 1946. The first reference is on the first page of the first chapter, titled "Black Music." The mere idea of this "missing link" sends Blesh into rapturous speculation: "What, then, must have been the effect of this African survival at its height, on the children and youths who, in future years, formed the first street bands? May not some of them have danced and sung, drummed or blown wooden trumpets in the historic square?"[21]

Marshall Stearns, in *The Story of Jazz* (1956), devotes several pages to Congo Square and maintains that the dances continued, on and off, from 1817 to 1885. He quotes Cable's article extensively, and confidently asserts that the writer "gives us the observations of an acute eyewitness."[22] In his 1968 book *Early Jazz*, Gunther Schuller concludes that a continuum from "the rituals of the Place Congo in New Orleans to the spread of 'jazz' as a new American music" is "well substantiated."[23]

All of these claims concerning the decisive role of Congo Square in the formation of jazz turn out to be founded on only two accounts: Hearn's and Cable's. Other descriptions of dances at the Place Congo exist but come from a much earlier time: 1799 to around 1845. Nevertheless, the testimony of two eyewitnesses, both living in New Orleans during the 1880s, is held to be convincing. But as we shall see, Hearn's account was not of Congo Square at all, and Cable's was an outright fraud.[24]

In 1884 New Orleans played host to the World's Industrial and Cotton Centennial Exposition, a kind of world's fair that attracted visitors from around the country. This event sparked interest in the unique history and culture of the Crescent City, and the New York editors of the *World* and *Century Magazine* solicited Hearn and Cable to write amusing and colorful stories about old New Orleans lore.

Hearn's article described a dance he witnessed not in Congo Square, but in a backyard on Dumaine Street. Nor was it conducted by throngs of African dancers, but by "a few old persons." The music consisted of a man beating a "dry good box and an old pork barrel," accompanying the chants of "some old men and women." Hearn confessed he knew "nothing about Creole music or Creole Negroes," and when he inquired about the words being sung, an old woman laughed and replied "C'est le Congo!"[25] Hearn describes Congo Square itself as "the last green remnant of those famous Congo plains where the negro slaves once held their bamboulas." This modest anecdote, in the course of being told and retold throughout the jazz literature, has been conflated into direct evidence that the Congo Square tradition remained alive throughout the latter part of the nineteenth century.[26]

Cable's account is even more chimerical. He had heard stories concerning wild dances in Congo Square occurring fifty years earlier, and tried to see if any old-timers could furnish him with details. Unfortunately he found no one whose memory stretched back that far. Undaunted, Cable decided to construct his exotic story from far-flung historical sources, including two books by the French politician and historian Médéric Moreau de Saint-Méry: *Description topographique de l'isle Saint-Domingue*, from 1798, and *De la danse*, from 1801.[27] According to Louisiana historian Jerah Johnson, even these texts are questionable, because both contained "second-hand descriptions of Saint-Domingue [now Haiti] dances."[28] Nevertheless, Cable used these descriptions as the basis for his *Century Magazine* piece, which has been reprinted throughout the jazz literature: "They pranced back and forth, leaping into the air and stamping in unison, occasionally shouting 'Dansez Bamboula! Badoum! Badoum!' while the women, scarcely lifting their feet from the ground, swayed their bodies from side to side and chanted an ancient song."[29] The musical instruments described include a "gourd partly filled with pebbles or grains of corn," "the jawbone of some ox horse or mule," long, hollow drums carved from a single piece of wood, a primitive marimba, and a four-string banjo. To these details Cable added further embellishments: "For the true African dance, a dance not so much of legs and feet as of the upper half of the body . . . there was wanted the dark inspiration of African drums and the banjo's thrump and strum."

Cable also apparently borrowed from an 1879 article, "The Congo Dance—A Glimpse of the Old Square of a Sunday Afternoon Sixty Years

Ago," in the New Orleans newspaper *The Picayune*.[30] This provided a handy discussion on the origins of the various dancers in Congo Square during its heyday. Cable incorporated this into his account, referring to "tall, well-knit Senegalese from Cape Verde, black as ebony, with intelligent, kindly eyes and long, straight, shapely noses; Mandingoes, from the Gambia river," and so on. All told, Cable includes the names of eighteen tribes in his *Century Magazine* article.

Most egregious of all, Cable maintained the fiction that the dances in Congo Square continued up to his present day, the mid-1880s—hence all the repeated attempts by jazz writers to connect the dances directly to Buddy Bolden. The 1879 *Picayune* article, intended for a strictly New Orleans readership, clearly states that the only drumming heard in the square at that time was of the "cicade on the tall sycamore tree." The article goes on to state, "Sixty years ago, on a Sunday afternoon, Congo Square would present a very different appearance, [but now] the tom-toms have long since been laid away."[31]

So what are the real facts concerning Congo Square? It is true that blacks congregated in open spaces for the purpose of dancing when New Orleans was under French and Spanish rule. A 1786 law allowed slaves to dance in public squares only on "Sundays and holy days until the close of the evening service." One visitor said the dancers were accompanied by three or four drummers beating on a "long kind of narrow drum of various sizes, from two to eight feet in length."[32]

The dances continued when New Orleans was ceded to the United States in 1804. An 1817 law retained Sunday as the appointed day for the festivities, but prohibited dancing after sunset. It further required that dances be held under police supervision, and only in one approved site. This location, chosen by the mayor, came to be known as Congo Square.

The site's previous name, the "Congo Circus," was based on outdoor theatrical performances that were organized by one Signore Gaetano of Havana and begun in 1816. Attractions included monkeys, a bear, and a tiger, plus a man who stood on the back of a galloping horse while drinking a glass of champagne. Ironically, the Signore's "Congo Circus" was open only to whites.[33]

There are some reliable eyewitness accounts of dances at Congo Square from the post-1817 period. One comes from the architect Henry Latrobe, best known for his work on the U.S. Capitol building. Latrobe had come to New Orleans to devise a plan for desalinating the drinking water. One Sunday in 1819, he happened upon the unforgettable sight of five to six hundred black people clustered into circular formations with groups of musicians and female dancers at the center. In one area a trio of instrumentalists performed. Latrobe wrote in his diary: "An old man sat astride of a cylindrical drum about a foot in diameter, & beat it with incredible quickness with the edge of his hands & fingers. The other drum was an open staved thing held between the knees & beaten in the same manner. They made an incredible noise. The most curious instrument, however, was a stringed instrument, which no doubt was imported from Africa. On the top of the fingerboard was the rude figure of a man in sitting posture, & two pegs behind him to which the strings were fastened. The body was a calabash." This last instrument would have been a kora, with a resonating body made from a dried gourd, often from the calabash tree. A forerunner of the banjo, the kora is traditionally used by West African griots to accompany their oral histories.

Two women danced "in a miserably dull & slow figure, hardly moving their feet or bodies," and "squalled out a burthen to the playing at intervals." A different instrumental group played in another corner of the square. Here Latrobe mentions a large wooden block "with a mortice [slit] down the center," which was "beaten lustily on the side by a short stick. In the same orchestra was a square drum, looking like a stool, which made an abominably loud noise."[34]

Even as early as Latrobe's visit to Congo Square in 1819, the dances had begun taking on other influences. Some observers mention hearing fifes, fiddles, Jew's harps, triangles and tambourines. Others tell of slaves dancing to fandangos and Virginia breakdowns, and musicians playing such popular minstrel songs as "Jim Along Josie," "Old Virginia Never Tire," and "Get Along Home You Yellow Gals." As music historian S. Frederick Starr notes, "By the 1820s the assemblies at Congo Square, though raucous and picturesque, were sufficiently altered for them to have been called 'balls' without irony."[35] Jerah Johnson concurs: "The 1820s saw the balance between traditional African dances and developing Afro-American dances tip in favor of the new forms."[36]

By 1829 residents were objecting to the crowds and noise, leading city fathers to outlaw the Sunday dances. A city directory of 1845 refers to Congo Square as a "place where the Negroes in olden times were accustomed to meet." Another account from the same time noted that the old "Congo" dances of the square's "primitive days" had ceased.[37]

If the dances in Congo Square did indeed survive into the 1880s, as Cable suggests, one would expect conga-like cylindrical drums to make an appearance in early jazz, instead of, or along with, the military-derived snare and bass drum. But the conga had to wait until the 1930s and 1940s to be reintroduced via Cuba into American music.

In any case, the idea that Buddy Bolden, or any other proto-jazz player of his era, could have witnessed dances in Congo Square is preposterous. The missing link in jazz proved to be just as fraudulent as that other famous missing link: the notorious Piltdown Man.

JIM CROW LAWS AND JAZZ

One of the most frequently cited "creation myths" concerning jazz purports to show how the music came about as a response to discriminatory racial legislation enacted in Louisiana during the 1890s. As the story goes, these laws forced the Creoles of New Orleans, mainly a professional class of mulattoes who spoke French and practiced Catholicism, into a grudging rapprochement with freed slaves and their descendants, who were Protestant and tended to be darker-skinned, poorer and less educated. Jim Crow laws had the effect of melding these two cultures by consigning all people of color to the lowest rung of society. Music was one of the few professional outlets open to them. Thus racism on the part of a white ruling class resulted in a harshly enforced separation of the races and created the oppressive conditions under which jazz was born.

This theory was first advanced by Alan Lomax in his book *Mr. Jelly Roll*, published in 1950. According to Lomax, "By the 1890s the Creoles of New Orleans were being pushed out of their old trades and down on the social scale. Soon they were to be eliminated from the skilled trades. Music had once been a hobby or at most the source of a few extra dollars; now those few dollars became the income for a family and music became a serious professional matter. On his way down the class scale the light-skinned Creole met the black-skinned American musician fighting his way out of the black ghetto. This meeting took place in Storyville, which opened in 1897 and offered regular, well-paid jobs to any musician who wasn't too proud to work in a barrelhouse."[38]

Despite this paragraph's huge influence on much subsequent jazz literature, just about everything in it is totally false. A cursory search through the city directories of New Orleans, or many published jazz texts for that matter, reveals unambiguously that Creoles did not lose their skilled trade work as a result of discriminatory legislation. Tinsmiths, such as Alphonse Picou, remained tinsmiths; Sam Dutrey still ran his pressing shop; Sidney Bechet's father, Omar, continued to make shoes; Freddie Keppard held on to his job in a jewelry store. Some trades, such as carpentry and cabinetmaking, masonry, house painting, and plastering, were in fact dominated by Creoles of color, and still are to this day.[39] Creoles were also teachers and school administrators, doctors and dentists, sextons and clergy.

It is true that the number of African-American musicians (both Franco and Anglo) steadily rose over the late nineteenth- and early twentieth-century. Census figures show that in 1870 people of color made up a mere five percent of professional musicians in New Orleans. By 1910 that figure was up to thirty percent, when blacks comprised less than a quarter of the total population.[40] But was this because of discriminatory legislation or in spite of it? Creoles and blacks (and combinations thereof) came to dominate the music scene in New Orleans. In many cases their bands were favored by the white upper crust, the same people often accused of shunning all people of color. As bassist George "Pops" Foster stated, "In New Orleans, the colored bands had most of the work."[41] Jazz historian Lawrence Gushee observes that as late as the 1920s there were frequent complaints "from white musicians in the musicians' union that black bands were being hired in preference to their own."[42]

Creole bands in particular had a near monopoly on society work for upper-class whites. John Robichaux and Armand J. Piron led the most successful society bands in New Orleans for a combined period of fifty years: Robichaux from 1893 until his death in 1939, Piron from 1913 to his death in 1943. During this period, both these organizations were regularly hired for the most prestigious and lucrative jobs in New Orleans, even though segregation was at its statutory peak. To suggest, as Lomax does, that music was an idle hobby for Creoles is ludicrous.

Robichaux was born in 1866 in Thibodaux, Louisiana, and raised by a white family who provided him with an excellent musical education. In 1891 he moved to New Orleans, and a few years later he was leading his own orchestra, which quickly became a mainstay at white society balls in the Garden District. In addition to playing at all the major hotels in New Orleans, and for dances at the then all-white Tulane University, Robichaux's band appeared regularly at the Southern Yacht Club and the New Orleans Country Club. During the teens he kept one band for stage shows at the Lyric Theatre, the largest African-American venue in town, while another made the usual rounds "up and down St. Charles Avenue" playing for his rich white clientele. As Pops Foster noted, "The rich also had music at the Audubon Club, the City Golf Club, and the West End Golf Club. John Robichaux got most of the dicty jobs like that around town. He had the rich people's jobs all sewed up for a long time. His band played the country clubs, restaurants like Antoine's or Gallatoire's where the rich people gave dinners and had dancing; private clubs like Jackson Square Gardens or the Harmony Club where they'd have parties."[43]

Armond J. Piron's career was no less extraordinary. His band was also a favorite at Tulane University dances and afternoon teas at the Country Club, and he enjoyed a ten-year run at Tranchina's, an exclusive restaurant at Spanish Fort, a white resort on Lake Pontchartrain. Clarinetist Lawrence Duhé and others recalled jobs with Piron at the Roosevelt Hotel Gold Room, Fabacher's Restaurant, the Pickwick Club, Antoine's, the Yacht Club, and the Italian Hall. Later in Piron's career, his band played at the whites-only Suburban Gardens and broadcast regularly over station WWL.

Nevertheless, as recently as 2000, the Geoffrey Ward and Ken Burns book *Jazz: A History of America's Music* (which accompanied Burns's PBS television series) recites the old canard that "even Robichaux found himself displaced by white musicians, forced to . . . for the first time compete on an even footing with blacks."[44] This statement, like Lomax's, is utter nonsense. Robichaux was not "forced" into an inferior status in the local music scene; his music had wide appeal across racial lines.

Furthermore, Lomax's description of the "black-skinned American musician fighting his way out of the black ghetto" is anachronistic. Ghettos arose later, during the period of the Great Migration. New Orleans had concentrations of ethnic groups in certain areas, but in the main people of all races and backgrounds lived side by side. The Protestant Buddy Bolden, the French-speaking Kid Ory, and the young Larry Shields, future clarinetist of the Original Dixieland Jazz Band, all lived within a block of each other (with Shields and Bolden only two doors apart).

Lomax is contradicted in his own book when he quotes Jelly Roll Morton saying, "You see, there wasn't no certain neighborhood for nobody to live in New Orleans, only for the St. Charles Avenue millionaires' district, and that's why anybody could go any place they wanted to."[45] Elsewhere in the same book, speaking of an area in which both white and black prostitutes lived, Morton stated, "There was no such thing as segregation in that section—in fact nowhere in New Orleans at that time."[46]

Lomax's fanciful ideas were elaborated in a succession of books by some of the most distinguished writers on jazz: Marshall Stearns, Charles Edward Smith, and Martin Williams among them. I am indebted to Louisiana historian Jerah Johnson, who painstakingly charted the layers of half-truths and falsehoods that sprouted up like weeds from Lomax's flawed analysis.[47]

Most of these embellishments attempt to show how specific Jim Crow laws directly affected early New Orleans jazz. Samuel Charters, in his book *Jazz New Orleans, 1885–1963*, wrote: "In 1894, the problem was aggravated by the enactment of legislative code No. 111, which included the colored Creoles in the broad restrictions of racial segregation. . . . The proud, volatile Creoles found themselves forced into the uptown neighborhoods and there began an intensive struggle to maintain some sort of status in the hostile atmosphere."[48] As Jerah Johnson points out, the law Charters refers to mandated separate train cars for white and black passengers traveling in first class only (and this legislation was passed in 1890, not 1894).

Charles Edward Smith was the first to connect the notorious *Plessy v. Ferguson* ruling of 1896 to jazz history. *Plessy* was the legal challenge to the same Louisiana train car ruling, and it took six years to work its way up to the Supreme Court. In this decision, the Court lent its imprimatur to the notion of "separate but equal," which was deemed constitutional for fifty-eight years until the landmark *Brown v. Board of Education* decision of 1954. Also implicit in this legislation was the concept of the "one drop rule," whereby a person with only a single drop of black blood is considered legally black. Other discriminatory laws followed in Louisiana: separate train cars led to separate railway station waiting rooms, and interracial marriage was banned. By 1898, 95 percent of blacks were eliminated from the voting rolls, and segregation became the law in hotels, theaters, bars, restaurants, social clubs, churches, brothels, streetcars, parks, libraries, playgrounds, drinking fountains, restrooms, hospitals, insane asylums and cemeteries.

But how did this legal barrage affect New Orleans jazz in its formative years? The answer is: hardly at all. As Johnson explains, "These regulations were not systematically enforced until near or during World War I, which meant that by the time segregation became effective, jazz had already developed." He further notes, "The effect of the new segregation was so deleterious that the jazz musicians began to flee . . . driven to more tolerant places where they were able to find again a spirit of free association." For the next forty years, until the Jim Crow era ended, jazz became an endangered species in the town that gave it birth.

There is another reason why the music profession remained immune from all this odious social engineering. Musicians in America have traditionally functioned very much as servants, albeit skilled ones. As everybody knows, no color line applies to the service sector. Well-to-do white households have always entrusted people of color with the most intimate and vital tasks, such as cooking, cleaning, and raising children (to the point of wet-nursing them). There are written records going back to colonial times of black musicians entertaining in white households. What was different in New Orleans was that, by the time of World War I, when conditions deteriorated, the better musicians were free to move on to greener pastures, unlike their enslaved forefathers.

A question remains: what did bring the Creoles and blacks together? The truth is that the two groups had been finding common cause since the conclusion of the Civil War. The legal distinction between slave and free person of color was eliminated by emancipation. One Creole leader wrote in 1864: "Our future is indissolubly bound up with that of the negro . . . and we have resolved . . . to rise or fall with them. We have no rights which we can reckon safe while the same are denied to the fieldhands on the sugar plantations."[49] Intermarriage between Creoles and English-speaking blacks was not uncommon by the late nineteenth century.

This is not to say that cultural differences and prejudices didn't exist. "The worst Jim Crow around New Orleans was what the colored did to themselves," related Pops Foster. "[The Creole] clubs and societies were the strictest. You had to be a doctor or lawyer or some kind of big shot to get in. The lighter you were the better they thought you were. The Francs Amis Hall was like that. That place was so dicty they wouldn't let us come off the bandstand because we were too dark. . . . There was a colored church in town that had seating by color."[50]

Attitudes of superiority on the part of the Creoles did inevitably filter into their musical judgments of blacks. Drummer Warren "Baby" Dodds put it this way: "At one time the Creole fellows thought the uptown musicians weren't good enough to play with them, because most of the uptown musicians didn't read music. Everybody in the French part of town read music. . . . When they went into music they were given money to get a teacher and they would learn music from the start. My brother and I were really exceptions in that we both got teachers and became reading musicians."[51] Louis Armstrong recalled, "Things were hard in New Orleans in those days and we were lucky if we ate, let alone pay for lessons."[52] It wasn't until Armstrong worked on the riverboats under a Creole leader, Fate Marable, that he began to master his reading skills.

But for all such statements emphasizing the rift between Creole and black musicians, there are others that call this divisiveness into question, and often from the very same people. Baby Dodds spoke of how "the musicians of those days were remarkable men. When the leader of an orchestra would hire a man, there was no jealousy in the gang. Everybody took him in like a brother, and he was treated accordingly." He went on to remark that he and Creole clarinetist Sam Dutrey "were close friends, just as his brother, Honore, was my best friend in the Oliver outfit later."[53] According to Albert Nicholas, "They all played together in the brass bands. Those were mixed bands, Creole and Uptown. In a brass band they were solid, they were one, you know. . . . They sounded a little different . . . but there were always many different styles of music in New Orleans."[54]

In the final analysis, there were two main reasons why Creole and black musicians came together: first, there was a growing demand at all levels of society for the hot new style of dance music that came to be known as jazz; and second, anyone who couldn't or wouldn't play it would be left out of a competitive and lucrative market. As we shall soon see, this same situation applied to white musicians as well.

On a more primal level, there was the irresistible appeal of the music itself. Historians and social critics, many of whom are just as passionately drawn to the music as the musicians themselves, never seem content to ascribe this passion to the power of the music alone. Other forces must be at work, whether social conditions, rebellion, or even cross-racial homoeroticism, as one recent scholar suggests.[55] They should pay more attention to the musicians' own testimony. Here the Creole clarinetist George Baquet, describing his first encounter with Buddy Bolden's band, eloquently captures the magnetic hold this strange new music exerted on him: "I'd never heard anything like that before. . . . I'd played 'legitimate' stuff before. But this—it was something that pulled me! They got me up on the stand that night, and I was playin' with 'em. After that I didn't play legitimate so much."[56]

I think Jerah Johnson deserves the final word on the subject: "Jazz had its origins not in segregation, but in the assimilative tradition of easy interaction of peoples that prevailed in New Orleans, undiminished by the . . . Jim Crow laws of the 1890s. Jazz is a music of urban civilization and complexity, not a music of cultural isolation or of racial singularity. It is a music of freedom and joy, not a music of repression and sorrow."[57]

BUDDY BOLDEN: SEPARATING FACT FROM FICTION

"We have no way of choosing between those who credit Buddy Bolden with the invention of jazz and those who either choose someone else or think the whole idea of an individual starting it all is crazy," writes jazz historian Lawrence Gushee.[58] Buddy Bolden is often cited as the "first man of jazz," which is the subtitle of Donald M. Marquis's excellent biography of this legendary and elusive figure. Common sense dictates that no one person could be responsible for the creation of such a momentous and complex cultural phenomenon as jazz. So what exactly was Bolden's role and his real contribution to the music?

Thanks largely to Marquis, we now know that much of the Bolden story as first reported in *Jazzmen* is false. He was never a barber; he never edited a scandal sheet called *The Cricket*; and "Tin Type Hall," where he supposedly played, never existed. Trumpeter Bunk Johnson, who supplied many of these colorful and misleading details, was simply too young to have worked in Bolden's band as he claimed.

According to Marshall Stearns in *The Story of Jazz*, "Bolden was born in 1868 in the rough-and-ready uptown section of New Orleans."[59] Marquis uncovered a baptismal record that proves decisively the cornetist was born in 1877.

Bolden is typically portrayed as the quintessential "uptown black" (as opposed to the more refined "downtown Creole"), meaning he was poor, uneducated, and the product of a largely insular black environment. As the English historian Eric Hobsbawm wrote (under the pen name Francis Newton), "We see him first, surrounded by legendary mist, as Buddy Bolden, the demon barber of Franklin Street, the blackest of black men, as the tale goes, 'a pure Negro' (for blackness means low status, even among Negroes), who found his cornet on the street."[60] Again, all these clichés are false.

The neighborhood Bolden spent virtually his entire life in was mixed both in terms of class (with an array of skilled and unskilled workers) and ethnicity. In the late 1880s it was predominantly Irish and German. Marquis characterizes it as a "well-integrated area" and notes that "steamboatmen, teamsters, carpenters, porters, teachers, plasterers, and longshoremen" formed the bulk of the population on Bolden's block.[61]

Stearns states that Bolden "couldn't read a note," yet many of the musicians cited by Marquis dispute that claim. In fact, it's highly likely that Bolden was a trained musician. He was listed as a "music teacher" in the city directory in 1901. At a time when education was not compulsory, Bolden not only attended but finished school, according to his friend Louis Jones. The school in his neighborhood, the Fisk School for Boys, had a solid music program in the European mold and the students even performed operettas such as Gilbert and Sullivan's *HMS Pinafore*.[62] (This is the same school that Louis Armstrong would attend a generation later, though only through the fifth grade.[63])

By the 1890s at least two professional musicians taught at the Fisk school, the brothers James and Wendell McNeil. Both worked for years with famed Creole bandleader John Robichaux. Wendell played violin and viola, while James played cornet and eventually became vice-principal of the school. James McNeil also led the Onward Brass Band, which enlisted as a unit to fight in the Spanish-American War. Before returning home to New Orleans, the band made a stop in New York and marched in a triumphant victory parade up Fifth Avenue, predating by two decades James Reese Europe's celebrated appearance in the World War I Armistice parade. Around the time of McNeil's New York visit, a cylinder recording of a cornet solo was made there by one "James McNeil." This presents the tantalizing possibility that, although no recording of Bolden has turned up, one by his putative teacher may exist.[64] (I have tried to locate this cylinder but so far to no avail. Almost assuredly the music is not jazz-related; most likely it's a typically polite Victorian cornet solo of the period.)

These possible associations between Bolden and his teachers—along with the many Creoles, including Kid Ory and Oscar Celestin, who lived in his neighborhood—contradict the familiar uptown/downtown, black/Creole dichotomies found in most jazz histories. Bolden is also listed as a plasterer in city directories from 1897 to 1900, and plastering was a craft dominated by Creoles of color. Creoles founded the plasterers' union around the turn of the century, and it's doubtful anyone without close Creole connections could have found work in this line. (Other Creole musicians who worked as plasterers include banjoist Johnny St. Cyr and Joseph Bechet, Sidney's older brother).[65]

To further confound the notion that Bolden was the prototypical uptown black, the exact nature of his "blackness" is open to question. In the 1870 census, Bolden's paternal family is listed as mulatto, the official mixed-race designation. Jelly Roll Morton described Bolden as "a light brown-skinned boy from Uptown."[66] Kid Ory mentions that he had reddish hair.[67] In 1902 Bolden married a mulatto woman, Nora Bass, and his in-laws included Ida Rose, pianist with the Bloom Philharmonic, a Creole concert orchestra.[68]

Getting back to more substantial matters, we need to confront the question of whether Bolden was in fact the "first jazz musician." Since there are no recordings of Bolden's band, this will always be an irresolvable question. But a substantial amount of testimony does support the claim that Bolden introduced the blues to an improvised form of ragtime and dance music, played primarily on band instruments. There's certainly no doubt that such a fusion was crucial to the formation of early jazz.

Cornetist and violinist Peter Bocage credited Bolden with "starting" jazz, because Bolden's band—whatever kind of music it played—improvised. Moreover, "He had a good style in blues and all that stuff. Blues was their standby, slow blues."[69] Clarinetist Lawrence Duhé agreed: "See Bolden put them [blues] out. That's how jazz come about."[70] According to Jelly Roll Morton, "Bolden's band was very popular because they were practically the only band (the best anyway) that played blues at that time."[71]

Where would Bolden have heard the blues? The African-American trumpeter Punch Miller recalled how, in the New Orleans of his youth, it was common to see "guys walking up and down the levee with guitars on their shoulders."[72] For itinerant blues musicians from the Mississippi Delta region, New Orleans was less than a day's journey away. The vocalist Lizzie Miles, born in New Orleans in 1895, spoke of obscure early blues singers such as Tillie Johnson, and one Ann Cook, who was "before my time."[73]

But Morton also insisted that Bolden was not the first to make the leap from vocal to instrumental blues. "The whole world with the exception of New Orleans was ignorant of the fact that blues could be played by an orchestra. [Charlie] Happy Galloway's orchestra played blues when I was a child. Also [Henry] Payton's accordion orchestra.[74] Their main tunes were different pairs of blues. Later Buddy Bolden came along, the first great powerful cornetist."[75]

It's interesting to note that Charlie "Happy" Galloway was born in 1869, close to Bolden's originally assigned birthdate, and he ran a barber shop, a profession often ascribed to Bolden. Galloway played stringed instruments (guitar, mandolin, and violin), but at one time his band had a recognizable jazz instrumentation including cornet, clarinet, valve trombone, and drums. Bolden worked for Galloway, as did two musicians who would later be in Bolden's band: clarinetist Frank Lewis and valve trombonist Frankie Dusen. According to a contemporary of Bolden's, Dude Bottley, Bolden formed his first band by luring these two men away from Galloway.[76]

Yet even if Galloway's orchestra, Payton's accordion orchestra, or other groups preceded Bolden in playing instrumental blues, there's no question that Bolden was the first to create widespread (albeit local) interest in the new style. If he was not precisely the "first man of jazz," he was its first sensation. As Marquis writes, "Bolden is the most talked about and best remembered personality" of his time and place.[77]

So Bolden made the most noise, both literally and figuratively (his other most famous trait, besides playing the blues, was the incredible volume he produced on cornet, an instrument typically described as "mellow"). Jazz still bears the stamp of the heartfelt, driving, spontaneous, blues-inflected music he made famous a century ago. For that he is worthy of his legendary reputation, despite all the fanciful folklore surrounding it.[78]

THE BIRTH OF BOP

The genesis of bebop is typically portrayed as a revolution: the sudden and unforeseen brainchild of Dizzy Gillespie, Charlie Parker, Thelonious Monk and a few others. What's more, this strange new music was supposedly a militant reaction against the bland, commercial pop styles of the day. To quote LeRoi Jones (Amiri Baraka), bebop was a "willfully harsh, antiassimilationist sound" that sought to "restore jazz, in some sense, to its original separateness, to drag it outside the mainstream of American culture."[79]

Martin Williams, in a widely quoted passage from *The Jazz Tradition*, writes that Charlie Parker was "called upon . . . to change the language of jazz, to reinterpret its fundamentals and give it a way to continue." He goes on: "The crucial thing about the bebop style is that its basis came from the resources of jazz itself, and it came about in much the same way that innovation had come about in the past. That basis is rhythmic, and it involves rhythmic subdivision. . . . We should not talk about harmonic exactness or substitute chords and the rest before we have talked about rhythm. Like Louis Armstrong, Charlie Parker expanded jazz rhythmically and although the rhythmic changes are intricately and subtly bound up with his ideas of harmony and melody, the rhythmic change is fundamental."[80]

Williams and Baraka agree, as do many others, that rhythm was the defining characteristic of bebop. Gunther Schuller asks whether the

penchant in "modern jazz" to feel the eighth note as a basic unit is in any way related to African music. It is certainly clear by now that one of Charlie Parker's most enduring innovations was precisely this splitting of the four beats in a bar to eight. Was this—like the emergence of some underground river—the musical reincarnation of impulses subconsciously remembered from generations earlier and produceable *only* when the carrier of this memory had developed his instrumental technique sufficiently to cope with it? Once again, the fact that no comparable trend has developed in European "art music" lends support to this theory.[81]

All of these writers maintain that the rhythmic (and hence African) dimension is more crucial to the development of bebop than the harmonic (Western) one. Of course rhythmic innovation was an essential and immediately recognizable characteristic of bebop. But rhythmic developments were inextricably linked to bop's new and equally characteristic melodic approach based on detailing harmonic progressions. Both harmony and rhythm are part of the same package, and it is impossible to determine which is the more essential element. But clearly, harmony was uppermost in the minds of the beboppers when discussing their new musical language.

Bill Doggett, the pianist and organist who knew Dizzy Gillespie when they were teenagers in Philadelphia, remembered how

> We'd sit around and talk music, chord changes; that was the real thing at that particular time. . . . There were several tunes that we used to play to show the virtuosity of a musician, and one of the tunes at that time was a tune called "Liza," where you changed chords almost every two beats. Like you'd go to a major and a diminish [diminished chord] up to a minor seventh and then up to another diminish, and up to a major. We would try running these chords as we were playing. Running them up, running them backward, running them upside down, and all kinds of ways. And then we would take a tune like "I Can't Get Started," which Diz made one of his great tunes. Now this was a slow ballad, and we would try to make different chords off of almost every note there was in the tune.[82]

When Gillespie and bassist Milt Hinton were members of Cab Calloway's band, they would go up to the roof of the Cotton Club to experiment with chord progressions. "We're gonna play 'I Got Rhythm' but we're gonna use these changes," Gillespie would tell Hinton. "Instead of using B-flat and D-flat, we're gonna use B-flat, D-flat, G-flat, or F and we change."[83]

During a three-month job in the Ozarks with commercial bandleader George E. Lee, a sixteen-year-old Charlie Parker devoted himself to the study of saxophone technique and harmony. He began practicing tunes in all keys, which gave him a harmonic fluency that few musicians possessed at that time. "Cherokee," with its constantly modulating bridge, became his tune of choice for exploring advanced harmonic concepts. In a famous interview, Michael Levin and John S. Wilson (paraphrasing

Parker's comments) wrote that he became "bored with the stereotyped changes being used then." They added, "Working over the 'Cherokee' changes with [guitarist Biddy] Fleet, Charlie suddenly found that by using higher intervals of a chord as a melody line and backing them up with appropriately related changes, he could play what he was 'hearing.'"[84]

Shortly after moving to New York, Parker took a job washing dishes at Jimmy's Chicken Shack in Harlem. Despite the pitiful wages, the young altoist was rewarded by hearing piano master Art Tatum play in the main room. Mary Lou Williams remembered, "Art inspired me so much. Chords he was throwing in then, the boppers are using now."[85] Tatum's harmonically sophisticated style even had a strong influence on Thelonious Monk. As pianist Billy Taylor recalled, "The first time I ever heard Monk, he was playing much more like Art than what he later became."[86]

What is obvious in all these citations is how profoundly these musicians were affected by popular songs of the era, especially those incorporating advanced harmonies. The music they heard all day on radio and played all night on the bandstand was largely culled from the "great American songbook," as it is known today. Virtually Art Tatum's entire repertoire consisted of standards. Duke Ellington's contract with Victor specified that half of his recorded output had to consist of current pop tunes.[87] And as we've seen, John Hammond supervised recordings of standards sung by Billie Holiday and targeted to the African-American market. To the beboppers, this repertoire was as ubiquitous as the air they breathed.

By a happy coincidence, the thirties—the decade in which the bop generation of musicians began to develop—also witnessed the rise of the American popular song to its highest peak of sophistication, both lyrically and harmonically.

Many tunes by the great song composers foreshadow devices that the boppers later standardized (and I must get a bit technical here): an increase in harmonic rhythm, with harmonic changes occurring as often as every two beats (in Gershwin, sometimes as much as every beat); chromatic harmony veering off to distant keys; a reliance on ii–V–I progressions; the melodic and harmonic use of upper intervals; tritone substitutions; and altered seventh chords. All of these techniques were frequently employed in film scores, even in arrangements recorded by commercial big bands, such as Glenn Miller's "Song of the Volga Boatman" (which concludes with a G-flat thirteenth chord resolving to an F minor eleventh with a raised seventh, written by the progressive arranger Bill Finegan).

The intimacy with which jazz players knew the standard repertoire is illustrated in an anecdote from pianist Junior Mance about a recording date with tenor saxophonist Ben Webster. Mance had worked with three giants of the tenor saxophone—Webster, Coleman Hawkins, and Lester Young—and all three stressed the importance of learning the words to standards. Webster stopped playing near the end of a flawless take. When asked why, Webster replied that he'd forgotten the words.[88]

Despite this wealth of personal testimony, a host of influential jazz writers have severely downplayed the influence this repertoire had on the boppers. According to Albert Murray, "Sophisticated blues musicians extend, refine, and counterstate pop music, especially the thirty-two bar show tune, in precisely the same manner as they do the traditional folk-type blues strain. Indeed, as the endless list of outstanding blues-idiom compositions derived from the songs of Jerome Kern, Irving Berlin, George Gershwin, Cole Porter, Harold Arlen, Vincent Youmans, and Walter Donaldson, among others, so clearly indicate, blues musicians proceed as if the Broadway musical were in fact a major source of relatively crude but fascinating folk materials!"[89]

But it wasn't the "traditional folk-type blues strain" that inspired Gillespie, Parker, and Monk to veer off in another direction. Instead they grafted their own advanced harmonic ideas onto the basic blues itself, which Parker often pejoratively referred to as "rice and beans music." To me it is obvious that these musicians worked diligently to come to terms with the harmonic implications of the pop tunes of their day, and to develop a way of improvising in which all the harmonic nuances found in these tunes could be brought out. After all, as Murray correctly notes, these songs and their bebop derivatives formed the core of their repertoire.

Note how early some of the famous tunes of this era were composed:

1930	But Not For Me, Embraceable You, I Got Rhythm, I've Got a Crush on You, I'm Confessin', Fine and Dandy, Love for Sale, My Ideal, Time On My Hands.
1931	Just Friends, Dancing in the Dark, Between the Devil and the Deep Blue Sea, I'm Through With Love, When Your Lover Has Gone, Out of Nowhere, Who Cares?
1932	Night and Day, Alone Together, April in Paris, Ghost of a Chance, How Deep Is the Ocean, I'm Getting Sentimental Over You, The Song Is You, Street of Dreams, Willow Weep for Me, You Are Too Beautiful.
1933	Don't Blame Me, Everything I Have Is Yours, Talk of the Town, Smoke Gets in Your Eyes, Sophisticated Lady, Yesterdays.
1934	Autumn in New York, Deep Purple, I Only Have Eyes for You, My Old Flame, What a Difference a Day Made.
1935	Ballad in Blue, East of the Sun, Just One of Those Things, September in the Rain, Stairway to the Stars, Summertime, My Man's Gone Now.

1936   Easy to Love, I Can't Get Started, Pennies from Heaven, The
        Way You Look Tonight, There Is No Greater Love, There's a
        Small Hotel, Ridin' High, Shall We Dance?
1937   A Foggy Day, Nice Work If You Can Get It, Gone With the
        Wind, Someday My Prince Will Come, Where or When, Have
        You Met Miss Jones?, My Funny Valentine, Too Marvelous for
        Words.
1938   Cherokee, Spring Is Here, You Go to My Head.
1939   All the Things You Are, Darn That Dream, I Didn't Know What
        Time It Was, Indian Summer, What's New?, I Thought About
        You.

It's impossible for a jazz buff to read through this list without being
reminded of countless classic jazz performances. Jazz players took these
tunes to heart because the harmonies delighted and challenged them. For
the bridge to his composition "Yardbird Suite," Parker used essentially
the same chords found in Gershwin's "Nice Work If You Can Get It."
For his tune "Salt Peanuts," Gillespie borrowed the progression for the
release to "Alone Together."

In addition to providing a handy blueprint for improvising, these
tunes also make use of many devices that would later be associated
with bop. The melody and harmony of "Fine and Dandy" and "Time
on My Hands" emphasize upper intervals, as do the majority of tunes
just listed. "Between the Devil and the Deep Blue Sea" and "Out of
Nowhere" feature unusual harmonic shifts (F to A going to the bridge
in "Devil," and G to E-flat in the opening bars of "Nowhere"). Half-
diminished chords are found in "April in Paris" and "Yesterdays." Most
of the ballads, such as "I've Got a Crush on You," "You Are Too Beautiful" and "Don't Blame Me," contain a harmonic rhythm of two beats
per bar. Hoagy Carmichael's "Ballad in Blue" is a study in chromatic
alterations.

An increased awareness of harmony on the part of jazz musicians
began even before the advent of bebop. The transition from thinking
"horizontally" to thinking "vertically" (i.e., melodically to chordally)
occurred in the thirties and is well documented in arrangements of the
period. Printed stock arrangements of the twenties typically indicate an
improvised solo by writing the melody along with a verbal cue such as
"solo—improvise." By the early thirties chords were spelled out on the
staff, and a few years later chord symbols appeared. This indicates that
by at least the mid-thirties, even soloists in the nameless commercial
bands that purchased these stocks were expected to have a basic working
knowledge of harmony.

The evolution from melodic to chordal thinking is also traceable on records. One has only to compare Louis Armstrong's 1930 version of Johnny Green's "Body and Soul" with Coleman Hawkins's rendition nine years later. Armstrong's performance is stirring and perfect in its own way, but his approach is basically melodic. His unfailing ear (Armstrong had perfect pitch) enabled him to play with consistent reference to all the underlying harmonies. But he makes little attempt to "get inside" the changes and delineate their differences, which is precisely the path Hawkins takes. The beboppers took things a step farther by focusing more intently on upper intervals, a further harmonically inspired development.

To me, Martin Williams's vaunted claim that bop's innovations were fundamentally rhythmic is a typical overreaching generalization by a nonmusician. The increased speed of the harmonic rhythm in such tunes as "Liza" or "Cherokee" encouraged Parker and Gillespie to adopt eighth-note phrases for spelling out the intricacies inherent in the harmony. No mysterious atavistic African impulse was at work, as Gunther Schuller, a musician who should know better, suggests. If you slow Parker's and Gillespie's phrases down, their syncopations are not that dissimilar from Armstrong's. The main difference is that the boppers thought in terms of shorter time spans dictated by faster harmonic rhythm. This resulted in increased rhythmic subdivision, longer phrases floating over a succession of changes, and greater complexity of line. In later years, John Coltrane further increased the speed of harmonic rhythm in jazz, which in turn contributed to smaller and more irregular subdivisions. Once again, harmony was a motivating factor.

Nothing I've said here should be interpreted as an attempt to diminish the enormous contributions made by the innovators of bebop. They took disparate elements from a variety of sources, as all great artists do, and created something entirely new and original. The importance and uniqueness of their vision cannot be overestimated. I am merely trying to show where this brilliant group of musicians found inspiration and—reversing Baraka's language—to drag bebop back into the mainstream of American culture.

In LeRoi Jones's play *Dutchman* a character says: "Charlie Parker? Charlie Parker. All the hip white boys scream for Bird. And Bird saying, 'Up your ass, feebleminded ofays! Up your ass.' And they sit there talking about the tortured genius of Charlie Parker. Bird would've played not a note of music if he just walked up to East Sixty-seventh Street and killed the first ten white people he saw. Not a note!"[90]

A writer once noted that bebop was being promoted as a "fighting" word for some. He asked Dizzy Gillespie, "Was this a 'fighting' music?" No, Dizzy replied, "It is a love music."[91]

SOURCES OF THE AVANT-GARDE

A popular Marxist slogan of the thirties was that "Art is a class weapon." Though LeRoi Jones didn't publicly embrace Marxism until the 1970s, much of his writing in the 1960s was already headed in that direction. He repeatedly attempted to link "revolutionary" music, meaning bebop and later "free jazz," with political revolution. For Jones and others, avant-garde jazz signified the transformation in black consciousness from Martin Luther King Jr.'s vision of nonviolent resistance to the Black Panthers' preference for armed resistance. The German jazz scholar Ekkehard Jost, in his 1975 book *Free Jazz*, wrote, "As a rule wholesale judgments on free jazz focused on its sociocultural and political background."[92] As strident as the music could be, it was frequently seen only as an accompaniment to the political climate surrounding it.

In an attempt to put a racial stamp on avant-garde jazz, Jones insisted it be called "New Black Music." Its African roots, in the form of ritualized group interaction, were stressed. At the same time, what Jost referred to as "the proclamation of an openly anti-European (or anti-American) slant by some of the most prominent exponents of free jazz"[93] served to deemphasize Western influences. "When black people first came to these shores," wrote Jones, "they didn't know much about harmony . . . that's a Western musical phenomenon. The new music reaches back to what jazz was originally." In 1966 the white Marxist critic Frank Kofsky wrote, "Today's avant-garde movement in jazz is a musical representation of the ghetto's vote of no confidence in Western civilization and the American Dream—that Negro avant-garde intransigents, in other words, are saying through their horns, as LeRoi Jones would have it, 'Up your ass, feeble-minded ofays!'"[94]

What these and many present-day jazz writers miss (or chose to ignore) is that the advent of avant-garde jazz would have been unthinkable without the Western concept of artistic modernism. The very label "avant-garde" suggests the European origins of the movement. Following the Second World War, New York replaced Paris as the international capital of the art world. And for the first time in its history, America began to take its role as cultural pacesetter seriously. As William B. Scott and Peter M. Rutkoff note in their book *New York Modern*, "By the early 1950s, abstract expressionists, along with beat poets and writers and postwar jazz musicians, formed a new American avant-garde as heirs to both the Greenwich Village rebellion and the bohemianism of the prewar Parisian Left Bank."[95] To the American public, abstract painters Jackson Pollock, Mark Rothko, and Robert Motherwell, "like Marilyn Monroe, Marlon Brando, and Joe DiMaggio . . . joined America's postwar pantheon of cultural icons."[96] In 1949 even *Life* magazine proclaimed Pollock the nation's most important painter. Stravinsky, Schoenberg, Bartók, and Varèse had all relocated to America by the end of the war. Modernism had found a new and nurturing home.

The mainstreaming of the modern was evident in new architecture springing up across America. In New York, the Museum of Modern Art moved into its present location in 1939. Le Corbusier's United Nations building was completed in 1947. In 1958 Mies van der Rohe unveiled his Seagram building. Sixth Avenue in midtown was rebuilt according to Bauhaus ideals. In 1959 Frank Lloyd Wright's Guggenheim Museum opened, and shortly thereafter a well-known photograph of John Coltrane was taken inside. In Chicago, Wright gave visible expression to the new aesthetic in such buildings as the Robie House, standing only a block from where the Association for the Advancement of Creative Music (AACM), the epicenter of Chicago's black jazz avant-garde, was formed. Even Fort Worth, Texas, where Ornette Coleman (the guiding force of the new jazz) grew up, was hardly a cultural backwater; the Modern Art Museum of Fort Worth is second in size only to New York's MOMA among the nation's modern art museums. In neighboring Dallas, from 1945 to 1949, the symphony was conducted by Antal Doráti, who championed the music of fellow Hungarian modernists Béla Bartók and Zoltán Kodály. On national television in the fifties and early sixties, Leonard Bernstein dissected the music of Stravinsky as well as American renegade composer Charles Ives.

Just as it was impossible to reach maturity in the thirties without being aware of the great American pop tunes of the era, so it was impossible for those coming of age after the war to escape the influence of modernism. The notion that art was engaged in an evolutionary march led by its avant-garde was simply the conventional wisdom of the day.

Of course, jazz from its beginning had grown up with modernism, and Buddy Bolden belongs to the same generation as Ives, Bartók, Stravinsky, Picasso, and James Joyce. In his book *Jazz Modernism*, Alfred Appel Jr. traces the parallel developments of the two, and rightly notes that modernist indeterminism has always been a feature of jazz. The freedom of improvisation—or at least the appearance of it through the abnegation of restrictive formal procedures—is an important element in all modernism. For a powerful demonstration of indeterminism in even prewar jazz, Appel cites Louis Armstrong's breathtaking solo on "Swing That Music" from May 1936.[97] On the last chorus, "Only a computer or an EKG could possibly calibrate and transcribe the way Armstrong's teeming miniscule rhythmic inflections variously fall on or just off the basic metric pulse."[98] I can attest to the truth of this observation, as I've attempted to transcribe (or more precisely, approximate) this solo on more than one occasion.

The close connection between jazz and modernism is also suggested by the term "modern jazz," which was loosely applied to various forms of postwar jazz. What Ornette Coleman and later jazz avant-gardists shared with cutting-edge modernism was a desire to break free of past artistic canons of beauty ("Ugly Beauty" as the title of Thelonious Monk's composition eloquently put it), along with time-honored means of achieving structural coherence.

The last line of James Joyce's virtually impenetrable novel *Finnegans Wake* is: A way a lone a last a loved a long the

Ornette Coleman was once asked to write his autobiography, and he submitted the following: Born, work, sad and happy and etc.[99]

Coleman's "motivic chain associations" (a term borrowed from Ekke-hard Jost) and Joyce's "stream of consciousness" are two sides of the same modernist coin. "I will try to express myself in some mode of life or art as freely as I can and as wholly as I can," says Joyce's protagonist Stephen Dedalus in *Ulysses*, and this could have been the motto for the jazz avant-garde as well.

Significantly, Jackson Pollock's 1947 painting *White Light* appears on the cover of Coleman's 1960 recording *Free Jazz*. One index of the close connection between avant-garde jazz and the Western modernist tradition is the number of musicians who took up painting, including Ornette Coleman, Pharoah Sanders, Muhal Richard Abrams, Bill Dixon, Roscoe Mitchell, and Lester Lashley (as well as the trans-stylistic Miles Davis).[100] Those who took up modernist poetry included Joseph Jarman, Archie Shepp, and Cecil Taylor.

The jazz avant-garde has never gained broad popular acceptance, leading to cries of racism. But Ornette Coleman and those who followed have suffered the same fate that other modernists had met before them: their work has been more often subjected to critical study than widespread approval. "I'm not loved because nobody is interested in what I'm doing," reflected Coleman. "They're only interested in writing and talking about it, not the music itself." Another jazz iconoclast Sun Ra once said, "I want to be the only thing I could be without anybody stopping me in America—and that is to be a failure. So I feel pretty good about it, I'm a total failure."[101] Public apathy, if not downright opprobrium, was already a well-worn path in the avant-garde tradition. Writers from Walt Whitman to Proust, Eliot, and Virginia Woolf had great difficulty getting their work published, and often did so at their own expense. The Joyce of *Ulysses* and *Finnegans Wake*—like the late-career Coltrane, with his forays into free jazz—was taken seriously due to his earlier and more accessible work. None of these authors made much money from their more experimental writing. And apart from school assignments much of their work is still not widely read.

Of all the species of avant-garde artists, only abstract painters enjoyed broad commercial success. This may be simply because viewing a painting requires less of a personal commitment in terms of time and attention than reading a novel or listening to a piece of music (especially one of Cecil Taylor's two-and-a-half-hour sets). Perhaps more importantly, fine art is a form of tangible property with transferable ownership, and therefore becomes a financial investment capable of paying much higher dividends than books or records.

Whether these avant-garde artworks turned a profit or not, they continue to be controversial. Their merits are still hotly debated, as may be the case forever. Whenever art veers off from direct communication and steps into the realm of incoherence, there will always be a handful of people willing to devote themselves to studying it, but the vast majority will simply ignore it. Cecil Taylor once stated, "The artist's first responsibility is to communicate with himself," not his audience.[102] The artist who doesn't strive to communicate to a large audience will rarely attract one.

The lack of widespread acceptance for avant-garde jazz is not a function of racism; it's a function of the more extreme forms of modernism. The home this music eventually found was in those interracial places that have traditionally harbored exploratory art: artists' communities in downtown New York (specifically the East and West Village and Soho), Europe and the universities.

One of the most interesting cultural phenomena of the 1970s was the rapid deployment of black avant-garde musicians to teaching positions in prestigious liberal arts colleges throughout America. These jobs opened up in conjunction with a new wave of black studies programs, which sought to bring more African-Americans into the university fold at a time of mounting social unrest. Avant musicians were hired in a host of departments, ranging from black studies to music, theater, and dance. Pianist Horace Tapscott, founder of the Union of God's Musicians and Artists Ascension (UGMAA) and the Pan Afrikan Peoples Arkestra, took a teaching post at the University of California, Riverside, as a result of protests by the university's Black Student Union. Archie Shepp joined the black studies faculty of the State University of New York (SUNY) at Buffalo in 1969, and moved on to a tenured position at the University of Massachusetts–Amherst in 1974. Makanda Ken McIntyre was appointed professor at SUNY at Old Westbury, and Sun Ra taught a course at the University of California, Berkeley. As for trumpeters, Bill Dixon taught at Bennington College from 1968 to 1996; Bobby Bradford at Claremont College; and Wadada Leo Smith at Bard. Cecil Taylor took positions at Glassboro State College, the University of Wisconsin, and Antioch College, where he was joined by the rest of his trio, alto saxophonist Jimmy Lyons and drummer Andrew Cyrille. For many years Anthony Braxton has taught in the ethnomusicology department at Wesleyan University, and his AACM associate Roscoe Mitchell is at the University of Michigan.

As Eric Porter wrote in his book *What Is This Thing Called Jazz?*, "Because of the revolutionary meanings associated with their music, jazz musicians who became teachers had an appeal across racial lines to politicized students who sought alternative intellectual training and a validation of black cultural practices. [Musician and author] Ben Sidran noted that by 1966 the new jazz and other black musics had gained increasing popularity with white college students who wanted to identify with black liberation struggles or who linked black musical expression to their own antiestablishment orientation."[103]

Many of these politicized students became the jazz history teachers of today, and through them the mythology of jazz has been transmitted to a new generation.

NOTES

1. Stearns, *The Story of Jazz*, 13.
2. Blesh, *Shining Trumpets*, 5.
3. Chernoff, *African Rhythm and African Sensibility*, 40.
4. Chernoff, 42.
5. "Metric modulation," a term first applied to the work of contemporary American composer Elliott Carter, refers to the use of a repeated rhythmic phrase—most commonly based on a triplet pattern in 4/4 time—to establish a new beat, either faster or slower than the original tempo. Rumor has it that drummer Tony Williams and bassist Ron Carter, while playing with the Miles Davis quintet, employed this technique to confound tenor saxophonist George Coleman and prevent him from overusing phrases based on running eighth notes.
6. Schuller, *Early Jazz*, 21.
7. Oliver, *Savannah Syncopators*, 36–37.
8. Charters, *The Roots of the Blues*, 127.
9. Lyons, *The Great Jazz Pianists*, 213.
10. Priestley, *Chasin' the Bird*, 48.
11. Gillespie and Fraser, *To Be or Not To Bop*, 485.
12. Dahl, *Morning Glory*, 271.
13. Hogan Jazz Archive, Tulane University. Ory interview conducted April 20, 1957.
14. Taylor, *Notes and Tones*, 242–243.
15. Monson, ed., *The African Diaspora*, 347.
16. Transcript of the Jelly Roll Morton Symposium held at Tulane University, May 7, 1982. Courtesy of Bruce Boyd Raeburn, curator of the Hogan Jazz Archive.
17. Ramsey and Smith, eds., *Jazzmen*, 7.
18. Ramsey and Smith, eds., 5.

19. Ramsey and Smith, eds., 9.
20. Goffin, *Jazz*, 14.
21. Blesh, 157–158.
22. Stearns, 39.
23. Schuller, 4.
24. Old myths die hard. In *The Power of Black Music*, author Samuel A. Floyd Jr. states in a footnote: "I have come across information demonstrating that Cable's description [of dances in Congo Square] was constructed from others' first-hand knowledge of such events. . . . But I have chosen to leave my statements as I have written them, since Cable's description, although imaginative, conforms to the essentials of actual reported accounts of such activities." Floyd, *The Power of Black Music*, 35.
25. This confession, made in a letter from Hearn to musicologist Henry Edward Krehbiel, is quoted in Henry Kmen, "The Roots of Jazz and the Dance in Place Congo: A Re-appraisal," *Anuario interamericano de investigación musical* 8 (1972): 12. Hearn would later go on to write books about Creole proverbs and Creole cuisine.
26. Kmen, "The Roots of Jazz and the Dance in Place Congo," 5–16.
27. Starr, *Louis Moreau Gottschalk*, 41.
28. Jerah Johnson, *Congo Square in New Orleans*, 40.
29. George Washington Cable, "Dance in Place Congo," *Century Magazine*, November 1883, 45.
30. Kmen, "The Roots of Jazz and the Dance in Place Congo," 13–14.
31. Kmen, "The Roots of Jazz and the Dance in Place Congo," 13.
32. Kmen, *Music in New Orleans*, 226.
33. Jerah Johnson, 33.
34. Kmen, *Music in New Orleans*, 227–229.
35. Starr, *Louis Moreau Gottschalk*, 40.
36. Jerah Johnson, 42.
37. Jerah Johnson, 42.
38. Lomax, *Mister Jelly Roll*, 79.
39. Much of the French Quarter as we know it today was originally built by Creoles of color. Many had fled the Haitian revolution of the 1790s and relocated in New Orleans just as the city was being rebuilt after the great fire of 1788.
40. Eric Porter, *What Is This Thing Called Jazz?*, 99.
41. Foster and Stoddard, *Pops Foster*, 61.
42. Gushee, *Pioneers of Jazz*, 314 (footnote 22).
43. Foster and Stoddard, 43.
44. Ward and Burns, *Jazz*, 16, 18.
45. Lomax, 52.
46. Lomax, 19.
47. Jerah Johnson, "Jim Crow Laws of the 1890s and the Origins of New Orleans Jazz: Correction of an Error," *Popular Music* 19, no. 2 (2000): 243–251.
48. Charters, *Jazz New Orleans*, 3.
49. Domînguez, *White By Definiton*, 135–136.
50. Foster and Stoddard, 65.
51. Dodds and Gara, *The Baby Dodds Story*, 13.

52. Armstrong, *Satchmo*, 187.

53. Dodds and Gara, 15, 24.

54. Max Jones, *Jazz Talking*, 26.

55. Krin Gabbard, professor of comparative literature and English at the State University of New York at Stony Brook, seems to be going for the academic trifecta by combining race, gender, and class within a single theory: he has written of the "homoerotic and voyeuristic element of fascination" on the part of white jazz fans, aroused by "black men as they enact their masculinity with saxophones, trumpets, guitars, and other phallic instruments." Krin Gabbard, *Black Magic: White Hollywood and African American Culture* (New Brunswick, NJ: Rutgers University Press, 2004), 203.

56. Originally published in an article by Frederic Ramsey Jr. in *Downbeat*, December 15, 1940, 10, 26. Reprinted in Gushee, 40.

57. Jerah Johnson, "Jim Crow Laws," 249.

58. Gushee, *Pioneers of Jazz*, 17–18.

59. Stearns, 68.

60. Newton, *The Jazz Scene*, 200.

61. Marquis, *In Search of Buddy Bolden*, 22.

62. Marquis, 18, 29.

63. Armstrong, 25.

64. Charters and Kunstadt, *Jazz*, 53.

65. Chilton, *Sidney Bechet*, 7.

66. Lomax, 60.

67. Hogan Jazz Archive. Ory interview conducted April 20, 1957.

68. Marquis, 96.

69. Marquis, 105.

70. Hogan Jazz Archive. Duhé interview conducted June 9, 1957.

71. Russell, *Oh, Mister Jelly*, 136.

72. Hogan Jazz Archive. Miller interview conducted August 20, 1959.

73. Hogan Jazz Archive. Miles interview conducted January 18, 1951.

74. The spelling is given as "Peyton" in Al Rose and Edmond Souchon's *New Orleans Jazz: A Family Album* (Baton Rouge, LA: Louisiana State University Press, 1978).

75. Russell, 485.

76. Barker, *Buddy Bolden and the Last Days of Storyville*, 9. Dude Bottley was the brother of Buddy Bottley, who booked bands in Lincoln Park (including Bolden's) and ran a popular hot-air balloon ride there.

77. Marquis, 53.

78. It's sadly ironic that Bolden, the iconic "first man of jazz," and Leon Roppolo, the first truly great white jazz musician to record, both ended their days in the same place: the Louisiana State Asylum for the Insane in Jackson.

79. LeRoi Jones, *Blues People*, 181.

80. Williams, *The Jazz Tradition*, 141.

81. Schuller, 25. Schuller's claim that the "penchant" for using the eighth note as a basic pulse has no corollary in "European art music" is hard to fathom. What does he make of the eighth-note motor rhythms in Bach, or the Baroque style in general?

82. Gillespie and Fraser, 51–52.

83. Gillespie and Fraser, 143.

84. Priestley, 27.

85. Shapiro and Hentoff, *Hear Me Talkin' To Ya*, 294–295.

86. Gitler, *Swing to Bop*, 103.

87. This contract, from 1940, will be discussed more fully in a section devoted to recording in the chapter "It's Strictly Business."

88. Conversation between Junior Mance and the author, 2007.

89. Murray, *Stomping the Blues*, 205.

90. LeRoi Jones, *Dutchman*, 34–35.

91. Gillespie and Fraser, 142.

92. Jost, *Free Jazz*, 8.

93. Jost, 8.

94. Kofsky, *Black Nationalism and the Revolution in Music*, 131.

95. Scott and Rutkoff, *New York Modern*, 290.

96. Scott and Rutkoff, 318.

97. Armstrong recorded "Swing That Music" twice in 1936, once on May 18 and again on August 7. Appel is clearly referring to the first recording.

98. Appel, *Jazz Modernism*, 189.

99. Litweiler, *The Freedom Principle*, 19.

100. White musicians of an earlier generation, such as Django Reinhardt, Pee Wee Russell, and Bob Haggart, also took to painting, perhaps revealing an earlier inclination to identify themselves as "artists." Drummer George Wettling was so serious about painting that he took lessons from the American modernist Stuart Davis. One artist who reciprocated in kind was painter Larry Rivers, who also played jazz saxophone.

101. Litweiler, 144.

102. Litweiler, 207.

103. Eric Porter, 234.

4

~

What Gets Left Out

"The past is not here to defend itself."

—Henry Steele Commager

By stressing the insularity of black culture, many inconvenient truths are swept under the ideological rug. White participation in jazz is viewed with suspicion, and obvious connections between jazz and mainstream American culture, or the Western artistic tradition, are downplayed if not simply ignored. Let's take a look at some aspects of the jazz story that are frequently left out of the history books.

BLACKFACE MINSTRELSY

Why start with minstrelsy? Conventional wisdom tells us unequivocally that minstrelsy was the embodiment of racism. Besides, it has only the slightest connection to jazz. Let me address this last point first.

In America there have been many marriages between the music of African and European descendants. The first such union produced the spirituals, which emerged from the 1780s to the 1830s, a period of religious revival known as the Second Great Awakening. The second union gave us minstrelsy. Minstrelsy, the direct ancestor of American musical theatre, lasted for nearly one hundred years as a major form of popular entertainment. Later musical hybrids would produce ragtime, jazz, R&B, and rock, to name only a few. A convincing case can be made that American music developed its own identity only after it took on influences stemming from its African-American populace.

Of all these musical traditions, minstrelsy stands out as the ugliest and most mean-spirited form of cultural abuse: a wholesale appropriation of the musical expression of an enslaved people, used to taunt and revile them. The specter of white men in blackface still haunts the American mind. It stands as a symbol not only of racism, but also of the willingness of whites to accept tawdry imitations of black culture for the real thing. To deny this claim in modern America seems tantamount to denying the Holocaust. As historian Ann Douglas says in her book *Terrible Honesty*, "Minstrelsy was racism in action: the expropriation and distortion of black culture for white purposes and profits."[1]

The same sorts of accusations have been leveled at the jazz world, implicating white audiences, white musicians, and white business interests throughout the history of jazz. Regardless of whatever degree minstrelsy is relevant to discussions on jazz, the subject arises with persistent frequency throughout the jazz literature, so I feel compelled to at least raise some points that are rarely, if ever, mentioned.

Was hatred of blacks the real driving force behind the mass appeal and longevity of minstrelsy? Does conventional wisdom match the real history of this curious institution?

Minstrelsy began in the abolitionist North. Many of its early song lyrics recount tales of the noble slave, his harsh life, and his ability to outwit the evil master. Other songs deal with the horrors of slave families being torn apart. Some are tender songs of love between a male and female slave. No less a figure than Frederick Douglass once expressed his approval of the idiom, albeit with some reservations: "It would seem almost absurd to say it, considering the use that has been made of them, that we have allies in the Ethiopian songs; those songs that constitute our national music. They are heart songs, and the finest feelings of human nature are expressed in them. 'Lucy Neal,' 'Old Kentucky Home,' and 'Uncle Ned' can make the heart sad as well as merry, and can call forth a tear as well as a smile. They awaken sympathies for the slave, in which antislavery principles take root, grow up and flourish."[2]

In 1828, the white entertainer Thomas Dartmouth "Daddy" Rice introduced a song and dance routine with the ominous title "Jump Jim Crow." Born in New York City, Rice toured extensively, even bringing his blackface routine to England. When he returned to the United States, minstrelsy was all the rage, particularly "Jump Jim Crow." "Never has there been such an excitement in the musical or dramatic world," gushed a reporter from the *New York Tribune* in 1855. As described by Eileen Southern in her book *The Music of Black Americans*, all the verses of Rice's song "share in common the one theme—to disparage the black man and his life style. And indeed, that was the theme of all the minstrel or Negro songs during the period."[3]

Yet others have seen the song quite differently. Historian Dale Cockrell writes, "Mockery and denigration, in this case, though, are strawmen, for there is a moral purpose to the story. . . . Some verses to 'Jim Crow' are staunchly antislavery."[4] One verse eerily portends the Civil War, still years away:

> Should dey get to fighting,
> Perhaps de blacks will rise
> For deir wish for freedom
> Is shining in deir eyes . . .
>
> I'm for freedom
> An for Union altogether
> Aldough I'm a black man,
> De white is called my broder.[5]

Rice once even played the character of Uncle Tom in a stage production of "Uncle Tom's Cabin," Harriet Beecher Stowe's 1852 antislavery novel. Another verse to "Jump Jim Crow" could almost be mistaken for a contemporary rap lyric:

> An' I caution all white dandies,
> Not to come in mya way.
> For if dey insult me.
> Dey'll in de gutter lay.

The dialect of these songs may put off many modern readers, yet we need to remind ourselves that these lyrics represent an attempt, crude as it may be, to capture the actual patterns and inflections of southern black speech. The African-American poet Paul Laurence Dunbar (1872–1906) wrote in dialect, and the librettos of many African-American musicals through the first four decades of the twentieth century employed similar vernacular, as does rap today.

Songs on the subject of forced separation by evil slaveholders form an entire genre of minstrel songs. Examples include "Farewell My Lillie Dear," "The Virginia Rose Bud," "Mary Blaine," and the most famous of all, "Darling Nellie Gray."[6] Another genre consists of tender and heartfelt love songs rendered from the standpoint of one slave to another. Among these were "Nelly Was a Lady," "Lubly Dine," "Angelina Baker," "Melinda May," and "Ella Ree."

Still another popular subject of minstrelsy was the unjust lot of the overworked slave, who could only find rest and refuge in death. Stephen

Foster's "Old Black Joe" falls into this category, as does the following lyric from the song "The Poor Old Slave":

> 'Tis just one year ago today,
> That I remember well,
> I sat down by poor Nelly's side,
> And a story she did tell.
> 'Twas about a poor, unhappy slave,
> That lived for many a year;
> But now he's dead, and in his grave,
> No master does he fear.[7]

The arduous journey up north to freedom is another familiar topic in minstrel songs. In "Ole Shady, The Song of the Contraband," an exultant slave sings:

> Goodbye hard work wid never any pay,
> Ise gwine up North where the good folks say,
> Dat white wheat bread and a dollar a day
> Are coming, coming; Hail mighty day.

"Tom-Big-Bee River" relates the story of a slave who constructs a canoe out of a gum tree and sails down the river with his "Julia so true," until they spy a ship waving a "flag of true blue" that tows them to freedom.

Perhaps the most surprising and fascinating minstrel songs are those that celebrate the end of slavery and express utter glee in turning the tables on cruel and unjust authority. Several were written by the white lyricist and composer Henry Clay Work (1832–1884). He and his father were staunch abolitionists, and their home in Middletown, Connecticut was an important stop on the Underground Railroad. Work's father was arrested and imprisoned for harboring fugitive slaves. Work is best known today for his Civil War tune "Marching Through Georgia" (celebrating Sherman's decisive routing of Confederate forces in his "march to the sea") as well as the perennial pop classic, "My Grandfather's Clock." But Work also penned a host of stirring antislavery songs. Many of these were introduced by Christy's Minstrels and became staples on the minstrel circuit.

The following lyric by Work appeared under the title "Babylon is Fallen":

> Don't you see de black clouds
> Risin' ober yonder,
> Whar de massa's ole plantation am,
> Nebber you be frightened—
> Dem is only darkies,
> Come to jine an' fight for Uncle Sam

Massa was de kernal
In de rebel army,
Ebber sence he went an' run away;
But his lubly darkeys,
Dey has been a watchin',
So dey take him pris'ner tudder day.

We will be de massa,
He will be de servant—
Try him how he likes it for a spell;

Chorus:
Look out dar, now!
We's gwine to shoot!
Look out dar,
Don't you understand?
Oh! Don't you know that Babylon is fallen!
And we's a gwine to occupy de land.

In another of Work's songs, "Kingdom Coming," the slave master gets suntanned to evade Union troops, but his slaves hunt him down and turn him in. They then take over the master's house and lock their dreaded overseer in the smokehouse cellar. The chorus depicts the merriment caused by this sudden reversal of fortune:

De massa run? Ha, ha!
De darkey stay? Ho, ho!
It mus' be now de kingdom comin',
An' der year of Jubilo!

"Wake Nicodemus" tells of a proud slave born in Africa and "never a sport of the lash," because none of his masters are "so brave or so rash." His dying request is to "wake me up for the great Jubilee," and the chorus joyously proclaims, "The good time coming is almost here!"

Songs that are still very much part of our living folk tradition originated as antislavery minstrel anthems. One famous example is "The Blue Tail Fly," in which a slave delights in his master's death from the bite of a blue tail fly. The slave's irreverent attitude is well expressed in the famous chorus: Jim crack corn and I don't care.

I'm certainly not suggesting that all minstrelsy was intended as abolitionist propaganda. Far from it. Ugly stereotypes and demeaning characterizations are more prevalent than the examples of compassion and understanding I've shown above. My point is that minstrelsy was a broad and evolving form of entertainment. One reason for its lasting appeal was that it could accommodate almost any attitude towards black people, from revulsion to respect to outright admiration to a desire to share in the joy and triumph of their eventual liberation.

African-Americans took up minstrelsy immediately following the Civil War, when it became relatively safe for blacks to travel in groups in many parts of the country. This suggests that they did not necessarily view this form of entertainment as demeaning. Black minstrel troupes, such as the Black Diamonds, Bohee Brothers, Harvey's Genuine Colored Minstrels, Lew Johnson's Plantation Minstrel Company, and the Hicks and Sawyer Minstrels, became part of a new tradition that would later spawn many blues and jazz stars, such as Ma Rainey, Bessie Smith, Johnny Dodds, Bubber Miley, and Coleman Hawkins. Even LeRoi Jones acknowledged in *Blues People* that "Early Negro minstrel companies like the Georgia Minstrels, Pringle Minstrels, McCabe and Young Minstrels, provided the first real employment for Negro entertainers."[8]

Several black writers of earlier generations also had positive things to say about minstrelsy, and believed it could help white audiences develop a taste for black entertainment. Author, poet, and civil rights activist James Weldon Johnson wrote in 1930, "The real beginnings of the Negro in the American theater were made on the minstrel stage. . . . Its history cannot be reviewed without recognition of the fact that it was the first and remains, up to this time, the only completely original contribution America has made to the theatre."[9] Johnson was not blind to the pernicious effects of depicting the African-American as an "irresponsible, happy-go-lucky, wide-grinning, loud-laughing, shuffling, banjo-playing, singing, dancing sort of being." But he noted that minstrel companies "did provide stage training and theatrical experience for a large number of coloured men," which they "could not have acquired from any other course."[10]

Noble Sissle, the African-American singer and bandleader (as well as lyricist for the 1921 hit show *Shuffle Along*) wrote in an unpublished memoir, "White minstrel shows had taught the general theatre-going public about our comedy and the popularity of our rhythmic dance expressions—the steps and music—both of which were sweeping the country like prairie fires."[11] Even the dignified and venerable James Reese Europe featured comedy drawn from "Ye Olde Fashion Minstrel" tradition in his 1911 Clef Club concert at Carnegie Hall.

By the 1890s minstrelsy had taken on a more nasty and vicious tone. This was the decade in which "Jim Crow" laws were enacted in the South, sparking the Great Migration, which in turn provoked fear and resentment in the North. Some of the leading academic institutions in America began espousing "scientific racism" that sought to "prove" white superiority. The new field of eugenics advocated forced sterilization of "inferior" races, including recent émigrés from Eastern Europe as well as African-Americans.

The comparatively benign "plantation melodies" of old gave way to "coon songs," in which black people were portrayed as ignorant, foolish, and dangerous. Songs that depict these newer, edgier stereotypes include "The Bully Song" from 1896, and "A Razor, Dat Am a Black Man's Friend" from 1904 (written, strangely enough, by African-American composer Ernest Hogan, who also came up with "All Coons Look Alike to Me").[12]

It is my opinion that the commonly held view of minstrelsy—that it is a perverse manifestation of a deep-seated and pervasive hatred for all things black on the part of a prejudiced white public—stems from this later period. The decade of the 1890s was a transitional and highly contradictory time. Blacks and whites lived in proximity in many cities, and ghettos had yet to be formed, but a new tide of fear and bigotry loomed on the horizon. Ragtime achieved widespread popularity throughout America, and in the early years of the twentieth century, black theater would establish a foothold in New York. Nevertheless, coon songs enjoyed a wide appeal and their message, certainly to our sensibilities, is primarily one of hatred and scorn.

For many modern observers, the image of whites made up in blackface is inherently racist. Of course, the theatrical practice of wearing masks goes back to ancient times; Elizabethans, for instance, were accustomed to women being portrayed by men. Still, there's something uniquely ugly about the spectacle of blackface. Even harder to fathom is the fact that black comedians "blacked up" all the way into the 1950s. Jack Schiffman, owner and manager of the famed Apollo Theater in Harlem, noted, "Almost every black comic in the United States worked in black face—burnt cork. It was not until the NAACP pressed for reform that this makeup was abandoned."[13] I'll leave it for others to determine whether this phenomenon signified self-hatred born of slavery and segregation, or a sense of connection to a once proud and vibrant tradition.

In any case, the legacy of minstrelsy, both black and white, is very convoluted and multifaceted. No simple cliché can sum it up. Nor can it be explained away simply as an emblem of white hatred for African-Americans and the wholesale denigration of their culture.

WHITE MUSICIANS IN NEW ORLEANS

Jazz, the companion book to Ken Burns's PBS documentary, devotes only two paragraphs out of the first fifty-two pages to early white musicians before the advent of the Original Dixieland Jazz Band.[14] Suddenly the ODJB appears, seemingly out of nowhere, claiming to be "the originators of jazz," and they're roundly condemned for this act of unconscionable hubris. The reader is given no hint that this band stemmed from an already well-established tradition.

How much of a tradition are we talking about?

Ray Lopez was the cornetist of Tom Brown's Band from Dixieland. This quintet of New Orleans musicians arrived in Chicago in 1915, the first white band to make the exodus north. After a shaky start at Lamb's Café in the Loop, they began to catch on with the show business set, and soon lines were forming around the block. A year later the Original Dixieland Jazz Band came to Chicago and won even greater acclaim after opening at Schiller's Café, on South 31st Street, at the edge of the city's burgeoning black belt.

After hearing this band, comprised of several old friends from home, Lopez pulled aside Eddie Edwards, trombonist with the ODJB, and asked him why Nick LaRocca was selected to bring to Chicago, "when there were so many good hot cornet players he could have gotten, like Emile Christian, his brother Frank, Pete Dientrans, Joe Lala, or Harry Shannon."[15] Still others in this pool of white New Orleans cornet/trumpet players who knew how to "fake" and play hot were Johnny Bayersdorffer, Johnny (Wiggs) Hyman, Lawrence Veca, Manuel Mello, Gus Zimmerman, Richie Brunies, Johnny Lala, Harry Knecht, Johnny DeDroit, Dominic Barocco, George Barth, "Doc" Behrenson, Pete Peccopia, Pete Dietrich, Freddie Neuroth, and slightly later, Abbie Brunies, Pinky Gerbrecht, Paul Mares, Bill Padron, Emmett Hardy, Wingy Manone, Sharkey Bonano, Tony Almerico, Dick Mackie, and Stirling Bose. Notice that this list includes Italian, German, Spanish, Jewish, French, English and Irish names. One scholar estimated that of all the first-generation jazz musicians born before 1900 (both black and white), a full third were of Italian extraction.[16]

The mere existence of so many early white jazz musicians presents a problem for jazz writers who subscribe to the notion that jazz grew up amidst, and perhaps because of, an oppressive and legally sanctioned separation of the races. If this paradigm were accurate, why on earth would so many whites want to play music associated with the most despised and denigrated class of people in New Orleans? How could white musicians even be exposed to this music if interracial contact was severely limited? Hard as it may be for some jazz scholars to accept, a sizeable number of white musicians played syncopated and improvised music during the first two decades of the twentieth century. So how can we account for them taking up this new style?

The answer is simple. White musicians played jazz, or an early version of it, for the same reason the Creoles did: there was a growing interest at all levels of society for this hot new style of dance music, and anyone who couldn't or wouldn't play it was left out of a competitive and lucrative market. As we've seen, African-American bands (Creole, black, and mixed) found favor even with the "St. Charles millionaires," and white bands had to adapt or lose out. Many first- and second-generation white jazz musicians avidly took up this challenge, as indicated by how many of them were nonreading improvisers.

For many white musicians in New Orleans, jazz became their specialty and principal form of musical expression. I must say I find it odd, even disturbing, that their story has received so little attention from jazz scholars. To date, no book chronicles their history. Samuel Charters's *Jazz New Orleans, 1885–1963* is typical in that it deals exclusively with African-American bands and musicians. Richard Sudhalter's exhaustive study *Lost Chords: White Musicians and Their Contribution to Jazz* begins in 1915 with the arrival of Tom Brown's band in Chicago.

The story of brass bands in New Orleans is usually told from the black perspective, but it's important to remember that African-American bands were a local manifestation of a nationwide phenomenon. According to one estimate, 10,000 brass bands and 150,000 bandsmen were actively performing in the early 1890s.[17] The band craze in America is usually traced back to one Patrick Sarsfield Gilmore, an Irish-born cornet virtuoso and composer of the Civil War anthem "When Johnny Comes Marching Home." Although there were many brass bands before his, he was the first to gain a national reputation. Gilmore was based in Boston, but traveled to New Orleans in 1864 after Union forces took possession of the city. There he organized an enormous festival in Lafayette Square, featuring a "Grand National Band" that consisted of 500 army bandsmen, local drum and bugle players, and a chorus of 5,000 children. Gilmore himself operated an electric button that fired off 36 cannons. His taste for theatricality helped launch a brass band boom that continued from the last three decades of the nineteenth century well into the twentieth.

It was also through Gilmore that the Fisk Jubilee Singers, the famed African-American choral ensemble made up of students from Fisk University, first attracted national attention. In 1872 Gilmore invited them to perform at the World Peace Jubilee, which he produced in Boston.[18] The following year Gilmore relocated to New York to lead a military band, and when he died in 1892 the baton was passed to John Philip Sousa. (Interestingly enough, Sousa lived in an interracial neighborhood in Washington, DC, on the same block where James Reese Europe grew up.)

After Gilmore's departure from New Orleans, the white brass band tradition continued to flourish in the form of ethnic groups (Irish, Italian, and German) and eventually ragtime bands capable of improvising.

The record clearly shows that bands of all racial hues shared more or less the same repertoire before the advent of jazz. In the latter part of the nineteenth century, this typically included European-derived dance music such as the schottische, mazurka, polka, waltz, and quadrille (a precursor to square dancing). Even Buddy Bolden played "waltzes and mazurkas, no ragtime, except in the quadrilles or late at night," according to trombonist Bill Matthews. "When it came to playing sweet music, waltzes, there was nobody in the country could touch him. . . . Everybody was crazy about Bolden when he'd blow a waltz, schottische or old low down blues."[19]

Henry Zeno was a drummer who played with Bolden, and later with a very young Louis Armstrong. Zeno's wife, Alice, was born a slave in 1864. From her mother, a full-blooded Wolof, Alice learned words and expressions in the Wolof language. Nevertheless, when asked what kind of music she remembered her husband playing, Alice Zeno spoke of waltzes, quadrilles, polkas and mazurkas.[20]

As jazz historian Lawrence Gushee explains: "Around 1890 a simplified type of dance began to be adopted, the two-step, which by the end of the century was often danced (in the United States at least) to syncopated ragtime pieces."[21] Given the primitive communications technology of that time, it's amazing how quickly this new fad spread across the country. The nascent recording industry was only a novelty for the rich. Nevertheless ragtime proliferated via sheet music, piano rolls, and live performances, and became virtually ubiquitous by the late 1890s. As James Weldon Johnson notes in his 1912 novel *The Autobiography of an Ex-Colored Man*: "No one who has traveled can question the world-conquering influence of rag-time, and I do not think it would be an exaggeration to say that in Europe the United States is popularly known better by rag-time than by anything else it has produced in a generation."[22] By the early twentieth century George M. Cohan featured ragtime songs on Broadway, and in 1911 Irving Berlin scored his first runaway hit with "Alexander's Ragtime Band." Two years later Berlin wrote "That International Rag," which proclaimed, "The world is ragtime crazy from shore to shore."

The appeal of ragtime was clearly as widespread as it was interracial. Bands of both races continued playing much the same repertoire, which now included rags. Even so, how closely did the early white bands in New Orleans resemble black bands in performance style? Answering this very nagging question requires a visit to the Hogan Jazz Archive at Tulane University. In 1958 the Ford Foundation provided funds to tape-record interviews with all surviving figures of the early New Orleans jazz scene, both black and white. This source brings us as close as we're likely to get to resolving the many mysteries surrounding the creation of jazz.

The interviewers were William Ransom Hogan, Richard B. Allen, and William Russell, the man who wrote the chapter on New Orleans jazz in *Jazzmen* and brought Bunk Johnson out of retirement. They prepared a standardized list of questions for all of their subjects, yet even here a certain bias crept in. Their questions varied slightly but significantly depending on the race of the person interviewed. White musicians were consistently asked about their early exposure to black bands, but black musicians were not similarly questioned. Thus that direction of cultural exchange was not explored, though it does occasionally surface in asides and digressions.[23] Nevertheless, the Hogan Archive is a vast, indispensable, and unique resource for anyone trying to make sense of a period that remains mired in so much myth and confusion. Nearly all of the following quotes are drawn from the archive's taped oral histories.

Jack Laine is often referred to as "the father of white jazz," because so many musicians, including those who went on to form the nucleus of the Original Dixieland Jazz Band, passed through his ranks. By 1900 he ran as many as five bands (some sources say ten) working simultaneously. Laine was interviewed twice for the Hogan Archive, and by that time he was already an old man, prone to making confused and contradictory statements. "We didn't have as much swing in the music in them days. In other words we played almost straight stuff," he stated. But later, referring to the bands of Paul Barbarin and George Lewis, both representatives of the quintessential traditional New Orleans jazz style, he says, "If you sit down and listen to them play music you can say right away, well, I heard Jack Laine's band play that, in the same style, same way."[24]

When asked about Bolden, Laine said he knew the cornetist only by reputation and couldn't recall actually hearing him. Laine was quick to point out that Bolden started playing in the 1890s, whereas Laine was leading improvising bands a decade earlier. In fact Laine thought he was "about the first one to ever have a ragtime band on the street. We'd tear it up . . . we'd rag it up . . . I mean as far as we could go."

Bolden biographer Donald Marquis writes, "It is a good guess that Bolden heard Laine and one of his Reliance bands some time before the turn of the century."[25] This poses a significant question: was Laine playing some sort of extemporized ragtime even before Bolden? I'm not suggesting that jazz originated from white bands such as Laine's, since the provenance of jazz clearly comes out of the African-American traditions of ragtime and the blues. But what is the chronology concerning Laine and Bolden?

The dates of Bolden's career have been somewhat problematic for jazz scholars. The only existing photo of his band was originally dated to sometime before 1895 by Bunk Johnson, but this information was later disproved.[26] Marquis believes 1905 is a more likely date. He charts Bolden's career as a professional musician starting around 1897, when the cornetist was about twenty. This proposition is borne out by accounts of Bolden playing just before the Spanish-American War of 1898.

New Orleans city directories also offer clues about the course of Bolden's career as a musician. From 1897 through 1900 he was listed as a plasterer; in 1901 he was a "music teacher"; and from 1902 to 1907 he was a professional musician.[27] According to Marquis, "Most people who heard him mention seeing him between 1900 and 1905."[28]

The claim that Laine's band played ragtime in the streets in the late 1880s may seem suspect, as the first published ragtime piece didn't appear until 1897. (This was the "Mississippi Rag," written by the white Chicago bandleader William Krell. Within a year, rags were published in St. Louis, New York, Cincinnati, and St. Paul, as well as New Orleans. 1897 was also the year that Scott Joplin, the most celebrated ragtime composer, completed his first ragtime composition.) Yet it's conceivable that bands in New Orleans played a form of syncopated and semi-improvised music prior to that date. The African-American composer and bandleader Will Marion Cook, in an interview for the *Chicago Defender*, said that "about 1888 marked the starting and quick growth of the so-called 'ragtime.' As far back as 1875, Negroes in questionable resorts along the Mississippi had commenced to evolve this musical figure."[29]

As Lawrence Gushee points out, "Whether the practice of playing dance music by ear was common ca. 1880 or before is as yet (and possibly for always) an unanswerable question: we didn't ask the right questions soon enough."[30] Few people interviewed for the Hogan Archive were even as old as Laine, so the further back we look, the colder the trail becomes. The verdict on how black and white bands compared in performance style likewise remains out: there is simply no concrete evidence to draw conclusions from. But it's entirely possible that both played some form of ragtime as early as the 1880s.

Jazzmen makes much of the fact that Jack Laine had two light-skinned African-Americans working in his bands: Dave Perkins and Achille Baquet. The inference is that these two musicians taught the others how to improvise. But ironically, one of Dave Perkins's key roles in the band was to help the white musicians learn to read music. Said Laine, "We all played by ear until we got . . . Perkins." As Johnny Lala put it, Perkins "was a straight reader, he wasn't no hot man."[31] Baby Dodds referred to him as a "straight man in music. Dave Perkins gave me the rudiments of drumming."[32] What's more, according to Pops Foster, "The whites had a musicians' union and my cousin, Dave Perkins was president of it."[33] Perkins reportedly held cards in both the black and white unions at the same time.

Achille Baquet's story is no less unusual. His brother George played with both John Robichaux and Bolden, and was later a member of the Original Creole Band, the first African-American jazz group to tour extensively on the white vaudeville circuit.[34] George's very few appearances on record include three dates with Jelly Roll Morton in 1929.[35] But the lighter-skinned Achille chose another route.

Achille Baquet joined one of Laine's earliest bands, by some accounts the very first. He traveled to New York and performed and recorded with Jimmy Durante's Original New Orleans Jazz Band in 1918 and 1919. Achille was obliged to pass as white in order to perform with both of these "white" groups. In 1920 he settled in Los Angeles; after that he falls off the radar screen and is barely mentioned in jazz history books.[36] Achille's playing on records is similar in style to other clarinetists of the day, such as Alcide Nunez or even Ted Lewis. Nothing in it suggests he was stylistically in advance of the other white musicians he worked with; in fact Larry Shields of the ODJB is a more interesting and soulful player.

Despite Jack Laine's reputation as a seminal figure in early white jazz, his were not the only white bands in New Orleans playing some form of semi-improvised ragtime. Among the others were Frank Christian's Ragtime Band, Heineman's Ball Park Ragtime Band, King Watzke's Dixieland Band, Morgan's Euphonic Syncopators, and the bands of Ernest Giardina, Johnny Lala, Joe Gallaty, Johnny Fischer, Johnny Stein, the Barocco brothers, the Brunies brothers, George "Happy" Schilling, and Mike "Ragbaby" Stevens. Moving closer to the 1920s, there were also the Triangle Jazz Band, the Jazzola Six, The New Orleans Jazz Band, and the New Orleans Jazz Babies.

As noted, ragtime took on a new twist when it became infused with the blues. But when did white musicians begin to follow suit?

As early as 1908 a New Orleans publisher, the Cable Piano Company, issued a tune by violinist Anthony Maggio under the title "I Got the Blues." This piece includes blue notes in the melody, and the first strain follows the classic twelve-bar blues form. The title page of the published sheet music bears the inscription: "Respectfully Dedicated to all Those who have the Blues." Maggio reportedly wrote this tune after listening to an itinerant black guitarist playing on the levee in Algiers, directly across the Mississippi from the French Quarter. The Hogan interviews contain several references to white bands playing the blues by the mid-teens. Tony Sbarbaro said that in 1914 and 1915, before he was drummer for the ODJB, he played with Ernest Giardina's band, and their repertoire included "blues and stuff."[37] Monk Hazel recalled that Emmett Hardy's band played the blues at the Tonti Aid and Social Club, a large open-air pavilion in a Creole section of town; starting at 11:00 p.m., "They'd play the blues for 45 minutes."[38] The ODJB recorded three blues tunes in 1917 and 1918, indicating that such pieces were already a staple in the repertoire of early white bands. In a 1917 lawsuit involving ownership of the tune "Livery Stable Blues," Nick LaRocca maintained the piece was composed in 1907. His adversary, clarinetist Alcide Nunez, claimed it went back five years earlier.

Evidence is sketchy, but it does indeed seem to indicate some sort of time lag from the time black bands incorporated the blues into their repertoire to when white bands did the same. Just how long this period was will probably always remain a matter of conjecture.

Some jazz writers have attempted to define differences in stylistic approach between early black and white jazz bands. Charles Edward Smith drew a distinction between those musicians who followed Bolden's "strong jazz beat" (of which no aural evidence exists) and the "Dixielanders," who "in their staccato style appear to have been influenced by syncopated ragtime."[39] While Smith doesn't specifically mention race, the inference is clear when he says, "The influence of Dixieland may still be discerned, especially as it has filtered through Bix [Beiderbecke] and Pee Wee [Russell], various Chicago combos and Red Nichols groups." At the same time, "One would never think of identifying the [King Oliver] Creole Jazz Band with Dixieland."

Yet when writers try to explain these perceived differences in musical terms, the results are far from satisfying. The author and history professor Burton W. Peretti states that early white bands, such as the ODJB, exhibit a style in which "syncopation . . . was comparatively slight."[40] This assessment is absurd, and can easily be refuted by listening to any of their recordings.

In the case of earlier New Orleans jazz, the absence of recorded evidence makes it impossible to distinguish between varieties of performance practice. This is not to say that significant differences didn't exist. What is certain, however, is that white and black bands did have numerous opportunities to absorb influences from each other. In the hotter months, entertaining was conducted outside, or at least with the windows wide open. Black and white bands paraded together during Mardi Gras and Labor Day celebrations. "Every musician in town was playing in one of the bands marching in the big Labor Day parade," recalled Armstrong.[41] Bands of both races played on advertising wagons and "ballyhooed" on the sidewalks in front of dance halls to draw in business. New Orleans musicians frequently played at sporting events, such as the boxing match where white clarinetist Tony Parenti heard Louis Armstrong, Johnny Dodds, and Kid Ory for the first time.[42] White bands even marched in traditional New Orleans funerals, to the point of playing ragtime on the way back from the burial.[43] The New Orleans classic "Didn't He Ramble," which Jack Laine remembered as "Did You Ramble," was part of his band's repertoire. "We heard it played somewhere or another and we played it," he said.

Many musicians of both races recalled hearing each other at the resorts on Lake Pontchartrain. According to Danny Barker, "Colored and white bands battled (or bucked) frequently."[44] Ray Lopez told of how "there were camps all along the lake with a colored band here and a white band there, all trying to outblast each other."[45] Creole drummer Paul Barbarin remembered these encounters as "honest musical rivalry."[46] Abbie Brunies recalled playing picnics in the Milneburg resort area from 9:00 a.m. until 6:00 p.m. His band would "take it easy until late in the afternoon, allowing other bands nearby, both colored and white, to blow hot."[47]

In a tape-recorded interview at the Hogan Jazz Archive, the following exchange occurred between Tony Sbarbaro and Emile Christian, both ex-members of the ODJB, recounting their early experiences at the lake:

> Sbarbaro: You'd be playing up against colored bands because one band would be here and maybe there would be about four bands, right? Playin' all day.
>
> Christian: All surrounded, see. Blowin' with each other all day. Years ago.
>
> Sbarbaro: There was no dissension or trouble.
>
> Christian: No trouble. Just blowin'.[48]

Sbarbaro goes on to mention how much he enjoyed hearing the bands of Manuel Perez, Freddie Keppard and King Oliver. In another taped interview, Paul Barbarin recalled hearing Emile Christian's band at the lake.

There were even occasions in New Orleans when African-American jazz bands played together with, and even substituted for, white bands. "Many times the Brunies Band would have a job for another band and they would call us," Pops Foster related. "They'd also use Jack Carey's band, Amos Riley's band, or someone else." Furthermore, the Brunies brothers "played for a lot of dances all around New Orleans where I'd be on the same bill with them." In his personal opinion, "The Brunies and their band played very good."[49]

Friendly relationships and mutual respect developed between many black and white musicians. Sharkey Bonano recalled that he bought his first cornet from Buddy Petit, "one of the finest cornet players to come out of New Orleans."[50] Bonano would follow parades just to listen to King Oliver, whom he also heard at the lake. His other favorite African-American cornetists were Sam Morgan and Kid Rena. Guitarist Louis Keppard recalled that when his brother Freddie led the Olympia band they would sometimes "buck" Sharkey's band. "Sharkey played good cornet at that time," said Louis, and "Freddie said he didn't know whether he was more afraid of Bunk [Johnson] or Sharkey."[51]

"The white and colored musicians around New Orleans all knew each other and wasn't any Jim Crow between them," maintained Pops Foster. "They really didn't much care what color you were, and I played with a lot of them around New Orleans."[52] Johnny Lala said he knew "where all the colored musicians lived in the 5th Ward—mostly ever' one of 'em."[53]

Lala, who grew up in the 5th Ward, specifically mentioned Oliver, Keppard, Buddy Petit, "Sugar Lips" Johnny Smith, Sam Morgan, and Chris Kelly. "I knew 'em all, cause I was just around 'em." Once, when Lala's cornet became bent and unplayable, Joe Oliver lent him one.

Johnny DeDroit said he "helped Louis Armstrong when he had patches in his pants." Ray Lopez recalled hearing and admiring "Oliver, [Manuel] Perez, who played sweet, Keppard and Armstrong" in addition to Bolden.[54] The black trombonist Roy Palmer said of his colleague George Brunis, "We came up together around here."[55] (George, the most famous of the original Brunies brothers, dropped the "e" in his last name on the advice of a numerologist.)

Red Allen remembered how he and Emmett Hardy, a white cornetist who was an early influence on Bix Beiderbecke, both studied with the Creole teacher Manuel "Fess" Manetta. Manetta claimed he devised a variation of the last strain of the tune "Panama"—a variation played by traditional jazz bands to this day—expressly for Hardy.[56] Allen described Hardy as "a great trumpet player. . . . I was coming up in those days and probably listened to everybody, and Emmett Hardy impressed me more than most. A kind of lyrical player, it was a pity he never made a record."[57] Sadly, in 1925, Hardy died at the age of twenty-two from tuberculosis. Allen also noted, "Right across the street from where I lived in Algiers lived the Brunies brothers—five of them. Now they all played great."[58]

"Speaking of the Red Light District and its Musicians," wrote Louis Armstrong, "I was lucky to have heard all of them who played there. . . . The White Boys were also Blowing up a Storm. There weren't as many white bands as the negro Bands in the District, but the ones who played there sure was good."[59]

The English writer Max Jones interviewed Wingy Manone and came away feeling that, "The strongest impression he carries of early New Orleans music is, rather surprisingly, one of racial integration, or, at any rate, nonsegregation." In Manone's words, "It was all mixed up there. Buddy Petit, Sidney Bechet, Freddie Keppard, Bunk Johnson, Nick LaRocca, the Bigards . . . we were all in one area. The musicians listened to each other, and sometimes played together in parades. . . . The young jazz musicians listened to everyone who came up who could play, white or colored."[60]

Early in my research I spoke with Richard B. Allen, at that time the last living interviewer for the Hogan Jazz Archive, and I asked him what he had concluded about racial interaction during the early period of New Orleans jazz. His response was, "[Musicians] lived together, they worked together in bands. How are you going to separate things when people live next door to each other and play in the same bands? The more you study it the more you realize that one thing mixed with another."[61]

THE CLASSICAL TINGE

Much of the jazz literature emphasizes a close connection between jazz and African music, while the more direct and demonstrable link between jazz and the European classical tradition has been largely ignored. I'm not saying that jazz belongs to this tradition, or that the language of jazz owes more to "white" culture than to black. What I am saying is that much of what we consider "black culture" is richly heterodox, and that the greatest exponents of jazz were curious and wide-ranging individuals who sought training and inspiration from a variety of sources. Jazz has repeatedly been able to renew itself by acquiring and transforming new musical influences—one reason for its worldwide appeal.

The linkage between classical music and jazz is perhaps most clearly revealed in the history of jazz piano. Ragtime is rooted in antebellum banjo styles, and in its day was already known and advertised as an "authentic" black style. Yet Scott Joplin, who brought the form to its highest level of artistry and refinement, studied harmony and technique with a German teacher. This man, whose name is lost to history, was so taken with the young pianist's talent that he refused to accept payment for lessons. According to Joplin biographer Peter Gammond, this anonymous teacher "also aroused Joplin's interest in music by playing him the compositions of the great composers."[62] Among Joplin's varied output were waltzes, marches, and "concert rags," as well as two operas.

James P. Johnson, often described as the dean of the Harlem stride piano school, studied with a professor named Bruto Giannini for four years as a teenager. Johnson authority Michael Montgomery wrote that the pianist "practiced various concert effects from Giannini; effects which he later built into his blues and rags."[63] James P. once used Liszt's *Rigoletto Concert Paraphrase* as an introduction to a stomp, and amused listeners with stride versions of Rossini and Grieg. Like Joplin, he wrote extended works in a concert vein, including *Harlem Symphony*, *Symphony in Brown*, *Yamekraw*, and a one-act "blues opera" with a libretto by poet Langston Hughes.

Johnson's protégé, Thomas "Fats" Waller, studied the classical repertoire first with Carl Bohm at Juilliard and later with Leopold Godowski, a concert pianist and brother-in-law of George Gershwin. In 1935 Waller said, "I consider the thorough-bass foundation I got in the study of Bach the best part of my training."[64] Lil Hardin once impressed Jelly Roll Morton—and by her account won a cutting contest with him—by playing Bach and Chopin.[65] Earl Hines developed his prodigious technique under the tutelage of another of the ubiquitous German music teachers, a Mr. Von Holz. According to Hines, this teacher "had me go through Czerny and big books of composers like Chopin."[66]

Teddy Wilson wrote, "My first contact with music was with the 'straight' or 'classical' kind, and my life in jazz has in no way diminished my interest in classical music. I learned to read music with great facility at an early age and I have successfully put my memory to the test since with such things as the Grieg *Piano Concerto*, Chopin etudes, Chopin preludes, Bach, and so on."[67]

Art Tatum, arguably the most technically adept of all jazz pianists, received classical instruction from one Overton G. Rainey, who was African-American and like Tatum, visually impaired. Rainey was not an improviser and didn't encourage an interest in jazz among his students.[68] Tatum was a lifelong fan of concert pianist Vladimir Horowitz, who in turn was a great admirer of Tatum. Bud Powell, the father of bebop piano, began studying the instrument at age six. According to his biographers Alan Groves and Alyn Shipton, "Until his mid-teens, he concentrated on European classical music, especially the works of Mozart. It wasn't until his teens that he exhibited any interest in jazz.[69]

For many jazz pianists, classical studies were a means of achieving technical mastery that would better enable them to express themselves through jazz. "What I went through as a student was probably what everyone else grooming himself for the classical field goes through— Czerny, Hanon, Dohnányi," said piano virtuoso Oscar Peterson. "All of these things just serve to broaden digital control. It was something I wanted to get behind me as quickly as possible."[70] McCoy Tyner received similar training at Philadelphia's Granoff School of Music, where he also acquired an abiding love for Debussy and Stravinsky. Herbie Hancock, at age eleven, performed a movement from a Mozart piano concerto with the Chicago Symphony Orchestra. "In fact," said the pianist, "I studied classical piano all the way through college, until I was twenty."[71]

Love of the classics was not just confined to pianists. Sidney Bechet "always retained fond memories of visiting the Opera House with his mother," writes his biographer, John Chilton, "and from childhood loved the sound of the tenor voice. Some of the first gramophone records that he ever heard were of Enrico Caruso."[72] The first records Louis Armstrong bought were also by Caruso, as well as the renowned coloratura sopranos Amelita Galli-Curci and Luisa Tetrazzini. Quotes from Verdi's *Rigoletto*, Leoncavallo's *Pagliacci*, and Bizet's *Carmen* show up in Armstrong's solos. The wide, pulsating vibratos of both Armstrong and Bechet, plus their overall imposing and dramatic approach to music, reveal a deep affinity for grand opera.[73] According to clarinetist Buster Bailey, even Freddie Keppard "loved to play *Pagliacci*."[74]

Coleman Hawkins started out on the cello and later practiced the Bach cello suites on his tenor sax. This not only helped develop technique on the horn, but also provided him with valuable lessons in harmony and voice leading. He once advised aspiring jazz musicians, "Do what I do every day. I spend at least two hours every day listening to Johann Sebastian Bach, and man, it's all there."[75]

Charlie Parker expressed his admiration for Bach, Beethoven, Bartók, Shostakovich, and Schoenberg. He often quoted from Stravinsky's *Petrushka* and *L'histoire du soldat* in solos. Once, when Stravinsky was in the audience at Birdland, Parker incorporated a phrase from *The Firebird Suite* in mid-solo and the composer roared in approval.[76] Drummer Ed Shaughnessy recalled, "Bird [Parker] was the first one to tell me I should buy the little scorebooks to the *Firebird* and *Rite of Spring* by Stravinsky, because he said, 'It seems that you like odd times and odd rhythms'—'cause I'd been studying East-Indian rhythms. And he said, 'I want you to follow the score and see how Stravinsky moves the time signatures around, because he's a master of that.'"[77] In a famous recorded interview with fellow alto player Paul Desmond, Parker spoke of a desire to study with composer Edgard Varèse.

Thelonious Monk, speaking of the beboppers in general, said, "We liked Ravel, Stravinsky, Debussy, Prokofiev, Schoenberg, and maybe we were a little influenced by them."[78] Saxophonist Jimmy Heath recalled, "Trane [John Coltrane] and I used to go to the Philadelphia Library together and listen to Western classical music. . . . We would play Stravinsky and people like that and listen to all this music that we could. We listened to the *Firebird Suite* and *The Rite of Spring* because we heard Parker was carrying around miniature scores of Stravinsky."[79] Another spiritual student of Stravinsky was cornetist and arranger Thad Jones, who incorporated some of the composer's spiky harmonies in his big band scores. Trombonist J.J. Johnson was proud of his nickname "Igor," denoting his favorite composer. Coltrane reportedly played tenor along with a recording of Bartók's *Concerto for Orchestra*. He was fascinated with Bartók's use of quartal harmony, which he and McCoy Tyner developed along with their own improvisational language. When Coltrane took up the flute, he practiced technique by playing Mozart.

Eric Dolphy and Charles Mingus also had strong classical backgrounds. Mingus started on the cello and played in a family trio alongside his two violin-playing sisters, Grace and Vivian. When he took up the bass he studied with one of the country's leading classical teachers, Herman Rheinshagen.[80] Dolphy played in orchestras through high school and majored in music at Los Angeles City College, where he performed with the school's symphony orchestra. He also studied briefly with Italian flute player Severino Gazzelloni. Luciano Berio, Pierre Boulez, and Stravinsky all wrote music for Gazzelloni, and the Dolphy composition "Gazzelloni," from the 1964 recording *Out to Lunch*, was named in his honor.[81] "[Dolphy would] spend more time practicing classical than jazz," said his friend

Buddy Collette, "so he had the fingering and had the difficult things always behind him."[82]

As I said at the outset, I don't wish to overstate the overall musical influence of classical music on jazz. As historian Lawrence Levine points out, "Black Americans have always had a penchant for refashioning the music they borrowed to fit their own aesthetic priorities and social needs."[83] But just as the blues has time and again been translated and retranslated to jazz, so too has Debussy, Stravinsky, and Bartók.

Of course the harsh reality for African-American musicians was that a career in concert music was, at least until relatively recently, out of the question no matter how hard they studied. "When I started out," recalled clarinetist Buster Bailey, "You couldn't even think, if you were a Negro, of making [a living in] symphony orchestras."[84] Only after the Second World War did blacks begin to appear in orchestras, and then only in very small numbers.

Yet African-Americans have continually shown great resourcefulness in forming orchestras of their own. As early as the 1830s a Negro Philharmonic Society was organized in New Orleans. Sixty years later cornetist Theogene Baquet established the Lyre Club Symphony, in which his sons Achille and George performed. In 1903 the Bloom Philharmonic was organized by Joseph Bloom (who, despite the name, was a Creole of color) and Luis Tio. Among the clarinet students of the Tios—Luis, his brother Lorenzo, and Lorenzo Jr.—are a virtual who's who of the New Orleans jazz clarinet: Jimmie Noone, Johnny Dodds, Sidney Bechet, Albert Nicholas, Omer Simeon, Darnell Howard, and Barney Bigard. Other musicians who passed through the ranks of these orchestras include Charles Elgar, Manuel Perez, Peter Bocage, Louis Cottrell Sr., Armand J. Piron, Alphonse Picou, and "professor" William J. Nickerson, an early teacher of Jelly Roll Morton.

Charles Elgar was one of the first New Orleans musicians to relocate to Chicago, and as early as 1916 his Creole Orchestra played concerts of classical and light classical music at the Municipal Pier (now Navy Pier). Elgar's Creole Orchestra also performed in 1918 and 1919 at Orchestra Hall, home of the Chicago Symphony.[85]

In New York, James Reese Europe formed the Clef Club Orchestra in addition to his better-known Society Orchestra. The Clef Club Orchestra was featured in sold-out performances at Carnegie Hall on three separate occasions. The programs consisted of concert works by Europe and the Afro-British composer Samuel Coleridge-Taylor as well as the French composer Camille Saint-Saëns. A reviewer from the *New York Age* noted, "Some of the leading white citizens sat in evening dress in seats next to some of our highly respected colored citizens, who were also in evening clothes."[86]

In the 1920s African-American musicians formed the Harlem Symphony, whose well-attended concerts featured staples of the orchestral repertoire, such as works by Mendelssohn and Brahms. Fletcher Henderson, James P. Johnson, and oboist William Grant Still (better known as a composer) performed at one time or another with this orchestra.[87]

Such hands-on exposure to classical music was a godsend for these working musicians, greatly expanding their range of skills. Prohibition required nightclubs to hide their illicit liquor sales under the cover of elaborately staged shows, and musicians needed to negotiate complex scores and accompany all manner of singers, dancers, and entertainers. The "straight" musical skills they acquired from being exposed to classical music would stand them in good stead when dealing with intricate arrangements written for large ensembles, which became the norm from the mid-twenties on.

Especially interesting is the positive way black audiences took to classical music, and the degree to which African-American musicians delighted in showing off their versatility. In the mid-1920s, at the 1500-seat Vendome Theater in Chicago, Erskine Tate conducted his "Little Symphony" in classical works such as the *William Tell* overture and the intermezzo from *Cavalleria Rusticana*.[88] Black entertainer Tommy Brookins stated that Tate "had collected the best musicians and was able to interpret to perfection any kind of music."[89] Even Louis Armstrong, who appeared with the Little Symphony in 1925, was called upon to render hot versions of themes from *Madame Butterfly*.[90]

In a 1956 interview, Armstrong explained how he switched from cornet to trumpet to meet these new challenges:

> The time I was playing in the symphony orchestra with Erskine Tate, he one day asked me to change from the cornet to the trumpet. Not that they don't sound good and all that, but they just don't look the same sitting in a symphony orchestra and I'm sitting there with a little cornet besides the trumpets. So I changed and I liked it better. I think it [the cornet] was more mellow a tone, see? A cornet's all right in a brass band and just plain dixieland, [but] a fellow don't want to be stamped as just a jazz player or something like that. But we tried to be musicians all around. That's why I proved I could play in this symphony orchestra.[91]

The Lafayette Theatre in Harlem presented the famed African-American actor Charles Gilpin performing Shakespeare, the opera *Faust* with an all-black cast, and Fats Waller playing Bach on the massive theater organ. Even in a nightclub that catered to blacks, such as the Elite Number 2 in Chicago, "you were listening to grand opera—the next minute to high class vaudeville," as reported in the *Indianapolis Freeman*.[92] Pianist Willie "The Lion" Smith remembered that at Leroy Wilkins's cabaret in New

York—where the owner initially tried to discourage white patrons, feeling that "mixing of the races was tindery"—Smith was hired to play "high-class" music: "operatic and semiclassical pieces [were] preferred."[93]

Even on the black vaudeville circuit, known as the TOBA (Theater Owners Booking Association), concert artists appeared alongside blues singers. One notice mentions a certain "Cherry Blossom, the Japo-Negro soprano who has been acclaimed by critics of Boston and the East as the greatest lyric soprano since 'Black Patti.'"[94] Black Patti was the legendary African-American concert soprano Sissieretta Jones (1869–1933), who took her stage name in tribute to the white opera singer Adelina Patti. Jones was widely acclaimed by both black and white audiences in the late nineteenth century. Even before Jones was the equally renowned Elizabeth Taylor Greenfield (1824–1876), known as the "Black Swan." It's worth noting that the two leading black-owned and run recording companies of the 1920s were named after African-American opera singers: Black Patti and Black Swan. Other concert singers who appeared on the black theater circuit were such now-forgotten names as Henrietta Loveless, Ravella Hughes, Carlton Boxhill, and Cecil Rivers.

Many African-American musicians working in northern cities took advantage of opportunities to study with the best teachers they could find. Louis Armstrong studied with a German teacher in Chicago, and Kid Ory and New Orleans trumpeter Tommy Ladnier also sought classical instruction there. Benny Goodman, Jimmie Noone, and Buster Bailey all studied with clarinet virtuoso Franz Schoepp, and drummers Lionel Hampton, Big Sid Catlett, and Gene Krupa took lessons from symphony percussionist Roy Knapp. Bassist Milt Hinton started his musical career playing violin, and became good enough to tackle Mendelssohn's Violin Concerto in E Minor. After switching to bass he studied with Dmitri Shmuklovsky of the Chicago Civic Opera Orchestra. "Whenever I think about him now," wrote Hinton, "I realize how strongly he affected my life. . . . For him, passing on his skill and knowledge was a solemn duty. It was a mission that went beyond music. And looking back, I know his greatest gift was to teach me this strong sense of responsibility."[95]

Another vital influence on Hinton's development was an African-American teacher, Major N. Clark Smith, who left a mark on an entire generation of black musicians. After serving as a major in the army, he graduated from Chicago Musical College and went on to lead the Tuskegee Cadet Marching Band. Smith then devoted himself to teaching and founded the music program at Lincoln High School in Kansas City. There he started Walter Page on bass (for years Page was the anchor of the Count Basie Orchestra) and trained many other K.C. notables, such as Harlan Leonard, Julia Lee, Lamar Wright, and DePriest Wheeler. The program that Smith directed at Lincoln would later produce Charlie Parker.[96] "Major N. Clark Smith taught all those great jazz musicians, but he never taught jazz," recalled Lionel Hampton. "The only time we'd play jazz was when Major N. Clark Smith wasn't in the room. He'd throw a stick at you in a minute. . . . He was a demon, about the greatest musician I guess I have ever known."[97]

During the twenties Smith led the music program at Wendell Phillips High School in Chicago, which produced (in addition to Hampton and Hinton) Eddie South, Happy Caldwell, Scoville Browne, Ray Nance, and Nat "King" Cole. In later decades, the school turned out the singers Joe Williams, Dinah Washington, and Lou Rawls, plus saxophonist Johnny Griffin. Smith arranged for his students to attend rehearsals of the Chicago Symphony, and even managed to have the orchestra with conductor Frederick Stock perform at school assemblies. Smith also worked out an arrangement with Chicago's leading music store, Lyon & Healy, to supply instruments for black schools throughout the South Side.

It should be remembered that traditional black colleges of the time taught music mainly in the Western classical tradition. Even the spirituals were for the most part performed in a grand concert style. Those fortunate enough to study in these institutions—such as Lil Hardin and Jimmie Lunceford at Fisk, and Fletcher Henderson at Atlanta University—received much the same instruction that white students received in comparable institutions. Though some excellent student jazz groups existed for a time at Fisk, Morehouse, Wilberforce, and Alabama State, these were formed on an ad hoc basis and received little or no support from the schools themselves. At times such groups were met with outright hostility from school officials.

LeRoi Jones complained about the lack of sympathy for indigenous African-American music among the faculty at many black colleges. "As one of my professors at Howard University protested one day," he recalled, "It's amazing how much bad taste the blues display."[98] Although trumpeter Donald Byrd taught some jazz classes there in the 1960s, it wasn't until the 1970s that Howard offered a jazz degree program, becoming the first historically black institution of higher learning to do so.

When Marshall Stearns was seeking a home for his extensive jazz collection—which ultimately became the nucleus of the world-renowned Institute of Jazz Studies at Rutgers University—he initially approached Fisk and Howard, but both universities turned him down. As we are about to see, the black middle class often looked down upon jazz as avidly as their stodgy counterparts in white society.

JAZZ AND MIDDLE-CLASS MORALITY

In the late 1910s and early 1920s, jazz, as performed by both black and white jazz bands, found itself in the crosshairs of moralists across the country. One infamous example was an 1921 article from *Ladies' Home Journal* entitled "Does Jazz Put the Sin in Syncopation?" The author, a certain Mrs. Marx E. Oberndorfer (writing under the more mellifluous pseudonym of Anne Shaw Faulkner) declared, "Welfare workers tell us that never in the history of our land have there been such immoral conditions among our young people, and in the surveys made by many organizations regarding these conditions, the blame is laid on jazz music and its evil influence on the young people of today." Furthermore she offered the following theory: "Jazz originally was the accompaniment of the voodoo dancer, stimulating the half-crazed barbarian to the vilest deeds."[99]

In *Etude*, a magazine aimed at professional music teachers and serious music lovers, a panel of "experts" was invited to comment on jazz in a two-part article from 1924 entitled "The Jazz Problem." The editors felt that jazz "in its original form . . . has no place in musical education and deserves none." One authority opined that jazz "represents, in its convulsive, twitching, hiccoughing rhythms, the abdication of control by the central nervous system."[100]

The General Federation of Women's Clubs expressed horror at the introduction of corset checkrooms in dance halls. This august group issued a statement which read in part: "Those under the demoralizing influence of the persistent use of syncopation are actually incapable of distinguishing between good and evil, between right and wrong."[101]

Although undertones of racism may be detected here—as in Faulkner's voodoo dancer stimulating the half-crazed barbarian—many of these denunciations originated in places where black jazz bands had never appeared before the public. In New York, public criticism became so vehement that the city passed an ordinance in 1921 banning jazz from nightclubs along Broadway after midnight. The next year Victor Records thought it prudent not to renew the contract of the Original Dixieland Jazz Band despite the overwhelming success of their hit records "Margie" and "St. Louis Blues."[102] It was largely through the public acceptance of Paul Whiteman, and his efforts to "improve" and perhaps "sanitize" jazz, that criticism of jazz on moral grounds finally started to subside.

All this is generally well known, but what gets lost in most jazz texts is that middle- and upper-class African-Americans—whose influence extended beyond their relatively small numbers—raised many of the same objections. These pillars of the black community were especially sensitive about being identified with the "lowly" culture of uneducated migrants from the South. Dr. M. A. Majors, editorial writer for the *Broad Ax*, a Chicago newspaper, complained about "ugly, low, nasty dances" as well as the gangs of black toughs who hung around pool halls "armed to the teeth."[103]

One reason black and white musicians commonly wore tuxedos during the 1920s was to lend an aura of respectability to their profession. As a budding violinist and bass player, Milt Hinton liked to "see these guys with their tuxes on. Everybody else was a porter or worked in the stockyards. Musicians were heroes."[104]

Others were not so favorably inclined toward jazz musicians, despite their formal dress code. As William H. Kenney notes in *Chicago Jazz: A Cultural History*, the music columnist and bandleader Dave Peyton, in his columns for the *Chicago Defender*, "condemned most jazz playing as rank musical ignorance, insisting that any trained musician could do it, while jazz performers simply could not play legitimate orchestral scores." Peyton also "advised musicians to abandon 'gut bucket' cabaret music with its 'squeaks, squawks, moans, groans, and flutters'; he insisted that a 'jazz-crazed public' and the 'hip liquor toter' had created the demand for such 'novelty,' 'hokum' music, leading race musicians to abandon concert hall instruments like the violin for louder, more vulgar instruments like the banjo."[105] Other African-Americans who attacked jazz in the Negro press include Maud Cuney-Hare of the NAACP's *The Crisis* and Lucien H. White of Harlem's *New York Age*.[106]

In New York, the blues were especially singled out for disfavor among the African-American elite. Francis "Doll" Thomas, active in black theater during the Harlem Renaissance, remembered, "The colored people hated you if you sang the blues. Blues was figured as the Devil's music."[107] Willie "The Lion" Smith recalled, "The average Negro family did not allow blues, or even raggedy music, played in their homes. . . . Many of the New York City colored folks, including quite a few of the musicians, did not go for the blues music."[108]

Ragtime, jazz, and blues were often lumped together as lower forms of entertainment representing a simple, hedonistic, and uneducated class. The African-American historian E. Franklin Frazier once characterized émigrés of the Great Migration as "ignorant peasant people without experience [in] urban living"[109] According to LeRoi Jones, "Any reference to the Negro-ness of the American Negro was frowned upon by the black middle-class in their frenzied dash toward the precipice of the American mainstream."[110] Jones was perhaps overstating his case in an attempt to raise political consciousness among the black bourgeoisie, but there's definitely some truth to his observation.

"Back in those early days churchgoing Negro people would not stand for ragtime playing; they considered it to be sinful," noted Willie "The Lion" Smith, referring to a time when "ragtime" and "jazz" were virtually synonymous terms.[111] This rift within black society is the subject of W. C. Handy's song "Aunt Hagar's Blues." The figure of Aunt Hagar is drawn from *Genesis*, in which Hagar is the Egyptian "handmaid" of Abraham's wife, Sarah, and the mother of Abraham's first son, Ishmael. African-American audiences in the early twentieth century would have understood Handy's inference that Hagar is a kind of mother figure for all black people. The lyrics are:

> Old Deacon Splivin',
> His flock was givin',
> The way of livin' right,
> Said he 'No wingin'
> No ragtime singin' tonight.'
> Up jumped Aunt Hagar,
> And shouted out with all her might
> 'Oh, 'taint no use o' preachin,'
> Oh, 'taint no use o' teachin,'
> Each modulation
> Of syncopation
> Just tells my feet to dance,
> And I can't refuse
> When I hear the melody they call the blues.
> Aunt Hagar's Blues.

In 1921 Handy and businessman Harry Pace founded the Black Swan record label, with the goal of providing "the only records made entirely by colored people." W. E. B. Du Bois was brought in as an advisor and investor. Handy and Pace were hoping to cash in on the blues craze, initiated the year before by OKeh's recording of singer Mamie Smith. But the patrician tastes of Pace and Du Bois (who favored opera) got in the way of achieving real success with the "race" market. They passed on Bessie Smith because she sounded too rough, too "black" to them. In 1923, as Smith's debut record for Columbia was on its way to reportedly selling 800,000 copies, Black Swan was driven into bankruptcy.

In 1927, Du Bois, then editor of the NAACP journal *The Crisis*, was so horrified at a budding romance between his daughter Yolande and Jimmie Lunceford (notwithstanding the future bandleader's degree from Fisk) that he called off the relationship and arranged a hasty marriage between her and the homosexual poet Countee Cullen. Cullen left for the honeymoon in Paris with boyfriend Harold Jackman, leading one Harlem newspaper to trumpet: "Groom Sails with Best Man." Yolande Du Bois Cullen had to make her own way to Europe, where the marriage soon dissolved.[112]

Members of the black intelligentsia called poet Langston Hughes a "sewer dweller" for using lower-class dialect and expressions in his poems, and for finding inspiration in the blues, which one of his accusers referred to as "trash reeking of the gutter."[113] Hughes was labeled "poet 'low rate,'" a play on poet laureate. He replied to their criticisms in *The Nation*, proclaiming: "Let the blare of Negro jazz bands and the bellowing voice of Bessie Smith singing Blues penetrate the closed ears of colored near-intellectuals until they listen and perhaps understand."[114]

Saxophonist and composer Benny Carter recalled, "We in music knew there was much going on in literature, for example, but our worlds were far apart. We sensed that the black cultural as well as moral leaders looked down upon our music as undignified." Of course Carter considered Langston Hughes an exception, and spoke of him as "a man who had much respect for and understanding of this music."[115]

Even as middle-class moralists vilified jazz and frowned upon its lower-class roots, white (and sometimes even black) recording executives pressured African-American musicians to focus on the blues. Billy Eckstine said, "Blues tunes have been good for me, but I know that white folks want to label all Negroes as blues singers. . . . The white man thinks that blues is all a black man should sing. He doesn't want you to do romantic stuff."[116] Joe Williams, long associated with the Count Basie Orchestra, voiced the same frustration. In the 1920s, Mayo Williams, the first black producer regularly employed by a white recording company, insisted that songwriters only submit blues material for his consideration.

The tastes of black audiences could be just as limiting. Eckstine brought his revolutionary bop big band, which included both Dizzy Gillespie and Charlie Parker, on tour through the South but discovered to his dismay that black audiences only wanted to hear the blues. This scenario repeated itself a few years later with Gillespie's newly-formed and struggling big band. Gillespie expressed chagrin at having to play for "unreconstructed blues lovers down South who couldn't hear nothing else but blues. . . . They wouldn't even listen to us. After all these years, I still get mad talking about it. . . . When we got back to New York, I broke up the band almost immediately."[117] In the sixties, jazz almost disappeared from the cultural landscape as its popularity was outstripped by forms of music more closely related to the blues: urban electric blues, rock and funk.

Jazz, throughout its history, has only been deeply understood and appreciated by a small group of admirers that has always cut across boundaries of race and class. I believe black and white musicians have often felt a strong kinship based on their devotion to this music, and this sense of common purpose and identity has been reinforced by the criticism heaped on them by conservative elements in both the black and white community. As one black eyewitness to the jazz scene in Chicago recalled: "The growth of hot jazz in Chicago during the twenties . . . brought about the spectacle of white and colored 'experts' meeting in order to further a common interest."[118]

NO ONE IS BORN PLAYING JAZZ; OR, STOMPING THE WHITE JAZZ MUSICIAN

Several jazz writers have tried to offer cultural explanations for why whites just aren't able to play the music very well. The Marxist writer Frank Kofsky, in his book *Black Music, White Business*, stated that whites are "culturally deprived" because they attach little value to acquiring "sophisticated rhythmic sensibility" through such childhood games as "patting juba" or playing "hambone."[119] Ben Sidran, in his 1971 book *Black Talk*, argued that black culture represents a fundamentally "oral" tradition, which is more conducive to jazz than the "literate" tradition of whites. Even black bands that read music are "employing oral techniques," as opposed to white bands, whose performances are merely "passive." Like Rudi Blesh and Hugues Panassié before him, Sidran believes that for a white person, attempting to play jazz is "like learning another man's language." Furthermore, "Whereas white society in America tends to be conformist, black culture is *collective*, or communal."[120]

The theme of the black musician as representative of a collective spirit, not privy to whites, is taken up by Jon Panish in his book *The Color of Jazz*. Written in 1997, it describes a country in which "racism persists, and racial inequality has worsened." In his opinion, the very concept of individuality is emblematic of white racism. He refers to "the white male's continued, unapologetic privileging of the dominant culture's individualistic ethic, from which he more than anyone else benefited." Once again, "white appropriation of black culture" has meant that "almost exclusively white musicians and businessmen [are] making money from it."[121]

And to revisit Martin Williams's comment: "Why is it really enlightened or unprejudiced to assume that Negroes could not have something called 'natural rhythm?' . . . It seems to me perfectly valid to say (whether the basis is racial, ethnic, environmental, or whatever) that black jazzmen in general have had fewer rhythmic problems than white jazzmen."[122]

An African-American musician, pianist Hampton Hawes, eloquently and definitively answered all these claims: "If I say that all colored people can play blues better than all whites, that would fit into the white racists' argument that 'all colored are alike.' To play the blues, to play jazz, you have to have the feeling. You can't study up on it. Some Negroes and whites have it, and some don't."[123]

Nevertheless, many still subscribe to these discriminatory views. And like all sweeping generalizations, there's a kernel of truth in them. Rhythm does figure more prominently in African-American culture than white. The average black dancer may indeed dance more gracefully than the average white. However, the average professional dancer, who has spent his or her life attacking the problems of moving the body gracefully through space, succeeds on the basis of individual talent and hard work; not on whether he or she grew up patting juba. The same principle holds for jazz musicians.

It's perhaps fair to say that African-Americans are somewhat more likely to start out approaching jazz from a more rhythmic angle, and whites from a more harmonic angle. If this is the case, then African-Americans may indeed have an edge, as rhythm is a more fundamental aspect of music, particularly in jazz. But the best players of either race are masters of all facets of music: rhythm, harmony, phrasing, sound, imagination, and so on. I agree with Leonard Feather that the main reason for the preponderance of great African-American players is that music (and especially jazz) has been one of the few professions open to them through the bulk of the twentieth century. As pianist Dick Katz noted, "It was almost impossible to make a living solely from playing jazz for a white musician. In some crazy way there were more opportunities for a black musician because there was nowhere else to go."[124] And I would add that society on the whole has more strongly encouraged African-American musicians to pursue jazz as a career. White musicians who didn't go into classical music tended to get shunted off into commercial work.

If we accept the common stereotype, it's hard to explain why Duke Ellington and Count Basie hired so many white drummers, including Louie Bellson, Buddy Rich, Dave Black, Ed Shaughnessy, Jake Hanna, Steve Little, Butch Miles, Greg Fields, Duffy Jackson, and Ed Metz Jr., among others. Any black musician will tell you that skin color is no guarantee of musical excellence, or even competence. There is a well-known story concerning an untalented black drummer who sat in with Roy Eldridge's group. After one painful tune, the trumpeter called a break and said to his musicians (most of whom were white): "We all got rhythm? Bullshit!"[125] Guitarist Freddie Green of the Basie band kept a long stick on his music stand in order to poke drummer Sonny Payne when he rushed the beat.[126]

As for the language analogy that many jazz writers are fond of, scientific evidence suggests that only the basic templates for language, and not any particular language, are hard-wired into the human brain. African-Americans carry no genetic memory of African languages any more than I do German or Hungarian. And despite my Austro-Hungarian ancestry I can assure you that Wynton Marsalis plays the Haydn Trumpet Concerto much better than I can. Based on my own admittedly unscientific observations, I believe that becoming a first-rate jazz musician requires years of experience playing with superior rhythm sections. This may be just as important as innate talent, or whatever cultural tradition the artist springs from. Those lucky enough to be granted these opportunities are likely to develop into the most accomplished players.

We have been told for the better part of a century that the blues and swing are endemic to black culture, yet many well-known jazz musicians have frankly admitted they had to sit down and learn these styles just as much as anyone else. Fletcher Henderson figured out how to play jazz by studying James P. Johnson's piano rolls, and though he accompanied a plethora of blues singers on record in his early career, he never really mastered the style. Vocalist Jimmy Rushing recalled the time when "Basie had come to the West with a show. He couldn't play the blues then."[127] The arranger Jimmy Mundy once had to coach Paul Robeson on how to sing the blues for a recording session. Despite Albert Murray's assertion that Coleman Hawkins turned the "blues into finespun glass,"[128] the saxophonist only began playing blues with any frequency in his fifties. His biographer Burnett James wrote, "To say that Coleman Hawkins was one of the small handful of undisputed jazz masters and yet was not a great blues player may well seem an inadmissible paradox."[129] But, like Art Tatum, Hawkins never had much affinity for the style. Billie Holiday never recorded more than a handful of blues and typically avoided them in her repertoire. To her, being called a "blues singer" was an insult. Even Dizzy Gillespie admitted, "I'm not what you call a 'blues' player. I mean in the authentic sense of the blues."[130]

Meanwhile the jazz literature is replete with one-sided images of whites painstakingly learning at the feet of African-American masters. In Marshall Stearns's *The Story of Jazz*, members of the ODJB are portrayed as "hanging around and listening open-mouthed" to the music of black bands.[131] But all jazz musicians, black and white, have sought inspiration from musical role models. Louis Armstrong recalled, "I would delight in delivering an order of stone coal to the prostitute who used to hustle in her crib right next to Pete Lala's cabaret. Just so's I could hear King Oliver play."[132] Twenty years later, a teenage Charlie Parker would stand night after night in the alleyway behind the Reno Club in Kansas City listening to his idol, Lester Young, play with the Count Basie band.

There are many familiar accounts of the young white Chicagoans, such as Eddie Condon, Dave Tough and Bud Freeman, gathering to hear King Oliver's band with Louis Armstrong. But many young black musicians underwent similar life-altering experiences in the presence of the same band. Saxophonist Garvin Bushell described his tour of the vaudeville circuit with singer Mamie Smith in a band that included cornetist Bubber Miley: "When we got to Chicago, Bubber and I went to hear King Oliver and his Creole Jazz Band at the Dreamland every night. It was the first time I'd heard New Orleans musicians to any advantage, and I studied them for the entire week we were in town. I was very much impressed with their blues and their sound. The trumpets and clarinets in the East had a better 'legitimate' quality, but the sound of Oliver's band touched you more. It was less cultivated but more expressive of how people felt. Bubber and I sat there with our mouths open. . . . That's where Bubber got his growling, from Joe Oliver. . . . It was in Chicago, after hearing Oliver, that Bubber changed his style and began using his hand over the tin mute that used to come with all cornets."[133] Miley would soon introduce this technique to Duke Ellington's band, where it would have a major impact in creating Ellington's new "jungle style."

Many critiques of white jazz musicians betray a basic contradiction: somehow they've been unable to master this fundamentally black music, but at the same time they've managed to "appropriate" it. As we've already seen, many white jazz players were active in New Orleans since nearly the beginning of the music. By the late teens and very early twenties, improvised hot music had become so ubiquitous in many parts of the United States that white musicians could cobble together their own jazz styles without any apparent black models. Many white musicians— among them guitarist Eddie Lang and violinist Joe Venuti in Philadelphia; Adrian Rollini from Astoria, Queens; and Frank Trumbauer of Carbondale, Illinois—were able to create distinctive improvisatory styles from the live music around them plus whatever was available on record, which had yet to include black jazz bands. Nevertheless, all of them, and others, had a direct effect on African-American jazz players. Ellington's baritone saxist Harry Carney was a great admirer of Rollini, as was Coleman Hawkins. Carney said he "tried to make the upper register sound like Coleman Hawkins and the lower register like Adrian Rollini."[134] Benny Carter, Lester Young, Buddy Tate, and Marshal Royal all acknowledged a debt to Trumbauer. "Adrian Rollini was, along with Bix and Trumbauer and Jimmy Dorsey, one of the guys we all listened to," recalled saxophonist Eddie Barefield.[135] The African-American guitarist Lonnie Johnson said admiringly that Eddie Lang "could lay down rhythm and bass parts just like a piano."[136]

"To discover whether a critic or cultural historian is concerned primarily with art or racial politics," wrote Alfred Appel Jr. in his book *Jazz Modernism*, "see what they say about Bix Beiderbecke's influence, and how quickly they gainsay the genius of George Gershwin and Astaire, downgrading their accomplishments as exploitations of black sources."[137] Beiderbecke's reputation has indeed suffered during the current era of political correctness. Stanley Crouch feels that "Bix is not worthy of inclusion in the pantheon."[138] Ben Ratliff, jazz critic for the *New York Times*, stated that Beiderbecke "could swing a bit," but "there is little funk in Bix's style."[139] Also in the *New York Times*, Rob Gibson, then the director of Jazz at Lincoln Center, wrote: "The great white historians can't understand why Bix Beiderbecke and Benny Goodman aren't in there [JALC concert programs]. My point is, what did they write?"[140]

Contrast these statements with those of Louis Armstrong: "Bix stood up and took a solo and I'm tellin' you, those pretty notes went all through me."[141] On many occasions Armstrong referred to Beiderbecke as a "born genius." He warmly reminisced about jam sessions they had together, stating, "I've never heard such good music since."[142] As for Gibson's claim that Bix was not a composer of consequence, Armstrong had this to say: "You couldn't find a musician nowhere in the whole world that doesn't still love Bix's [piano composition] 'In a Mist.'"[143] Other African-American musicians who had the opportunity to hear Beiderbecke live were equally lavish in their praise. Adolphus "Doc" Cheatham stated, "Bix opened my eyes to a lot of things. [He] played something I'd never heard before. Bix just changed the whole scene around when it came to jazz. Nobody had the talent he had."[144] "In my book Bix was a once-in-a-million artist," said cornetist Rex Stewart, with whom Beiderbecke once shared a locker at the Roseland Ballroom in New York. "I doubt if what he played will ever be surpassed on the trumpet. He was one of the all-time giants, and I feel his gifts remain today as unsullied and strikingly refreshing as when he lived."[145]

The great African-American trumpeter Clark Terry once told me, "I'm always confronted with these situations where people like to pit, in our craft of jazz, black against white, and I think it's so wrong because we've all been inspired by one person or the other. There are people who are determined to turn that around. There's always this controversy of the black against the white and I always say just to steer clear of all that: a note doesn't give a damn who plays it whether he's black or he's white as long as he plays it good."[146]

NOTES

1. Douglas, *Terrible Honesty*, 76.
2. Blassingame, ed. *Frederick Douglass Papers Vol. 3*, 48. Taken from an address delivered by Douglass in Rochester, New York, on March 19, 1855.
3. Southern, *The Music of Black Americans*, 91.
4. Cockrell, *Demons of Disorder*, 89.
5. Cockrell, 89.
6. This tune was revived in 1937 on a recording by Louis Armstrong and the Mills Brothers, and was also performed on Armstrong's Fleischmann's Yeast Hour radio program.
7. These lyrics and all others cited in this section are included in *Minstrel Songs: Old and New* (Boston: Oliver Ditson Company, 1882), editor unknown.
8. LeRoi Jones, *Blues People*, 86.
9. James Weldon Johnson, *Black Manhattan*, 87.
10. James Weldon Johnson, *Black Manhattan*, 93.

11. Contained in the Flournoy Miller collection at the Schomburg Center for Research in Black Culture, New York Public Library.

12. "The Bully Song" and "A Razor, Dat Am a Black Man's Friend" were published by Helf & Hager Co., New York. "All Coons Look Alike To Me" was published in 1896 by the more prestigious firm of M. Witmark and Sons, and reportedly earned its composer over $26,000 in royalties.

13. Schiffman, *Uptown*, 123.

14. And even these are typically skewed. Mention of Jack Laine, the man usually credited as the "father of white jazz" in New Orleans, comes directly after a detailed recounting (in eleven paragraphs) of the notorious Robert Charles riot. That melee was initiated when a black man, Robert Charles, shot and killed seven people (including two white police officers) and wounded twenty. The book quotes drummer Paul Barbarin saying "there was an honest, friendly rivalry" between black and white musicians, then states that following the riot, "that honest rivalry would sometimes turn poisonous." Yet Barbarin's comments were describing the racial climate in New Orleans a decade and a half after the Charles incident.

15. Dick Holbrook, "Mister Jazz Himself: The Story of Ray Lopez (1889–1970)," *Storyville* 64 (April–May 1976): 146. To be fair to LaRocca, there was bad blood between him and Lopez concerning the composer credits to "Livery Stable Blues," which led Lopez to challenge LaRocca in court. This matter is described in chapter 9.

16. Bruce Boyd Raeburn, "Stars of David and Sons of Sicily," *African American Review* 29, no. 2 (Summer 1995): 231–232. The scholar cited is Guido Festinese.

17. Badger, *A Life in Ragtime*, 20.

18. Southern, 229.

19. Marquis, *In Search of Buddy Bolden*, 101, 107.

20. Hogan Jazz Archive. Alice Zeno interview conducted November 14, 1958.

21. Gushee, *Pioneers of Jazz*, 8.

22. James Weldon Johnson, *Autobiography of an Ex-Colored Man*, 87.

23. You can hear the displeasure in William Russell's voice when trombonist Ike Rodgers expresses his admiration for Tommy Dorsey.

24. Hogan Jazz Archive. Laine interview conducted March 26, 1957.

25. Marquis, 34, 78.

26. This date of "sometime before 1895" was presented in Orrin Keepnews and Bill Grauer Jr., *A Pictorial History of Jazz* (New York: Crown Publishers, 1955), 6.

27. Marquis, 46–47.

28. Marquis, 47.

29. Peress, *Dvořák to Duke Ellington*, 37.

30. Gushee, 50.

31. Hogan Jazz Archive. Lala interview conducted September 24, 1958.

32. Dodds and Gara, *The Baby Dodds Story*, 71.

33. Foster and Stoddard, *Pops Foster*, 61.

34. And by one account George Baquet was the only reading member of that band.

35. The Morton recordings with Baquet were made on July 9, 10, and 12, 1929, and include such titles as "Burnin' The Iceberg" and "New Orleans Bump." It was

formerly thought that Baquet also recorded for Bessie Smith, but recent investigations discount this claim.

36. To show how ecumenical the New Orleans music scene could be, Achille Baquet claimed he'd learned some techniques from one Monte Korn, a clarinetist raised in the local orphanage for Jewish boys.

37. Hogan Jazz Archive. Sbarbaro interview conducted February 11, 1959.

38. Hogan Jazz Archive. Hazel interview conducted July 16, 1959.

39. Hentoff and McCarthy, eds., *Jazz*, 36.

40. Peretti, *The Creation of Jazz*, 80.

41. Armstrong, *Satchmo*, 134.

42. Gushee, 78.

43. Hogan Jazz Archive. Laine interview conducted May 23, 1960.

44. Hogan Jazz Archive. Barker interview conducted June 20, 1959.

45. Hogan Jazz Archive. Lopez interview conducted August 30, 1958.

46. Ward and Burns, *Jazz*, 25.

47. Hogan Jazz Archive. Brunies interview conducted October 19, 1957.

48. Hogan Jazz Archive. Sbarbaro and Christian interview conducted February 11, 1959.

49. Foster and Stoddard, 64.

50. Hogan Jazz Archive. Bonano interview conducted November 9, 1966.

51. Hogan Jazz Archive. Louis Keppard interview conducted August 4, 1957.

52. Foster and Stoddard, 63.

53. Hogan Jazz Archive. Lala interview conducted September 28, 1959.

54. Hogan Jazz Archive. DeDroit interview conducted Deember 4, 1969.

55. Hogan Jazz Archive. Palmer interview conducted September 22, 1955.

56. Hogan Jazz Archive. Manetta interview conducted August 26, 1959.

57. Chilton, *Ride Red Ride*, 7.

58. Hoffman, *The Henry "Red" Allen & J. C. Higginbotham Collection*, 20.

59. Brothers, ed., *Louis Armstrong, in His Own Words*, 33.

60. Max Jones, *Jazz Talking*, 147.

61. Taped interview with Richard B. Allen, 2000.

62. Gammond, *Scott Joplin and the Ragtime Era*, 29.

63. Michael Montgomery, liner notes to *James P. Johnson 1917–1921*, Biograph BLP-1003Q.

64. Hadlock, *Jazz Masters of the 20s*, 153.

65. Shapiro and Hentoff, *Hear Me Talkin' To Ya*, 93.

66. Dance, *The World of Earl Hines*, 14.

67. Teddy Wilson, *Teddy Wilson Talks Jazz*, 3.

68. Lester, *Too Marvelous for Words*, 38.

69. Groves and Shipton, *The Glass Enclosure*, 10.

70. Lyons, *The Great Jazz Pianists*, 132.

71. Lyons, 271.

72. Jones and Chilton, *Louis*, 5.

73. The use of a prominent vibrato is characteristic of many African-American singers and instrumentalists across a spectrum of musical genres, and it's worth noting that vibrato is virtually nonexistent in traditional West African music.

74. Shapiro and Hentoff, 91.

75. Chilton, *Ride Red Ride*, 367.

76. Appel, *Jazz Modernism*, 60.

77. Taped interview with Ed Shaughnessy, 2004.

78. Newton (Eric Hobsbawm), *The Jazz Scene*, 206.

79. Lewis Porter, *John Coltrane*, 63.

80. Collette, *Jazz Generations*, 21, 25.

81. Horricks, *The Importance of Being Eric Dolphy*, 19, 48.

82. Collette, 89.

83. Levine, *Black Culture and Black Consciousness*, 196.

84. Shapiro and Hentoff, 331.

85. Paul Eduard Smith, ed., *Esquire's 1946 Jazz Book*, 22.

86. Badger, 67.

87. Lewis, *When Harlem Was in Vogue*, 103.

88. Bergreen, *Louis Armstrong*, 32.

89. Shapiro and Hentoff, 107.

90. Bergreen, 266.

91. Louis Armstrong radio interview for Voice of America, c. July 1956, transcribed by Ricky Riccardi.

92. Kenney, *Chicago Jazz*, 10.

93. Willie "The Lion" Smith, *Music On My Mind*, 88, 96.

94. Taken from an announcement in the *New Orleans States* newspaper, March 28, 1923. Reprinted in Lynn Abbott, "'For Ofays Only': An Annotated Calendar of Midnight Frolics at the Lyric Theater," *The Jazz Archivist: A Newsletter of the William Ransom Hogan Jazz Archive* 17 (2000): 8.

95. Hinton, *Bass Line*, 101.

96. Driggs and Haddix, *Kansas City Jazz*, 38–39.

97. Hampton, *Hamp*, 20.

98. LeRoi Jones, *Home*, 108.

99. Walser, ed., *Keeping Time*, 32–36.

100. Walser, ed., 41–54.

101. Smith and Guttridge, *Jack Teagarden*, 40–41.

102. Brunn, *The Story of the Original Dixieland Jazz Band*, 175.

103. Kenney, 26.

104. Taped interview with Milt Hinton, ca. 1990.

105. Kenney, 56–57.

106. Bruce Boyd Raeburn, "New Orleans Style: The Awakening of American Jazz Scholarship and its Cultural Implications" (PhD diss., Tulane University, 1991), 9.

107. Kisseloff, *You Must Remember This*, 303.

108. Willie "The Lion" Smith, 101.

109. Osofsky, *Harlem*, 139.

110. LeRoi Jones, *Home*, 109.

111. Levine, 178.

112. Lewis, 75, 202; Marks and Edkins, *The Power of Pride*, 232.

113. Paul Johnson, *A History of the American People*, 706.

114. Lewis, 191.

115. From an interview with Benny Carter conducted by Ed Berger in liner notes to Carter's 1992 CD *Harlem Renaissance*, Musicmasters CIJD65080Y.

116. DeVeaux, *The Birth of Bebop*, 335.

117. Gillespie and Fraser, *To Be or Not To Bop*, 223.

118. Kenney, 109.

119. Kofsky, *Black Music, White Business*, 127–141.

120. Sidran, *Black Talk*, 51, 76.

121. Panish, *The Color of Jazz*, 3, 13.

122. Williams, *The Jazz Tradition*, 67–68.

123. Hentoff, *The Jazz Life*, 73.

124. Taped interview with Dick Katz, 2005.

125. Conversation between Joe Muryani and the author, 2006.

126. Hentoff, *The Jazz Life*, 150.

127. Dance, *The World of Count Basie*, 20.

128. Murray, *The Omni-Americans*, 206.

129. James, *Coleman Hawkins*, 66.

130. Gillepsie and Fraser, 310.

131. Stearns, *The Story of Jazz*, 72.

132. Bergreen, 47.

133. Bushell, *Jazz from the Beginning*, 25.

134. Sudhalter, *Lost Chords*, 172.

135. Sudhalter, *Lost Chords*, 172.

136. Sudhalter, *Lost Chords*, 152.

137. Appel, 60.

138. Conversation between Stanley Crouch and the author, 1994.

139. Ben Ratliff, *Jazz: A Critic's Guide to the 100 Most Important Recordings* (New York: Times Books, 2002), 18.

140. Theodore Rosengarten, "Songs of Slavery Lifted by a Chorus of Horns," *New York Times*, February 23, 1997.

141. Lion, *Bix*, 191.

142. Evans and Evans, *Bix*, 384.

143. Shapiro and Hentoff, 158.

144. Taped interview with Doc Cheatham, c. 1993.

145. Stewart, *Jazz Masters of the 30s*, 18.

146. Taped interview with Clark Terry, c. 1995.

5

~

The Road to Radicalism

"Whatever crushes individuality is despotism."

—John Stuart Mill

How did jazz go from a dynamically evolving art form to a music in which the importance of blazing new trails was widely and openly discounted? When did sociological relevance begin to overtake musical content in the minds of many jazz cognoscenti? And how much has the issue of race been a factor in this transformation?

Perhaps we should start by looking at the changing role society has assigned to jazz. Jazz enthusiasts are generally familiar with the progression of musical styles from traditional jazz to swing to bebop to avant-garde, and so on. Less widely recognized is the changing status of jazz itself within American cultural life. Like vast tectonic shifts, these changes are more elemental and work at a slower and more all-encompassing scale.

In terms of how society has viewed its cultural role and significance, jazz has moved through three major epochs in the course of the twentieth century. When jazz first appeared on the American scene it was taken as a form of popular entertainment, widely enjoyed by various strata of society, sometimes pilloried by moralists, often misunderstood, and in general taken to be a passing fad not worthy of serious attention. Many of its leading practitioners did in fact create great art in the process of seeking to entertain their audience, but commercial concerns were paramount. A flourishing nightclub scene was driven by the underground world of Prohibition, and the nascent recording industry, prospering from a booming economy, could take chances on obscure artists and niche markets.

The populist appeal of swing in the thirties only strengthened the overall perception of jazz as entertainment. As Duke Ellington once said, "We weren't out to change the world musically. We wanted to make a living and get as much self-satisfaction out of our work as we could."[1]

All this began to change in the late thirties, when a chorus of influential writers argued that jazz was America's one true native art form. The deal was sealed following the Second World War, as America emerged as the world's leading economic and political power. The focus of the art world shifted from Paris to New York, and for the first time in its history, America began to take its role as cultural arbiter seriously. Jazz, though receiving next to nothing in the way of institutional support, was nonetheless elevated in the popular imagination to a high art whose merits were considered and debated by people of learning and sophistication. It was hip to be hip. This was also the time when the State Department began sending jazz artists on tours abroad as "goodwill ambassadors." But it was also the most feverish and fecund period of creative experimentation in the music's history. Just as the postwar abstract expressionist painters pushed the boundaries of nonrepresentational art to its farthest reaches, and science offered up startlingly new concepts of the atom and the universe, so Ornette Coleman, Sonny Rollins, and John Coltrane engaged in a "space race" of their own to explore the outer limits of jazz. In 1961 Nat Hentoff stated, "As Miles Davis, Thelonious Monk, and Ornette Coleman have proved, it has become 'commercial' (in the denotative sense of the word) to be as uncompromising as one wants to be."[2]

With any shift in the public's perception of a cultural movement, there are winners and losers when criteria for acceptance and recognition change. As jazz became a self-conscious art form, many greats of the swing era and earlier found themselves regarded as hopelessly out of date and largely irrelevant. Men in their forties and fifties were declared stodgy old-timers. Trumpeters Roy Eldridge, Buck Clayton, and Oran "Hot Lips" Page found their work drying up and considered leaving the business. Louis Armstrong, in the estimation of many critics, was relegated to the same nostalgic niche as Bunk Johnson, that hoary relic of a bygone era. Duke Ellington was one of the few to successfully span both epochs, graduating to large-scale suites even as he continued to turn out popular hits like "Satin Doll." Emblematically, Ellington presided over small-group dates with both John Coltrane and Louis Armstrong in the early sixties. But even Duke had been largely taken for granted by the cognoscenti until his "comeback" at the 1956 Newport Jazz Festival.

Aside from encouraging innovation, the postwar jazz-as-art era was the most color-blind that jazz has ever known. Much of the Jazz Age of the twenties was economically driven by a well-to-do white public that viewed imbibing bootleg liquor and indulging in Negro music as bites from the same forbidden fruit. It was unthinkable for a white musician to make a living playing jazz alone. In the thirties, both black and white bands had to appeal to the common denominator of mass public taste, but the playing field was far from level. Black swing bands encountered many forms of discrimination as they traveled throughout the country, and faced restrictions from record companies as to the material they could record.

But when artistic excellence became the driving force of jazz, the field was open to all who had a fresh point of view, regardless of race, color, or creed. Independent record labels, such as Orrin Keepnews's Riverside, reissued classic jazz while offering a forum for Thelonious Monk, George Russell, and Bill Evans. Major companies such as Columbia and RCA Victor also repackaged the old masters (with notes stressing their artistic and historical relevance) while issuing new music by Dave Brubeck, Sonny Rollins, Miles Davis, and Ellington. Brubeck, Ellington, and Monk all appeared on the cover of *Time*, indicating the new status of jazz within American society. The integrationist era, as embodied in Martin Luther King Jr.'s civil rights crusade, was reflected in the many collaborations between black and white jazz artists: Miles Davis with arranger Gil Evans, Sonny Rollins, and guitarist Jim Hall, the dual trombones of J.J. Johnson and Kai Winding, the duo of trumpeter Ruby Braff and pianist Ellis Larkins, the Thad Jones/Mel Lewis Orchestra, Clark Terry and Bob Brookmeyer, Gabor Szabo and Charles Lloyd, Cannonball Adderley with both Bill and Gil Evans, Laurindo Almeida with the Modern Jazz Quartet, and so on.

Critics and a critical mass of the public cheered on bold developments as jazz began evolving at an ever-dizzying pace. No sooner had people warmed to bebop, cool jazz, hard bop, and modal jazz than they had to come to terms with—to cite just one artist—Coltrane's "sheets of sound," his extra-tonal harmonic explorations, and finally his forays into free jazz. But the masses, in their never-ending thirst for music-as-entertainment, increasingly turned away from jazz and toward new and simpler forms of danceable music. By the mid-sixties, rock—which aimed to satisfy the elemental need for mass entertainment, while assuming the mantle of art for itself in the work of the Beatles, Bob Dylan, and Jimi Hendrix—threatened to push jazz off the cultural map altogether.

The overwhelming popularity of rock represented an even greater threat to the livelihood of jazz musicians than the Great Depression. Many jazz players suffered a crisis in confidence as they questioned their ability to please themselves and the public as well. Several sought refuge in Europe, where serious art generally enjoys greater appreciation. Through the seventies, jazz sought its identity in art-driven free jazz and entertainment-driven fusion (which morphed into offensively inoffensive "smooth jazz"). Meanwhile, the mainstream jazz of Freddie Hubbard, Woody Shaw, Joe Henderson and others made haphazard appeals to both camps.

At the dawn of the eighties, another seismic shift would confer a new societal role to jazz. This new age was to see jazz enshrined as a cultural icon representing the black experience. The music itself was to be a celebration of past achievements, guided largely by a young generation of well-dressed, well-spoken African-American musicians. The outer boundaries of jazz would be defined and set, and the goal of a jazz musician would be to reassert and revive the glories of "the tradition." New ideas would be largely unwelcome, as would older black musicians and most white musicians of any age.

As already noted, the major record companies were complicit in legitimating this trend. The recording industry's attempt to create a youth market for jazz, along with society's desire to improve conditions for African-Americans, converged and reinforced one another in the promotion of young black jazz players.

To understand how jazz went from an art form to an icon of black achievement, we need to review some basic American, and particularly African-American, history. This radical transformation was almost entirely motivated by the extrinsic needs of a society desperately trying to heal itself from racial divisions—not the intrinsic needs of an art form.

Now I must do just what I've criticized others for doing: namely, addressing social issues as context for better understanding a musical phenomenon. But that's exactly what's required if we're to grasp the fateful transition from art to icon. Bear with me as we review some crucial historical currents that are typically omitted from jazz discussions.

The Great Migration brought along wrenching social changes for both blacks and whites in the North. It's customary to think of the first half of the twentieth century as a period of unremitting racial tension and strife, but it was also a time of significant economic gains for many African-Americans. By the 1920s black belts had formed throughout major cities and a rising black middle class began to assert itself, forming political power bases and a variety of institutions calling for equal rights and protections under the law.

These new urban black communities, despite attempts by white interests to rein in their boundaries, might have continued to flourish if not for the Great Depression of the 1930s, which had a disastrous and longlasting effect on the black urban population. Harlem the ghetto became Harlem the slum, and other black belts suffered similar fates. By the end of the decade prospects again improved, as labor unions admitted blacks to accommodate a recovering U.S. economy. With the onset of the Second World War a struggling black middle class got a significant boost when President Roosevelt, under the threat of a march on Washington organized by A. Phillip Randolph, signed an executive order mandating desegregation of defense industries.

In the 1940s, 87 percent of black families still lived below the official poverty line, and income levels were less than half that of white families. But the next thirty years saw unprecedented economic advances: by 1960, the poverty rate among blacks had fallen almost in half, to 47 percent, and by 1970 the figure was down to 30 percent.[3] During the same thirty-year period the percentage of African-Americans in professional occupations more than doubled, and per capita incomes steadily rose.

By the 1950s the black vote had become a major force in American politics. The growing civil rights movement led by Martin Luther King Jr., aligned with mounting support among a white constituency in the North, brought significant pressure to bear on the federal government, which responded by enacting a series of sweeping rulings and legislation aimed at eliminating discrimination throughout the country: the 1954 *Brown v. Board of Education* Supreme Court decision calling for equal access to public schools; the 1964 Civil Rights Act; the 1965 Voting Rights Act; and the 1968 Fair Housing Act. But the period of euphoria over these wide-ranging accomplishments was short-lived.

One of the great hinge events in American history was the civil unrest of the 1960s, particularly the devastating riots that swept through inner cities from 1964 to 1969. Only two weeks after the signing of the Civil Rights Act, Harlem became the first flashpoint. In the following weeks, six other northern cities erupted in violence. The following summer, riots occurred in twenty-one urban centers, among them the Watts section of Los Angeles, which was left a smoldering ruin. Other major disturbances took place in Tampa, Cincinnati, Buffalo, Dayton, Des Moines, Kansas City, and Philadelphia. Newark suffered property damage in excess of $10 million, Detroit as much as $45 million. Nationwide in 1967, eighty-six people died, with 2,000 serious casualties and 83,000 arrests. Following the assassination of Martin Luther King Jr. in March 1968, riots broke out in 126 cities from Washington, DC, to Oakland, and another forty-six people lost their lives. The National Guard was called out in Chicago, Detroit, Pittsburgh, and Boston, as well as the nation's capital.

The underlying causes of these riots, the worst civic unrest in the U.S. since the Civil War, have been debated ever since. Why were significant elements of the black population so consumed with rage that they took to the streets to ravage their own neighborhoods just as a legal framework was instituted to end centuries of discrimination? Did new feelings of hope engender a sudden painful realization of the privations and humiliations black people had suffered for so long? Was racism so entrenched in white society that it would take a revolution to even begin to confront it?

The African-American sociologist William Julius Wilson suggests some other basic factors that lay behind the urban trauma of the sixties. A new wave of immigrants from the South poured into the already overpopulated urban black belts of the North for a thirty-year period from 1940 to 1970. The number of central-city black teenagers aged sixteen to nineteen rose by 75 percent in the decade from 1960 to 1969, compared with only a 14 percent rise for whites. Blacks aged twenty to twenty-four increased by nearly two-thirds.[4] At the same time the economic base of northern cities was transitioning from industry to services, and the demand for unskilled labor was drying up. Gone were the entry-level positions, regulated by union wages and benefits, that an earlier generation of African-Americans had found. An unprecedented number of black youths were without work or not enrolled in school, and they became a source of increasing delinquency, crime, and unrest. Their disaffection was only amplified by the strident political rhetoric of the day.

Wilson argues that the riots were the result of a deep, festering, and unfocused despair and frustration among these young people. In some ways the riots had the aspect of an internal civil war against the black middle class. Studies showed that the race of a ghetto storeowner had little impact on how a business fared during a riot.[5] It was also widely perceived that the benefits of the civil rights revolution did not extend to the truly disadvantaged; hence the NAACP was mockingly called the National Association for the Advancement of Certain People.

President Johnson recognized the urgent need to address this unprecedented urban conflict, and sought explanations for the riots from a blue-ribbon panel chaired by Governor Otto Kerner of Illinois. The conclusions of the Kerner Commission differed drastically from the later findings of Wilson, but would set the tone for much of the racial dialogue for the remainder of the century. Despite polls that showed nearly three-quarters of all Americans in support of the Civil Rights Act, the Kerner Commission laid the blame squarely on white racism.[6] Many influential black leaders characterized the riots as targeted political protest, and affirmed that the rioters represented black America as a whole. As the commission's report declared: "What white Americans have never fully understood—but what the Negro can never forget—is that white society is deeply implicated in the ghetto. White institutions created it, white institutions maintain it, and white society condones it."[7]

In effect, the commission sent a signal to angry young blacks that they were right to blame the sum total of their anger and frustration on white society. Tamar Jacoby, in her book *Someone Else's House: America's Unfinished Struggle for Integration*, traces the capitulation of liberal white officials to the ideology of a core group of black radicals: "Instead of talking candidly about what was necessary to heal the ghetto—some combination of white help and black acculturation efforts—the president's establishment panel had encouraged blacks to blame whites, and to wait angrily for whites to make things better." The panel's conclusions "sent a message about rage and responsibility that would haunt the nation for decades to come."[8]

Government and intellectual leaders, both white and black, increasingly adopted the received wisdom of the Kerner Commission's analysis. The demands and denunciatory rhetoric of a handful of black radicals would form the basis of a new agenda, in which the ideals of integration and racial harmony were abandoned.

Even before Martin Luther King Jr.'s assassination, his program of nonviolent social change was vilified by black militants. Commenting on King's "I Have a Dream" speech, Malcolm X said, "What is a dream to you is a nightmare to us." Integration, he felt, was just another term for white domination, a way to further rob blacks of their culture and identity. Malcolm also mistrusted the help of white liberals, who in his view were "foxes" that "show their teeth to the Negro but pretend that they are smiling." For Malcolm, the only workable proposal was "complete separation" of the races.[9]

A younger generation of radicals followed Malcolm's lead and derisively referred to the figurehead of the integration movement as Martin "Loser" King. Stokely Carmichael called for "Black Power," which would "smash everything Western Civilization has created." As head of the Student Nonviolent Coordinating Committee, Carmichael managed to shift that organization's centrist civil rights positions to an espousal of "Hatred for All Things White." Fellow SNCC leader James Forman, in his "Black Manifesto" of 1969, wrote that the U.S. was "the most barbaric country in the world, and we have a chance to bring this government down." He looked forward to "long years of sustained guerilla warfare inside this country" and declared, "Africa is our motherland."[10]

This militant stance also drew support from young white radicals. A 1967 cover of *The New York Review of Books* featured a diagram showing how to make a Molotov cocktail. The writer of the accompanying article, Andrew Kopkind, opined, "Martin Luther King and the leaders who appealed to nonviolence are all beside the point. . . . Morality, like politics, starts with the barrel of a gun."[11] Many members of America's cultural elite, including Norman Mailer, Leonard Bernstein, Susan Sontag, Jane Fonda, Candice Bergen, and Yale president Kingman Brewster, openly expressed sympathy and admiration for black militants. The University of California at Santa Cruz awarded Black Panther cofounder Huey Newton an honorary PhD. Susan Sontag, in her famous 1969 article "What's Happening in America," declared, "The white race *is* the cancer of human history." Afterward she amended her statement somewhat, but only to say it was an insult to cancer![12]

The only remaining course for white leaders and liberal sympathizers was to accede to the less violent demands of black militants. The loudest and most vehement of these activists were often taken to be true spokespeople for the Negro masses, when polls clearly indicated this was not the case. One study from 1964 found that 88 percent of black metropolitan residents believed that Martin Luther King Jr. had "done most to help Negroes," as compared to 1 percent for Malcolm X. When asked to name people they didn't like, 48 percent selected Malcolm, whereas only 1 percent chose King. In New York, where Malcolm was best known, his disapproval rating was even higher: 55 percent.[13] In the summer of 1966, only 5 percent of blacks approved of "black nationalism" and 63 percent disapproved. Only 11 percent felt that blacks should give up working together with whites.[14] A poll conducted in 1968 showed that a full 80 percent of the urban black population held on to the goal of integration, and wished to work, live, and send their children to school along with whites.[15] Yet more and more, "community control"—a key demand of black separatists—was being granted to radical leaders who had learned that angry confrontation yielded power.

Mayor John Lindsay of New York, who'd been a member of the Kerner Commission, oversaw the firing of scores of white teachers, to be replaced by black "role models." The core curriculum was shelved in favor of teaching race consciousness and racial pride. Over the next twenty years, many primary and secondary schools from New York to California adopted Afrocentrist curricula that taught, in effect, that behavior is innately determined according to race, and that Western civilization is in fact the "stolen legacy" of Africa.

The Black Arts Movement, largely founded by LeRoi Jones in the mid-sixties, advocated a "neo-African" aesthetic that stood opposed to "European or Western essentialism," which was "masked under the rubric of 'universality.'"[16] These ideas were taken up in the black studies departments that sprung up on campuses across the country in the late sixties. Expressing a view commonly held in academia, scholar Henry Louis Gates Jr. wrote, "The rhetoric of liberal education remains suffused with the imagery of possession, patrimony, legacy, heritage, inheritance—call it cultural geneticism. At the same moment, the rhetoric of possession and lineage subsists upon, and perpetuates a division: between us and them, we the heirs of our tradition, and the Others, whose difference defines our identity."[17] In other words, black and multicultural studies are a necessary antidote to white, male Western hegemony.

The purpose and efficacy of these black studies programs is still much debated. To economist and social commentator Thomas Sowell, teachers were initially selected with "little or no regard to the wholly inadequate numbers of academically qualified people to staff so many departments established simultaneously." Further, many of these professors "would lead such departments in nonacademic or even anti-intellectual directions."[18]

As one academic observer put it, most universities have ceded the humanities departments to the "political activists and extremists, leaving undisturbed their nonhistoricized scientific disciplines, which is where the meat and money are."[19] Identity politics, commonly taught under the guise of multiculturalism, reaffirm many of the ideological stances first espoused under the banner of "black power," namely, racial solidarity, a belief in a separate and distinct black culture, distrust of all things "white," and a surrender of individual identity to group identity. These ideals, according to one professor, have "produced a culture in which identities of students are *totalized* by their minority status."[20] By 1972, as another academic saw it, colleges had all the intergroup harmony of Beirut, resulting in near total racial segregation on campus outside the classroom.[21]

The government did its part to encourage these separatist trends, though arguably with the best intentions. The riots of the sixties convinced successive administrations in Washington, both Democrat and Republican, that it was necessary to catapult as many African-Americans into the middle class as quickly as possible. In a famous speech at Howard University in 1965, President Johnson borrowed a metaphor from Dr. King, describing a person "hobbled by chains" who, once liberated, is asked to compete in a race. Noting that such competition is inherently unfair, he called for "affirmative action" to help blacks advance in society. Johnson's programs were primarily aimed at education and job training, but under the Nixon Administration affirmative action was extended to the business world. From 1969 forward, affirmative action became official policy throughout corporate America, regulated by the Labor and Justice Departments as well as the Equal Employment Opportunity Commission.

Along with earlier civil rights legislation, affirmative action has been largely successful in achieving rapid social and economic advancement for a great number of African-Americans. Young educated black Americans now earn as much as similarly qualified whites, and the median income of black female professionals now exceeds that of their white counterparts.[22] Between 1965 and 1977 the number of blacks attending college quadrupled. From 1964 to 1974, black elected officials in the South grew from 70 to 1,600. By the early 1980s nearly 300 black mayors were serving in cities throughout America, including New York, Chicago, and Los Angeles.[23] African-Americans won congressional seats in every district where they formed a majority of voters. A poll conducted nationally in 1994 showed that 74 percent of blacks felt that the United States was "the very best place in the world to live."[24]

Despite claims to the contrary, the public at large supported this effort to bring blacks into the mainstream. One study found that 70 percent of whites were in favor of affirmative action "provided there are no rigid quotas," as were 80 percent of blacks.[25] Every president since Johnson has supported affirmative action. It wasn't until 2003 that George W. Bush sought to challenge racial preferences in university admissions. In response, the Supreme Court—in a decision echoing public opinion—ruled that universities are justified in ensuring admission of a "critical mass" of minority students provided these selections are not based on a predetermined formula.

In effect, the government did succeed in addressing many underlying social and economic issues that tore the country apart in the racial strife of the sixties. But rather than erasing the fault line between the races, attempts at racial redress often deepened it. In the *Bakke* decision of 1978—the first case challenging the legality of racial preferences to reach the Supreme Court—Justice Harry Blackmun's majority opinion read, "In order to get beyond racism, we must first take account of race. There is no other way. And in order to treat some persons equally, we must treat them differently."[26] In other words, Americans were asked to sacrifice, at least for a time, the sacred principle of equality before the law for what was presented as the greater good: offering a helping hand to African-Americans whose rights had been denied for so long.

Efforts to achieve racial redress filtered into virtually every aspect of American life and assumed many guises: political correctness, multiculturalism, attacks on notions of individuality, attacks on "Westernized" standards of excellence, identity politics, and appeals to historical victimization. Fundamental to these propositions is the notion that racism is still prevalent throughout the land, and that racial privilege continues to be overwhelmingly bestowed on whites. Joe R. Feagin, in his book *White Racism*, argues, "Racism is a fundamental part of U.S. culture and is spread throughout the social fabric." He refers to a "Law of Racial Thermodynamics," a theory advanced by legal scholar Richard Delgado in which "racism is never destroyed but always comes back in new forms."[27] As one university charter solemnly intoned: "The multicultural curriculum requires . . . awareness of the fundamental importance of race, ethnicity, gender, class, special needs, sexual orientation, language, religion, and age in understanding social reality." Further, this curriculum is meant to overcome "what may be called 'exclusive' curricula, whether these be Euro-centric, Anglo-centric, or male-centric. The problem with 'exclusive' curricula is that they equate the values of a dominant group with 'universality' and falsely present the experience of a dominant group as a formula for all other groups."[28]

Many commentators have recognized the not-so-hidden dangers inherent in encouraging this "balkanization" of American society. As historian Arthur Schlesinger Jr. noted in his book *The Disuniting of America*, "The cult of ethnicity exaggerates differences, intensifies resentments and antagonisms, drives ever deeper the awful wedges between races and nationalities. The endgame is self-pity and self-ghettoization."[29] Jim Sleeper, author of *Liberal Racism*, maintains, "Constraining us all to define our citizenship and even our personhood more and more by race and ethnicity in classrooms, workrooms, courtrooms, newsrooms, and boardrooms, today's liberalism no longer curbs discrimination; it invites it. It does not expose racism; it recapitulates and, sometimes, reinvents it."[30] Increased polarization of racial attitudes was evident in a series of high-profile media events: the Tawana Brawley affair, the Crown Heights disturbances, the LA riot following Rodney King's arrest, and the O. J. Simpson double murder case.

Social critics also point out that though many African-Americans have prospered, the black underclass continues to fall behind, widening the class gulf within the black community. With the help of fair housing legislation, middle-class blacks have been able to abandon the ghetto, leaving it largely to its own devices. "By the 1980s," writes linguist and Manhattan Institute scholar John McWhorter, "the ghetto had become a ruthless war zone, where black people were their own worst enemies."[31] Rap music became the angry soundtrack accompanying an epidemic of drug abuse, AIDS, and out-of-wedlock births. Many civil rights leaders clung to the notion articulated in the Kerner Commission report that white racism still lay behind the crisis conditions of the ghetto.

Others saw a Faustian bargain in the works, which would prove deleterious to blacks of all classes as well as American society as a whole. In his *Harper's* article "The Age of White Guilt and the Disappearance of the Black Individual," the African-American social commentator Shelby Steele argues, "We allowed ourselves to see a greater power in America's liability for our oppression than we saw in ourselves . . . To go after America's liability we had to locate real transformative power outside ourselves. Worse, we had to see our fate as contingent on America's paying off that liability. We have become a contingent people ever since, arguing our weakness and white racism in order to ignite the engine of white liability. And this has mired us in a protest-group identity that mistrusts individualism because free individuals might jeopardize the group's effort to activate this liability."

Steele also identifies a moral neediness on the part of white America that works hand-in-glove with the politics of minority grievance:

> Two great, immutable forces have driven America's attitudes, customs, and public policies around race. The first has been white racism, and the second has been white guilt. The civil-rights movement was the dividing line between the two. . . . White guilt is literally a vacuum of moral authority in matters of race, equality, and opportunity that comes from the association of mere white skin with America's historical racism. It is a stigmatization of whites and, more importantly, America's institutions with the sin of racism. Under this stigma white individuals and American institutions must perpetually prove a negative—that they are not racist—to gain enough authority to function in matters of race, equality and opportunity. If they fail to prove the negative, they will be seen as racists. Political correctness, diversity politics, and multiculturalism are forms of deference that give whites and institutions a way to prove the negative and win reprieve from the racist stigma. . . . Thus it was a symbiosis of both white and black need that pushed racial reform into a totalitarian model where schemes of 'the good' are imposed by coercion at the expense of freedom.[32]

The politics of racial redress and group identity would find fertile ground in the world of arts and letters. The influential French philosopher Michel Foucault argued that language and literature were primarily means of exercising power and authority, paving the way for modern hermeneutics, semiotics and deconstructionism, all of which sought to undermine notions of objectivity, and hence a common sense of shared humanity.

At the very same time American society was asked to sacrifice its fundamental tenet of equality in an effort to achieve racial redress, the art world willingly jettisoned its own hitherto sacred principles of individuality and merit. The "who" became vastly more important than the "what," as artistic individuality was increasingly overshadowed by group identity, and artwork was judged by its usefulness in legitimating group claims to exceptionalism, free of any "elitist" notions of universal artistic excellence. Art and culture critic Robert Hughes wryly paraphrased this line of thinking: "The idea of 'quality' in aesthetic experience is little more than a paternalist fiction designed to make life hard for black, female, and homosexual artists, who must henceforth be judged on either ethnicity, gender, and medical condition rather than the merits of their work."[33] Melville Herskovits's dream of cultural relativism was now enshrined in academia and had crept its way into conventional wisdom.

This attempt to commandeer the arts to achieve social change has typically produced bad art, in much the way Soviet efforts to force science to prove socialist dogma produced bad science. But never mind; art was now in service to a higher moral authority, a greater good. And the effect on the jazz world would be far-reaching indeed.

NOTES

1. Hentoff, *The Jazz Life*, 34.
2. Hentoff, *The Jazz Life*, 41.
3. Sowell, *Black Rednecks and White Liberals*, 241.
4. William Julius Wilson, *The Declining Significance of Race*, 92.
5. Thernstrom and Thernstrom, *America in Black and White*, 163.
6. Jacoby, *Someone Else's House*, 43.
7. Jacoby, 141.
8. Jacoby, 144–145.
9. Wolfenstein, *The Victims of Democracy*, 13–14.
10. Malcomson, *One Drop of Blood*, 155–156.
11. Podhoretz, *Breaking Ranks*, 217. Kopkind's statement is a play on Mao Tse Tung's famous dictum that "political power grows out of the barrel of a gun."
12. Kramer, *The Twilight of the Intellectuals*, 230.
13. Thernstrom and Thernstrom, 169–170.
14. Thernstrom and Thernstrom, 169.
15. Jacoby, 149.
16. Gates, *Loose Canons*, 101.
17. Gates, 109.
18. Sowell, 238–239.
19. Beckwith and Bauman, eds., *Are You Politically Correct?*, 159.
20. Post and Rogin, eds., *Race and Representation*, 161.
21. Schlesinger, *The Disuniting of America*, 106.
22. Webster, *The Racialization of America*, 110–111.
23. Jacoby, 382.
24. Thernstrom and Thernstrom, 179.
25. Post and Rogin, eds., 352.
26. Post and Rogin, eds., 20.
27. Feagan, Vera, and Batur, *White Racism*, 219.
28. Beckwith and Bauman, eds., 73–90.
29. Schlesinger, 18.
30. Sleeper, *Liberal Racism*, 2.
31. John H. McWhorter, "How Hip-Hop Holds Blacks Back," *City Journal*, Summer 2003.
32. Shelby Steele, "The Age of White Guilt and the Disappearance of the Black Individual," *Harper's Magazine*, November 2002, 41.
33. Hughes, *Culture of Complaint*, 6.

6

～

Radical Ideas
and Retro Music

"Didn't we do it good enough the first time?"

—Miles Davis

Individuality was the cornerstone of jazz from its earliest days. As trumpeter Henry "Red" Allen said, "The great thing we talked about in New Orleans was to be yourself musically. You didn't have to see which guy it was playing the trumpet solo, you knew who it was before the band came around the corner. So, naturally, I tried to make my playing different from the others."[1] But more recently, individuality took a backseat to group identity. Jazz became widely touted as a product of a hermetically sealed black environment. The importance of originality and innovation would be replaced by a new aesthetic calling for a celebration of bygone heroes and a recapitulation of the jazz tradition.

In the past there hadn't been a "tradition" so much as a succession of iconoclastic individuals, such as Armstrong, Ellington, and Charlie Parker, who expressed the music in their own unique ways. Each of them spoke out against any attempt to rigidly define jazz. Duke Ellington famously stated: "'Jazz' is only a word and really has no meaning. We stopped using it in 1943. To keep the whole thing clear, once and for all, I don't believe in categories of any kind."[2] In the course of a 1948 "blindfold test" for the magazine *Metronome*, Charlie Parker said there was "no such thing as jazz. You can't classify music in words—jazz, swing, Dixieland, etc.; it's just forms of music; people have different conceptions and different ways of presenting things. Personally, I just like to call it music, and music is what I like."[3]

To serve an agenda promoting group identity and cultural exceptionalism, activists needed fixed boundaries for jazz; to claim a territory, one must first delineate its borders. Proselytizing the new jazz aesthetic to the public required a charismatic though necessarily controversial spokesman. With a legion of corporate sponsors and their powerful publicity machines behind him, Wynton Marsalis became the new voice of jazz and was able to attain a level of influence the jazz world had never seen before. As pianist Mulgrew Miller, a fellow alumnus of the Art Blakey band, said, "Wynton Marsalis—and I can say this without reservation—became the most highly *promoted* musician in the history of jazz. When we think of Duke Ellington and Louis Armstrong, those guys became celebrities because they endured. It wasn't until after many years that they became big celebrities. But Wynton received all of this promotion behind his first recording. And so, I don't think that has any precedence in jazz."[4]

In 2000, the *New York Times* jazz critic Peter Watrous wrote, "Over the last twenty years, through his considerable skills as a conservator and popularizer, he [Marsalis] has become the public face of jazz in America. He has seen himself sainted and vilified. Along the way, Mr. Marsalis has championed a vision of jazz that is at the same time deeply radical and deeply conservative, placing the music securely in black American culture."[5]

To fully understand the Marsalis phenomenon, it is important to remember that before the trumpeter came on the scene, many in the jazz community were fearful that young blacks were no longer attracted to the music, especially when so many other professional opportunities were opening up to them. In his 1978 article "Are Blacks Deserting Jazz?" Leonard Feather discussed how few blacks were taking advantage of the new jazz programs in colleges across the country, and how many of the most talented black musicians were forsaking jazz for studio or commercial work. Feather quotes the drummer Mel Lewis: "Even Count Basie hasn't been able to find people. If the guys who are with him now all quit, and he had to reorganize, he'd have to hire mostly white guys in order to put it back together." The Thad Jones/Mel Lewis Orchestra was also having difficulty maintaining its racial balance. Feather ended his piece rather melodramatically: "The choice is theirs. Meanwhile, the survival of jazz as a medium for creative artists in the tradition of Armstrong, Tatum, and Parker hangs precariously in the balance."[6]

So even before Wynton Marsalis arrived on the scene, many jazz critics seemed to be hungering for a new black messiah to save the music from extinction. The record companies were also well aware that the jazz legends of former years—Miles Davis, Dizzy Gillespie, Sarah Vaughan, Ella Fitzgerald, and others—would not be around forever. Something new was needed to revitalize the entire jazz industry.

Marsalis grew up in a musical family in New Orleans and from an early age exhibited prodigious talent and dogged determination. At the age of fourteen he was invited to perform with the New Orleans Philharmonic, and at seventeen he became the youngest musician ever admitted to Tanglewood's Berkshire Music Center. He accepted a scholarship to Juilliard in 1978 and moved to New York City. In 1980 he apprenticed in Art Blakey's band, and a year later he signed with Columbia Records. His first two albums, one classical and one jazz, garnered Grammy awards in both fields, an unprecedented feat. His early advances from Columbia were reportedly $1 million per recording, though in subsequent years this figure went down to $100,000.[7] In 1987 he was appointed musical director of a new jazz program at Lincoln Center, which in 1993 was granted full status alongside the New York Philharmonic, the Metropolitan Opera, and the New York City Ballet. In 2004 Marsalis presided over the opening of a new home for Jazz at Lincoln Center, a 100,000-square-foot performance and rehearsal space in the new Time Warner building at Columbus Circle. This venture required $131 million in start-up funds, and has an annual operating budget of around $34 million. Marsalis's annual salary as director was just under $1 million as of the fiscal year 1998–99.[8] To date Marsalis has received a total of nine Grammy awards; a Pulitzer Prize (the first ever awarded to a jazz musician) for his extended work *Blood on the Fields*; twenty-nine honorary degrees from universities, including Columbia, Brown, Princeton, and Yale; the National Medal of Arts; and numerous awards from other countries. He was also named one of "America's Best Leaders" by Harvard's Kennedy School of Government in conjunction with *U.S. News and World Report*. As of 2006, United Artists was considering a biopic based on the trumpeter's life, starring Will Smith.

Marsalis's brother Branford, the renowned saxophonist, acknowledged there was something suspect about Wynton's meteoric rise to fame: "Why was Wynton successful? Being good had nothing to do with it. They look for trends. The trend was young, black, well dressed, glib. 'So find me a bunch of young black kids who are glib and well dressed. Or we'll dress 'em.' You know? Being a good musician, I mean, that's too subjective. How the fuck do they know? They're all accountants. They have to look for things that they can understand. Music is not one of them."[9]

Ironically, Marsalis's interest in jazz only began at age fourteen, even though his father was a professional jazz pianist. Marsalis biographer Leslie Gourse recounts that when Stanley Crouch first met the young trumpeter, "He [Crouch] was astounded at how great Wynton's prowess on the trumpet was and how little Wynton knew about the jazz tradition." Marsalis freely admits that as a teenager he viewed Louis Armstrong as an Uncle Tom, and was turned off by Dizzy Gillespie's "thin tone." He credits Crouch for being "one of the first people who made me understand the value of the historical perspective in jazz music and the fact that there's a philosophy behind any type of aesthetic statement."[10]

I'm in no way proposing that Wynton Marsalis is unworthy of serious attention. I'm only suggesting that the degree of acclaim he has received is out of proportion to his real achievements, considerable though they are. In many ways, he is belatedly reaping benefits that were not afforded to earlier jazz masters; Marsalis's Pulitzer Prize, for example, was widely seen as recompense for the 1965 fiasco in which Duke Ellington was selected by the jury but snootily rejected by the Pulitzer Board. I believe that the public role that's been thrust upon Marsalis clouds a true evaluation of his work, which, despite its limited vision, is often exceptional and displays the highest standards of musicianship. He is unquestionably a virtuoso trumpeter and a skilled if not particularly distinctive composer. His initial success launched a whole new interest in traditional acoustic jazz. Even critics of his Lincoln Center jazz program have to admit that, without him, it probably wouldn't exist at all. He is a tireless and fiercely determined advocate for jazz. And many times he has exhibited that quality so extolled by his mentors Albert Murray and Stanley Crouch: extraordinary grace under pressure. (Crouch has shown considerably less grace under fire, engaging in three physical altercations with fellow writers.)

My concern is more with the social and ideological dynamics of the Marsalis phenomenon—how the forces beyond him and his music have in large measure created his enormous stature, and how he has exploited those forces to pursue his own (and Murray's and Crouch's) agenda. Though this power has been conferred upon Marsalis from a variety of sources, whose motives will be examined presently, Marsalis has never shied away from wielding it. He seems to believe it is his right and duty to exercise unprecedented control over the jazz community. His influence has limits, of course, but has been felt in all corners of the globe where jazz is performed, and especially in America. In short, Marsalis's tireless proselytizing has indeed helped raise the profile of jazz in the public mind, but in other ways, his influence has been divisive and, I would argue, detrimental to the continued health and vitality of the music.

Marsalis and his apologists often express a belief that the very concept of innovation in jazz is a sham and a distraction from the true nature of the music. "Jazz doesn't have to move forward," the trumpeter stated. "The point I want to make is the development of jazz is not tied to the development of European music in any way. . . . We have to understand jazz music is half African, there's African components, and when I say African I don't mean in a generic sense, I'm talking about the fundamental rule and philosophy of the music that gives it its functional and ritualistic component. And that component does not have to change because it addresses mythology."[11]

His associate Stanley Crouch agrees, titling one of his articles, "The Jazz Tradition Is Not Innovation." He writes that certain individuals can effect "dramatic reinterpretations of the present language," but their significance is limited to how well they can "add fresh choice to the community and to their idiom. They do not necessarily advance music." Thus, once again, the individual's role is framed as ultimately subservient to the group.[12]

Even Ben Ratliff, currently jazz critic for the *New York Times*, has gone on record as saying: "Newness—as in music that has never been heard before is a very tricky idea. I don't trust it anymore." Instead he feels that the truly "delicious side" of jazz lies in "refining its tradition."[13]

The jazz writer Tom Piazza—who, like Crouch, owes much of his credibility in the jazz world to his relationship with Marsalis—has fashioned himself into a fierce advocate of stagnation. "Jazz as innovation is a myth," he maintains. "In times like these, the new, as the critics mean it, is not what saves art. What saves art is an attempt to rediscover its wellsprings or to redefine its roots." Echoing Marsalis's concept (by way of Crouch and Murray) of the collective, ritualistic nature of jazz, Piazza says, "Within the realm of the arts, enduring forms constitute a kind of collective unconscious, without the use of which the artist is powerless."[14] Should we feel nostalgia for the strong individual personalities of jazz in former times, Piazza tries to set us straight: "Strong individualism is an extension of the group dynamic, and it is the work of the group that gives the individual statement context and meaning. The self-immolating genius/iconoclast image that many of the reviewers subscribe to, and think is so democratic and American, is really more of a French elitist conception—the alienated art-for-art's-sake martyr figure blazing his own existential trail into unintelligibility and sainthood."[15] Piazza lacks the imagination to see the range of creative possibilities that lies between recapitulating the past and unintelligibility.

It is not enough that Marsalis does not aspire to be an innovator: in the opinion of Piazza and Crouch, no one else is allowed to have new ideas either. Piazza's anti-individualism is also reflected in the dogmas of the academic left; Jon Panish's book *The Color of Jazz*, for instance, states: "In the most generalized terms, white texts tend to romanticize the jazz musician's experience, stereotype jazz heroes, dehistoricize and decontextualize the development of the music, and emphasize competitive individualism over any sense of community. . . . One of the principle ways black cultural values were transformed through white texts was to ratchet up the significance of individualism, the white male's continued unapologetic privileging of the dominant culture's individualistic ethic, from which he more than anyone else benefited."[16] In other words, the very concept of individualism represents nothing more than a power play on the part of whites to suppress minorities.

Shelby Steele has illuminated the motives behind such pronouncements: "Black politics, since the sixties, has been based on this hidden incentive to repress individuality so as to highlight the profitable collective identity. The greatest threat to the grievance elite is a society in which the individuality of blacks supersedes their racial identity in importance. The iron law of the racialist elite is that race is contingency and individualism is nothing. . . . Group identity in oppressed groups is always very strategic, always a calculation of advantage."

Jaded and retreatist views of art have become so prevalent that many tend to forget just how radically reactionary they are. Looking at the big picture of artistic change and evolution, historian Paul Johnson reminds us that the role of the creative artist is

> breaking free of the canon and its restrictions, carrying society and the public with them—not necessarily immediately, but in time—and thus eventually creating new canons. It is in the nature of the greatest artists to do things in a new way, and to carry their point. Hence, to understand art, we must look for the moments of tension before a creative innovator rejects the present and shapes a new future, study what precedes, accompanies and follows the revolution, and weigh its balance of gain and loss. These climactic moments in art history are what make it so exciting to study, and so rewarding, because it is precisely the contrast between the intervals of canonical calm, in which artists bring a particular mode to perfection, and the dramatic caesurae leading to a new way of working and seeing, which enables us to penetrate deep into the nature of art. For art is Janus-faced, tradition and novelty fighting for supremacy.[17]

I think the jazz world is likely poised at one of Johnson's "climactic moments," and if anything, conditions are ripe for change.

Many observers have expressed their dismay and frustration with the conservatism that has reigned over the American jazz scene since the 1980s. As the late Eric Nisenson wrote in his 1997 book *Blue: The Murder of Jazz,* "The clearest indication that jazz is fading as an art form is the increasing diminution of genuine artistic vitality. Indeed, there seems to be a wholesale avoidance of the kind of fresh inventiveness and risk-taking that had always kept jazz a vital and continually stimulating art form. At times there seems to be a conscious attempt to prevent jazz from being as fiercely creative and innovative as it has been in the past. This violence to the driving motor of jazz is what I, and a number of other longtime lovers of this music, consider to be nothing less than the murder of this one-time feverishly fecund and innovative art form."[18]

Several European writers have been very pointed in their criticism of neoconservative jazz trends in the U.S. In Germany's weekly news magazine *Die Zeit,* Konrad Heidcamp stated: "The USA has slithered into a musical provinciality. It produces great instrumentalists but no new approaches." British jazz journalist Richard Williams wrote, "If Wynton Marsalis is its creative figurehead, then jazz is probably really dead this time."[19]

A host of well-respected jazz musicians have spoken out against Marsalis's confining strictures. "I'm not happy about the idea of limiting jazz and discouraging jazz musicians from the freedom to [experiment] with other music or instruments," said pianist Herbie Hancock, who employed Marsalis in the early eighties. "I think when you limit jazz you destroy jazz at the same time. Because jazz is not limited . . . I think jazz expresses the heart and human emotions. That's why people all over the world from different cultures can relate to jazz. When you start limiting it, you're getting away from its true meaning."[20]

Trumpeter Terence Blanchard spoke of an atmosphere permeating that jazz world that discourages creativity. "It's amazing how the whole notion of being a jazz musician is to be experimental, but in this certain climate of the business, when you do that you're viewed as being unfaithful to the music. It seems to me that there's a certain tendency for people to not want you to be adventurous. It's like they want you to stay within a certain niche, because they think that's what jazz is."[21]

Others have told of the excessive control Marsalis exercises even over his own musicians. Charles Fambrough, the bass player in one of Wynton's early bands, noted that it "didn't have the freedom of Art Blakey's. It was all about what Wynton thought the music should sound like. He didn't give any real consideration to the individual musicians. The band I was in was actually lucky. You can hear the cats playing the way they wanted to. But he was standing behind, saying, 'Don't do this, don't do that.' . . . That was the beginning of a problem Wynton was going to have in the future."[22]

The alto player Donald Harrison had this to say: "What's frustrating for me about Wynton is that he thinks he is the only one who knows something about this music. . . . I mean, I love that he's doing well and that he's successful at it; just don't put anyone else down."[23]

What is the source of Marsalis's combativeness and divisive opinions? Some attribute these tendencies to growing up in a family with seven boys competing for their parents' attention. Others peg Marsalis's feelings of dissatisfaction to his relentless perfectionism. But in interviews, the trumpeter has cited other reasons for his discontent. As recently as 2006 he told an interviewer:

> As I grew up, I had to deal with a lot of racism. I was very, very angry for a long time. Very angry. It made me so mad. Once I was at CBS Records, and the singer, Bill Withers, came to me, he said, "Man, I look at you, I understand how angry you are." He said, "I'm going to tell you, that anger will kill

you and there's a lot for you to be happy about. Turn your mind onto that."
I said, okay, a lot happened I didn't like, but a lot happened that I did like.
People did things to me that were unjust and unkind, but people always did
a lot of kind things. So it's a matter of adjustment. It's hard to do.[24]

So despite all the positive attention (gracing the covers of the *New York
Times Magazine* and *Time*, which named him one of the twenty-five most
influential Americans) and the embrace by corporate America (from Columbia Records to PBS to Lincoln Center), not to mention the acquisition
of untold wealth, Wynton Marsalis still seems to identify himself as a
victim of racism.

Marsalis has been accused of pursuing a discriminatory, antiwhite
agenda at Lincoln Center, though he deflects such criticism by asking
rhetorically, and more than a little disingenuously, "Why are you asking?
What's your stake in the question?"[25] He has been quoted saying blacks
make better jazz players: "Crouch says 'they [blacks] invented it.' People
who invent something are always best at it."[26] (As jazz historian Rich
Johnson remarked in response to these and similar comments, the fact that
blacks didn't invent basketball doesn't make Michael Jordan any less of a
player.[27]) Despite being descended from Creoles of color in New Orleans,
a group that often owned slaves in antebellum times, Marsalis also stated:
"The fact that the ancestors of one group lived in slavery and the ancestors
of the other did not was critical [to jazz] at the point of inception."[28] In 1997
a writer for the *New York Times* asserted, "Over the past decade, in large
part because of Wynton Marsalis's efforts, jazz has been widely celebrated
as an essential element of the African-American cultural heritage and white
practitioners have been increasingly seen as interlopers."[29]

Marsalis's views on race have unquestionably matured and mellowed
over the years, perhaps as a result of increasing contact with the white elites
providing financial support for his Lincoln Center program. But like any
successful politician, he sometimes modifies his statements to fit his audience, leaving one to wonder where his heart truly lies. In an article for *Ebony*
magazine, entitled "Why We Must Preserve Our Jazz Heritage," Marsalis
stated: "Jazz is an art form and it expresses a Negroid point of view about
life in the twentieth century. It is the most modern and profound expression of the way Black people look at the world. . . . It is the nobility of the
race put into sound; it is the sensuousness of romance in our dialect; it is the
picture of a people in all their glory, which is what swinging is."

Where Marsalis, Crouch, and their mentor Albert Murray depart from
Amiri Baraka's radical separatist stance is in upholding the universal
significance and appeal of jazz. Murray seems to believe that America's
very salvation lies in understanding the true lessons of "the blues" and
"swing" as models for achieving grace through triumph over adversity.

"America's only hope," said Murray in an interview with Robert Boynton for the *New Yorker*, "is that the Negroes might save us. . . . We're trying to do it with Wynton and Stanley. That's all we are, just a bunch of Negroes trying to save America."[30]

All three men walk an ideological tightrope, aiming to be all-inclusive while simultaneously stressing the African-American provenance of their beliefs and the superior ability of African-Americans to attain this desired state of grace. To achieve this philosophical sleight of hand, all three are constantly affirming the importance of race even as they deny it. Marsalis, for example, bases many of his works on African-American historical themes: *At the Octoroon Balls*; *Big Train*; *All Rise*; *Congo Square*; the three-part *Soul Gestures in Southern Blue*; *In This House, On This Morning*, depicting a black church service; *Blood on the Fields*, dealing with slavery; and most recently, *From the Plantation to the Penitentiary*. But as a *New York Times* article on the premiere of *Blood on the Fields* rather coyly noted: "[Marsalis] concedes that as a black artist he draws on his own personal experience but insists that the theme of his work is universal. He points out that he never identifies his characters as Africans. Nor does he use the term white man, or black. . . . Mr. Marsalis tried simultaneously to acknowledge and transcend race."[31]

What accounts for all of this racial posturing and its simultaneous denial? One explanation lies in the racially charged interactions between African-American artist-intellectuals and their white benefactors and public. Shelby Steele describes the dynamic thus: "One's group identity is always a mask—a mask replete with politics."

Steele tells the cautionary tale of writer James Baldwin, who, "in blatant contradiction of his own powerful arguments against protest writing, became a protest writer." In the process, he "submitted his artistic vision—his 'private view'—to the authority of the group." As a result, "Nothing he wrote after the early sixties had the human complexity, depth, or literary mastery" evident in his earlier work. Nevertheless,

> [h]is fame was out of proportion to his work, and if all this had been limited to Baldwin himself, it might be called the Baldwin phenomenon. But, in fact, his ascendancy established a pattern that would broadly define, and in many cases, corrupt, an entire generation of black intellectuals, writers, and academics. And so it must be called the Baldwin model.
>
> The goal of the Baldwin model is to link one's intellectual reputation to the moral authority—the moral glamour—of an oppressed group's liberation struggle. In this way one ceases to be a mere individual and becomes, in effect, the embodiment of a moral imperative. . . . The protest intellectual positions himself in the pathway of the larger society's march toward racial redemption. By allowing his work to be framed by his protest identity, he articulates the larger society's moral liability. He seems, therefore, to hold the key to how society must redeem itself.

> Today the protest identity is a career advantage for an entire generation of black intellectuals. . . . Inflation from the moral authority of protest provides an irresistible incentive for black America's best minds to continue defining themselves by protest.

Finally, Steele asks, "What happened in America to make the Baldwin model possible? The broad answer is this: America moved from its long dark age of racism into an age of white guilt."[32] Thus an unhealthy symbiotic relationship between black grievance and white guilt made possible a new model of success for ambitious African-Americans, involving the submersion of individuality to group identity and the adoption of an oppositional protest ethos.

Given these powerful cultural undercurrents, it seems almost unfair to hold Marsalis personally responsible for assuming the exalted position that society so eagerly conferred upon him. Barely out of his teens, he was asked not only to save jazz but also to help heal the nation's racial wounds. Society required him to be a voice and role model for the downtrodden black masses, even as it showered him with fame, money, and prestige. The contrast between what he was and what he was held to represent couldn't have been starker. Thus we are treated to the spectacle of a man who feels he is still the victim of racism even as he enjoys a degree of celebrity and wealth few artists in history have ever attained. And he has always been all too willing to assume this contradictory role, despite all its personal and political pitfalls.

It also troubles me that while Marsalis has reached out to children, the black community, and audiences around the world, he has never reached out to fellow musicians in his adopted home of New York. He is the artistic director of the largest jazz institution the world has ever seen, yet he seems blithely unaware of what other musicians are doing right next door. Negative comments concerning Jazz at Lincoln Center are typically met with accusations of racism, casting white critics as meddlers attempting to mold the program in an image more to their liking. I am well aware that any jazz program, especially the one with the highest public profile, can't please everybody. And Jazz at Lincoln Center has shown signs of enlarging its artistic vision by including concerts honoring the legacies of Ornette Coleman and even Benny Goodman. Nevertheless, to the vast majority of working jazz musicians, Jazz at Lincoln Center remains an unwelcoming and tightly closed shop.

There is yet another way in which jazz musicians, both black and white, have suffered from the Marsalis phenomenon. The relentless promotion of Marsalis and the "Young Lions" who followed in his wake has led to a cultural backlash in Europe. Every American jazz musician I've talked to, regardless of the particular genre they specialize in, says their work in Europe has seriously declined over the past ten years. This trend can partially be attributed to weakened economies, high airline prices, and the imposition of tariffs on foreign artists. But U.S. jazz musicians are also facing considerable rejection on aesthetic and ideological grounds for the first time in the music's history. As the English writer Stuart Nicholson writes in his book *Is Jazz Dead? (Or Has It Moved to a New Address)*, "We are at a key moment in jazz history. The music is being reshaped and re-imagined beyond the borders of the United States through the process of glocalization [*sic*] and transculturation with increasing authority by voices asserting their own cultural identity on the music." He notes the irony of how, from the beginning of the twentieth century, jazz helped liberate Europeans from the aesthetic dead ends of their own perhaps overly refined musical tradition. "Now," Nicholson states, "the jazz tradition is stifling America."[33]

Starting in the 1980s, recording labels were looking to make stars out of musicians who were, in the words of Branford Marsalis, "young, black, well dressed, glib." Bassist Christian McBride relates, "Because of the young lions era . . . any jazz musician under the age of twenty-five was offered a recording contract."[34] Saxophonist Javon Jackson added, "Now guys of only nineteen or twenty are coming up and they get record contracts and go out with their own bands and they haven't played with anybody. You have these people saying, 'this is the next Coltrane, the next Miles,' it's absurd. But that's the nature of the business."[35]

The hunt to sign young black jazz musicians could go to incredible, and at times ludicrous, lengths. In 1986 Wynton Marsalis met sixteen-year-old trumpeter Roy Hargrove and invited him to sit in during an engagement in Hargrove's hometown of Fort Worth, Texas. Shortly after, manager Larry Clothier offered to represent Hargrove and invited him to participate in an all-star package at the North Sea Jazz Festival in The Hague. When the young man returned to Texas, he entered the twelfth grade. Enter Bruce Lundvall, who had originally signed Marsalis to Columbia, and was now an executive at Blue Note Records, formerly the premier independent jazz label but since acquired by media giant EMI. Lundvall tells what happened next:

> I brought Roy to New York, straight from his high school band in Texas. He stayed with [trumpeter and producer] Don Sickler for about a week, and Sickler opened him up to people like Kenny Dorham and to other trumpet players he hadn't heard before. . . . Then we brought Roy over to Mount Fuji [a major Japanese jazz festival], where he played with Bobby Watson, and he recorded with Bobby. . . . At that point, I felt he wasn't ready to be signed. He had a scholarship offered him by Berklee School of Music, and Rufus Reid, who's the head of the jazz department at William Paterson [University],

New Jersey, called me and said, "This is a very gifted and natural player, he shouldn't be going to Berklee, he should be with us. Is there a way you could pay his tuition?" I said, "Well, that's difficult, he's not signed here." He said, "We can pay his room and board, but not his tuition." I went to Roy and said, "Look, I want to make a kind of deal I've never made before—I want to sign you as a sideman, with an option to sign you as a leader, when you're ready." He liked it, his mother didn't. . . . Then I brought him back when he was at Berklee, because every Monday night we used to have a Blue Note night at the old Birdland on 105th Street, and I brought Roy down to play—he was good, but he still wasn't ready to be signed. I met with Larry Clothier, and was looking at a ridiculously expensive deal, and I passed. Roy ended up at RCA. So we lost him. I thought Roy had a sound that was great, and hopefully he would develop.[36]

Hargrove's first album on the RCA Novus label was titled *Diamond in the Rough*, as if even his new record company openly admitted the trumpeter still wasn't ready. Nevertheless, their formidable publicity department went to work making him a new jazz sensation. I went to the Village Vanguard to hear the young trumpeter at his first major New York booking, which occurred even before his first album was released. Long lines of people waiting to get in stretched down Seventh Avenue. Immediately I realized that a new phenomenon was afoot: Wynton Marsalis would not be one lone megastar, but would soon be joined by a constellation of other young and basically inexperienced jazz players destined to inherit the jazz world.

I was impressed by Hargrove's precocity and his undeniable feel for the music, but as with Marsalis, I heard little in the way of originality. More than twenty years later I still don't, even if Hargrove has developed into a highly proficient and soulful player. His most recent recording—with another apologetic title, *Nothing Serious*—sounds as if it could have been made years before the trumpeter was born.

Through the eighties and nineties the major labels, all subsets of major corporations, dominated the entire business of jazz. Signing young players was widely believed to be the best way to court the youth market. "I thought if I went after young artists at least it would pique the interest of kids," said George Butler of CBS.[37] Publicity departments of the majors felt they could create overnight jazz stars much as they had done for decades in the realm of pop music. Musicians were selected as much for projecting an approved "image" as for their ability to play. The Black Music department at Columbia, which handled Wynton Marsalis—and, for a time, his brother Branford, as well as Terence Blanchard and Donald Harrison—was also promoting Michael Jackson, Lisa Lisa and Cult Jam, and other pop acts. Though Steve Backer of RCA denied that jazz departments of the majors were operating "in lockstep," one industry observer, Richard Cook, noted, "At a time when a world of diverse music was becoming more available to consumers than ever before, a dreadful homogeny was beginning to sweep through dealings of the major record companies."[38]

A much smaller number of white musicians, such as pianist Benny Green and organist Joey DeFrancesco, were approached by the majors. (Green was dropped by Blue Note because, as Lundvall explained, "His records were selling OK, but not enough to justify the escalating expenses."[39]) Older white musicians, Joe Lovano and Dave Douglas being the prime examples, attracted major label support only in the 1990s, after years of apprenticeship. Lovano was signed to Blue Note in 1991 at the age of thirty-eight, Douglas to RCA at thirty-seven. Both of their careers really took off after receiving the kind of support only a major label could provide. Strong evidence of the record labels' intent to focus on African-American jazz artists can be found by looking at the winners of the annual Thelonious Monk International Jazz Competition, the most prestigious talent contest in the jazz world. Winners are selected by a panel of noted jazz professionals on the basis of artistic merit, yet those offered recording contracts have nearly always been black. Jacky Terrasson, Marcus Roberts, and Joshua Redman all signed major label contracts, whereas Ted Rosenthal, Jon Gordon, and Bill Cunliffe did not. Of the young white first-place winners, only trumpeter Ryan Kisor was awarded a deal (by Columbia), but he was dropped after only two recordings.

Older African-American musicians also suffered as a result of the new youth orientation of the major labels. Such renowned veterans as pianists Tommy Flanagan and Hank Jones were ignored by the majors during this period, as were saxophonists Frank Wess and Jimmy Heath. Middle-aged trumpeter Jon Faddis had no record deal even though at one time two of his young students did. The venerable saxophonist and composer Benny Carter, with seven Grammy nominations and two wins under his belt, was similarly passed over.

The major labels did, for the most part, select extremely talented individuals to be the new jazz stars. I happen to be a fan of Joshua Redman, Branford Marsalis, and particularly Nicholas Payton. But the arbitrariness of their choices, even regarding young black musicians, was also apparent. Such accomplished players as saxophonist Steve Wilson, pianist Kenny Drew Jr., and trombonist Wycliffe Gordon were all overlooked, even though their music was just as strong—and, I would say, more individual—than most of the over-hyped "young lions."

Apart from controlling distribution of recordings and churning out expensive publicity, the majors had other ways of rigging the market on behalf of their clients. Jazz periodicals were dependent on them for advertising revenue. Though the jazz press strove to maintain editorial autonomy, the line between feature articles and advertising promotion grew increasingly fuzzy. And of course any recordings released by the majors were automatically reviewed and given serious attention.

Record companies were able to manipulate club and festival appearances as well. Promotional expenditures for new artists included offering them gratis to a jazz venue, or as part of a package with more desirable and established musicians. With nightclubs, record companies would simply buy out the room, pay for the club's publicity, or sponsor record release parties when the venue would otherwise be dark. Record companies also worked in tandem with major booking agencies, which, as Stuart Nicholson reported, "effectively decide musicians' careers: who's in and who's out, who is on the top and who is going down."[40] All costs pertaining to recording and promotion were then charged against the young artists' future earnings. Obviously, musicians without similar backing did not face a level playing field. Such business practices in other industries would be considered unfair competition, or even "illegal dumping." But in the virtually unregulated music business everything was considered fair game, and ethical questions were routinely ignored in the jazz press.

The result of all this high-powered manipulation is that an air of artificiality permeates the jazz world, hanging over it like a thick smog. Musicians have become either brand names or invisible men (or women), with very few in between. (Miles Davis's name was actually trademarked posthumously by his lawyer.) Without the backing of a corporate record label, musicians have been largely unable to get bookings and reviews that translate into name recognition and drawing power. The jazz world of today is more about who's been granted a chance than who has the most to say. Musicians fortunate enough to receive such attention may have great abilities, but their musicianship has become secondary to their perceived marketability. We are left with a jazz scene nearly devoid of creativity and risk-taking, and rife with stale tribute concerts and albums. And as in the classical world, the bulk of the money goes to a few "stars" who are endlessly written up in the popular and music press.

Of course major label dominance came to a grinding halt in the 2000s as Internet downloading replaced CD sales, an outcome I discuss in the final chapter. However, the distorted musical landscape created by corporate record departments in the 1980s and 1990s is still very much with us.

Paul Johnson notes a depressingly similar trend that seized the art world from the 1980s onward. He writes of a

> self-reinforcing, self-perpetuating oligarchy, which includes art magazines, critics, professional patrons and, most important, museum directors. These work in conjunction with state bodies which dispense public funds to deserving artists, or the judges who award prizes. . . . The artist becomes

institutionalized in turn, and figures in the art histories and dictionaries of art and artists. Thus enduring fame is acquired in ways which would have astonished Raphael and Michelangelo, who innocently believed it was the result of creating beautiful works of art. The opportunities for intolerance and censorship are obvious.

Modern art establishments wield much more power than anything practiced in the times of, say, [Charles] Le Brun or [Jacques-Louis] David: the power to create and to render invisible. They do not burn paintings, as Hitler did, or send artists to the gulag, as was the wont of Stalin. Nor do they manipulate mobs of Red Guards to butcher sculptors and craftsmen in the streets. But they do break the hearts and impoverish the lives of artists who do not conform to their meretricious criteria. Writers and editors who resist these establishments quickly find themselves without jobs or platforms. The opportunities for corruption are obvious.[41]

Art critic Robert Hughes also spoke out against these tendencies, which have striking parallels in the jazz world: "The American art world is in gridlock today. Its museum directors are still in thrall to the market, its supposed variety a myth, since it clings to the '80s star system; its institutions march in lockstep, imposing a uniformity of taste that has few parallels in American cultural history." As with jazz, a few institutions and corporations hold the key to an artist's success or failure, and overwhelmingly support a status quo "designed to appease a populist mentality that contents itself with the easy task of supporting ethnicity and gender differences in the arts instead of the hard one of looking for real excellence."[42] Hughes points to the inflated reputation of the young African-American graffiti artist Jean-Michel Basquiat, who died of a drug overdose at age 27 and became the subject of a major motion picture. Hughes quotes the director of the Whitney Museum saying that "lingering racist presumptions seriously cloud the ability of many to understand Basquiat," the implication being that anyone who doesn't like his work must be racist.

Similarly, as Stuart Nicholson points out, "Marsalis rejected criticism in a way that suggested it was an attack on jazz and thus African-American culture itself."[43] One gets the feeling Wynton has convinced himself that—to paraphrase the famous comment of a General Motors executive in the 1950s—what's good for Wynton Marsalis is good for jazz.

Despite attempts to claim jazz as the cultural birthright of the black masses, even Marsalis acknowledges the widening gulf that separates jazz from the average African-American. In 2000 he noted, "In terms of African-Americans, under no circumstances do they support jazz music at any level."[44] Fellow trumpeter Terence Blanchard gloomily remarked, "Black radio ain't doing nothing."[45] Even as jazz is widely promoted through the mainstream media as "black music," blacks themselves are

showing only moderate interest, especially among the younger generation. "It's a black thing that few African Americans give a damn about,"
said culture critic Greg Tate.[46]

Ideology met reality one night in 1997, when Marsalis attended a free
outdoor performance by veteran trumpeter Clark Terry at Grant's Tomb
in New York. Stanley Crouch described the incident: "As Wynton Marsalis observed . . . when the master trumpeter Clark Terry, who was having
problems with his black, uptown audience . . . went into the great *Jeep's
Blues*, assuming to communicate through the time-honored form [Albert]
Murray has celebrated and described as so basic to Negro American culture and what it has to offer the world, 'It was amazing.' Marsalis added,
'Those Negroes had no idea what he was playing. They had no feeling
for the form and no emotional rapport at all. He could have been playing to the wind.'"[47] Crouch attributed their lack of interest to American
cultural blight, a "decadence that knows no limits of skin tone or class or
anything else." He goes on to chide black academics for failing to teach
Murray's theories of the "blues aesthetic" to young blacks. He never
questions whether these theories are faulty and out of touch with reality
themselves.

NOTES

1. Chilton, *Ride Red Ride*, 51.
2. Duke Ellington, *Music Is My Mistress*, 452.
3. Eric Porter, *What Is This Thing Called Jazz?*, 75.
4. Magro, *Contemporary Cat*, 48.
5. Peter Watrous, "Wynton Marsalis: A Jazzman on the Run," *New York Times*,
January 30, 2000.
6. Feather (1980), 80–83.
7. Watrous, "Wynton Marsalis: A Jazzman on the Run."
8. Watrous, "Wynton Marsalis: A Jazzman on the Run."
9. Magro, 48.
10. Gourse, *Wynton Marsalis*, 107.
11. Nicholson, *Is Jazz Dead?*, 49.
12. Stanley Crouch, "The Jazz Tradition Is Not Innovation," *JazzTimes*, February 2002, 26.
13. Nicholson, 20.
14. Piazza. *Blues Up and Down*, 170.
15. Piazza, 99.
16. Panish, *The Color of Jazz*, xix.
17. Paul Johnson, *Art*, 5.
18. Nisenson, *Blue*, 134.
19. Nicholson, 19, 24.
20. Magro, 140.

21. Magro, 139.

22. Gourse, 147.

23. Magro, 49.

24. Marcia Stepanek, "Wynton's War," *Contribute: The People and Ideas of Giving* 1, no. 2 (May/June 2006): 38–44.

25. Theodore Rosengarten, "Songs of Slavery Lifted by a Chorus of Horns," *New York Times*, February 23, 1997.

26. Nisenson, 40.

27. Conversation between Rich Johnson and the author, 2006.

28. Rosengarten, "Songs of Slavery Lifted by a Chorus of Horns."

29. Nicholson, 26.

30. Nicholson, 66. Originally printed in Robert S. Boynton, "The Professor of Connection: A Profile of Stanley Crouch," *New Yorker*, November 6, 1995.

31. Rosengarten, "Songs of Slavery Lifted by a Chorus of Horns."

32. Shelby Steele, "The Age of White Guilt and the Disappearance of the Black Individual," *Harper's Magazine*, November 2002, 37–38.

33. Nisenson, 239–40.

34. Nicholson, 7.

35. Derek Ansell, "Javon Jackson," *Jazz Journal International* 53, no. 4 (March 2000): 8.

36. Cook, *Blue Note Records*, 228.

37. Nicholson, 6.

38. Cook, 220.

39. Cook, 221.

40. Nicholson, 234.

41. Paul Johnson, *Art*, 729.

42. Hughes, *Culture of Complaint*, 199–201.

43. Nicholson, 45.

44. Nicholson, 45.

45. Magro, 145.

46. Yuval Taylor, ed., *The Future of Jazz*, 39.

47. Crouch, *Always In Pursuit*, 161–162.

7

~~

The Biggest Myth of All

"I don't play for any black people. Every place I go to—Japan, Switzerland, New York—playing at the Blue Note. The black ones can't afford it and the kids got into their own thing and it became a separate thing and it's sad.[1]"

—Milt Hinton

Without presenters and audiences there would be no jazz musicians. What most jazz texts don't reveal is the great degree to which black musicians have benefited from and even depended upon the efforts of white presenters and the appreciation of white audiences. The more these dynamics are taken into account, the clearer it becomes that jazz has been an interracial phenomenon throughout most of its history.

One of the least studied aspects of jazz is its audience, and consequently a mistaken conventional wisdom has filled the void. Many writers seem to assume jazz was sustained almost exclusively by the black community until after the Second World War. But whites have supported jazz almost from its beginning, and the truth is that all the major jazz figures—including Louis Armstrong, Duke Ellington, Billie Holiday, Charlie Parker, and Miles Davis—spent the bulk of their careers performing for white audiences. The jazz audience, in choosing where to spend its money, has exerted an enormous influence on the music's development. There's much truth to the old adage that he who pays the piper calls the tune.

Musicians have always been keenly aware of the decisive role their listeners play. "I study the audience," said trumpeter Adolphus "Doc" Cheatham. "I can tell by the audience what I should play—I see the expressions on their faces. That's an old system. Louis did that—all them old trumpet players did that."[2] The contemporary trumpeter Dave Douglas thinks of the audience as the fourth member of a trio or the fifth member of a quartet.[3]

The history of whites employing black musicians stretches back to colonial times. "In the North black musicians provided much of the dance music for the colonists of all classes," writes music historian Eileen Southern. "All over the South slaves played for the dancing of their masters at balls, assemblies, and special 'Entertainments' in the plantation ballrooms and 'palaces' of the colonial governors."[4]

In New Orleans, people of African descent provided music for white society throughout the nineteenth century. Even at the notorious quadroon balls, which flourished until the mid-1900s, music was typically furnished by nonwhite musicians while upper-class white males selected Creoles of color to be their concubines. "Indeed the colored male musician was the one exception to the prohibition against colored males being present at these balls," writes Henry Kmen in his book *Music in New Orleans: The Formative Years 1791–1841.*[5]

When syncopated dance music took the country by storm at the turn of the twentieth century, African-American bands enjoyed overwhelming popularity. As already noted, the orchestras of John Robichaux and Armand J. Piron were the two leading society bands in New Orleans for decades. To revisit Pops Foster's comment on Robichaux, "He had the rich people's jobs all sewed up for a long time. . . . In New Orleans, the colored bands had most of the work."[6]

Robichaux and Piron were not isolated cases, but part of a nationwide trend. In New York City James Reese Europe, besides conducting a symphony, led a society orchestra that rapidly became a favorite among elite families whose names are still familiar today: Rockefeller, Wanamaker, Pinchot, Gould, Astor, Vanderbilt. Europe's band played regularly at such prestigious locations as the Waldorf Astoria, Sherry's, Delmonico's, Martin's, Rector's, the Hotel Astor, and the Ritz-Carlton. "Since the turkey trot craze," *Variety* reported in 1913, "the colored musicians in New York have been kept busy dispensing syncopated music for the Four Hundred."[7] In 1910 Europe helped organize the Clef Club, a guild for African-American musicians. Europe was elected president, and membership eventually numbered in the hundreds. At a time when blacks made up only around 2 percent of New York City's population, the Clef Club booked in excess of $120,000 in business for a single year.[8]

James Weldon Johnson wrote that the Clef Club bands performed at "nearly all the best functions, not only in America, but in London and Paris," adding that they held a "monopoly of the business of entertaining at private parties and furnishing music for the dance craze which was beginning to sweep the country. . . . The colored musicians, all members of the Clef Club, had every amusement place outside of [the] legitimate theaters sewed up."[9]

In 1914 Europe began his collaboration with the white dancing team of Vernon and Irene Castle, the most famed proponents of the new dance craze that captivated the entire country. Europe's reputation was so widespread that the *New York Tribune* noted he had "all but secured complete control of the cabaret and dance field in the city."[10] In Boston, his brother John Europe led a band in the Copley Plaza, the largest and most luxurious hotel in the city. In Washington, DC, Louis Thomas—an inspiration to the young Duke Ellington—sent out various groups under his own name, and became so busy he occasionally hired white musicians. According to pianist Claude Hopkins, Thomas was getting "all the society work around Washington."[11] Thomas's success enabled him to purchase a building for the headquarters of his "Capital City Clef Club."

Ford Dabney operated yet another entertainment bureau based in New York for African-American musicians, and for years he led bands in such wealthy enclaves as Palm Beach, Miami, and Newport, Rhode Island. In Chicago it was not unusual to find African-American bands playing in all-white clubs or hotels. Bandleader William Samuels was a favorite among socialites along the Gold Coast. During the 1910s a black instrumental quartet played at Chicago's Hotel Normandy, and the New Orleans pianist Tony Jackson could be heard at the Congress Hotel. Luckey Roberts and Noble Sissle enjoyed success as society bandleaders on the East Coast even into the 1950s. The tradition of black musicians entertaining elite white society continued right up until 2005, when Bobby Short, perhaps the last great African-American cabaret star, died.

There's little question that jazz in its very earliest days was indeed the product of the black community in New Orleans. According to his biographer Don Marquis, Buddy Bolden "played all over town for different stratas of black society and for every conceivable function."[12] Bolden worked at dance halls, honky-tonks, and outdoor amusement parks that catered specifically to black audiences.

A black cultural context was obviously critical to the formation and character of jazz early on. But whites were not immune to its appeal, and Bolden attracted the attention of at least some. As Marquis states, "First of all, he would have been seen and heard in the street parades that wandered over great areas in the city. Papa John Joseph said he played 'mostly for colored,' implying that he may have played a few jobs for whites; Willie Foster said when he was a kid he heard Bolden and took some white friends to Lincoln Park to hear him play; Frank Adams stated simply, 'Bolden was tops, famous, and played for white and colored.'"[13] Pops Foster, recalling the evening festivities at Lincoln Park in which

Bolden figured so prominently, said, "You couldn't tell who it was for, there were so many whites."[14] The white trumpeter Johnny Lala remembered hearing Bolden's band play in 1898 for the embarkation of troops during the Spanish-American War.

Circling the famed vice district Storyville was a chain of cabarets. Some catered to a black clientele, mainly workers in the district, but the majority were patronized by free-spending whites. The instrumental blues tradition was carried on by King Oliver and Louis Armstrong, who played for black audiences at the Big 25, Segretta's, and other such places. But both men also probably played much the same music in establishments catering to whites, such as Pete Lala's and Tom Anderson's. Johnny Lala explained the hiring practices of the nightclub owned and run by his distant cousin Pete: "I didn't play there because he had colored musicians . . . he had white business, but he had colored, he didn't ever hire no white band."[15]

Black bands were employed exclusively at all the clubs surrounding Storyville from its establishment in 1897 until around 1912 or 1913, when a few white bands began working there as well. Storyville was created for white patronage, and blacks who did not work there were not welcome. The only exceptions were a string of storefront "cribs" where black prostitutes operated, and a handful of cabarets. As Louis Armstrong reminds us, "The Negroes were only allowed to work in the Red Light District. Most of the help was Negroes. They paid good Salaries and had a long time job. The pay was swell, no matter what your vocation was. Musicians—Singers and all kinds of Entertainers were always *welcomed* and *enjoyed*. Just stay in your place where you belonged. No *Mixing* at the *Guests Tables* at *no time*. Everybody understood Everything and there weren't ever any mix-ups, etc."[16]

There were still other neighborhoods in New Orleans where black jazz bands were hired by whites. The Creole drummer Paul Barbarin told of working frequently for Irish people in the Irish Channel district. Baby Dodds recalled how much "the Irish people liked the colored music." He played for them regularly in trombonist Jack Carey's outfit, which was also hired for white fraternity parties at Tulane University.[17] Pops Foster also remembered playing at lawn parties for "white and colored on different nights." Drummer Tony Sbarbaro related, "A colored band could play a white picnic and always did play 'em, but no white band ever played a colored picnic."[18] Kid Ory led a band including Louis Armstrong that worked every Saturday night at the all-white New Orleans Country Club.[19]

Jelly Roll Morton spoke of a place called "The Frenchman's," which he visited as early as 1902. "All of the girls that could get out of their houses was there. The millionaires would come listen to their favorite pianist. There weren't any discrimination of any kind. They all sat at different tables or anywhere they felt like sitting. They mingled together just as they wished to and everyone was just like one big happy family."[20] Morton also recalled similar establishments: "Many times you would see St. Charles millionaires right in those honky-tonks. Called themselves slumming, I guess, but they was there just the same, nudging elbows with all the big bums—the longshoremen and the illiterate screwmens [dockworkers who stowed, or "screwed," cargo into the hold of a boat] from down the river."[21]

When Louis Armstrong was fourteen, he lived for a time with his father and stepmother. As he wrote in his autobiography *Satchmo*, "On quiet Sunday nights I'd lay on my bunk listening to Freddie Keppard and his jazz band play for some rich white folks about half a mile away."[22] One of Keppard's first professional jobs was playing with Johnny Brown's band at the whites-only Spanish Fort amusement area on Lake Pontchartrain. Later, with the Olympia Orchestra, he had plenty of white society work. He also performed in Storyville cabarets, notably at Pete Lala's for white customers, as well as some uptown black dance halls. By 1912 he was touring the white Orpheum vaudeville circuit with the Original Creole Band. After landing in Chicago, he played for six years with Doc Cook's band at Paddy (Patrick) Harmon's all-white Dreamland dance hall.[23] Keppard alternated in pit bands in some black theaters, but not for long. He then led a band at Bert Kelly's Stables on Rush Street, once again playing for white audiences. By the time he died prematurely at age 43 in 1933, he had spent virtually his entire professional career performing for whites.

The expanding and increasingly interracial audience for jazz would have a direct effect on the music. Baby Dodds explained how a band's repertoire might be tailored to fit the tastes of even an international audience: "In those days we used to play all kinds of numbers. New Orleans is a seaport town and boats would come in from all parts of Europe. Many of the fellows had been on boats for three to five months when they came in and they were glad to find a dance hall and fast women in the district. Then we'd play 'Over the Waves' for the sailors and different nationality songs."[24]

The story of the Tuxedo Orchestra is a good illustration of how African-American musicians in New Orleans actively pursued the lucrative white market. Bill Ridgely played trombone, but during the day he ran a clothes cleaning and pressing shop. A white costumer suggested that Ridgely form a band and name it the Tuxedo Orchestra, with the musicians dressed in formal attire. Ridgely's friend and sometime helper, drummer Henry Zeno, worked out a deal with a tailor shop on Rampart Street: the shop would supply the band with tuxedos, and in exchange, the band would advertise the shop by playing on its balcony for two months. The arrangement paid off. According to Samuel Charters, "Ridgely's contacts among the white families in New Orleans and the idea of tuxedos gave the band a lot of society work, and they became very popular."[25] The Tuxedo Orchestra managed to stay working from 1916 to 1924, and its ranks included such notable jazz figures as Louis Armstrong, Jimmie Noone, and Johnny Dodds. In a famous photograph, the bandmembers pose at a function alongside the white family that hired them.[26]

Bands of both races played on excursion steamboats that plied the Mississippi, but once again the clientele was overwhelmingly white. Pops Foster explained the protocol: "Monday night out of St. Louis was for colored. There were as many white as colored on Monday nights and you couldn't hardly get on the boats that night. In New Orleans no colored were allowed on the boats."[27]

The phenomenon of slumming took hold in many urban centers from the late nineteenth century on, giving new impetus for whites to seek out black entertainment. Slumming initially focused more on Italian, Jewish, and Chinese enclaves but later shifted to black neighborhoods. In cities such as San Francisco, Los Angeles, New York, Chicago, and Kansas City, many African-Americans were consigned to poor neighborhoods at the edge of "tenderloins," meaning established vice districts. Venues that provided musical entertainment in these black communities were often racially mixed, calling to mind Morton's description of The Frenchman's in 1902.

The notorious Barbary Coast section of San Francisco flourished from 1906 until 1921, when it was closed down by local authorities. Sid Grauman (later the owner of Hollywood's famous Grauman's Chinese Theatre) began his show business career there escorting groups of white tourists and slummers to such places as Purcell's and Red Kelly's, where black bands played for mixed audiences. Such well-known patrons as Al Jolson, Mary Pickford, and Fatty Arbuckle lent these establishments an aura of show-biz glamour. In 1917 Jelly Roll Morton and his first wife, Anita Gonzales, opened a cabaret in Los Angeles called the Jupiter. "My place was a black-and-tan," said Morton, "for colored and white alike."[28]

The vogue for slumming was reflected in two epochal musicals on the New York stage: Charles Hoyt's *A Trip to Chinatown* from 1891, and Bob Cole and Billy Johnson's *A Trip to Coontown* from 1898. The latter was the earliest musical staged in New York that was written, directed, and performed by blacks for white audiences. After a shaky start at the modest Third Avenue Theater, the show moved to such prestigious locations as the Casino Roof and the Grand Opera House, and then crossed the country on road tours for over three years. Cole and Johnson's success with white audiences engendered a wave of African-American stage productions that lasted through the 1920s. Among the more successful black shows were *Shuffle Along* (1921) and *Chocolate Dandies* (1924), both with music and lyrics by Eubie Blake and Noble Sissle; James P. Johnson's *Runnin' Wild* (1923), which introduced the "Charleston"; Will Vodery's *From Dixie to Broadway* (1924); The *Blackbirds* revues (1928–1939), mounted by white producer Lew Leslie; and Fats Waller and Andy Razaf's *Hot Chocolates* (1929), which introduced the hits "Ain't Misbehavin'" and "Black and Blue" and made Louis Armstrong a star to the white theatergoing public in New York.

A favorite hangout for the elite African-American theatrical crowd in the early years of the twentieth century was the black-owned Marshall Hotel on West 53rd Street. Here Jim Europe, Will Marion Cook, Bob Cole, Billy Johnson, Bert Williams, and others talked business and socialized. "Gradually," writes New York historian Luc Sante,

> white show people, composers, and songwriters began to drop by, absorbing the musical innovations that came through from the South and West, and the influences began to show up in their work, initially and notably in Irving Berlin's first great hit, "Alexander's Ragtime Band," which introduced the world at large to ragtime. Soon the dance craze was on, and the usual motley crowd of financiers, gigolos, gangsters, heiresses, prostitutes, pimps, actors, and ward bosses began practicing the steps of the bunny hug, the grizzly bear, the turkey trot, the one-step, and that import from the slums of Buenos Aires, the tango. Soon the established Broadway lobster palaces began converting their premises to allow for large dance floors.[29]

As the black population shifted uptown, the Marshall was succeeded by Happy Rhone's at 143rd and Lenox Avenue in Harlem. The African-American owner, bandleader Arthur "Happy" Rhone, presented black floor shows for mixed audiences, which included celebrities such as John and Ethel Barrymore, Charlie Chaplin, W. C. Handy, Ted Lewis, and Ethel Waters. James Weldon Johnson was of the opinion that *The Darktown Follies*, an all-black show staged at the Lafayette Theatre in 1913, kicked off the white "invasion" of Harlem. As he wrote in his book *Black Manhattan*, this production "drew space, headlines, and cartoons in New York papers; and consequently it became the vogue to go to Harlem to see it . . . the beginning of the nightly migration to Harlem in search of entertainment."[30]

On Chicago's South Side similar developments were taking place. The Pekin Inn started attracting entertainers and "sporting" people of both races, and by 1910 the *Chicago Defender* noted that it "caters much at present to white people."[31] In 1916, theater seats were taken out to make way for a dance floor. New Orleans trumpeter Manuel Perez led a band there in 1919, with clarinetist Alphonse Picou and bassist Ed Garland. Later bookings included King Oliver's band and pianist Tony Jackson's group featuring Sidney Bechet. The Pekin became a popular hangout for white gangsters, and in 1920 two policemen were shot on the premises. The club was shut down for good a few years later, but it set the pattern for Chicago's South Side black-and-tans.

Black-and-tans became a nationwide institution once Prohibition was enacted. They distinguished themselves from other music venues by offering floor shows, part of an elaborate ritual meant to disguise the club's primary purpose: the sale of alcohol, or overpriced "set-ups" (mixers, ice, etc.) for drinks. The "black" in black-and-tan referred to the musicians and help, while the "tan" applied to the showgirls ("tall, tan, and terrific," as the Cotton Club advertised). The expense of mounting these productions, which became increasingly popular and lavish as the twenties progressed, meant that such places catered primarily to upscale white patrons.

Another attraction of the black-and-tans was that they remained open into the early morning hours. As guitarist Danny Barker explained, "At about 2:00 a.m., when the famous clubs, theaters, and entertainment places closed for the night downtown and about town, it was the custom for good-time swinging people to come uptown. . . . Some officials were paid off and the after-hours joints stayed open until after daylight, not bothered by the police." Barker witnessed a familiar scene in which "everybody sat around half asleep" until a "slick doorman" alerted the staff that a party of "prosperous-looking people" was about to enter. Suddenly, "Everybody went into action; the band swinging, waiters beating on trays, everybody smiling and moving, giving the impression the joint was jumping."[32]

The Cotton Club in New York has become a part of American folklore, but less commonly known is just how widespread the black-and-tan phenomenon was. In addition to Harlem's Cotton Club, there was Al Capone's Cotton Club in Cicero, Illinois, and Frank Sebastian's Cotton Club in Los Angeles. By the late twenties, Cotton Clubs had appeared in such middle-American cities as Indianapolis, Cleveland, Akron, and Ashtabula, Ohio.

All of these establishments grew up independently (unlike the large restaurant chains of today), but in response to the same set of circumstances: the unpopular Volstead Act outlawing the sale of alcohol, and the subsequent rise of organized crime. Local authorities were generally willing to turn a blind eye to various forms of vice as long as they were confined to the newly emerging black belts. Some other famous black-and-tans of the era were the Sunset Café, the Grand Terrace, and the Nest Club (later known as the Apex Club) in Chicago; Connie's Inn, Small's Paradise and the Saratoga Club in New York; a Club Alabam and a Kentucky Club in both New York and Los Angeles; and Plantation Clubs in New York, Chicago, St. Louis, and Los Angeles.

The famed Sunset Café in Chicago, which launched Louis Armstrong's career as a bandleader, started off catering to black customers. But as Chicago jazz historian William Howland Kenney notes, by the time Armstrong arrived, "black musicians who worked there and white musicians who sat in with them concur that nearly all of the customers were white."[33] Diagonally across the street King Oliver led his Dixie Syncopators at the Plantation Café, another exclusive black-and-tan. In 1926, a reporter from *Variety* visited both venues and stated, "The dusky patrons are but a small percentage of the trade," adding that a glass of ginger ale sold for $1.25.[34] Next door to the Plantation, clarinetist Jimmie Noone worked at the Nest Club, which also, according to Kenney, "catered to a wealthy white clientele."[35] At Connie's Inn in New York, where Fletcher Henderson and later Louis Armstrong appeared, the average tab was $15, a substantial sum for the time.[36] At the Cotton Club black customers were barred altogether, except for a handful of celebrities.

Even the exact demographics of the Lincoln Gardens, where Armstrong made his northern debut in King Oliver's band, are open to question. It's widely assumed throughout the jazz literature that the Gardens catered almost exclusively to blacks. The venue did in fact advertise regularly in the *Chicago Defender*, a black newspaper, at the time Oliver was there. But though the Lincoln Gardens is often depicted as a dance hall, it featured floor shows, a hallmark of the black-and-tan. Johnny Lala, on a visit up north, remembered the Gardens as "white and colored, you know, black-and-tan."[37] Hoagy Carmichael also referred to it as a black-and-tan, and one black patron remembered it having "Jim Crow seating."[38] The white bandleader Art Landry told jazz scholar James T. Maher that 80 to 100 white couples danced there every night.[39] An African-American entertainer, Tommy Brookins, provided this description: "People belonging to all classes of society attended: doctors, lawyers, students, entertainment people, musicians, people of all colors were found there."[40]

Some black-and-tans made an effort to attract more black customers by lowering prices on "Blue Mondays," offering matinees from 3:00 to 7:00 p.m. for those coming home from work, and hosting breakfast dances from 4:00 a.m. to mid-morning on Sundays. Louis Armstrong spoke of one Chicago establishment, the Fiume, which catered to blacks but hired a white jazz band.[41] Nevertheless, it was the money of upper-class whites that largely bankrolled the black-and-tan phenomenon.

Black-and-tans became the primary locus of black jazz in the twenties and attracted its greatest exponents. Louis Armstrong worked the Sunset Café in Chicago, Connie's Inn in New York, Sebastian's Cotton Club in Los Angeles, and the Suburban Gardens in New Orleans. Earl Hines worked with Armstrong at the Sunset and went on to work for Jimmie

Noone at the Apex. After that he began a ten-year residency as big band leader at the Grand Terrace. All these places catered to white audiences.

Duke Ellington and Fletcher Henderson launched their bandleading careers at the Kentucky Club and Club Alabam respectively, both black-and-tans in midtown Manhattan. In 1927 Ellington brought national fame to the Cotton Club and vice versa. Henderson was featured at Connie's Inn from 1930 to 1931, and appeared in midtown at the Roseland Ballroom for a slightly less well-to-do white audience from 1924 to 1942. Fats Waller also performed at Connie's Inn, where his revue *Hot Chocolates* was originally staged.

Cab Calloway spoke out about the exclusive racial policies at the Cotton Club, where he began his career as a bandleader: "I don't condone it, but it existed and was in keeping with the values of the day. It couldn't happen today. It shouldn't have happened then. It was wrong. But on the other hand, I doubt jazz would have survived if musicians hadn't gone along with such racial practices there and elsewhere."[42]

Although white musicians were frequent visitors to the black-and-tans, they were almost never hired to perform in them. Thus a color line was drawn that excluded white musicians from the only real jazz work of the 1920s. The Original Dixieland Jazz Band created a short-lived sensation in Chicago and New York in the late teens, but after Prohibition was instituted they found their popularity waning fast. The New Orleans Rhythm Kings enjoyed a seventeen-month run at the Friar's Inn in Chicago, but were fired when management decided to install floor shows and discovered the band couldn't read well enough to handle written arrangements for specialty acts. Typically white jazz players had to seek employment in large, commercial dance bands that used jazz to spice up their musical fare, but not as the main course. Those who resisted this kind of employment didn't work regularly at all: saxophonist Bud Freeman was unable to secure a steady playing job until 1933, and drummer Dave Tough until 1936.[43] In his 1946 article "Chicago Jazz History," Paul Eduard Miller and George Hoefer wrote of a "refusal of white nightlifers to support white jazz . . . While the white jazzmen struggled against the odds to play his kind of music, the Negro musician found strong support for jazz."[44]

Cabarets that retained a predominantly African-American clientele in the twenties tended to be smaller, humbler affairs than the grand black-and-tans of jazz lore. In Harlem, many such cabarets were located in the ground floor of brownstone residences, much like the clubs that would line 52nd Street a decade later. Most of them hired no more than a pianist and perhaps a singer, though musicians were sometimes welcome to sit in and jam. However, as John Hammond pointed out, "With tenants living above the ground-floor . . . an inordinate amount of noise from brass instruments and drums was not permitted."[45] Salaries in such places were low to nonexistent and musicians often worked for tips alone.

Some of these small clubs, such as Edmond Johnson's Cellar in New York, were considered "the last stop on the way down in show business," as Ethel Waters put it. "After you worked there, there was no place to go except into domestic service."[46] Jelly Roll Morton's wife Mabel stated that "the colored places couldn't afford him," but "he was so liked by the white people that he never had to play a colored engagement."[47] Consequently there are no ads for a Jelly Roll Morton performance in the *Chicago Defender*, even though he lived in that city from 1922 to 1928.

To be sure, there were a handful of clubs that catered almost exclusively to black patrons and hired bands. Among these were the Bamboo Inn and the Lenox Club in Harlem. They are barely mentioned in the jazz literature, however, for the simple reason that they could only afford to hire such peripheral acts as McRae's Ebony Stompers or bands led by June Clark or Cliff Jackson. Some first-rate musicians, Jimmy Harrison and Bubber Miley among them, passed through the ranks of these groups, but only for brief periods on their way to bigger and better things (Harrison ended up in Fletcher Henderson's band, Miley in Ellington's).[48]

James Weldon Johnson wrote that most Harlemites were "ordinary, hardworking people" who had "never seen the inside of a night club," and were occupied with "the stern necessity of making a living, of making ends meet, of finding money to pay the rent and keep the children fed and clothed."[49] In 1923 music publisher and bandleader Clarence Williams told a black publication, the *New York Clipper*, that entertainment-hungry blacks bought so many records precisely because the best live performances occurred in prohibitively expensive or racially exclusive clubs.[50] The white journalist and novelist Konrad Bercovici related that at Barron Wilkins's Exclusive Club in Harlem, "A hundred-dollar bill will not go far and is not intended to do much service in this luxuriously fitted-out cabaret."[51] The small black upper class, which could perhaps afford such extravagance, was seldom interested in jazz at all, and most writers of the Harlem Renaissance barely recognized its existence.

Aside from the black-and-tans, black bands were also popular in many white dance halls. In 1919, Louis Brecker, great-uncle of the contemporary jazz musicians Michael and Randy Brecker, opened the Roseland Ballroom at the corner of 51st and Broadway in New York. His policy was to feature two bands alternating half-hour sets, and from 1924 on he consistently hired African-American bands to work opposite white bands. Armand Piron's orchestra was the first black band to appear, and after Piron returned to New Orleans, Brecker hired Fletcher Henderson, whose run lasted off and on until 1942.

Other white dance halls across the country picked up on this trend. McKinney's Cotton Pickers, a black band managed by white bandleader Jean Goldkette, began a long residency at the Greystone Ballroom in Detroit in April 1927. In Chicago, Paddy (Patrick) Harmon employed Charles Elgar's band for his whites-only Dreamland ballroom from 1921 to 1928. Dreamland, as already noted, was also the home of Doc Cook's orchestra, featuring Freddie Keppard and Jimmie Noone. A band led by clarinetist Darnell Howard played at Harmon's other location, the Arcadia Ballroom on the North Side. Elgar and Howard also worked at the appropriately named White City Ballroom. Albert Wynn, Jimmy Wade, and Eddie South ("the Dark Angel of the Violin") led orchestras at the elegant Moulin Rouge Café on Wabash Street in the heart of downtown Chicago.

One of the most unusual establishments of the time was Bert Kelly's Stables, just north of the Loop. The club was a favorite hangout for white bohemians and college students, plus the usual complement of gangsters. The Stables almost seems a prototype for the jazz club as we know it today, except that it included a dance floor along with cabaret seating. King Oliver worked there for three months in 1922, followed by Freddie Keppard, billed as "The World's Greatest Colored Jazz Cornetist." Keppard's drinking made him an unreliable leader and the job was turned over to Johnny Dodds, who enjoyed a six-year run from 1926 to 1932.[52] Kelly paid his musicians well: Dodds was reportedly making $175 a week as leader in 1930, enough for him to purchase apartment buildings on Chicago's South Side.

Of course the black community also supported their own musicians and entertainers in theaters on the TOBA circuit, as well as black dance halls such as the Savoy Ballrooms in New York and Chicago. But in these places jazz was typically only one type of music among several performed. African-American musicians were fond of showing off their versatility, and playbills indicate that black audiences responded to a wide variety of entertainment. Among the acts appearing at the Lyric Theatre in New Orleans were not only the singers Ethel Waters, Ida Cox, and Bessie Smith, but also Butterbeans and Susie, the popular comedy team; "Jailhouse" Tolliver, "the world champion negro roller skater"; Sunshine Sammy, who later became famous as a cast member in the *Our Gang* films; John Pamplin, described as "a mustachioed negro juggler"; The Black Valentino, a "dashing Senegambian," and his "warbling and tangoing wife"; and Sandy Burns, the comedian who supplied Ferdinand Morton with his nickname "Jelly Roll."[53]

Many TOBA shows also became popular with whites, and black theaters responded by initiating special "Midnight Frolics" for white audiences. As early as 1920, black theaters in New Orleans, Atlanta, Memphis, Houston, Dallas, Greenville, South Carolina, Winston-Salem, North Carolina, and Pensacola, Florida, hosted midnight shows for whites only.

In the thirties the audiences in black theaters became increasingly integrated. Jack Schiffman, whose father Frank owned the Apollo Theater from 1935 to 1977, wrote, "Although it is uncommon to see more than a sprinkling of whites at an Apollo show today, it was not so in the thirties. Despite an increasingly sinister reputation, the Harlem of the Depression years and early forties was popular with whites. Whole generations of Columbia students, for instance, knew the theater intimately. . . . At the Wednesday night amateur shows, at least half the house was customarily white and, at the Saturday midnight shows in years gone by, as many as four out of five customers were white."[54]

Black dance halls became integrated as well. In 1929 Cab Calloway said the "crowds were 90 percent colored at the [New York] Savoy."[55] By the mid-thirties, whites were increasingly joining in. As David Stowe writes in his book *Swing Changes*, the Savoy

> had a policy of welcoming and encouraging white dancers and spectators. A report on the redecoration and modernization of the Savoy in the fall of 1936 reported that the ballroom "now resembles any other downtown palace except for the fact that about 20 percent of the crowd is colored. Ofays have muscled in something awful." During his sojourn in Harlem in the early 1940's, Malcolm X estimated that one-third of the sideline booths off the dance floor contained whites, mainly spectators, but some of whom danced, a few even with blacks. According to poet Langston Hughes: "The lindy-hoppers at the Savoy even began to practise acrobatic routines, and to do absurd things for the entertainment of the whites, that probably would never have entered their heads to attempt merely for their own effortless amusement. Some of the lindy-hoppers had cards printed with their names on them and became dance professors teaching the tourists. The Harlem nights became show nights for the Nordics."[56]

Though the fabled Kansas City jazz scene is often depicted as by and for blacks, it too followed the black-and-tan model. As such it was dominated by white gangsters and catered mostly to thrill-seeking whites. "Like Lerner and Loewe's *Brigadoon*, the celebrated mythical hamlet, Kansas City jazz is an enigma, more myth than fact,"[57] write Frank Driggs and Chuck Haddix in their comprehensive study on the city's jazz history. The town was controlled by its corrupt mayor Tom Pendergast with an assist from crime syndicate boss Johnny Lazio, an associate of Al Capone. After the Kansan Harry Truman met Stalin in Potsdam at the end of World War Two, he commented that the Soviet dictator was "as near like Tom Pendergast as any man I know."[58]

The thriving nightlife scene in Kansas City continued full blast through the Depression, its illicit nature undimmed by the repeal of Prohibition, as gang activity simply turned from alcohol to narcotics. This helps explain why Charlie Parker became addicted to heroin there in 1936 (to relieve pain suffered from an auto accident), a full decade before the drug made its way to the streets of Harlem, where Billie Holiday and so many others became hooked. It's no coincidence that the legendary period of Kansas City jazz ended with the collapse of the Pendergast regime. In 1938 Pendergast, after amassing millions, was sent to Leavenworth Penitentiary and fined his remaining assets.

Buster Smith, lead altoist with Count Basie at the famed Reno Club and an early mentor of Charlie Parker, stated, "In Kansas City, all them big clubs were [run by] them big gangsters and they were the musicians' best friend."[59] Driggs tells of prostitutes at the Reno, "perched in the balcony like exotic birds, dispensing knock-out drops to unsuspecting cattle men."[60] As Nathan W. Pearson notes in his book on the Kansas City jazz era, "Most of the better nightclubs of the period, even those run by blacks, were for white patrons exclusively. Blacks were often allowed into the balcony on certain nights, or to sit on the bandstand with the musicians.[61] According to pianist and bandleader Jay McShann, with whom Charlie Parker made his first commercial recordings, "The top clubs they always catered to the white audience and the mediocre clubs they let blacks in."[62]

A scene in Robert Altman's 1996 movie *Kansas City* depicts a black band entertaining an almost exclusively black audience at a fictional "Hey Hey" club in the 1930s. But as was the case in New York and Chicago in the 1920s, Kansas City's bigger bands and best musicians played for a largely white clientele. The actual "Hey Hay Club" was owned by Milton Morris, son of Russian Jewish immigrants and another Pendergast crony. According to Driggs, the Hey Hay "became a popular destination for both locals and tourists hungry for a taste of Kansas City nightlife."[63] Customers sat on bales of hay in a room decorated with corn shucks, and ordered whiskey shots or marijuana sticks for twenty-five cents each. The Hey Hay became a notorious gang hangout, and like so many similar establishments throughout the country, relied on black talent to entertain a white audience eager to indulge in recreational sin.

Small group jazz found a home in the basement clubs of brownstones lining New York's famed 52nd Street. The first of these, the Onyx, started in 1927 as an illegal speakeasy where white musicians could relax and jam after work (the password was "I'm from 802," the number of the local musicians' union). The club officially opened to the public in 1934, shortly after repeal. "It would never cease to amaze me," said owner Joe Helbock, "how they would come in complaining about some leader that kept them for rehearsals ten minutes longer than expected. Then they would stay in my place playing all night long—for free."[64] The Onyx began hiring musicians for extended engagements, and eventually launched the New York careers of an interracial galaxy of jazz stars: Art Tatum, Maxine Sullivan, Joe Sullivan, the Spirits of Rhythm, John Kirby, Stuff Smith, and Louis Prima.

By the late thirties, jazz clubs lined both sides of 52nd Street between 5th and 6th Avenues, a stretch that came to be known as "Swing Street." While the Street probably featured more black than white musicians, its customers were almost uniformly white until the war years. As Leonard Feather recalled, "I resented the exclusion of black people as customers. The clubs could not exclude black musicians with whom they were familiar. But by and large, they tried to keep everything as white as possible. . . . It was not until 1943–1944 that the raised eyebrows began to disappear."[65] Pianist Billy Taylor witnessed the changing racial climate when he first arrived in New York in 1943: "What made 52nd Street was not just the number of music clubs, but the variety of the music you could hear and the interchange between musicians. There is no substitute for free interchange. Fifty-second Street had it. Color was no hangup. When I took a job I was free to hire anybody I wanted. I remember Shelly Manne coming into a club in his Coast Guard uniform—it was during the war—and sitting in with a mixed group. Nobody thought anything of it."[66]

In Chicago, a strip of nightclubs much like Swing Street sprang up along a two-block stretch of Randolph Street, just west of State Street in the Loop. Such jazz greats as Art Tatum, Roy Eldridge, Jack Teagarden, Lionel Hampton, Red Allen, and Eddie South appeared regularly at these clubs, which included the Preview, the Latin Quarter, the Band Box, the Brass Rail, the Hollywood Lounge, and the Garrick Showbar. Close by was the famed Three Deuces, where Bix Beiderbecke and the Chicagoans had jammed in the twenties. In the thirties, Roy Eldridge attained national notoriety via nightly radio broadcasts from the Deuces, and Wingy Manone, Zutty Singleton, and Art Tatum appeared there as bandleaders. Once again, many African-American artists were steadily employed to perform for largely white audiences.

Some club owners—such as Barney Josephson, who had two Café Society locations in New York, and Billy Berg in Los Angeles—made a point of encouraging African-American patronage. Impresario Norman Granz insisted on integrated seating at his Jazz at the Philharmonic concerts, which started in 1944 and featured mixed bands. Milt Gabler also fostered race mixing at his informal jazz concerts in New York. "We mixed the personnel right from the beginning. Also audiences," Gabler recalled. "For that matter, I used mixed bands on my Commodore recordings. The problem was to get blacks—musicians included—to bring their wives downtown. They weren't used to socializing outside of Harlem."[67]

The "swing era" of the 1930s and early 1940s was of course dominated by the rise of the big bands. The economics of the music industry changed, and jazz was increasingly dictated by popular tastes, as opposed to those of the wealthy minority that patronized the black-and-tans in the twenties. Big bands of both races had to appeal to a more common denominator, and black bands suddenly found themselves at a disadvantage. Their focus on hot jazz had carved out a niche market that had served them well over the previous quarter-century. But now attempts to broaden their audience and repertoire were often rebuffed by recording executives who wanted them to remain faithful to their core fan base. Bandleader Andy Kirk told of his struggle to convince Jack Kapp of Decca Records to let him record a ballad. He quotes Kapp as saying, "Andy, what's the matter with you? You've got something good going for you. Why do you want to do what the white boys are doing?" After much arm-twisting, Kapp agreed to let Kirk record a rendition of "Until the Real Thing Comes Along," which hit pay dirt. "We jumped from 10,000 sales to 100,000. 'Real Thing' was to widen our territory, open up new areas for jobs and help us to reach people of all levels. It was our real breakthrough from race records."[68]

The stereotype of the African-American as hot jazz musician became a liability in this new and much more commercial environment. Meanwhile, criticism of the swing bands from the newly emerging jazz cognoscenti reinforced the old stereotype that whites played (and profited inordinately from) a watered-down version of jazz. As we've already seen, most of these early writers from the mid- to late-thirties looked askance at new attempts to "commercialize" jazz, and held many white bandleaders personally accountable. Criticism was also leveled at black bandleaders thought to sound "too white," such as Ellington, Chick Webb, and Jimmie Lunceford.

White swing bands typically enjoyed more widespread appeal, as they were granted more flexibility to play and record both sweet and swinging dance tunes. What's more, radio had become the premier medium of mass entertainment, and commercial sponsors, fearful of alienating southern audiences, only awarded contracts to the leading white bands. Cigarette companies, based in the South, were the prime sponsors of big bands on radio through the thirties and early forties.

Despite all the disadvantages faced by black bands, the gross incomes of the top black and white bands were surprisingly similar over the long haul. In the early forties, the orchestras of Glenn Miller, Benny Goodman, and Artie Shaw each grossed around $700,000; a few years later, Cab Calloway pulled in $750,000 and Ellington $600,000.[69] In any case, all through the "swing era" it was the sweet bands, not the swing bands, that enjoyed the greatest commercial success. Not even Benny Goodman could touch the heights reached by Guy Lombardo, who is reputed to have sold as many as 25 million records. Lombardo's was the only name band to have a sponsored, primetime network radio show every year from 1930 to

1945.[70] Lombardo was a perennial favorite at dance halls throughout the U.S. and Canada, and even held the attendance record for a single night at the Savoy Ballroom in New York.[71]

Journalists of the time, particularly from the black press, were indignant that white bands were enjoying a broader range of work than black bands. While there's truth to this complaint, which has been echoed by jazz writers up to the present day, it's again important to distinguish between jazz and non-jazz work. Take hotel work, for example. In an article for *Harper's Magazine* in 1941, Irving Kolodin noted that Count Basie, Jimmie Lunceford, Louis Armstrong, and other black bandleaders were "almost never encountered in a prominent hotel," even though their names were familiar to white audiences.[72] Some hotels occasionally hired black bands in the thirties—including the Congress Hotel and Hotel Sherman in Chicago, the Park Central in New York, the William Penn in Pittsburgh, and the Ritz-Carlton in Boston—but most did not. Scott DeVeaux, in his book *The Birth of Bebop*, argues that the "exclusion from prominent hotels was far more deleterious" to black bands than the lack of radio sponsorship, even though, as he admits, "major white bands, such as Glenn Miller's or Tommy Dorsey's actually lost money over the course of an extended [hotel] engagement."[73]

The truth is that hotels were never hospitable to jazz. In 1935 the new Benny Goodman Orchestra was booked into the Roosevelt Grill (at the Hotel Roosevelt in midtown New York) following a long and successful run by Guy Lombardo's band. As Goodman's vocalist Helen Ward recalled, "The place was impossible for what we were trying to do. How softly can you play 'King Porter Stomp?' The people were absolutely totally unnerved. They were used to this sweet music, and so they couldn't hear each other over dinner."[74] After the first set the band was summarily fired. Most white bands that did secure steady hotel jobs were saccharine society bands like those of Ozzie Nelson, Vincent Lopez, Dick Stabile, Mal Hallett, and Jan Savitt. Swing bands largely had to forsake their jazz repertoire, or were off-limits entirely.

Today when we think of the swing era we're apt to recall Benny Goodman's classic hits, such as "King Porter Stomp" or "Bugle Call Rag." But his better sellers were pop confections like "The Glory of Love" and "This Year's Kisses." As America approached wartime there was an increasing demand for romantic ballads. Trumpeter Harry James, who made his reputation as a fiery jazz soloist with Goodman, formed his own orchestra and scored a moderate hit in 1938 with a hot version of the old jazz classic, "I Found a New Baby." Yet it wasn't until he recorded such syrupy numbers as "I Don't Want to Walk Without You" and "Sleepy Lagoon" that he achieved real commercial success, and from then on he was consigned to playing overripe ballads to keep his band going. (Goodman once told me that he would have fired James if he'd played that way in his band.) The ever-resourceful Duke Ellington rode out this trend by recording some of the greatest ballads of the era: "Sophisticated Lady," "Solitude," and "I Got It Bad (And That Ain't Good)." Just as with Goodman and James, these romantic tunes turned out to be much more commercially successful than the swing classics he's known for today, such as "Rockin' In Rhythm," "Caravan," and "Take the A Train."

By the late thirties public tastes had largely turned away from jazz. The more commercially oriented bandleaders, such as Glenn Miller and the Dorsey brothers, accepted this turn of events in stride. As Miller said, "I haven't a great jazz band, and I don't want one. Some of the critics among us . . . point their fingers at us and charge us with forsaking real jazz. Maybe so. Maybe not. It's all in what you define as 'real jazz.' It happens that to our ears harmony comes first. A dozen colored bands have a better beat than mine."[75]

But for those leaders who were at heart jazz players, the increasing commerciality of the swing era was a bitter pill. Benny Goodman and Artie Shaw both disbanded at the height of their popularity; Gene Krupa gave up his big band in the late forties after being hounded by drug agents; and Harry James retreated into alcoholism. After declaring bankruptcy, Bunny Berigan died from the effects of alcoholism in 1942 at the age of thirty-three.

The war years were difficult even for bandleaders who managed to avoid the draft. The move toward integrating bands—which Benny Goodman and Charlie Barnet famously began in the mid-thrities (though others, such as Leo Reisman, had done it before, in the late twenties)—picked up speed during the war years. As more and more musicians were drafted, both black and white bandleaders were forced to make a virtue out of necessity to fill their ranks. Gender as well as racial barriers were broken, as Woody Herman hired a twenty-two-year-old lead trumpeter named Billie Rogers and vibes player Marjorie Hyams, while Lionel Hampton brought in saxophonist Elsie Smith. Largely because of wartime tax regulations limiting personal income, many bandleaders decided to pour extra profits into hiring full string sections. In the final years of the war, Harry James, Tommy Dorsey, and Earl Hines all employed lavish string sections comprised mostly of female musicians.

Starting in December 1946, in the space of only a few weeks, eight big bands broke up due to high overhead costs and declining business. These bands were led by some of the top names of the era: Benny Goodman, Woody Herman, Harry James, Tommy Dorsey, Les Brown, Jack Teagarden, Benny Carter, and Ina Ray Hutton. Many disbandments would follow, and a spate of once-prominent bandleaders declared bankruptcy. The history of musicians filing for bankruptcy is a long one and includes

the names of Jean Goldkette, Red Nichols, Jack Teagarden, Claude Hopkins, Billy Butterfield, Ruby Braff, and Woody Herman. (Of course this
list probably pales in comparison to the number of nightclubs and independent record companies that have gone under.)

The war years also witnessed the rise of jazz clubs catering specifically
to the African-American community. Count Basie's longtime lead altoist
Marshal Royal described a situation in Los Angeles that repeated itself
across the country: "The whole context of black people changed during
the war. All those people came out here from the South and went to work
in aircraft factories and the shipyards and made more money than they
ever thought existed in their lives. Some of them worked two eight-hour
shifts a day, making that dough."[76] Suddenly bars in the black neighborhoods of Los Angeles, New York, Chicago, Detroit, Pittsburgh, Indianapolis, and other urban centers began hiring bands to attract customers.
The government imposed a wartime tax on dancing, so many dance halls
converted into "listening rooms."

Minton's and Monroe's, the famed incubators of bop, were part of this
new wave of black clubs but still attracted a measure of white musicians
and customers. As George Avakian recalled, "Minton's was a mixed
crowd—more black but there was no segregation on the part of anybody.
No feeling of anything being strange. Harlem was very cool."[77]

The great era of black jazz clubs lasted perhaps less than a generation.
Even at its height, the appeal of rhythm and blues posed strong competition for jazz within the black community. In the early fifties, John Coltrane
worked in Philadelphia with a succession of R&B acts, including Daisy
Mae and the Hep Cats and vocalist Bullmoose Jackson's band. Coltrane
not only sang back-up vocals but soloed while ambling across the club's
bar—a practice known as "walking the bar." After the development of the
semi-portable Hammond organ in the early forties, the organ-tenor trio, a
musical hybrid of jazz and R&B, became extremely popular in black clubs
throughout the country.

Ornette Coleman explained the manner in which jazz was accepted in
his hometown of Fort Worth, Texas, in the early fifties: "There was an
audience for bebop to this extent: When you were playing around town,
a band that played for black people, you were going to hear a mixture of
bebop and rhythm and blues. A guy could double-time a chorus when we
were playing 'Stardust.' But there was no club where you could go hear
a band just play *jazz*."[78]

Following the war, black neighborhoods suffered another economic
slump as the defense industry scaled back sharply. New housing laws
permitted middle-class blacks to relocate in more upscale neighborhoods,
and the live music scene in the black community gradually withered
away. Whatever remained by the mid-sixties was threatened by an influx

of hard drugs and virtually finished off by the riots. Anyone looking for remnants of the once vital music scene in Harlem, Chicago, Los Angeles, or Kansas City is likely to come across vacant lots where legendary music venues once stood.

Bebop found its first commercial success on 52nd Street. In 1945 Dizzy Gillespie led a mixed group at the Three Deuces (named after its Chicago predecessor) with Charlie Parker, Al Haig on piano, Curley Russell on bass, and Stan Levey on drums. (Gillespie was already a presence on the Street, having participated in clarinetist Joe Marsala's interracial jam sessions at the Hickory House, and sat in with Coleman Hawkins and Benny Carter at the Deuces.) Dizzy's quintet generated such excitement that within a week their pay nearly doubled, record deals were offered, and radio host "Symphony" Sid Torin and promoter Monte Kay made plans to present the group at two Town Hall concerts, both of which were near sell-outs. Shortly thereafter Leonard Feather managed to get Gillespie signed with RCA Victor, and also produced concerts featuring Parker and Gillespie at Carnegie Hall.

Despite all this success, Gillespie wrote: "Jazz never attracted a real big audience, like rock 'n' roll or the singers that came along. We never carried big crowds because jazz is strictly an art form, and so there was always a division between jazz and what other people were doing who were not really participating in a creative art form."[79] He also noted, "Regarding friendships across racial lines, because white males would sometimes lend their personal support to our music, the bebop era, socially speaking, was a major concrete effort of progressive thinking black and white males and females to tear down and abolish the ignorance and racial barriers that were stifling the growth of any true culture in modern America."[80] In 1949, one African-American writer described Gillespie's audience as highly integrated, comprised of African-American and white youths plus whites from the "Persian-lamb-mink-coat gang." He also reported that members of the "respectable black bourgeoisie were conspicuously absent."[81]

By the late forties, jazz in New York was moving west to clubs in the Broadway area, such as the Royal Roost, Bop City, the Metropole, and most famously, Birdland. All of these places were decidedly interracial both on and off the bandstand. Audiences continued to be predominantly white, however, and even more so at the new upscale jazz "supper clubs," such as Basin Street, The Embers, and the Roundtable in New York; Basin Street West in San Francisco; and the London House in Chicago.

Jazz had established a foothold in New York's artsy Greenwich Village since at least the early thirties. Black musicians played for largely white audiences at the Hot Feet Club and the Black Cat, where John Hammond discovered guitarist Freddie Green for the Count Basie band. In the forties, fifties, and sixties, the Village became a home for both traditional and cutting-edge jazz. Tourists and local residents, again almost exclusively white, filled such moderately priced rooms as Nick's and Eddie Condon's to hear classic jazz. The Village Vanguard, Café Bohemia, and the Half Note—and in the East Village, the Five Spot and Slugs'—presented such famous (or soon-to-be famous) names as Thelonious Monk, John Coltrane, Lennie Tristano, Ornette Coleman, and Cannonball Adderley in front of more mixed crowds.

The postwar era saw the rise of the jazz musician as freelancer, the former sideman as star. Among the first of this breed was Coleman Hawkins, who struck out on his own after returning from Europe in 1939. That same year Charlie Parker came to New York as a member of Jay McShann's band. Following stints with the big bands of Earl Hines and Billy Eckstine, Parker began his career as a freelance jazz musician. Musicians like Parker were "independent" in the sense that their reputation was based solely on the music they themselves created, while their livelihood still depended on a network of bookers, managers, club owners, record producers, and even the New York City police department, which could prevent them from working by rescinding their all-important cabaret card. And success meant appealing to a largely mixed, but again, predominantly white audience.

The new jazz soloists also realized that drawing power, and hence asking price, was largely determined by hit records, much the same as with the big band leaders of the previous generation. It wasn't until George Shearing recorded "September in the Rain," Art Blakey "Moanin'," Horace Silver "Doodlin'," Dave Brubeck "Take Five," Stan Getz "The Girl From Ipanema," John Coltrane "My Favorite Things," Lee Morgan "The Sidewinder," and Cannonball Adderley "Mercy, Mercy, Mercy," that their careers really took off. Despite the pull of commercialism, the importance of establishing one's own sound—while reaching as broad an audience as possible—remained paramount.

Miles Davis and Thelonious Monk benefited hugely from the publicity machine of Columbia Records, which landed Monk on the cover of *Time* magazine in 1963. (Louis Armstrong had been the first in 1949, then Dave Brubeck in 1954 and Duke Ellington in 1956, the latter two also as a direct result of their associations with Columbia.) Producer George Avakian, who oversaw the rise of Davis and the resurgence of Ellington at Columbia, pioneered the idea of the "concept album" in jazz, striking gold with *Louis Armstrong Plays W. C. Handy* (1954), *Ellington at Newport* (1956), and the first Miles Davis-Gil Evans LP collaboration, *Miles Ahead* (1957). When Avakian left Columbia for RCA, he quickly signed Sonny Rollins and produced one of his bestselling albums, *The Bridge*. Jazz was becoming more a part of mainstream America's cultural life and its audience was expanding accordingly. Record sleeves of the time reveal how the major labels marketed jazz alongside their prestigious classical and bestselling pop releases.

For working jazz musicians without popular-selling records it was often touch and go, feast or famine, with the usual piecemeal rounds of work. Many former swing musicians, both black and white, found themselves playing Dixieland to make a living. Trumpeter Buck Clayton recalled the humdrum commercial work he was sometimes obliged to accept: "I liked working with Joe [Kane] because he was one society bandleader that dug jazz and many times he'd also use Roy Eldridge and Zoot Sims to help him swing the bar mitzvahs."[82] To subsist in the music business within a strictly African-American milieu, a black musician would almost have to forsake jazz for rhythm and blues, or at least one of its "jazzier" derivatives.

Many jazz musicians avoided such indignities by emigrating to Europe. Trumpeter Art Farmer recounted his reasons for expatriating in 1968: "In the sixties during all the social strife going on the United States I was working in a little circuit, which was a rut; going from this little club to that little club. Just around the East Coast—occasionally out to Chicago. When I was in New York I was getting some studio work too, but I felt it was really a rut playing a little place on the Lower East Side and a little place in Philadelphia, ghetto places; places in parts of town where people were afraid to go at night. And I started spending more time in Europe."[83] Farmer would make Vienna his home base until his death in 1999. Increasingly Europe and Japan became essential markets for American jazz musicians. "No Europe, no jazz," impresario George Wein famously declared.

Both musicians and aficionados got a big boost in the fifties with the advent of the jazz festival, largely Wein's creation. Starting in 1950, Wein operated a club called Storyville in Boston's posh Copley Square Hotel. In 1955 he chose the exclusive, lily-white domain of Newport, Rhode Island, as the site for the country's first major jazz festival. The festival always roused a certain degree of tension within the community, but in later years Newport did elect an African-American mayor, Paul Gaines, no doubt partially thanks to Wein's efforts to foster interracial harmony.

Despite LeRoi Jones's unsuccessful attempts to relocate "free jazz" to Harlem, the music found its real home in the artists' communities stretching from Soho to the East Village in lower Manhattan. Through the 1970s, experimental jazz flourished in the informal environments of loft apartments owned by the musicians themselves. Places such as Sam Rivers's Studio RivBea, Ornette Coleman's Artists House, and drummer Rashied Ali's Ali's Alley attracted primarily college-age audiences of every racial hue. Overseas performances were also crucial to the survival of the avant-garde school.

In the eighties, climbing real estate prices in major cities, particularly New York, forced jazz clubs to raise prices precipitously. Attending clubs became a luxury, a splurge on a special night out, or a lark for tourists out on the town, much like a Broadway show. Cover charges became financially out of reach for most musicians. Where clubs had once been hotbeds of experimentation, or at least unbridled extemporization, many now resorted to tried-and-true formulas and well-established "names."

One welcome exception was Smalls, located a few blocks from the Village Vanguard. For years it charged a $10 admission price, and didn't serve alcohol. This attracted a very young audience, something sorely needed in the jazz world today. (Today the club serves liquor, but the cover and minimum is a modest $20.) Another unique location was the Knitting Factory, which provided a space for creative bands trying out experimental material for a youthful and mixed audience. Musicians worked for a share of gate receipts. For the last several years, however, the Knitting Factory has focused almost exclusively on underground rock. The club Tonic, originally associated with composer and saxophonist John Zorn, took up some of the slack by giving a platform to adventurous improvising musicians, but its doors closed in 2007. Since then Zorn has opened a new club, the Stone, dedicated to the experimental and avant-garde.

In 2002, Ben Ratliff of the *New York Times* noted, "In New York, the most fertile and adventurous small-club scenes for jazz—Smalls, the Cornelia Street Café, the Internet Café—are almost totally white," both in terms of performers and audience.[84] In an article for *The New York Post* entitled "Black Culture Blends to a Newer Hue," African-American columnist Michael Meyers told of how even the renascent jazz clubs in Harlem were attracting mostly white audiences. "Today, 90 percent of the Lenox Lounge's customers are white . . . In fact, it's been an open secret that whites have been maintaining and nurturing black culture for decades."[85]

Record companies in the 1980s and 1990s were quick to spot this dependence on white audiences. Richard Cook noted that when Wynton Marsalis was initially signed in 1981, "the black audience showed little sign of any new interest," but "a middle-class white audience had begun to investigate jazz once again."[86] Twenty years later, Matt Pierson, head of the jazz department at Warner Brothers, gloomily complained, "The audience for straight ahead jazz is made up of aging white males. In ten years, after they've all had heart attacks, it'll be left with no audience."[87]

African-American musicians have also commented on the racial makeup of the core audience that supports them. "For so long, jazz has been outside of the community that it came from, and now it's almost lost," said trumpeter Nicholas Payton. "Jazz, sad to say, probably has no social significance to most black people's lives . . . As far as the race thing—well, I know a lot of black people will say, 'Well, this is expensive.

I'm not paying $17 plus a $10 drink minimum to see, you know, Terence [Blanchard] at the Vanguard.' OK, that's expensive, but if Snoop Dogg is at Madison Square Garden, they'll pay fifty-five bucks to see him. The whole concept of just listening to music is gone. It's got to be a show. And jazz has a stigma that it's just for older people to come to a club and sit in a seat and just listen."[88]

Fellow trumpeter Terence Blanchard stated, "One of the most frustrating things for me is to play a gig and the majority of people there are not black. It's disappointing but at the same time I understand it. A lot of these kids grew up with no respect for themselves *and* others. The things that they deal with every day do not have anything to do with jazz." Bassist Christian McBride vowed that, "As long as I'm a musician, my all-time goal is to try to draw more black people to the music, especially young black people."[89]

Reprising Dizzy Gillespie's comment about the small number of truly knowledgeable jazz fans, Branford Marsalis said, "When jazz is played at its best level, very few people know what's going on. You get blank looks—from black people, from white people—but you'll have five people in the back going, *'Yeah!'* And they can be any color because they can *hear* it. So it ain't got nothing to do with being mad when there are no black people there. I'm just happy when I see five people who know what you're doing. You know, *if* I can find five I'm lucky."[90]

In 1992, jazz scholar Scott DeVeaux conducted a survey of the jazz audience for the National Endowment for the Arts. He concluded that the audience for jazz had grown significantly since previous surveys of 1982 and 1985. DeVeaux came up with a profile of an essentially "affluent, well educated, youthful, and ethnically diverse" fan base. One of his more controversial findings was that the sample of respondents who said they consistently attended live jazz performances was "strikingly black in comparison with the general population." This did not mean that blacks outnumbered whites in the jazz audience, only that blacks were disproportionately represented: "Although blacks make up 11 percent of the adult population, between 16 and 20 percent of the audience for various forms of participation in jazz is black." Furthermore, "More than half (54 percent) of the adult African American population reports liking jazz, compared with only a third (32 percent) of whites. Roughly 16 percent of African Americans like jazz 'best of all'—only religious music captured a larger proportion—compared with 4 percent of whites."[91]

What are we to make of these findings, which are so at odds with the other empirical evidence? For one thing we have to assume that "jazz" for many respondents (both black and white) was a blanket term that included various forms of instrumental pop. What the survey does clearly indicate, I think, is the importance of jazz in the black psyche as a source of racial pride. How much this translates into a real involvement with the music is open to debate.

In any event, jazz has attracted a diverse audience from nearly its very beginning. A significant subset of the white population in the U.S., and overseas, has always appreciated and supported the music, whether as fans, entrepreneurs, or scholars. One of the attractions of jazz is its ability to cross all boundaries of race, gender, and class. Sometimes this attraction lies in its perceived exoticism: northern audiences have been captivated by its southern appeal, whites by its African-American allure, foreigners by its American-style freedom. But for the most ardent and informed fans, I think the appeal of jazz is much more personal. For these aficionados, jazz is the intimate and direct expression of one soul to another. And for them there simply are no racial boundaries.

NOTES

1. Taped interview with Milt Hinton, 1990.
2. Taped interview with Doc Cheatham, 1990.
3. Taped interview with Dave Douglas, 1995.
4. Southern, *The Music of Black Americans*, 43.
5. Kmen, *Music in New Orleans*, 231.
6. Foster and Stoddard, *Pops Foster*, 61.
7. Charters and Kunstadt, *Jazz*, 32.
8. James Weldon Johnson, *Black Manhattan*, 123.
9. Badger, *A Life in Ragtime*, 69.
10. Badger, 120.
11. Tucker, *Ellington*, 48.
12. Marquis, *In Search of Buddy Bolden*, 56.
13. Marquis, 73.
14. Foster and Stoddard, 64.
15. Hogan Jazz Archive. Johnny Lala interview conducted September 24, 1958.
16. Brothers, ed., *Louis Armstrong, in His Own Words*, 24.
17. Dodds and Gara, *The Baby Dodds Story*, 13–14.
18. Hogan Jazz Archive. Tony Sbarbaro and Emile Christian interview conducted February 11, 1959.
19. Armstrong, *Satchmo*, 152.
20. Lomax, *Mister Jelly Roll*, 42.
21. Lomax, 52.
22. Armstrong, 52.
23. Not to be confused with the Dreamland Café in Chicago, a black-and-tan. Charles "Doc" Cook (sometimes spelled "Cooke") got his nickname by earning a doctorate from the Chicago Musical College.
24. Dodds and Gara, 10.

25. Charters, *Jazz New Orleans*, 69.

26. This photograph is reproduced in Ward and Burns, *Jazz*, 36–37.

27. Foster and Stoddard, 113.

28. Stoddard, *Jazz on the Barbary Coast*, 52.

29. Sante, *Low Life*, 95.

30. James Weldon Johnson, *Black Manhattan*, 174.

31. Kenney, *Chicago Jazz*, 7.

32. Barker, *A Life in Jazz*, 134.

33. Kenney, 21.

34. Wright, *"King" Oliver*, 59. The article appeared in the April 21, 1926, issue of *Variety*.

35. Kenney, 21–23.

36. Lewis, *When Harlem Was in Vogue*, 211.

37. Hogan Jazz Archive. Johnny Lala interview conducted September 24, 1958.

38. Kenney, 104.

39. Interview with James Maher, 2002. Maher gave much the same information in a 1996 interview for the Ken Burns *Jazz* series: "They [standard jazz accounts] never told you that once you got inside [the Lincoln Gardens] there were 150 white couples dancing every night."

40. Shapiro & Hentoff, *Hear Me Talkin' To Ya*, 98.

41. Brothers, ed., 67.

42. Calloway and Rollins, *Of Minnie the Moocher & Me*, 90.

43. Kenney, 109.

44. Miller, ed., *Esquire's 1946 Jazz Book*, 14, 31.

45. Hammond and Townsend, *John Hammond On Record*, 117.

46. Anderson, *This Was Harlem*, 128.

47. Lomax, 208.

48. See liner notes by George Hoefer for the Columbia box set *Jazz Odyssey Volume III* (C3L 33, 1964).

49. James Weldon Johnson, *Black Manhattan*, 161.

50. Kenney, 122.

51. Anderson, 172.

52. Kenney, 33.

53. Lynn Abbott, "For Ofays Only: An Annotated Calendar of Midnight Frolics at the Lyric Theater," *The Jazz Archivist: A Newsletter of the William Ransom Hogan Jazz Archive* XVII (2003): 1–29.

54. Schiffman, *Uptown*, 49–50.

55. Calloway and Rollins, 71.

56. Stowe, *Swing Changes*, 42–43.

57. Driggs and Haddix (2005), 1.

58. Paul Johnson (1997), 805.

59. Pearson (1994), 95.

60. Driggs and Haddix, *Kansas City Jazz*, 136.

61. Pearson, *Goin' to Kansas City*, 106.

62. Taped interview with Art Farmer, 1993.

63. Driggs and Haddix, 132.

64. Shaw, *52nd St.*, 60.

65. DeVeaux, *The Birth of Bebop*, 286.

66. Shaw, 173.

67. Shaw, 247.

68. Kirk and Lee, *Twenty Years On Wheels*, 84–87.

69. Berger, Berger, and Patrick, *Benny Carter*, 239.

70. McCarthy, *The Dance Band Era*, 66.

71. McCarthy, 64. See also Walter C. Allen, *Hendersonia*, 277. According to Allen, Lombardo's Savoy attendance record held until 1939 when it was beaten by Glenn Miller!

72. DeVeaux, 147.

73. DeVeaux, 148.

74. Firestone, *Swing, Swing, Swing*, 130.

75. Stowe, 120.

76. Bryant et al., eds., *Central Avenue Sounds*, 47.

77. Taped interview with George Avakian, 2003.

78. Litweiler, *Ornette Coleman*, 44.

79. Gillespie and Fraser, *To Be or Not To Bop*, 230.

80. Gillespie and Fraser, 282.

81. Eric Porter, *What Is This Thing Called Jazz?*, 90.

82. Clayton and Elliot, *Buck Clayton's Jazz World*, 183.

83. Taped interview with Art Farmer, 1993.

84. Yuval Taylor, ed., *The Future of Jazz*, 29.

85. Michael Meyers, "Black Culture Blends to a Newer Hue," *New York Post*, August 21, 2001.

86. Cook, *Blue Note Records*, 213.

87. Richard B. Woodward, "Kind of Blue: Jazz Competes with Its Past, Settles for the Hard Sell," *Village Voice*, January 16, 2001. Reprinted in *Rhythm and Business*, ed. Norman Kelley, 189.

88. Magro, *Contemporary Cat*, 144.

89. Magro, 145.

90. Magro, 146.

91. Portions of the DeVeaux study are reprinted in Walser, ed., *Keeping Time*, 389–95. The original study appeared as "Jazz in America: Who's Listening?" National Endowment for the Arts Research Division Report no. 31 (Carson, CA: Seven Locks Press, 1995).

8

∽

It's Strictly Business

"There are always two sides to every story, but an ignorant person just won't cope with either side."

—Louis Armstrong

There's no question that many blacks have been mistreated by the music business. But have they as a group been singled out for exploitation? Or has the jazz business relentlessly pursued its own bottom line at the expense of anyone who can be taken advantage of, regardless of color?

This is an enormous subject that really requires a book of its own. All I can do here is discuss some pertinent aspects of this question, especially those usually absent from standard jazz texts. I will try to delineate the real winners and losers in the jazz business and discern the reasons behind such disparities. Many of these issues are not as simple as black and white, and we are about to enter a lot of gray territory.

RECORDING

The recording business has been vital to the dissemination of jazz. The two grew up together, and it's doubtful that an art form so dependent on improvisation could have flourished without recording. But there has always been an unseemly side to this relationship. Record companies are often seen as exploitative of talent, especially African-American talent. There's much truth to this assertion. But like so many businesses, the recording industry has been an equal opportunity exploiter. And on occasion, it's been an honest broker in the distribution of artistic goods.

The following statements from two leading industry representatives serve to illustrate the dishonest side of the record business, and its neutrality to race. The first testimony comes from Mayo (Ink) Williams, an African-American executive for Paramount Records, and later Decca. The second is from Walter Yetnikoff, president of CBS Records from 1975 to 1990. These two men describe situations occurring over a half-century apart, but little seems to have changed in the cavalier way artists were treated.

When Mayo Williams joined Paramount Records (owned by the Wisconsin Chair Company, and no relation to the movie company), he became the first African-American employee of a white-owned recording company. In the early 1920s Williams convinced Paramount executives to let him create and supervise a catalog aimed at the burgeoning "race" market. "I've got a good bit of Shylock in me," he admitted, noting that an industry axiom of the time was "Screw the artist before he screws you." Paramount was unusual for its time in providing artist royalties, at least on paper. Contracts stipulated that artists were entitled to a one-cent payment for each "net" record sale. "That one cent 'net' covered a multitude of sins," said Williams. In what was to become standard industry practice, the "net" sale was calculated after deducting various expenses, most of them figments of creative bookkeeping. According to Williams, nine out of ten Paramount artists received no royalty at all, regardless of record sales.

"I was better than 50 percent honest, and in this business that's pretty good," Williams said. "If anybody was pitchin' a curve, I was pitching it in padding my expense accounts." Paramount's initial outlay to artists ranged from $25 to $50 per side. Featured accompanists were paid $10 per tune, other sidemen received as little as $5, and some got nothing at all. Paramount earned $100,000 in its most profitable year, but sloppy bookkeeping did the company in. After failing to file an annual report with the government in 1926, Paramount had to forfeit its corporate status and was forced out of business.[1]

Fast-forward some sixty years, to when Walter Yetnikoff was asked what overall philosophy drives recording companies:

> Pay the artists as little as you can. Tie up the artist for as long as you can. Recoup as often as you can. I am sure, in my day, that royalties were never paid on 100 percent sales. You paid on 85 percent and called the other 15 percent breakage—even though the breakage applied to shellac records from the forties and fifties. What's more, you pay artists half royalties on their overseas sales. You say that's due to the cost of setting up your subsidiaries. Even when those costs have diminished, though, you keep paying the lower

rate. On foreign sales, the company benefits from a tax credit on the artists' royalties. The royalties have nothing to do with the company, but the company pays less taxes. Meanwhile the artist doesn't even know it's happening. . . . You charge the artist the cost of packaging. That could be 10 percent—or one dollar on the wholesale ten-dollar price of a CD—when actual packaging costs might be a quarter. It goes on and on. Or at least it did in the music world of the seventies and eighties.[2]

Yetnikoff was asked if he thought such practices were corrupt. "Morally maybe. But legally it was written out in documents no one bothered to read. There are ways to pump up those costs on paper so that royalties are delayed or even permanently denied. . . . Did I condone these practices? Yes, like everyone else in the industry." Yetnikoff claimed that when CBS Records let him go, the company was making "$450 million a year in pre-tax bottom-line net profits." He went directly from his exalted position at CBS into rehab to recover from years of drug abuse. As he wrote in his autobiography, his position as CBS president "went to my head, went to my dick, and over a period of years turned me into a madman. The more powerful I became, the greater the rewards, the deeper my lunacy."[3]

Teddy Reig, a jazz producer for various labels through the fifties and sixties, wrote: "Jazz has always been mistreated by the record companies. Every few years there's a resurgence of jazz. All the companies jump into action and scrape up all the garbage and repackage it. The next thing you know, there's an overflow in the stores and they start complaining that jazz doesn't sell. And it dies again. Then somebody comes along and creates a little stir, and the whole thing starts all over."[4]

As trumpeter Art Farmer stated, "It's hard for me to be respectful of business people. The record companies don't give you the right figures, they don't push the records, and then some of them tell you what to play and if it doesn't sell they blame you."[5] The situation is rather like a card game in which the musician holds one card and the recording company holds the other fifty-one.

It's often assumed that recording companies ignored black artists until the advent of "race" catalogs in the early twenties, but this wasn't the case. Historian Tim Brooks writes, "Though often overlooked today, a remarkable array of African-Americans had recorded commercially during the first thirty years of the industry, going as far back as 1890."[6] These artists include singer George W. Johnson, perhaps the first black ever to record; comedian Bert Williams; Booker T. Washington delivering his famous 1908 Atlanta Exposition speech; boxer Jack Johnson describing his 1910 championship win over white opponent James Jeffries; and various spiritual vocal groups such as the Fisk Jubilee Singers. In the teens, records were made by several black bands, including those of Eubie Blake, Wilbur Sweatman, Ford Dabney, and James Reese Europe.

By the early twenties the recording industry had come to recognize that African-Americans were a growing consumer base, and that black artists also had an appeal across racial lines. "It is interesting to note," wrote a columnist for the trade publication *Talking Machine World* in 1924, "that although Bessie Smith sings selections written especially for the colored trade and generally written by colored composers, her Columbia records enjoy a considerable demand among white people. This has been especially true among white entertainers, who seem to recognize and appreciate her unique artistry."[7] As *Variety* reported, "Not only do the disks enjoy wide sales among the colored race, but have caught on with the Caucasians. As a result, practically every record making firm, from Victor down, has augmented its catalogs with special 'blues' recordings by colored artists."[8] However, it was also widely believed that the niche market of "race records" extended only as far as "Negro music": gospel, blues, and jazz. Mayo Williams related that if an artist submitted a pop-style ballad for consideration, "I would very quickly say: 'Well, we can't use it. Write me a blues.'"[9]

The record companies bought into the same segregation of styles already evident throughout the live music scene. This probably explains why white musicians, such as Bix Beiderbecke and Frank Trumbauer, were the first to record jazz ballads. But Beiderbecke's career suffered from the inverse of these black stereotypes. He left a scant seventeen jazz titles under his own name, as opposed to seventy-seven by Louis Armstrong from 1926 through 1929 alone. The white Chicagoans recorded even less. And African-American artists who didn't adhere to accepted "Negro styles" weren't recorded at all (Ethel Waters, who branched out into other material, was one of the very few exceptions). These policies may explain why the great stage actress and singer Florence Mills never recorded.

How did pay compare for black and white artists? A unique window into early business practices of the record industry is provided by a cache of Victor recording contracts from the 1920s and 1930s, collected by bandleader and jazz historian Vince Giordano. These contracts indicate that in many cases African-American performers earned roughly as much as their white colleagues. And when white musicians were paid more, this was often just a reflection of higher anticipated sales, since work assigned to whites was generally aimed at a broader and more strictly commercial market.

In 1923 the duo of Noble Sissle and Eubie Blake made $200 per approved master, from which copies would then be pressed. Two years later, white bandleader Jean Goldkette signed a contract guaranteeing $225 per selection, but to be divided among a fifteen-piece band. This same figure was granted to white drummer Ben Pollack in 1926 for records with thirteen pieces plus a vocal trio. Pay seems to have been a function of fame more than color: Sissle and Blake were already well known to white audiences from their hit Broadway show *Shuffle Along.*

Turning to the more jazz-oriented white groups, Red Nichols was paid $200 per side in 1927. Jack Pettis, former saxophonist of the New Orleans Rhythm Kings, earned the same figure in 1928. A 1929 contract for King Oliver offered virtually the same terms: $175 per selection, plus an additional $25 per arrangement. A contract for Earl Hines leading an eleven-piece band also paid $200, as did a 1930 contract for McKinney's Cotton Pickers. George Avakian remembers that Louis Armstrong's contracts for the famous Hot Fives and Hot Sevens with OKeh Records also paid $200 per title. Contracts such as these had no royalty clause, so the recording company owned its product free and clear after the initial payment. Nevertheless, Avakian was able to negotiate new agreements with Columbia (which acquired OKeh in 1926) enabling Armstrong and Duke Ellington to collect royalties from reissues of their earlier recordings. Of course both artists were signed to Columbia at the time, which might explain the label's willingness to share income from material it already technically owned.

Ellington also received $200 dollars per side in the late twenties, though he might have received more if he'd been willing to sign an exclusive contract with Victor. His agent, Irving Mills, wanted him free to record for a wide variety of labels. Still, the longer Ellington was with Victor the better his terms became. In 1940 he was receiving an advance of $500 against a royalty of three cents per title. By 1941 he was up to a five percent royalty. He had also earned enough clout to demand that no other artist be coupled with him on the flip side of his recordings. Nevertheless, he still had to answer to management in his choice of material. Frank B. Walker, vice president of RCA Victor, sent him a letter in 1940 stating, "On the matter of recording your own compositions, we are in agreement with this, but inasmuch as both you and I know the absolute necessity of recording a certain amount of popular hits in order to get records on the dealers' shelves, we must limit the use of your personal compositions to not more than 50 per cent of the number of selections to be recorded under your contract."[10]

Bands outside of New York were generally paid less, sometimes by as much as half. Jelly Roll Morton's classic Red Hot Peppers titles, done in Chicago, earned him only $100 per side (which, as pertains to all these figures, paid for the entire band). This same amount was given to Bennie Moten's band out of Kansas City.

Of course no bandleader, black or white, could touch the unprecedented success of Paul Whiteman, who pulled in $450 per selection for an eight-piece band as early as 1920. By 1928, when he employed a twenty-piece band, Whiteman received an annual guarantee of $75,000. But his sales merited the advance, often going as high as 100,000 copies of a single disc, and sometimes exceeding the $120,000 mark.

Small independent labels devoted more or less exclusively to jazz first appeared in 1937 and would leave behind a vital legacy. Most—like the very first, Milt Gabler's Commodore Records—were a labor of love and operated on a shoestring budget. Among the most famous indie jazz labels were Alfred Lion and Francis Wolff's Blue Note Records and Bob Weinstock's Prestige. Some hit the jackpot by tapping into the emerging R&B and soul market; Ahmet Ertegun's Atlantic Records, for example, signed Ray Charles and Aretha Franklin, in addition to John Coltrane and the Modern Jazz Quartet. But many more ended in bankruptcy, such as Orrin Keepnews and Bill Grauer's pioneering Riverside Records. All of these labels fostered the early careers of numerous jazz artists, most of them African-American. Most paid only union scale, and some even less. Some of the men running these labels were loved by their artists, and some were loathed. "We were all friends in the music business, except for Herman Lubinsky," recalled George Avakian.[11] Lubinsky, the founder of Savoy Records, earned his dismal reputation by paying musicians as little as possible and demanding as much as he could squeeze out of them. Many musicians turned to him when they needed money to support drug habits. Be that as it may, in its twenty-year history Savoy documented an interracial array of important artists, including Charlie Parker, Fats Navarro, Charles Mingus, Stan Getz, Miles Davis, Lennie Tristano, Archie Shepp, and Sun Ra.

By the mid-fifties, the appeal of jazz was reaching far and wide into American society. Armstrong, Brubeck, Ellington, and Miles Davis were all recording for Columbia, to be joined in 1962 by Thelonious Monk. In 1961 Sonny Rollins negotiated a contract with George Avakian at RCA Victor and secured an advance of $90,000. Impulse! Records, a subsidiary of ABC-Paramount, attracted Coltrane and Charles Mingus with generous contracts. Jazz musicians, and most notably African-American artists, began to receive as much attention from the publicity departments of these labels as stars in the pop and classical fields were accustomed to.

But just as these leading jazz figures were getting used to riding high, the bottom fell out of the market with the rock revolution of the mid-sixties. Big corporate labels turned away from jazz almost completely. By then many of the independents had gone out of business, having been outspent and outwitted by the majors. Many of the original owners of independent labels were also disillusioned by the turns jazz had taken, both musically and politically. The love seemed to have gone out of the business. In the opinion of Blue Note's famed recording engineer Rudy Van Gelder, avant-garde music plus the increasingly militant temperament of some musicians drove Alfred Lion to give up his label.[12] From 1964 to 1968 Bernard Stollman operated his label ESP-Disk to help document and promote New York's avant-garde musicians. During one session Stollman was physically assaulted and threatened with death by clarinetist Giuseppi Logan.[13]

The seventies were a relatively fallow period for jazz recording in America, and many musicians sought refuge with European labels. Others, such as Miles Davis, Herbie Hancock, and Chick Corea, maintained their major-label connections by courting the mainstream pop audience. Some musicians took matters into their own hands by forming their own labels, a tradition that had started decades before. From 1945 to 1947 Mezz Mezzrow operated the King Jazz label, which recorded himself, Sidney Bechet, and Hot Lips Page. In 1951 Dizzy Gillespie tried his hand with his own company, Dee Gee Records. The following year Charles Mingus, his then-wife Celia, and drummer Max Roach founded Debut Records, which is best known for releasing the 1953 Massey Hall concert featuring Charlie Parker, Gillespie, and Bud Powell along with Mingus and Roach. Other musician-owned labels included Jazz Records (Lennie Tristano), Mars (Woody Herman), and Saturn (Sun Ra).

In nearly all cases, musician-run labels failed to turn a profit. The main reason was that the majors still controlled the principle channels of distribution, so musicians ended up giving a hefty chunk of their album earnings to the very companies that neglected them in the first place. Sun Ra's records were sold by mail order out of his home address, but he had difficulty filling orders as he traveled to perform.

Suddenly in 1977 Columbia signaled a willingness to reenter the straight-ahead jazz market. Dexter Gordon's return to the U.S. after fifteen years abroad had been a media event, and Gordon's Columbia album "Homecoming" sold well enough for the label to consider expanding its jazz roster. Aware that most of the remaining jazz superstars were in declining age, Columbia began casting about for young and unknown musicians to promote. In 1980 they discovered Wynton Marsalis, and the rest, as they say, is history.

Marsalis ushered in a whole new era of major-label interest in jazz. Young and black was in. The so-called young lions, such as saxophonist Joshua Redman, trumpeter Roy Hargrove, and pianist Marcus Roberts, initially sold as many as 75,000 copies of their new releases. But expenses involved in establishing these artists were always high. "It costs between $15,000 and $60,000 to make a record, depending on how much you pay the sidemen," said Matt Pierson, head of the jazz department at Warner Brothers, in 2001. "But with touring, advertising, and promotion, you're talking about at least another $30,000 to $50,000 to market a record."[14]

In the late 1990s the industry went into a slump, and jazz was one of the first genres to feel the pinch. "Virtually any young critical favorite you can name—James Carter, Joe Lovano, Joshua Redman, Maria Schneider,

Danilo Perez, [Jacky] Terrasson, Greg Osby, Kenny Garrett, David San-chez, Dave Douglas, Geri Allen, Roy Hargrove, Brad Mehldau—is lucky to sell 15,000 records domestically in a CD's eighteen-month shelf life," wrote journalist Richard B. Woodward in 2001. "Usually they fail to do even that. Ditto for legends Sonny Rollins, Tommy Flanagan, Joe Hen-derson, or Oscar Peterson. And as well-publicized and richly rewarded as Wynton and Branford Marsalis have been, their recent sales figures are no better than anyone else's."[15]

By that time the majors were down to four: EMI, whose jazz imprint was Blue Note; Universal, which included the jazz label Verve; Sony-Bertelsmann, formed by the merger of CBS and RCA; and Warner Broth-ers, the only U.S.-owned company. The bestselling jazz artists on these labels were vocalists with crossover appeal, such as Diana Krall, Cassan-dra Wilson, John Pizzarelli, Harry Connick Jr., Dianne Reeves, and later Norah Jones (who is not really a jazz artist, but kept Blue Note Records in the black).

The Internet has revolutionized the way music is disseminated. Now a musician can create, mass-produce, distribute, market, and promote a re-cording without the aid of an established record company. Websites such as CD Baby, Amazon, and iTunes can distribute products for independent artists. Musicians who self-produce their recordings can sell them on jobs and pocket the full price. They own the recordings in perpetuity, and need not fear that their product will be deleted from a company's catalog. The playing field is now as level as it's ever been, but it's entirely up to the musicians' own resources—both financial and emotional—to make things happen. With fewer hands involved in the distribution of artistic creations, there is less room for exploitation of musicians, regardless of race.

THE STUDIOS

It is often remarked that white jazz musicians have made more money than their African-American counterparts. A following chapter on money will take up the truth of this question specifically within the jazz sphere. But I think what is often meant by this much-repeated claim is that a wider range of work has traditionally been open to white musicians. Has this been attributable only to racism, or does it simply reflect the fact that whites make up the majority of the population and want to hear music that suits their tastes? Certainly African-Americans have influenced those tastes enormously over the years, yet even today, for every white person who loves jazz, there are probably fifty who prefer country-and-western.

Work in radio, movie, or television orchestras was a lucrative source of income for musicians from the late 1920s until the early 1970s, when the studio staff system was dissolved. With very few exceptions these bands, whether in New York, Chicago, or Los Angeles, were all white. When most jazz musicians were struggling to get by on whatever work they could scrounge up, staff musicians were enjoying a steady paycheck plus the added benefit of keeping normal business hours like any other member of the professional class.

But there was always a downside to staff work. For one thing, it was commercial in the extreme. Historian Philip Eberly writes that a studio band "might be called upon to accompany a classical singer, to glide through a lilting Strauss waltz, or to perform a rousing Sousa march."[16] Daytime radio programming catered to stay-at-home housewives, and in the early thirties ushered in a new musical era of romantic ballads played by syrupy sweet dance bands.

Also, staff work didn't pay as spectacularly as one might suppose. For a few years, when network broadcasting was in its infancy, musicians did make a lot of money playing in radio bands on a freelance basis. But soon the broadcasting companies grew wise and initiated a staff system whereby musicians were hired as employees on a fixed salary. Studio salaries were decent, especially during the Depression years, but hardly extravagant, hovering around $100 a week. The Chicago local musicians' union, under the iron hand of James Petrillo, was able to negotiate the highest scale, from $120 to $150 per week in 1931, but more staff jobs were located in New York or Los Angeles. Staff musicians were contracted to work five days a week and had to be available eight hours a day, though they were only required to perform for four hours. They were forbidden from accepting outside work on days off, a regulation that was relaxed somewhat by the 1950s. By the late 1960s the networks had increasingly farmed out programming to independent production companies, which usually decided that live orchestras were an expendable luxury. When the last staff orchestra was disbanded in New York in 1971, its weekly salary had risen to only $250 a week per sideman. As the 1970s progressed, only a handful of live bands remained on television, such as those on the Johnny Carson, Dick Cavett, and Merv Giffin shows.

Another thing to remember about staff work is that most jazz musicians didn't respond well to its corporate regimen. As Benny Goodman wrote in 1939, "None of us had much use for what was known then, and probably always will be, as 'commercial' musicians. The saddest thing always was a recognized hot man who went into that sort of work because he made good dough and got steady work around the studios . . . I have seen more than a few fellows crack up for this one reason."[17] Willie "The Lion" Smith noticed, "Several of the musicians who used to visit me at Pod & Jerry's were working in the big radio studios. They couldn't wait to get loose from the job and run over to a speak for a taste."[18]

Many radio conductors, particularly in the early days of broadcasting, looked askance at jazz musicians, believing, perhaps correctly, that many harbored negative and unprofessional attitudes. Some feared that jazz musicians were likely to "turn Bolshevik." Trumpeter Chris Griffin recalled, "We did a lot of drinking. What else can you do in three hours [between broadcasts] if you don't play cards? So we'd stand with our foot up against Jim and Andy's bar."[19] Longtime studio guitarist Bucky Pizzarelli explained, "When you're on a radio program it had to be right, so I guess the guys that felt insecure started drinking. It's different when you're on the air. Making a record you can make a mistake and stop and do it over again; you can still try for it. But when you're doing a live performance that's it."[20] Drinking became a crutch for many musicians to calm nerves and relieve boredom. It's a small wonder that many jazz musicians abandoned successful studio careers at their first opportunity to pursue other work. Many popular bandleaders of the swing era—including Goodman, Artie Shaw, Glenn Miller, Bunny Berigan, and Tommy and Jimmy Dorsey—had left staff work to pursue a highly uncertain future.

Moreover, the requirements of jazz and studio playing are exactly opposite: a jazz player strives to establish a unique sound and identity, whereas a studio player needs to "fit in" with any musical setting. Both occupations demand the highest standards of musicianship, but in entirely different ways. The jazz player aims to be an artist, the studio player an artisan.

The difference between jazz and studio playing is well illustrated by an incident that George Avakian relates in his liner notes for *What Is Jazz?*, an educational record narrated by Leonard Bernstein: "Mr. Bernstein required the demonstration of a saxophone phrase played first with vibrato and then without. Coleman Hawkins, the man who literally introduced the saxophone into jazz, did the first part of this beautifully, but couldn't cut out his classic vibrato to save his soul! After a few attempts, Hawk was laughing so hard at himself that he had to give up, so on a subsequent studio date we asked Romeo Penque, a versatile musician with a feeling for jazz, to record these two examples."[21]

Many white jazz musicians were either ill-equipped for studio work or simply not interested. In the early thirties this number included Bud Freeman, Jimmy McPartland, Pee Wee Russell, and Dave Tough. In 1930 Bix Beiderbecke played for a time on the *Camel Pleasure Hour*, but on one broadcast, as he stood up to play his allotted eight-bar solo, he blacked out. Frank Cush, a trumpeter active in New York at the time, recalled, "It finished him in radio."[22] Pianist Dick Katz, himself never comfortable in the studio environment, noted that a later generation of white jazz players also had an uneasy relationship with this kind of work, even when it was available to them: "Some tried the studios but couldn't take the discipline. To be a studio musician, just to be able to read good wasn't enough. You had to be a smiling, affable character to go along with the program. A lot of guys couldn't do that. Stan Getz tried it and he couldn't take it. Tony Scott didn't last long at all because he was a wild, temperamental guy."[23] Chet Baker, Art Pepper, and Lee Konitz were also among those who eschewed the studio scene. Some, like the largely forgotten but very talented West Coast trumpeter Stu Williamson, barely bothered with studio work at all. Gil Evans could have made a fortune during a period when television and recording studios needed arrangements on a daily basis, but he preferred to lead a financially marginal existence, writing only what and when he wanted.

Becoming known as a studio musician could also tarnish a jazz musician's reputation. Even the highly regarded trumpeter Clark Terry experienced problems maintaining his credibility within the jazz world after achieving success in the studios. "There are a lot of cats who sort of put you down for playing studio type music. They refer to you as a square and as one who has gone over to the other side. They got all sort of things to call you, but for the most part the guys who complain to this extent are guys who either haven't prepared themselves to do a variety of work, or guys who just don't really care to do it because they think it's unhip."[24]

Terry also spoke of prejudice against African-Americans inside the studio world, noting that some in the scene "refer to us as 'them,' saying, 'They don't fit' or 'They can't play our type of music.'"[25] Lee Young, a percussionist and brother of Lester Young, was the first African-American musician to be regularly employed by the Hollywood studios. He worked for MGM and Paramount from 1938 to 1940, then for Columbia Pictures from 1944 to 1948. A handful of black musicians, such as Harry "Sweets" Edison, Plas Johnson, Bill Green, and Buddy Collette would eventually follow him. As late as 1971, Collette pored through a year's worth of union recording contracts and found that African-American musicians had played on just one percent of the work.[26]

Saxophonist Plas Johnson felt that he was able to land studio jobs because he had a niche talent white players of the time didn't possess:

I was there because of what I did—if there had been white players who could have played really good rhythm and blues solos at the time I probably wouldn't have been there. It was obvious that black players didn't have a future in the recording industry, or training to do it. It's different today. I don't think that young black players have it as hard as someone like Marshal Royal [the longtime lead altoist with Count Basie's orchestra].[27] What they did have was a lot of good blues guitar players who were white and respectable jazz players of the time, like Barney Kessel and Howard Roberts. These were great players but they were blues pickers also. So the opening was really more for saxophone players. And hey, I was the best. Eventually I got hired to play in sections.[28]

Plas Johnson is best known as the saxophone soloist on the "Pink Panther Theme," one of many high points in a thirty-year career in the studios.

A small number of African-American composers and arrangers made inroads in Hollywood. The little-known composer Calvin Jackson wrote for a dozen films between 1943 and 1947, and the equally obscure Phil Moore wrote soundtracks for dance sequences around the same time. Benny Carter began his film composing career in 1943 with *Stormy Weather*, featuring an all-star, all-black cast of Fats Waller, Cab Calloway, Lena Horne, and Bill "Bojangles" Robinson. Carter went on to write for a succession of films and TV shows, including the highly popular series *M Squad* and *Ironside*. Carter was also a mentor for a younger generation of jazz musicians doubling as Hollywood composers, including Quincy Jones, Oliver Nelson, J.J. Johnson, and Lalo Schifrin.

The new employment opportunities offered by radio, and the awarding of these jobs exclusively to white musicians, did not go unnoticed in the black press. Bandleader Walter Barnes, who replaced Dave Peyton as music columnist for the *Chicago Defender*, wrote in 1929: "Our folks buy, in proportion, more radios and allied equipment and Victrolas than any other group and even this seems to be overlooked when it comes to giving out contracts for broadcasting. It seems to be the belief among whites that the Race is still in the cotton fields and cannot sing or play anything else but cotton songs and blues. This is a great mistake. We are music lovers and enjoy all types and forms of music."[29]

In 1932 John Hammond attempted to gain steady employment for a mixed band on radio, and he might have succeeded if not for his confrontational tactics. He arranged for a New York station, WEVD, to sponsor an all-star band featuring Red Allen on trumpet, Benny Carter on reeds, Art Tatum on piano, and Artie Bernstein on bass. The broadcast emanated from a studio in the Claridge Hotel, and management insisted that the musicians use the freight elevator. Hammond interpreted this policy as racial discrimination, even though to this day New York hotels customarily require musicians to use service entrances. Hammond organized a picket line and the job was lost.[30] I wonder if the musicians shared in Hammond's zeal. Unlike Hammond, they weren't beneficiaries of independent incomes, and might have gladly used the freight entrance in exchange for steady employment, especially at the height of the Depression.

But Hammond rightly deserves credit for keeping alive the issue of admitting blacks into the studios. He wrote a series of articles on this subject for *New Masses* and later for the short-lived publication *Music and Rhythm*. In 1942 Hammond demanded a meeting with David Sarnoff, then head of NBC and a member of President Roosevelt's Fair Employment Practices Committee. Sarnoff arranged for the contractors of all three networks to meet with Hammond. Through these efforts a small number of African-American musicians were put on staff, among them drummer Cozy Cole, trumpeters Emmett Berry and Bill Dillard, trombonist Benny Morton, and bassist Israel Crosby.[31] More would follow throughout the forties and into the fifties and sixties, but never in substantial numbers. In 1968, only nine of the 180 musicians employed in New York's three network television orchestras were black.[32]

Trumpeter Joe Wilder was one of those nine, having been on the ABC staff since 1956. Wilder testified to a general belief that "black players could play jazz but not read" and "jazz players weren't dependable because of drugs."[33] To this day Wilder always appears neatly dressed in a jacket and tie, thus shielded from unwanted stereotypes.

But even those African-American musicians who made it into the studios expressed as much ambivalence toward the work as their white counterparts. Buddy Collette, who devoted the bulk of his career to working in recording and film studios, said, "I did studio work not because I thought it was the greatest, but because I was challenged by it. . . . I just didn't see any future in clubs as much as I did studio work, because I'd met a lot of guys who did studio work and they had homes and investments. Very few musicians working the clubs had that; they were worrying about the rent."[34]

Some African-American musicians were simply not interested in playing such commercial music. Tenor saxophonist Harold Ashby freelanced in Kansas City and Chicago before coming to New York in 1957: "When I came to New York it was a different thing altogether. I came in with a tenor and cats would be handing out their cards saying 'reeds.' And they played all the horns and played in any situation. I wanted to play jazz—go up on the stand and blow my horn."[35] Ashby went on to work with the Duke Ellington orchestra in 1960 and regularly from 1968 to 1975. Buck Clayton once explained, "I could have been on a studio job by now, but I wouldn't like sitting in one place, going to work, and doing the same thing. If you do the same thing for fifteen, twenty years, getting up at the same time every morning, catching the same old train, and coming home at the same time, it ages you."[36] Of course other musicians prospered in the hothouse studio environment, which had the rewards of working with other top-notch musicians and facing new musical challenges daily.

By 1971 the networks had eliminated staff orchestras but recording work in New York and television and movie work in Los Angeles was still relatively plentiful. That same year a sociologist named Robert R. Faulkner published a study of Hollywood studio musicians. Though most of these musicians made a very healthy income, Faulkner found that many were plagued by anxiety and doubt. "The greatest fear in this business is the fear of the unknown. You never know what they're going to throw at you to play," said one musician.[37] "You can't hide too long in this business," related another. "So you can lose it all in a day; I honestly believe it. You can come in a bar too soon, like you play a perfect recording and miss a note or a page-turn and the guy looks up and says, 'I won't use him anymore.'"[38]

Some expressed pride in their ability to negotiate a wide range of music. As one trumpeter put it, "You're pounding out high notes like we were last week for a couple of hours and all your blood is gone out of your lips and then they have you turn right around and play something soft and delicate, in the upper register, or play a little jazz, or a bugle call with finesse. Not many guys can make it come off."[39] But others were quite candid about the low opinion they held of their profession: "I compare my business to that of a prostitute. I'm a callman, you see. I go where I'm called and I get paid. There's no emotional involvement there. It's very convenient. I perform my duties to the best of my abilities and I don 't get involved."[40] One studio player offered up a standard lament of all commercial musicians: "It's a way of making a buck, one of the *only* ways in this society for the musician."[41]

Faulkner's study once again underscored the stark difference between studio playing and jazz playing, especially in terms of emotional commitment. Some wonderful and underrated white jazz players came to tragic ends despite thriving studio careers. Trumpeter Nick Travis, a solid lead player as well as an excellent jazz soloist, died at age thirty-eight in New York after suffering from ulcers and years of drug abuse. Though he appeared on hundreds of albums, he made just one under his own name. In Los Angeles the lyrical improviser Don Fagerquist drank himself to death at forty-six; like Travis, he left behind exactly one jazz album of his own.

Before leaving this subject it's important to clear up the distinction between staff work and studio work. Musicians hired on a regular salaried basis by the major TV and radio networks or movie studios were said to be "on staff." But recording studio work has always been conducted on a freelance basis. African-American musicians have always been part of the studio scene for jazz and its derivatives. Some musicians, especially in the fifties and sixties, found it more financially rewarding to work as freelance recording artists and turned down offers to join staff orchestras. Milt Hinton routinely made as much as $750 a week from recording dates, and by 1962 could have retired at age fifty-one with a lump sum of $49,000 from his union pension. When an NBC representative belatedly called to offer him a staff position, Hinton politely replied, "Well, thank you very much, but my schedule just wouldn't permit it."[42]

Freelance jazz orchestras that recorded throughout the integrationist era of the 1950s and early 1960s tended to be highly integrated themselves. Among these were bands assembled by Gil Evans and Oliver Nelson, to name just two examples. But as sentiment became more militant in the sixties, Nelson found himself criticized by other African-Americans. "I made about five or six records with Oliver Nelson," related the white drummer Ed Shaughnessy. "He told me personally that because he'd always use Phil Woods and myself and Bernie Glow he got a lot of static from guys who would give him phone calls and push pictures of slave ships under his door. To his credit he didn't change who he used, but it made him very unhappy. In fact when he told me this story he had tears in his eyes and he said, 'I'm just trying to find the guys who play my music the best. I have no other agenda whatsoever.'"[43]

In *Blues People*, LeRoi Jones accused white musicians of doing nothing to help their black colleagues enter the studio field, but this is utterly false. "The Negro musicians complained bitterly about the discrimination [in the studios]," wrote Jones, "but the white musicians never attempted to help them, and the contractors hired the men they wanted."[44] In reality, almost every black musician working for a broadcast or film studio initially had at least one white sponsor recommending him for the job: Joe Wilder had trumpeter Billy Butterfield; Buddy Collette had contractor Jerry Fielding; Plas Johnson and Harry "Sweets" Edison had Frank Sinatra, Nelson Riddle, and Henry Mancini; Grady Tate had Ed Shaughnessy; Specs Powell had contractor Lou Shoobe; Benny Carter had film composer Alfred Newman; and Quincy Jones had Mancini, director Sidney Lumet, and Irving Green, who also hired Jones to be the first African-American vice president of a major label, Mercury Records.

In short, staff work was considered undesirable by many creative musicians, and those who submitted to its regimen could be unfairly stigmatized as "commercial" players. Staff orchestras provided steady work with reasonable compensation, but resourceful and in-demand musicians, both black and white, could often make more money on a freelance basis. African-American musicians had the added problem of facing prejudice and discrimination as they strove to fit into the corporate environment of the major networks. Milt Hinton on the East Coast, and Buddy Collette on the West, gave free instruction on musicianship and comportment to up-and-coming black instrumentalists, in an effort to prepare them for whatever professional situations they might encounter. But in the end, too few were given a chance to prove their mettle.

AGENTS AND MANAGERS

It's easy to paint those on the business side of jazz as rapacious parasites who profit handsomely from the hard work and talents of others. Some did indeed meet this description, but there were many others who had the artists' best interests at heart and struggled diligently to further their careers. There's no question that a few very ingenious and industrious people were responsible for bringing the great African-American jazz figures before the general public, and allowing them to thrive at a time when representation by savvy white businessmen was absolutely necessary. Are we to damn these middlemen in light of contemporary standards of morality, or hail them for their groundbreaking work on behalf of their artists? Often it's a matter of viewing the cup as half-empty or half-full, but all too often these musicians' representatives are seen as morally empty vessels.

George Wein practically invented the jazz festival and for decades ran the most successful jazz booking agency in the world, Festival Productions. "As for the musicians," he stated, "I have always treated them as artists. But I discovered that, no matter how friendly I tried to be, I could not help but be aware of a sense of distrust. To them, I was the Man."[45]

In the early days of jazz, there was no clear business model for those who represented musicians and bands. Agents and managers quickly became vital liaisons for artists in dealing with employers, record companies, the press, and the public. Some were quite creative in inventing new methods for procuring work and public recognition. Many of these methods have since become standard practice.

Some of the earliest agents were music publishers. During the 1920s music publishers were intimately involved with record companies, which needed to keep up on the latest stream of hits. The Melrose brothers, Walter and Lester, were among the first publishers to initiate recordings and, to a lesser extent, arrange gigs for jazz bands.

Melrose Music specialized in jazz, publishing both sheet music and band orchestrations, later known as "stock" arrangements. The Melroses also saw to it that the music they published was recorded not only by the composer but also by as many different bands as possible. Jelly Roll Morton's "Wolverine Blues," published by Melrose in 1923, was recorded by Morton and also the Benson Orchestra of Chicago, Albert E. Short and his Tivoli Syncopators, Gene Rodemich and his Orchestra from St. Louis, and the New Orleans Rhythm Kings.

Thanks partly to the influence of Melrose Music, Chicago became known as the jazz capital of the country in the early to mid-twenties. The Melrose brothers had a hand in the seminal recordings of King Oliver, Jelly Roll Morton, and the New Orleans Rhythm Kings. They published an entire folio devoted to Morton's compositions, plus the very first edition of transcribed improvised solos: Louis Armstrong's *50 Hot Choruses*. Melrose also published King Oliver classics such as "Doctor Jazz" and "Snag It," as well as the work of Richard M. Jones and the blues and gospel composer Thomas A. Dorsey. The work of early white jazz composers was also an important part of the Melrose catalogue, including "Tin Roof

Blues," by the New Orleans Rhythm Kings; "Sobbin' Blues," by Chicago bandleader Art Kassel and drummer Vic Berton; and "Copenhagen" and "Jimtown Blues" by Indianapolis bandleader Charlie Davis. Many of these tunes were recorded by both black and white bands, and stock arrangements were widely available to any band that wanted them, serving to blur racial divisions in jazz.

Melrose Music brought Jelly Roll Morton and the New Orleans Rhythm Kings together for a landmark interracial recording in 1923. Joe Mares, brother of NORK trumpeter Paul Mares, explained how this date came about: "The New Orleans Rhythm Kings was a popular band but Jelly Roll was floating around. The Melroses advised him to see Mares about his tunes. Paul liked 'Mr. Jelly Lord' and 'London Blues.' Jelly came to a rehearsal and there he wrote the intro and verse to 'Milenberg Joys.'"[46]

Morton was also a paid employee of Melrose for a time, though his exact duties remain obscure. Clarinetist Barney Bigard said that whenever Morton needed money, "It was no problem. He and Walter Melrose were like brothers—Melrose the publisher. So, anytime he wanted money he'd go to Melrose and get a thousand dollars. In those days it was a lot of money, and he would tell Melrose, 'I'll write you a tune, we'll make up for it.'"[47] Others, like the white clarinetist Volly (Voltaire) DeFaut, who made some trio recordings with Morton in 1925, saw things differently: "[Walter] Melrose was quite a finagler. He was in and out of every place. He'd get a piece of this and a slice of that. I think Jelly lost a tremendous lot of money to Melrose. I don't think Jelly was much of a businessman. It was the general impression all around jazz circles in Chicago that he was really taken by Melrose, that he never got much for what he'd done."[48]

In Howard Reich and William Gaines's 2003 book *Jelly's Blues*, which covers the ups and downs (mostly downs) of Morton's career, the Melrose brothers are graphically portrayed as unscrupulous exploiters of black musicians. Other authors have expressed more charitable views. Chicago jazz historian John Steiner argues that Walter Melrose "played a major role as a liaison man, manager, agent, promoter, and all-round friend to most of these musicians. He got them jobs, tied in recording and publishing deals—he did a lot."[49] The exact nature of Morton's business dealings with Melrose will probably always be open to conjecture.

The same could be said for Duke Ellington's complex relationship with Irving Mills. Like Melrose, Mills started out with his brother, Jack, in the publishing business. There's no question that Irving Mills played a huge part in Duke Ellington's meteoric rise to international fame. As Ellington's longtime drummer Sonny Greer explained,

> It was imperative that we have a man like that, a front man, because I don't think we could have done it alone without his guidance. When anything

important pertaining to Ellington came up, he was there in person. He didn't send someone else out. When he made the second European trip with us, he was so sick he had to have a doctor in attendance twenty-four hours a day, but he made it every step of the way. He was a businessman, sure, but he always saw to it we had the best transportation. The band didn't know what a bus looked like in the early days. We had private Pullman cars, with "Duke Ellington" on the side, and a private baggage car, through every state of the union, and we were the only band in the country, white or colored, that had that.[50]

The partnership between Mills and Ellington lasted thirteen years, from 1926 to 1939. Mills discovered the Ellington band at the Kentucky Club in New York when he was out club-hopping with Sime Silverman, the founder of *Variety*. "I was immediately and profoundly impressed by this young man who, it soon became obvious, was not just another pianist or bandleader, but a truly creative artist, with the latent potential for an unlimited career," said Mills.[51] Ellington himself wrote, "He had always preserved the dignity of my name. Duke Ellington had an unblemished image, and that is the most anybody can do for anybody."[52]

Mills encouraged Ellington to create original music, which Mills then published. He landed recording dates for the Ellington band with a dozen low-budget labels. Then, within a year of becoming Duke's manager, he engineered a contract with Victor records and secured a long-term engagement at the Cotton Club. As was the custom with most publishers (including Melrose), Mills paid for all the band's arrangements himself. He also produced the shows at the Cotton Club and enabled Ellington to enlarge his band from ten to eleven, twelve, and eventually fifteen pieces. "I paid the salaries of the additional musicians out of my share of the project," said Mills.[53]

In 1930 and 1931 Mills booked the band into important midtown theaters, including the prestigious Paramount, where Ellington shared a two-week double bill with matinee idol Maurice Chevalier. Mills also took the band on lucrative cross-country tours, leading one entertainment columnist to declare Ellington "one of the outstanding stage attractions in the country."[54] The Ellington orchestra was the first African-American band to play in scores of locations, including the luxurious Congress Hotel in Chicago. "He [Mills] broke down so many darned barriers for Negro musicians you couldn't count them," wrote Cab Calloway, another longtime client of Mills.[55] Mills's financial acumen can be seen in the payout figures for bands booked for a week's work at the Apollo Theater in Harlem: in 1932 the Ellington band received $4,700, whereas two years later Earl Hines got $1,900, Jimmie Lunceford $1,750, and Fletcher Henderson only $900; still later, Charlie Barnet could only command $1,000.[56]

Bill LeBaron, head of RKO pictures, came to the Cotton Club on several occasions at Mills's behest, leading to the Ellington band's movie debut *Black and Tan*, a short subject from 1929. The next year the band appeared in a full-length motion picture, *Check and Double Check*. While working on this picture the band received a salary of $5,000 a week plus expenses. In 1933 and 1934 Mills negotiated contracts with Paramount for two feature films plus three shorts. One was a remarkable nine-minute film, *Symphony in Black: A Rhapsody of Negro Life*, devoted entirely to Ellington and featuring the first screen appearance of Billie Holiday. In 1935 the Ellington band received $18,249 from Paramount alone.[57] Mills also supervised Ellington's triumphant tours of England and the continent, which cemented the bandleader's stature as a figure of international acclaim and importance.

With the exponential growth of Ellington's reputation, Mills came under fire for his business practices, mainly from the black press but also from John Hammond. Adam Clayton Powell Jr., before he became a congressman, stated, "Duke Ellington is a musical sharecropper." Powell claimed that Ellington's salary was "around $500 a week," but "at the end of the year, when Massa Mills cotton has been laid by, Duke is told he owes them hundreds of thousands of dollars."[58]

Many took exception to Mills listing himself as the lyricist on many Ellington compositions (some sixty in all) to increase his share of royalties. Mills was already entitled to 50 percent as publisher, but a cocomposer credit upped his take to 75 percent. Porter Roberts, writing in the Pittsburgh *Courier*, complained that most of Ellington's earnings were going to Mills, adding: "No Negro writer has written the lyrics for any of Duke Ellington's melodies since he has been under the Mills banner. What's the matter, Duke? House rules?"[59]

As already discussed, Hammond flip-flopped on his views toward Mills, at one time calling him a "vulture," and another time "a man who saved black talent in the 1930's." Ellington himself was always circumspect about his personal and business dealings, but writer Barry Ulanov had access to all the parties involved when he wrote his 1946 Ellington biography. Ulanov claimed that a contract, presumably dating from around 1927 or 1928, was drawn up "giving each [Ellington and Mills] 45 per cent of a new corporation, Ellington, Inc., and giving lawyer Sam Buzzell the remaining 10 per cent. Duke, in turn, was given a share of some other Mills properties."[60] Statements by Mills and Ellington's son, Mercer, confirm this basic arrangement. Cab Calloway, who made a similar deal with Mills in 1931, spelled out the details in his autobiography:

> I owned 50 percent of the corporation [Cab Calloway, Inc.] and Irving Mills owned the other 50 percent. I read recently in Duke Ellington's book, *Music*

Is My Mistress, that he owned 50 percent of Irving Mills' half of the corporation, so I guess that Irving Mills owned 25 percent, Duke owned 25 percent, and I owned 50 percent. All of the business that I did and that the band did went through the corporation. I had a contract with the corporation where I received $500 per week as a straight salary, the corporation paid the band and took care of all traveling and other expenses, and at the end of the year I received 50 percent of the corporation's profits. By the end of 1931 I was making about $26,000 in salary and about an equal amount from the profits of the corporation—more than $50,000 a year in the middle of the Great Depression. God, what money. Betty and I had all the clothes and cars and fast living that you could want."[61]

By the mid-1930s, Ellington's finances were somewhat in disarray. He was clearly making good money, but, as was his wont, he recirculated most of it into his band. He took it upon himself to pay medical expenses for both his parents, as well as two of his former trumpeters, Arthur Whetsol and Freddie Jenkins. Ellington was devastated when his mother died in 1935, and he focused less and less on business affairs.

In 1938 Ellington visited Mills's office and asked to see the books. As the story goes, Ellington carefully scrutinized every page, got up and never returned, eventually severing his ties to Mills. One variant of this account relates that Ellington asked Mills to buy a $5,000 casket for his mother's funeral. Instead Mills spent $3,500—still a vast sum at the height of the Depression, but not top-of-the-line. In any case, Ellington had other reasons to break with Mills. As Ellington's son, Mercer, explained, "The Cotton Club was very beneficial to him [Ellington] at one stage of his career, but later it became a handicap. The syndicate that ran it gave him a contract with options, so that as his popularity increased he couldn't always take advantage of lucrative outside dates. When he did go out it was usually for a short time, and in the early days he had to hire the Cab Calloway band to go into the club in his place!"[62] Ellington's partnership with Mills necessitated uncomfortable business relationships with gangsters such as Owney "The Killer" Madden, owner and manager of the Cotton Club. While such associations were undoubtedly useful in establishing Ellington's career, they became liabilities as his fame and opportunities increased.

Ellington's publicly stated reason for leaving Mills was "lack of attention." At the time they dissolved their relationship, Mills was booking over a dozen other bands—including the Hudson-DeLange Orchestra, the Mills Blue Rhythm Band, and the orchestras of Cab Calloway, Lucky Millinder, and Ina Ray Hutton—as well as entertainers like singer and comedienne Martha Raye. Mills had also become deeply involved in the recording business by buying up the old Brunswick studio and initiating his own labels, Master and Varsity.

As for the charge that Mills contributed nothing to songs on which his name appears as cowriter, the facts are not as clear-cut as they might first appear. Cab Calloway unequivocally stated, "Irving Mills and I wrote 'Minnie the Moocher,' and whammo, I had my first big hit. . . . One day Irving Mills came to me and said, 'Cab, it's about time you had a theme of your own. You're on national radio, you're doing national tours. The band needs a tune that it can be identified by.' Then Mills and I got together on the lyrics. . . . We created her as a rough, tough character, but with a heart as big as a whale."[63] As with Ellington, Mills encouraged Calloway to develop his talents as a songwriter. "He was a complete manager, and he knew the business up and down," Calloway maintained. According to Sonny Greer, "Irving did wrong when he put his name on so many of Duke's songs. But Duke looked at it like it was sort of a bonus that Irving was giving himself. And Duke felt he was entitled because he had made Duke a star, got his music published and so forth."[64]

In the accounts of both Ellington and Mills, their parting was amicable. Mills reportedly even negotiated the terms for Ellington's new contract with the William Morris Agency. "I want to state that our close friendship and personal relationship never has come to an end," wrote Mills. "Every time he comes to Hollywood, Duke always spends a long, friendly visit with me at my home."[65] For his part Ellington stated, "We dissolved our business relationship agreeably and, in spite of how much he has made on me, I respected the way he had operated."[66] As Mercer Ellington saw it, "There is no point now in debating who profited more from the association, but it's clear that Irving served Ellington well in the formative stages of his career."[67]

As with Ellington and Mills, Louis Armstrong's destiny was intricately entwined with that of Joe Glaser, his agent and manager from 1935 until Glaser's death in 1969. And the exact details of their association are just as murky, and will likely remain so.

Armstrong met Glaser in 1926 at the Sunset Café in Chicago. As Louis wrote in his inimitable style: "Mr. Joe Glaser was the Boss of the Place. In fact he was the Owner of the whole place and Still owns the Building.[68] I always admired Mr. Glaser from the first day I started working for him. He just *impressed* me different than the other Bosses I've worked for. He seemed to understand Colored people so much."[69] After Glaser died, Armstrong amended these sentiments somewhat, confiding to George Wein: "When we started we both had nothing. We were friends—we hung out together, ate together, we went to restaurants together. But the minute we started to make money, Joe Glaser was no longer my friend. In all those years, he never invited me to his house. I was just a passport to him."[70]

According to Glaser, Armstrong was "broke and very sick" when he returned from Europe and Glaser took him on as a client. But by Armstrong's account, Glaser was "down and out" at the time, and he decided to work with Glaser partly out of pity: "He had always been a sharp cat, but now he was raggedy ass," said Armstrong. His directive to Glaser was: "You get me the jobs. You collect the money. You pay me $1,000 every week free and clear. You pay off the band, the travel and hotel expenses, my income tax, and you take everything that's left."[71]

"Joe Glaser and Louis had a special arrangement. They never had a contract; they had a handshake agreement," said Arvell Shaw, Armstrong's longtime bassist. "Joe Glaser and Louis were almost like partners and he took care of Louis, and me being with Louis, I got the benefit of it. As far as Joe Glaser was concerned, Louis could do no wrong. They had what's known as a client's account. Joe Glaser took a salary and Louis Armstrong took a salary and the rest of the money went into the client's account, and at the end they split it up between Louis's family and Glaser's family. And they both wound up multimillionaires from Louis Armstrong alone."[72]

Their wills tell a slightly different story. Glaser left an estate valued at $3 million, whereas Armstrong died with a total net worth of only $530,775.[73] However, royalties continue to pour into Armstrong's estate, which regularly donates over a million dollars annually to various educational and cultural projects.

Glaser certainly enjoyed the good life, with an apartment in Manhattan's East Fifties and choice box seats at Yankee Stadium. He raised champion schnauzers in his spare time, and gave a pair to the Armstrongs. He also lavished more extravagant gifts on his client, including a "big long Rust Colored Packard Car" early on in their relationship. He looked after Armstrong's affairs with great care and accompanied the band on tours, sometimes even bringing along his personal physician, Dr. Alexander Schiff. Glaser negotiated all of Armstrong's contracts for recordings, book deals and appearances in radio, film, and television. Armstrong began to receive sustained attention from the mainstream press, and became probably the first African-American to have a regularly sponsored network radio show. During the period Glaser represented him, Armstrong appeared in thirty feature films as well as several short subjects. Armstrong broke the color bar in numerous prestigious hotels, supper clubs, and theaters, as well as the show lounges of Las Vegas. It was even at Glaser's suggestion that Armstrong adopted "Sleepy Time Down South" as his theme. There's no doubt that Armstrong's career received a significant boost from Glaser's efforts.

Like Irving Mills, who maintained mob connections through his association with the Cotton Club, Glaser exploited his ties to organized crime as a not-too-veiled threat against anyone who might consider harming his clients. In the rough-and-tumble band business at mid-century, this clout was probably necessary. Armstrong had experienced run-ins with the mob in Chicago and New York, and knew the value of such strong-arm tactics. He famously recalled some advice he received as a teenager in New Orleans (the words have been variously ascribed to drummer "Black Benny" Williams and to "Slippers," the bouncer at Matranga's, where Louis worked): "When you go up north, Dipper [Armstrong's nickname], be sure and get yourself a white man that will put his hand on your shoulder and say, 'This is my nigger.'"[74]

George Avakian negotiated with Glaser for Armstrong's Columbia releases. Glaser was "very gruff and made a big show of it," said Avakian. "He wanted everybody to know that he was tough; [he was] very abrupt in his manner. But if you had something you really wanted to talk to him about he was not difficult to talk to."[75] Arvell Shaw drew a similar picture: "Everybody made their own deal for salary. He was a tough, hard man. He was not a generous man. He got you for as little as he could. He got a kick out of arguing money; he liked to negotiate with you. If you took what he offered you he'd look at you like you were some kind of a nut. He always offered you much less than what he was going to pay you. He'd joke around with you but when you'd get down to the nitty-gritty, the money thing, he was as serious as a heart attack, and a massive one. When you agreed on the money the sense of humor would return. He was a stone businessman." Shaw added, "If he promised you something it was as good as in the bank."[76]

Armstrong seemed content with his relationship with Glaser until the very end. In 1969, both were patients at Beth Israel Hospital in New York. Armstrong was in for lung surgery and would live for another two years; Glaser lay in a coma after suffering what proved to be a fatal stroke. When Armstrong learned that Glaser was in the same hospital, he insisted on being wheeled to his manager's bedside. Armstrong later wrote, "It was a toss up between us, who would cut out first. Man, it broke my heart that it was him."[77] Louis returned to his room where he began to write a touching memoir about his loving relationship with the poor Jewish Karnofsky family during his childhood in New Orleans. This was to be part of a never-completed autobiography, which Armstrong dedicated to "my manager and pal, Mr. Joe Glaser; The Best friend That I've ever had. May the Lord Bless Him; Watch over him always."[78]

Following Glaser's death, Armstrong soon discovered that his ex-manager had left his business, the Associated Booking Agency, to those left running it without providing Louis a share. Armstrong was incensed, telling George Wein, "I built Associated Booking. There wouldn't have been an agency if it wasn't for me. And he didn't even leave me a percentage of it."[79] By that time Associated Booking had grown into one of the country's major talent agencies, representing Duke Ellington, Barbra Streisand, Pearl

Bailey, Dave Brubeck, the Kingston Trio, Benny Goodman, Stan Kenton, Creedence Clearwater Revival, the Rascals, Josh White, Miriam Makeba, and even Mr. Television himself, Milton Berle. The real and unvarnished truth about Armstrong and Glaser's business dealings is locked away in the books of a company that continues doing business to this day.

As Duke Ellington wrote, "At first glance you might think Louis was the horse doing all the pulling while Glaser was in the driver's seat of the cart. Obviously, a cart is a most convenient place to stash the gold. Then you realize that in spite of how well Joe Glaser did for himself, Louis still ended up a very rich man, maybe the richest of all the 'trumpet Gabriels.' This is not a fact to be ignored, for what more can one man do for another: Joe Glaser watched over Louis like the treasure he was, and saw to it that his partner was well fixed for the rest of his life."[80]

Before judging the business practices of a Glaser or a Mills too harshly, we should consider that their duties went way beyond the traditional roles of agent and manager, enabling Armstrong and Ellington to devote themselves entirely to their music without having to worry about long-term or even day-to-day business operations of their bands. Contrast this to the experiences of Benny Goodman and Artie Shaw, who relied on more traditional management charging the standard 10 to 15 percent share of gross income. Both men suffered nervous breakdowns at the height of their careers and, for greater or lesser periods, quit the music business. (In later years both Ornette Coleman and Sonny Rollins also retreated from the music business for lengthy intervals to escape personal and professional pressures.)

Perhaps Ed Fox better fits the stereotype of the evil manager. In December, 1928, Fox opened the Grand Terrace in Chicago, installing Earl Hines as its resident bandleader. Hines would remain there for over a decade. Once again we have conflicting statements from various sources as to the nature of this relationship. Hines stated, "Whatever else I may say about him, I have to say he was one of the finest nightclub managers I ever ran into. He had a good system and stuck to it."[81] Fox promised that everyone in Hines's band would receive a full salary for the first year of the club, regardless of whether it turned a profit. By facilitating radio hookups and recordings for Victor, Brunswick, and Decca, Fox helped Hines earn a national reputation.

According to Hines, the trouble started around 1930 when the mob moved in and demanded a percentage. "They practically ran the place," said Hines, and Al Capone became a regular visitor. "It wasn't until the gangsters moved in that I got a lifetime contract at the club. . . . He [Fox] sold us down the river. . . . I was getting $150 a week and the boys were making $75, $80, or $90." Hines also stated that their salaries remained fixed even when Fox booked the band for lucrative tours: "Fox was getting $3500 a week for the band [on the road] when he was paying us that [regular salary] so he really made money."[82]

Chicago jazz historian Dempsey Travis claims that Hines's contract froze his salary at $150 a week in perpetuity and was transferable to Fox's heirs in the event of his death. It wasn't until 1941 that Hines took the matter to James Petrillo, president of the American Federation of Musicians. According to Travis, Petrillo wasted no time in voiding the contract, declaring it "not worth the paper it is written on."[83] Hines's salary quickly shot up to $500 a week, but he soon chose to sever ties with Fox altogether.

At New York's Savoy Ballroom, owner Moe Gale held similar sway over the bands he employed there. He managed to keep salaries low for both in-house and traveling bands: $40 for sidemen and $60 for the leader weekly, according to Local 802's executive board minutes of March 17, 1932. "Gale affects the life of every Negro maestro," read a 1941 report in the *Saturday Evening Post*, "even those not under his wing, because most of them can't come out ahead without playing six to twelve weeks a year at the Savoy."[84] Benny Carter complained, "Playing the Savoy was expected to lead to other things, so a band was supposed to be glad to be there. In fact, the owners and managers felt they were doing the bands a favor. They thought of us—in management and remuneration—as maybe a cut above the waiters."[85]

Moe Gale extended his operations into the field of personal management. Among his clients were Carter, Coleman Hawkins, Cootie Williams, Ella Fitzgerald, and even opera singer Robert Merrill. Fitzgerald's contract with Gale extended all the way from 1935, when she started as band singer for Chick Webb, to 1953. Gale kept her working but failed to catapult her to superstardom, which eventually came about through the efforts of Norman Granz. When Granz took over as Fitzgerald's manager, he soon discovered that Gale had neglected her tax bills. The singer owed a huge amount to the government and Granz settled the matter out of his own pocket.

Granz was, by most accounts, one of the good guys who strove to improve working conditions as well as the bank accounts of those in his care. He started out as a film editor in Los Angeles, but often traveled east to pursue his interest in jazz. He was a regular customer at Milt Gabler's Commodore Music Shop, and attended jam sessions run by Gabler and his brother-in-law, Jack Crystal (father of comedian Billy Crystal). The interracial nature of these jam sessions, both on and off the bandstand, inspired Granz to initiate his Jazz at the Philharmonic (JATP) concert series, which eventually toured coast to coast. Dizzy Gillespie wrote that JATP was "the original 'first class' treatment for jazz musicians. . . . You traveled 'first class,' stayed in 'first class' hotels and [Granz] demanded no segregation in seating."[86] Granz showed that it was possible to become wealthy producing jazz without taking advantage of the musicians. At various times Granz managed Lester Young, Oscar Peterson, Roy Eldridge, Dizzy Gillespie, Art Tatum, Ben Webster, and Count Basie. These and many other artists were featured on a succession of record labels that Granz either owned or produced for.

There were many other managers and agents whose interests clearly lay beyond simply enriching themselves. Among these were the Shribman brothers, Charlie and Si, who owned a string of ballrooms in New England and arranged tours throughout the Northeast during the 1920s and 1930s for both black and white bands. The Shribmans booked Ellington as early as 1924, and continued to do so for years, especially in the slow-business months of January and August. Ellington expressed his thanks in his book, *Music Is My Mistress*, saying they "never owned a piece of any band or anybody. . . . I cannot think of what would have happened to the big bands if it weren't for Charlie Shribman."[87] George Simon, the indefatigable chronicler of the big band era, noted that the Shribmans lent money to get bands started and kept them working until they could succeed on their own. "Leaders loved Si Shribman," wrote Simon, "not only for what he did for them but also because of the quiet, gentlemanly way in which he treated them."[88] The Shribmans were particularly helpful to Fletcher Henderson, and did much to establish the bands of Artie Shaw, Glenn Miller, Woody Herman, Tommy Dorsey, and Claude Thornhill.

Another mutually beneficial arrangement existed between the enormously talented Fats Waller and his last manager, Ed Kirkeby. In his book *Ain't Misbehavin'*, Kirkeby writes movingly about their close relationship. Together they endured frigid weather in unheated cabins in upper Wisconsin and the indignities of segregation in the South; in Florida Kirkeby was threatened by a gun-toting sheriff who refused to let any whites into the dance hall where Waller was scheduled to perform. Both prospered from triumphant radio, theater, and movie appearances as Waller reached his career peak, pulling in as much as $5,000 a week.[89] They shared the same sleeping compartment the night Waller died of pneumonia; "the saddest journey I ever remember," wrote Kirkeby.[90]

As the thirties progressed, the booking of bands became increasingly dominated by a few large and impersonal agencies. The first and biggest was the Music Corporation of America, founded in 1922 by Jules C. Stein and Ernie Young. MCA initially operated out of Chicago and booked pioneering tours for King Oliver and Jelly Roll Morton. "We toured all through Iowa—Pennsylvania—Maryland—Illinois—etc.," wrote Louis Armstrong. "A very nice tour I thought. King Oliver's Band was the first, All Colored Band to sign up with the MCA."[91] In 1926 the company moved its headquarters to New York. Though it booked a later tour for

King Oliver's Dixie Syncopators, MCA was turning its attention to more commercial bandleaders, such as Meyer Davis, Jan Garber, Eddy Duchin, and its most profitable discovery, Guy Lombardo.

It was a young booker for MCA, Willard Alexander, who steered the corporation back towards representing jazz-oriented groups in the mid-thirties. He signed Benny Goodman in 1935, and a year later, Count Basie. "Willard deserves as much credit as I for the [Basie] band's escape from Kansas City to national prominence," noted John Hammond.[92] But MCA—once described by *Variety* as the "Star Spangled Octopus"—was also branching into the film business, and many bandleaders felt they were given short shrift. Some, like Basie, followed Willard Alexander to the William Morris Agency, which was eager to capitalize on the band craze. As already noted, Ellington also sought refuge there. Others represented by the Morris agency included Paul Whiteman, Dizzy Gillespie, Boyd Raeburn, and Billy Eckstine. But William Morris was, like MCA, primarily a theatrical agency and their interest in bands was short-lived. After the war Willard Alexander struck out on his own and played a crucial role in maintaining the success of big bands through the ensuing, difficult decades. Among his roster of big band leaders were the ever-loyal Basie, the Dorseys, and later, Buddy Rich and Maynard Ferguson.

At the height of the big band era, the third most powerful agency, after MCA and William Morris, was the General Artists Corporation (GAC), originally named Rockwell-O'Keefe after its two founders. Tommy Rockwell started in the record business as an A&R man for OKeh, where he presided over recordings of Bix Beiderbecke and Louis Armstrong, among others. Rockwell played a significant role in Armstrong's career by bringing him to New York in 1929, booking him as a solo act, placing him on Broadway in *Connie's Hot Chocolates*, and steering him toward recording standards. Their relationship dissolved after Rockwell booked Armstrong into Sebastian's Cotton Club in Culver City, California. The details are murky, but apparently Rockwell enlisted Johnny Collins, a small-time hood, to oversee Armstrong's engagement at Sebastian's. Collins decided to take over Armstrong's management and a struggle for control ensued, involving various ominous threats from mob characters. Finally, in 1932, Armstrong fled with Collins at his side to Europe, where they eventually parted company. When Armstrong returned to America he began his longtime association with Joe Glaser.

Despite this contretemps, Rockwell-O'Keefe/GAC became a leading force in the band business, attracting such names as Artie Shaw, Bob Crosby, Woody Herman, and Glenn Miller. Many bandleaders switched from agency to agency through the course of their careers. Benny Carter is a good example, having been at various times represented by all the major players: Irving Mills, Joe Glaser, Moe Gale, GAC, MCA, and William

Morris. It's important to note that these agencies booked both black and white bands simultaneously. How much they may have favored one over the other is hard to determine, but the top name bands of both races only increased in stature throughout the big band era.

Billy Shaw, a former trumpeter and bandleader himself, apprenticed with Moe Gale and Willard Alexander before founding his own company, Shaw Artists. Shaw's operation was among the first to book bop musicians, such as Charlie Parker and Dizzy Gillespie. According to Gillespie, it was Shaw's idea for Billy Eckstine to front a big band. Shaw also booked Gillespie and Parker's West Coast debut at Billy Berg's club in Los Angeles. Shaw is immortalized in the classic Gillespie composition "Shaw 'Nuff." (Earlier, in 1938, Mary Lou Williams saluted Joe Glaser in her tune "Little Joe from Chicago.") Shortly after Shaw took on Parker he was obliged to buy his client a new horn, after Parker threw his alto out of an upper-floor window. In 1951 Parker lost his cabaret card and was prevented from working in New York nightclubs. Shaw booked him on a road tour with the Woody Herman band, but the wayward Parker failed to show up for some of the dates. Shaw and Parker dissolved their business relationship, but the following year Shaw agreed to book him as a nonexclusive artist. Other agents, such as Moe Gale and Norman Granz, stepped in to arrange dates for the increasingly troubled artist. Shaw died from a heart attack in 1956 at age fifty-two, only fifteen months after Parker succumbed. Ross Russell—author of the Parker bio *Bird Lives!* and founder of Dial Records, for which Parker recorded—felt that the stress of dealing with this brilliant, affable, yet uncontrollable musician contributed to Shaw's own demise.[93] Shaw Artists continued after Shaw's death, and at its height handled Miles Davis, Horace Silver, Art Blakey, John Coltrane, Sonny Rollins, Sonny Stitt, Roland Kirk, Oscar Peterson, Wynton Kelly, Hank Crawford, Shirley Scott, Milt Buckner, Wild Bill Davis, Bill Doggett, and Jimmy McGriff, as well as numerous emerging rock acts.

Teddy Blume was Parker's personal manager for four years, and Bird celebrated their tumultuous relationship with his tune "Bloomdido." "He nearly drove me nuts," said Blume, "scared my wife half to death with calls at all hours of the night." Blume met the altoist when he was concertmaster for the string section on the *Bird with Strings* recordings and performances in 1950. "I used to play violin for him late at night. It soothed him. He loved the violin. I loved Charlie Parker. I'd forgive him anything. The only way I got free was, he died."[94]

For the last year of his life, following Parkers' death, Billy Shaw represented Miles Davis. As Miles wrote in his autobiography, "I told them [Shaw and his bother Milt] from the beginning—they were white—what *I* wanted them to do. I wasn't going to be doing what *they* wanted me to do. Because back then white men always told black guys what to do so I wasn't having none of that and told them right up front. They assigned a guy named Jack Whittemore to work with me. We became good friends after a while, but I had Harold Lovett [Davis's lawyer and sometime manager] watch him like a hawk, because regardless of the fact that I grew to like Jack, I didn't want him trying to take advantage of me."[95]

Jack Whittemore proved to be an effective and considerate manager who guided Davis's career through its period of greatest acclaim. Following an impressive appearance at George Wein's Newport Festival in 1955, Davis was signed to Columbia by George Avakian, who worked with Whittemore to promote the trumpeter. According to Avakian, "Miles's work was skimpy when I signed him, essentially small clubs mostly in the East. He was a dead duck in some cities like Chicago—they wouldn't touch him. In New York the only place he could work for a while was Monday nights at Birdland."[96]

Whittemore negotiated the hiring of Davis's personnel, from John Coltrane to the later quintet with Wayne Shorter. When Coltrane went out on his own, he chose Whittemore to represent him. Davis stuck by his faithful manager until 1967, when he suddenly and unexpectedly fired him. "Jack had no contract with Miles," wrote George Wein, "but they had worked together for years. He accepted his dismissal without complaint. This self-effacing behavior was atypical of agents, who are commonly portrayed as cold-blooded, but wholly typical of Miles's followers. Jack loved Miles Davis to the point of masochism, and Miles took full advantage of it."[97]

An equally selfless and dedicated manager was Harry Colomby, who began representing Thelonious Monk in 1955. Colomby stayed with Monk through his steep rise to success and slow mental decline. Colomby later went into television and movie production, and switched from managing jazz musicians to managing actors such as Michael Keaton.

Among the first African-American managers, apart from Harold Lovett, were the Carpenter brothers, Charles and younger brother Richard. The two worked separately, with Charles handling Earl Hines, Lester Young, and John Kirby, and Richard for a time taking on Miles Davis and Dizzy Gillespie. The 1980s and 1990s witnessed a surge of female and African-American managers. Mary Ann Topper's agency, The Jazz Tree, has represented many successful jazz artists, including Jim Hall, Geoff Keezer, Christian McBride, Joshua Redman, and Diana Krall. Wynton Marsalis was managed from 1983 on by Ed Arrendell. "It was providential when I met Ed," said Marsalis. "The Lord was looking out for me."[98]

Perhaps the most prominent African-American manager is John Levy. Levy began as a bassist, working in the popular George Shearing quintet and serving as road manager. (Shearing, a blind English-born pianist, had one of the most "diverse" jazz groups of all time, with female vibraphonist

Marjorie Hyams and African-American drummer Denzil Best, as well as Levy.) In 1954 he founded John Levy Enterprises and went on to handle Shearing, Cannonball and Nat Adderley, Billy Taylor, Ahmad Jamal, Wes Montgomery, Freddie Hubbard, and vocalists Nancy Wilson, Joe Williams, Betty Carter, Roberta Flack, and Abbey Lincoln. In 2006 Levy, at the age of ninety-four, was awarded the prestigious Jazz Master Award from the National Endowment for the Arts.

With the recent decline of interest in jazz among the major record companies, many full- and part-time managers have left the business. The grand old agencies of the past have either disappeared or abandoned jazz altogether. William Morris has recently handled a few jazz artists, such as Herbie Hancock, Arturo Sandoval, and vocalist Karrin Allyson, plus a few in the smooth-jazz category, like Kenny G and Chris Botti. Joe Glaser's Associated Booking still administers the Louis Armstrong Educational Foundation and represents artists primarily in the blues and R&B (or "adult contemporary" if you prefer) field, including B. B. King, Teddy Pendergrass and Dr. John. Only George Wein's Festival Productions remains as a major agency dedicated to jazz within the United States.

What's the verdict in terms of fair business practices, especially for African-American artists? It's all a matter of who you're talking about, who you ask, and whether the last check cleared. But undoubtedly, Louis Armstrong, Duke Ellington, and Miles Davis (among many others) would not have come near the career heights they attained were it not for their hard-working business representatives. These businessmen unquestionably enriched themselves in the process, but the bottom line is: they delivered.

EVEN JEWS GET THE BLUES

In reviewing the history of those who have conducted the business of jazz, one can't help but notice the preponderance of Jewish business figures who chose to work in this unusual and highly uncertain field. Among them were the above-mentioned agents and managers Walter and Lester Melrose, Irving Mills, Joe Glaser, Moe Gale (born Moses Galewski), Ed Fox, Jules Stein, William Morris, Charlie and Si Shribman, Billy Shaw, Teddy Blume, Harry Colomby, Norman Granz and George Wein. Jews who ran jazz-leaning venues include nightclub owners Barney Josephson, Max Gordon, and Billy Berg; Lou Brecker of Roseland; Frank Schiffman of the Apollo Theater; Morris Levy and Oscar Goodstein of the original Birdland; and in Chicago, Sol Tannenbaum of the Beehive and Joe Segal of the long-running Jazz Showcase. Those that founded independent jazz labels include Milt Gabler of Commodore, Herman Lubinsky of Savoy,

Bob Weinstock of Prestige, Moses (Moe) Asch of Folkways, Lester Koenig of Contemporary, Bernard Stollman of the avant-garde ESP-Disk, and of course Alfred Lion and Francis Wolff of Blue Note. Jewish entertainment moguls include Ted Wallerstein and William Paley of CBS and David Sarnoff and Eli Oberstein at RCA.

So why were so many Jewish people involved in the jazz business?

Economist Thomas Sowell sheds some light on this matter in a discussion of what he terms "minority middlemen."[99] He defines such figures as members of a minority group who act as intermediaries, in both a social and economic sense, between producers (in the case of jazz, the artists) and consumers. Minority middlemen bring together disparate groups of people who communicate better through an intermediate third party. Thus Jewish agents and managers provided a necessary link between black performers and white audiences. The "capital" required by middleman minorities often amounts to nothing more than their own intellectual and interpersonal skills, and many, though not all, of the Jewish movers and shakers in the music industry came from humble beginnings. In the process of bettering themselves these businessmen provided a necessary service to the public, while opening up unprecedented opportunities for African-American artists.

Many of these relationships were certainly not equitable, especially by current standards. But as Sowell points out, "It seems clear—painfully clear—that they [middleman minorities] have been most hated where they have been most essential."[100] Sowell further notes, "Middleman minorities have often been accused of 'taking over' large portions of a country's economy, even in situations where it was they who largely—or solely—*created* particular businesses and industries."[101] Their role is often seen as parasitic, when in fact they've made a vital contribution to society as a whole. In the case of jazz, a middleman minority was crucial to the progress of the music from honky-tonks to concert halls and festivals, and to the ensuing fame and fortune of a multitude of jazz stars past and present.

NOTES

1. Stephen Calt, "The Anatomy of a 'Race' Music Label: Mayo Williams and Paramount Records," *78 Quarterly* 1, nos. 3–4 (1989). Reprinted in *Rhythm and Business*, ed. Norman Kelley, 86–111.

2. Walter Yetnikoff, *Howling at the Moon*, 288–289.

3. Yetnikoff, 84.

4. Reig and Berger, *Reminiscing in Tempo*, 73.

5. Taped interview with Art Farmer, 1993.

6. Tim Brooks, liner notes to *Lost Sounds: Blacks in the Birth of the Recording Industry*, Archeophone 1005 (2005).

7. "Bessie Smith Renews Contract," *Talking Machine World*, May 15, 1924. Reprinted in Tim Gracyk, *Pages from Talking Machine World*, self-published.

8. Charters and Kunstadt, *Jazz*, 96.

9. Calt, "The Anatomy of a 'Race' Music Label."

10. The letter from the Vince Giordano collection is dated January 24, 1940.

11. Taped interview with George Avakian, 2003.

12. Cook, *Blue Note Records*, 188.

13. Clifford Allen, "Bernard Stollman: The ESP-Disk Story," All About Jazz, http://www.allaboutjazz.com/php/article.php?id=19661, posted November 21, 2005.

14. Richard B. Woodward, "Kind of Blue: Jazz Competes with Its Past, Settles for the Hard Sell," *Village Voice*, January 16, 2001. Reprinted in *Rhythm and Business*, ed. Norman Kelley, 185–91.

15. Woodward, "Kind of Blue."

16. Eberly, *Music in the Air*, 23.

17. Goodman and Kolodin, *The Kingdom of Swing*, 110.

18. Smith and Hoefer, *Music On My Mind*, 202.

19. Taped interview with Chris Griffin, 2005.

20. Taped interview with Bucky Pizzarelli, 1995.

21. George Avakian, liner notes to *What is Jazz?*, Columbia CLP91A 02053.

22. Lion, *Bix*, 256.

23. Taped interview with Dick Katz, 2005.

24. Wilmer, *Jazz People*, 107–108.

25. Wilmer, 106–107.

26. Collette and Isoardi, *Jazz Generations*, 174.

27. See Royal, *Marshal Royal*, 123. Royal's autobiography doesn't mention any difficulties breaking into studio work, but perhaps he chose not to dwell on unhappy aspects of his career. Instead, he talks of making many rhythm-and-blues records after the war, and, after leaving Basie in 1970, recording with "just about every big name you can think of."

28. Taped interview with Plas Johnson, 1995.

29. Kenney, *Chicago Jazz*, 156.

30. Chilton, *Ride Red Ride*, 67.

31. Hammond and Townsend, *John Hammond On Record*, 239–241.

32. Wilmer, 110.

33. Taped interview with Plas Johnson, 1995.

34. Collette and Isoardi, 142.

35. Taped interview with Joe Wilder, 1990.

36. Wilmer, 127.

37. Faulkner, *Hollywood Studio Musicians*, 104.

38. Faulkner, 109.

39. Faulkner, 140.

40. Faulkner, 147.

41. Faulkner, 171.

42. Taped interview with Milt Hinton, 1990.

43. Taped interview with Ed Shaughnessy, 2004.

44. LeRoi Jones, *Blues People*, 164.

45. Wein and Chinen, *Myself Among Others*, 85.

46. Hogan Jazz Archive. Joe Mares interview conducted April 8, 1960.

47. Russell, ed., *Oh, Mister Jelly*, 460.

48. Russell, ed., 389–390.

49. Sudhalter, *Lost Chords*, 40.

50. Dance, *The World of Duke Ellington*, 69.

51. Irving Mills, liner notes to *The Ellington Era, 1927–1940*, Columbia C3L27.

52. Tucker, ed., *The Duke Ellington Reader*, 273.

53. Tucker, ed., 274.

54. Hasse, *Beyond Category*, 161.

55. Calloway and Rollins, *Of Minnie the Moocher & Me*, 106.

56. Schiffman, *Uptown*, 151.

57. Reported in *Variety*, January 15, 1936.

58. Nicholson, *Reminiscing in Tempo*, 194.

59. Ulanov, *Duke Ellington*, 206.

60. Ulanov, 58.

61. Calloway and Rollins, 110.

62. Mercer Ellington, *Duke Ellington in Person*, 41.

63. Calloway and Rollins, 111.

64. Michael P. Zirpolo, "In Duke's Head," *IAJRC Journal* 33, no. 3 (Summer 2000): 20.

65. Tucker, ed., 274.

66. Tucker, ed., 273.

67. Mercer Ellington, 82.

68. According to Earl Hines, Glaser's mother actually owned the building, and the club was managed by Sam Dreyfus and Ed Fox. "Joe Glaser had nothing to do with running the club," said Hines, "but he was always around." See Dance, *The World of Earl Hines*, 11.

69. Brothers, ed., *Louis Armstrong, in His Own Words*, 99.

70. Wein and Chinen, 300.

71. Berrett, ed., *The Louis Armstrong Companion*, 87.

72. Taped interview with Arvell Shaw, 2000.

73. Berrett, ed., 90.

74. Bergreen, *Louis Armstrong*, 175.

75. Taped interview with George Avakian, 2003.

76. Taped interview with Arvell Shaw, 2003.

77. Wein and Chinen, 299.

78. Brothers, ed., 6.

79. Wein and Chinen, 300.

80. Duke Ellington, *Music Is My Mistress*, 234–235.

81. Dance, *The World of Earl Hines*, 57–58.

82. Dance, *The World of Earl Hines*, 66–67.

83. Travis, *An Autobiography of Black Jazz*, 45–46.

84. DeVeaux, *The Birth of Bebop*, 138.

85. Berger, Berger, and Patrick, *Benny Carter*, 188.

86. Gillespie and Fraser, *To Be or Not To Bop*, 405–406.

87. Duke Ellington, *Music Is My Mistress*, 99.

88. Simon, *The Big Bands*, 47.
89. Smith and Hoefer, 229.
90. Kirkeby, *Ain't Misbehavin'*, 230.
91. Brothers, ed., 63.
92. Hammond and Townsend, 172.
93. Priestley, *Chasin' the Bird*, 127.
94. Reisner, *Bird*, 56.
95. Davis and Troupe, *Miles*, 195.
96. Taped interview with George Avakian, 2003.
97. Wein and Chinen, 463.
98. Gourse, *Wynton Marsalis*, 93.
99. Sowell, *Black Rednecks and White Liberals*, 65–86.
100. Sowell, 102.
101. Sowell, 83.

9

~

Copyrights: Accounting Without Accountability

"Never sell a copyright."

—Joe Davis, music publisher

Other than an instrument (and perhaps a tuxedo), copyrights are the only work-related property a jazz musician is likely to own. But like all property, copyrights can be sold or even stolen, and they don't always end up in the hands of their rightful owners. More often than not, the composer shares his earnings with people who were in no way connected with the actual creation of the musical composition. Any time property is up for grabs, and those in the know are in a position to take advantage of those who aren't, there's plenty of room for chicanery.[1]

How much has race been a factor in appropriating the artistic property of African-American musicians? The record seems to show that those who have reaped ill-gotten gains by way of copyright "protection" have come in all colors. And many times the offenders have been the musicians themselves, both black and white.

Copyright protection is provided for in the U.S. Constitution. Article 1, section 8 stipulates that Congress must "promote the progress of science and the useful arts, by securing for limited times to authors and inventors the exclusive right to their respective writings and discoveries."[2] The Copyright Act of 1790 followed English legal precedent by establishing a twenty-eight-year term of ownership, which has by now been extended to the life of the creator plus seventy years. In 1870 the Library of Congress became the clearinghouse for copyrights. Such early jazz luminaries as King Oliver, Louis Armstrong, and Bix Beiderbecke dutifully sent in lead sheets of their compositions, often in their own hand, to secure owner-ship of their work.[3] Since 1978, any "fixed medium of expression," from a recorded CD to even a computer file, is sufficient to establish ownership.

There are still many gray areas in copyright law, particularly in regard to jazz works. For instance, copyrights typically apply only to recogniz-able melodies and not to solos, which to this day have no legal protection. A particular recording can be copyrighted, though its ownership usually resides with the record company. Many copyrights are considered "works for hire," a notion enshrined in the Copyright Act that gave rise to a host of sins. When an established bandleader records a sideman's tune (which happened frequently during the swing era) it's perfectly legal, however morally dishonorable, to put the bandleader's name on the composition. Likewise, if a publisher commissions a tune and arranges for it to be recorded (as was often the case in the 1920s and 1930s), the composition may be considered a "work for hire." So however distasteful it might have been for Irving Mills to attach his name to so many Duke Ellington compositions, technically Mills was within his legal rights.

Royalties are split equally between the writer (or writers) and publisher in accordance with longstanding industry practice. However unfair this may seem to the creators of a musical work, bear in mind that galleries typically take a 50 to 80 percent commission on art sales, and publishers typically award their authors no more than a 10 to 15 percent royalty. Race played no part in the original formulation of these policies, though of course those holding the reins on the business side of the equation have traditionally been white.

Music publishers have a clear advantage over composers in the way earnings are distributed. Record companies would rather send checks to a few publishers than to a horde of composers, so payments are sent as a lump sum directly to the publisher. The publisher then deducts a 50 percent cut before turning the balance over to the writer(s). Obviously a composer has no way of knowing whether he's getting a fair share of his earnings, short of a full accounting of the publisher's books.

Until around the Second World War, publishers lived up to their name by printing sheet music copies of the compositions in their catalog. But more and more, publishing concerns have been reduced to collection agencies whose sole source of revenue is direct payment from record-ing companies and the music rights licensing agencies, such as ASCAP (the American Society of Composers, Authors and Publishers) and BMI (Broadcast Music, Inc.). Although publishers rarely, if ever, expend money on printing music anymore, their 50 percent share still remains the industry standard.

ASCAP was formed in 1914, but it took another three years of litiga-tion, going all the way to the Supreme Court, before it was authorized to levy charges wherever music was "performed publicly for profit." Its original membership, which consisted of 170 writers and 22 publishers, included only two African-Americans: composer Harry T. Burleigh and writer James Weldon Johnson. By the mid-twenties only eight more had been admitted.[4] New members had to be recommended by existing ones, and then approved by committee. Royalty rates were determined by a Byzantine, and ultimately arbitrary, classification system based on the "number, nature, and character" and "popularity and vogue" of a member's works, as well as the member's seniority within the organization.[5] Concert and theater music were favored, and the vast majority of black songwriters found it nearly impossible to get in. Fats Waller became a member in 1931, and Duke Ellington only in 1935. The prolific Jelly Roll Morton tried to gain membership in 1928 and again in 1934, only to be turned down. In 1939 he was finally let in, but with a low classification and correspondingly low royalty rate. Morton felt obliged to sue, and ASCAP responded by slightly upping his share.[6]

By this time ASCAP was back in federal court fighting for its very existence. The organization stood accused by radio networks of violating antitrust laws, and out of this battle emerged BMI, an alternative music rights licensing organization. BMI immediately adopted an open admission policy, and many black and country-and-western artists found a new and powerful ally to protect their rights.[7] A court-ordered consent decree forced ASCAP to abandon its classification system in favor of one based almost solely on frequency of performances. These new policies were well timed to coincide with a shift in public tastes to country, R&B, and eventually rock music.

In the early days of jazz in New Orleans there was little concern about ownership of a particular tune. Bands simply played their own versions of pieces other bands played. As in any folk music, many tunes developed over time, their precise origins unknown. So it's understandable that when jazz was first recorded, and copyright ownership became an issue, lots of legal wrangling ensued. King Oliver claimed "High Society," as did Clarence Williams, Armand J. Piron, Walter Melrose, and Roy Palmer. They all probably thought the tune was in the public domain, when in fact it had been written and copyrighted by Porter Steele in 1901. Sidney Bechet put his name on "Egyptian Fantasy," which had been written in 1911 by Abe Olman and published as "Egyptia" (the tune was widely performed by the Original Creole Band on tour). Bechet also claimed Charles "Doc" Cook's 1914 composition "Blame It On the Blues" under the title "Quincy Street Stomp."[8] The white New Orleans trumpeter Johnny DeDroit recorded "Washington and Lee Swing" as "The Swing"; he was sued and settled for the modest sum of $50.[9] The Creole bandleader Oscar Celestin recorded "Some of These Days" as his own composition, under the title "My Josephine."

The vagaries of copyright practices in those days are well illustrated by the career of W. C. Handy. Handy is known as the "Father of the Blues," but he was as much a "stenographer of the blues," to use music historian Ian Whitcomb's memorable phrase. Handy openly admitted to copyrighting tunes drawn from the music of "Negro roustabouts, honky-tonk piano players, wanderers, and others of their underprivileged but undaunted class from Missouri to the Gulf."[10] One such borrowed strain ended up in his first hit, "Memphis Blues." After being turned down by several publishers, Handy sold all rights to the tune for $50. After "Memphis Blues" became immensely popular, Handy decided to form his own publishing company. The success of this venture was ensured by the publication of his classic "St. Louis Blues." Handy maintained that the composition was his own creation, but some of the lyrics were taken from songs he'd heard during travels through the South.

The concept of "ownership" of folk material was relatively undeveloped when Handy began his business in 1914, so perhaps he may be excused for not giving full credit to his original sources (if they could even be traced). Less forgivable were the questionable practices of folklorist Alan Lomax, who listed himself or his father as cocomposer of many classic Huddie Ledbetter ("Leadbelly") songs, such as "Rock Island Line" and "Goodnight Irene," and also claimed publishing rights.

The Original Dixieland Jazz Band's February 26, 1917 Victor recording—usually cited as the very first issued jazz recording—was the subject of two separate lawsuits claiming copyright infringement. The final strain of "Dixieland Jass Band One-Step" was lifted from ragtime pianist and bandleader Joe Jordan's 1909 composition, "That Teasin' Rag." The matter was settled with an unspecified payment plus the addition of the subtitle "introducing 'That Teasin' Rag'" to the labels of subsequent record issues.[11]

The flip side, "Livery Stable Blues," engendered a ten-day court case in Chicago in October 1917. Alcide Nunez had been the original clarinetist with the ODJB until Nick LaRocca fired him for excessive drinking[12] (Nunez's first recording under his own name was "Alcoholic Blues"). The clarinetist maintained he and cornetist Ray Lopez were the true composers of "Livery Stable Blues," which includes some horn impressions of livestock animals. The press had a field day, one headline proclaiming "Barnyard Syncopation to Edify Judge." The *Chicago Journal* carried the sarcastic headline, "Jazz Band Masterpiece Authorship in Dispute: Dominic [LaRocca] Claims Alcide Purloined His Tone Picture of Emotions of Lovesick Colt." The article concluded with: "When the thirty-five witnesses have completed their testimony, and Judge Carpenter has heard from jazz experts, cabaret owners, and livery stable keepers, the composer of the world's greatest jazz music will be identified. The 'Livery

Stable Blues,' along with the Shakespeare-Bacon controversy, will have become history."[13]

Judge Carpenter finally weighed in with his opinion: "No living human being could listen to that result on that phonograph and discover anything musical in it, although there is a wonderful rhythm, something that will carry you along especially if you are young and a dancer."[14] As for his legal verdict, Carpenter ruled that the melody was too insubstantial, and probably existed in some form before either claimant came upon it. A music critic called in as an expert witness maintained that all blues are alike, and if played simultaneously would "produce perfect harmony." In effect, the trial failed to resolve the dispute. But from then on, record companies were careful to list composers on their labels, an industry practice that continues up to the present day.

No tune has created more authorship controversy than "Tiger Rag." The ODJB were the first to record it and claimed it as their composition. In an interview with discographer Brian Rust, LaRocca was quite specific, though a bit unconvincing, about the musical sources he drew on: a few bars of the hymn "The Holy City," a few more of "La Paloma," and for the chorus, the "National Emblem March."[15] (Jazz historian Dan Morgenstern notes that the chords to the final strain are also identical to "Bill Bailey" from 1902, and very similar to "Over the Waves" from 1889.) Jelly Roll Morton famously stated that he converted "Tiger Rag" into a jazz piece from a nineteenth-century French quadrille.[16] The French jazz writer Hugues Panassié claimed to possess a copy of the original French tune, though it never turned up after his death, and no one else has ever seen it. Jack Laine maintained that the tune was a staple of his repertoire even before LaRocca worked for him, and that it went under the title of "Reliance Rag" and "Meatballs."[17] Meanwhile, the African-American trombonist Jack Carey, brother of trumpeter Mutt Carey, claimed his band originated the tune.[18] The truth will probably never be known.

Louis Armstrong learned the value of holding onto a copyright early in his career. In 1918 he was working at Pete Lala's with Kid Ory's band and came up with a feature number called "Keep Off Katie's Head." Armstrong sang and played the tune while demonstrating a new dance, the "Shimmy." "One night, as I did the number," Louis recalled,

> I saw this cat writing it all down on music paper. He was quick, man, he could write as fast as I could play and sing. When I had finished he asked me if I'd sell the number to him. He mentioned twenty-five dollars. When you're making only a couple of bucks a night that's a lot of money. But what really put the deal over was that I had just seen a hard-hitting steel gray overcoat that I really wanted for those cold nights. So I said, "Okay," and he handed me some forms to sign and I signed them. He said he'd be back with the cash. But he never did come back.[19]

That man was music publisher Clarence Williams, and Armstrong never forgave him for his transgression. The tune went on to become a huge hit with new lyrics under the title "I Wish I Could Shimmy Like My Sister Kate." When the two met again in Chicago some six years later, Armstrong still expected Williams to broach the subject, but it never came up and Louis simply let it drop.

Another famous tune also got out of Armstrong's hands. In a taped interview with Dan Morgenstern and Jack Bradley in 1965, Armstrong stated that he, and not Kid Ory, was the composer of "Muskrat Ramble." He never attempted to claim the tune and only mentioned his authorship in passing. But there is no reason to doubt Armstrong's assertion, especially since he had nothing to gain by it. There is some doubt surrounding "Weatherbird Rag," which is credited to Armstrong on King Oliver's 1923 recording for Gennett, but to Oliver on Armstrong's 1928 recording for OKeh (where it is titled simply "Weather Bird"). The lead sheet on file in the Library of Congress is clearly in Louis's own hand. And why is "Dipper Mouth Blues" (sometimes retitled "Sugar Foot Stomp") credited as an Oliver-Armstrong composition on the Oliver recordings, but listed without Armstrong's name on the Melrose sheet music and the Fletcher Henderson version featuring Armstrong? We'll probably never know.

Several other tunes that Oliver recorded are in dispute. Creole clarinetist Alphonse Picou claimed he sent some of his compositions to Oliver, who then added a few touches, changed some titles, and credited Picou only as cocomposer on the recordings. "Snake Rag," "Chattanooga Stomp," "New Orleans Stomp," and "Alligator Hop" are among the tunes in question.[20]

Armstrong became embroiled in a lawsuit over copyright ownership with his ex-wife, Lil Hardin Armstrong. As Louis recalled, "I used to sit on the back steps of Lil's home and write five and six songs a day . . . just lead sheets . . . and Lil would put the other parts to them . . . cornet, clarinet, trombone, etc. . . . Then I would sell them to the recording company outright."[21] By this account, Armstrong's wife functioned more as an arranger, though she did sometimes compose as well. For her part, Lil Armstrong stated, "When we wrote those tunes . . . we didn't think it important to get our songs copyrighted or anything like that. We just put our names on them and thought about the immediate cash. Now I live off them, but it only happened after years."[22] Apparently both Armstrongs, by then divorced, recovered the copyrights when they came up for renewal, at which point Lil sued Louis. Louis, who generally handled his divorces by granting all previous assets to his former wife, turned over his copyrights to Lil, and she ended up owning such classics as "Struttin' with Some Barbecue" and "Hotter Than That."[23] The original OKeh labels did credit "Hardin" as the composer of both these tunes, but Louis's fingerprints are all over them.

The case of Jelly Roll Morton was an even more tangled state of affairs. *Chicago Tribune* jazz critic Howard Reich went to great lengths in his book *Jelly's Blues* to show how Morton was ripped off by his publishers, notably the Melrose brothers, as well as ASCAP. But Morton's business affairs were often untidy, and he was not above claiming compositions by others as his own.[24] In 1924 he recorded "Fish Tail Blues," credited to himself and trumpeter Lee Collins, who was on the date. "Jelly took that number from me and later recorded it as 'Sidewalk Blues,'" recalled Collins. "When I went back to New Orleans and saw an orchestration come out of 'Sidewalk Blues' and played it down once, I saw it was my own number, the number I'd been playing around New Orleans so many years. Roy Palmer warned me not to play it until I had it copyrighted, but I didn't take his advice. All I wanted to do was make the record. It was my first one."[25]

Like Beethoven before him, Morton would sometimes change the title of a composition and sell it to multiple publishers. "London Blues" became "Shoe Shiner's Drag," "Soap Suds" reappeared as "Fickle Fay Creep," "Tom Cat Blues" was changed to "Midnight Mama," and "Big Fat Ham" turned into "Ham and Eggs." More serious charges were leveled against Morton by one Harrison Smith, a West Indian man who shared an office with the composer in New York during the late twenties. According to Smith, of the twenty-four tunes Morton claimed as his own and recorded for Victor from December 1929 to October 1930, eighteen were in fact written by others; likewise, three titles released by General Records in 1940 as Morton's were not his own.[26] Smith claimed that "Blue Blood Blues" was originally "Majestic Stomp" by saxophonist Hector Marchese, and that Marchese also wrote "Pontchartrain" and the classic "Sweet Substitute." "Majestic Stomp" was never recorded, but according to Smith it was performed frequently on coast-to-coast broadcasts by Arnold Johnson and his Majestic Hour Orchestra featuring Marchese on alto sax. Smith said that he himself was the lyricist for "Gambling Jack," "Smilin' the Blues Away," and "That's Like It Ought To Be," and that these tunes were originally composed by one Ben Garrison, of whom virtually nothing is known. It is probably impossible at this point to determine the veracity of Smith's claims.

Early in his career, Morton does seem to have pirated "Mama's Got a Baby" from "Dixie Queen" by Robert Hoffman; "Don't You Ever Leave Me" from Hoffman's "Alabama Bound" (a different song than the one most people know); and "Buddy Bolden's Blues" from "The St. Louis Tickle" by Barney and Seymore. All of these tunes had been published and were available in New Orleans between 1899 and 1905.[27]

What about Howard Reich's claim that Melrose Music took advantage of Morton by buying his tunes outright and not granting him royalties? This is undoubtedly true, but Morton may have been complicit in this arrangement. Louis Armstrong expressed the view of many musicians of the time when he stated, "They [publishers] used to either buy the tune outright, or ask us if we cared to collect the royalties. . . . P.S. Of course you don't have to make any guesses as to our decisions . . . Aye? . . . Sure. . . . Our slogan was, A bird in hand gathers no moss [ellipses in original]."[28] Drummer Paul Barbarin, who played on several Morton recording dates, noted that Jelly was a compulsive gambler: "Then, when he needed money, he'd go down to Melrose, who published his tunes. . . . Yeah, that was his downfall—easy come, easy go."[29] It's not surprising that musicians didn't put much trust in a royalty system monitored by publishers, and preferred a cash-in-hand lump sum. Furthermore, many performers like Morton led a nomadic lifestyle that made receiving checks and royalty statements difficult at best. Morton himself said that his original contracts with Melrose were "lost with trunks" containing other possessions.[30] Morton assigned his later Victor material to Ralph Peer's Southern Music, which was notorious for buying compositions outright—a further indication that Jelly Roll consented to this kind of deal. It was only with the enormous success of Benny Goodman's recording of Morton's "King Porter Stomp" that Jelly Roll realized he'd made a terrible mistake.

The inaccuracy of composer credits is well illustrated by another composition from the Morton canon. Apparently Morton was the sole composer of "Wild Man Blues," but Louis Armstrong's name was attached when Melrose published a stock arrangement, which included a transcription of Armstrong's improvised chorus from his OKeh recording.

The swing era ushered in a new wave of questionable copyright claims as bandleaders added their own names to tunes written by sidemen. Often writers were happy to share composer credit with big-name leaders in order to get a well-promoted recording of their work. It's hard to tell just what, if anything, Benny Goodman contributed to many of the tunes that bear his name. Goodman is listed as sole composer of "A Smooth One," "Benny's Bugle," and "Slipped Disc" (named for his recurrent back problems). "Air Mail Special," "Seven Come Eleven," and "Solo Flight" were probably the work of guitarist Charlie Christian, who is listed as co-composer along with Goodman and arranger Jimmy Mundy. Goodman's name is also on Lionel Hampton's "Flying Home," as well as "Stompin' at the Savoy," which also credits bandleader Chick Webb before listing perhaps its true composer, Webb saxophonist Edgar Sampson. (Rex Stewart claimed that the tune existed even before Sampson wrote it down.) Sampson also wrote "Don't Be That Way," on which Goodman's name also appears.[31]

Guitarist, trombonist, and arranger Eddie Durham was a key member of the Count Basie orchestra and contributed many important titles to the band's library, only some of which he received credit for. Even before his tenure with Basie, Durham had written the jazz classic "Moten Swing," but bandleaders Bennie and Buster Moten assumed credit and ownership. For Basie, Durham wrote or at least contributed to "Swingin' the Blues," "Jumpin' at the Woodside," and "Sent for You Yesterday," all three of which are credited only to the bandleader. Basie's theme, "One O'Clock Jump," was put together by Durham along with saxophonist Buster Smith, though it "borrowed" its concluding (and main) theme from a 1929 arrangement of "Six or Seven Times," as recorded by The Little Chocolate Dandies. That tune lists Fats Waller and the ubiquitous Irving Mills as cocomposers, though neither sought legal redress.

Fats Waller was especially negligent in claiming his own compositions. He preferred selling all rights for quick cash to avoid sharing his income with an avaricious ex-wife. Waller even chose jail time over keeping up with his alimony payments. The often-heard claim that Waller and lyricist Andy Razaf are the true composers of "I Can't Give You Anything But Love,"—not the songwriting team of Dorothy Fields and Jimmy McHugh—is simply impossible to verify at this point.[32]

"In the Mood," sometimes called the "anthem" of the swing era, has a particularly tortuous history. The principle riff theme probably floated around for years before it was first recorded as "Tar Paper Stomp" by trumpeter Wingy Manone in 1930, with Manone listed as composer. The melody next shows up in 1931 on a Fletcher Henderson recording under the title "Hot and Anxious," credited to Don Redman. In 1938 the Edgar Hayes band recorded it as "In the Mood," listing the composer as Joe Garland, the band's saxophonist. That attribution has stuck ever since. In the following year Glenn Miller recorded his famous rendition, as arranged by Eddie Durham with Miller making some final adjustments. Reportedly Miller and Victor paid off Wingy Manone to drop a lawsuit.[33] In his autobiography, Manone says only, "I had a little legal fuss over it many years after I disked it."[34]

The adage that "success has a hundred fathers" could equally apply to Hoagy Carmichael's "Stardust." A persistent rumor holds that the song was the work of an itinerant black pianist, sometimes identified as Eltee Loving.[35] Loving, who attended Indiana University Law School at about the same time Carmichael was enrolled there, insisted throughout his entire life that he was the song's true composer. But Loving is not known for composing any other tunes, whereas Carmichael produced a string of hits, including "Georgia on My Mind," "Rockin' Chair," and "The Nearness of You," to name but a few. Others claimed to have written the verse of "Stardust," including Don Redman and even cornetist Sharkey

Bonano. But it's widely believed that Carmichael wrote the haunting tune, and especially the verse, under the spell of Bix Beiderbecke's romantic lyricism.

The example of Duke Ellington demonstrates the futility of assigning precise credit to compositions that originated from a variety of sources and developed over time. "Most of Duke's compositions from the 1920s and 1930s were composed with the musicians assisting," recalled Cootie Williams. "If any member of the band wrote a tune it was thought of as an honor for the band to play it; we didn't think of the money value or nothing like that. Everybody contributed something on their own also—[Juan] Tizol, [Johnny] Hodges, [Barney] Bigard, [Harry] Carney, and myself—but Duke would still get the credit and all the money. I did 'Echoes of Harlem' and 'Concerto for Cootie' and they were entirely mine, but Duke got his name on the label. I didn't mind."[36] As Ellington's son, Mercer, recounted, "Although Ellington was already established as a composer, he did not do very much writing in these formative years because of the men in the band who didn't read well. The arrangements were usually created orally, and I know that Mills used to complain when he had nothing on paper to copyright."[37]

Ellington recirculated his royalties back into the band's payroll and was able to keep his organization afloat even during the leanest times, such as the early 1950s, when almost every other big band leader had thrown in the towel. Some of Ellington's most loyal and longstanding musicians received extra pay for their contributions to the band's library. Many were happy with this arrangement but some, like Johnny Hodges, voiced displeasure. As Mercer Ellington wrote, "In the past, he [Hodges] had sold his rights to songs for $100 or $200, just as Fats Waller and Ellington had done when they were young and gullible. When Pop turned some of these songs into hits, Rab [Hodges's nickname was 'Rabbit'] wanted the deal changed, and when he was refused he became unhappy. That explains why he would sometimes turn toward the piano onstage and mime counting money."[38]

Ellington had learned the ins and outs of the publishing business from the slickest music mogul of the period, his own manager Irving Mills. (Mills and Ellington had an unusual business arrangement, described in the previous chapter.) Beyond holding publishing rights on Ellington's tunes, Mills also sometimes wrote, commissioned, or bought up lyrics that entitled him to a greater share of the royalties. Mills's name appears on such Ellington standards as "In a Sentimental Mood," "Mood Indigo," "Prelude to a Kiss," "Solitude," and "Sophisticated Lady."

The feisty valve-trombonist Juan Tizol managed to hold onto the rights for his compositions "Caravan" and "Perdido," but he was the exception. (According to Charles Mingus, Tizol once pulled a knife on him, ending the bass player's short engagement with the Ellington band.[39]) More typical were the Ellington-Bubber Miley collaborations, which, according to Miley's friend Roger Pryor Dodge, started out as Miley originals. Dodge reported that Miley got his inspiration for "Black and Tan Fantasy" from the spiritual "The Holy City," which his mother used to sing. (Nick LaRocca cited "The Holy City" as a source for "Tiger Rag," and musician and jazz scholar David Sager noted paraphrases of this spiritual in the Oliver-Armstrong composition "Canal Street Blues" as well as Oliver's "Chimes Blues."[40]) Dodge also wrote:

> Miley told me that the inspiration for the 'East St. Louis Toodle-Oo' came one night in Boston as he was returning home from work. He kept noticing the electric sign of the dry-cleaning store Lewandos. The name struck him as exceedingly funny and it ran through his head and fashioned itself into
>
> > Oh Le-wan—dos
> > Oh Le-wan—dos[41]

Clarinetist Barney Bigard said he brought Ellington "a slip of paper with some tunes" given to him by his old teacher from New Orleans, Lorenzo Tio Jr. On one tune, according to Bigard, "I changed some of it around, for instance the bridge on the second strain." Ellington wrote out another opening strain, mostly based on the harmony of Bigard's chorus but with some interesting twists.[42] Ellington then scored the melody for an unusual voicing of muted trumpet, trombone, and low-register clarinet, and the result was "Mood Indigo." Other tunes that originated from sidemen and were dressed up by Ellington include Harry Carney's "Rockin' in Rhythm" and Lawrence Brown and Otto Hardwick's "Sophisticated Lady."[43]

Saxophonist Rudy Jackson brought in another signature Ellington tune, which nearly resulted in a lawsuit. In 1923 Jackson participated in King Oliver's recording of the Oliver composition "Camp Meeting Blues." Presumably without telling Ellington its previous history, Jackson presented the tune as his own and shared writing credits with Ellington, who developed it in his own inimitable way. Released as "Creole Love Call," the piece earned Ellington his first significant hit.

King Oliver was moved to send the following letter, dated April 30, 1928, to the copyright department of Victor Records:

> Gentlemen,
>   I have recently listened to a recording by your company under the title of Creole Love Call, played by Duke Ellington's band.
>   Permit me to bring to your attention the fact that this number was written by me and copyrighted Oct. 11, 1923; #570230 under the title of Camp Meeting Blues.

The writer also recorded this particular number on the Columbia records and has collected royalties for same.

Will you, therefore, be good enough to forward me a contract covering Creole Love Call and should you desire further information, the same will be given, gladly.

Anticipating your earliest attention to this matter as well as a reply, I am

Very truly yours,
Jos. Oliver[44]

Sadly, Oliver's paperwork was not in order, as was the case for so many artists. The copyright number he lists is for "Temptation Blues," not "Camp Meeting Blues," which he may simply have never gotten around to registering.[45]

Ellington once ended up on the other end of a copyright controversy, ironically the victim of plagiarism by one of his sidemen, saxophonist Jimmy Forrest. In 1952 Forrest adapted a theme from "Happy-Go-Lucky Local," part of Ellington's *Deep South Suite*, into the hugely popular R&B tune "Night Train." Ellington initiated a suit, but a settlement for an undisclosed sum was negotiated out of court.[46]

"Satin Doll" gave rise to a bizarre lawsuit, initiated by the estate of Billy Strayhorn against the Ellington estate after both men had died. In an unusual decision, the court awarded Strayhorn half the composing credit for providing the harmonization to Ellington's melody.[47] During his lifetime Strayhorn was obliged to share composer credits with Ellington on several of his own tunes, such as "Day Dream." He did not seem particularly bothered about this and accepted their relationship as standard industry practice. But that would change in 1946 when Ellington was given sole credit for writing the score to the Broadway musical *Beggar's Holiday*, to which Strayhorn had contributed the lion's share of material. Strayhorn relocated to Paris and didn't work for Ellington again for another four years. In fairness to Ellington, it should be noted that he was always generous to Strayhorn and even granted him ten percent of his own publishing company, Tempo Music. Ellington was likewise lavish in his praise for Strayhorn, but nevertheless careless in giving specific credit for Strayhorn's work.[48]

Problems of attribution were compounded in the bebop era when many musicians were willing to sell tunes for instant cash in order to support drug habits. The standard procedure of cutting the bandleader in for a share of composer credits or publishing rights also remained widely accepted throughout the forties and fifties, and continues to a certain extent today, mostly in the pop field. Cootie Williams got his name on Thelonious Monk's "Round Midnight" by using the piece as his theme song. It is widely suspected that Coleman Hawkins, who employed Monk in his quartet, received credit for other Monk compositions, including "Stuffy," which Monk later recorded as "Stuffy Turkey." Hawkins also recorded Monk's "Hackensack" as "Rifftide," listing himself as composer. But Monk was not above doing some borrowing of his own, even from his friend, pianist Mary Lou Williams. A phrase from a Williams arrangement of "Lady Be Good" became Monk's "Hackensack" (or Hawkins's "Rifftide" if you prefer), and a phrase from the second chorus of her tune "Walkin' and Swingin'" evolved into "Rhythm-a-ning." "Eronel," attributed to Monk, was in fact composed by Idrees Sulieman and Sadik Hakim.[49]

Drummer Kenny Clarke maintained that "Epistrophy" began as his own composition "Fly Right"—originally recorded under that title in 1942—and that Monk only helped develop it.[50] Both share composer's credits, but the tune is typically thought of as a cornerstone of the Monk canon. What really riled Clarke, however, was not receiving credit for "Tenor Madness," usually attributed to Sonny Rollins. Clarke recorded this tune as early as 1946 under the title "Rue Chaptal," the street address of Hugues Panassié's Hot Club of France.

Another famous tune associated with Rollins, "St. Thomas," started out as the Danish folk song "Det Var En Lørdag Aften." The Virgin Islands were a Danish possession until 1917, and Rollins's grandmother, who hailed from St. Thomas, sang the tune to him as a child. Rollins first recorded it in 1956, but a year earlier pianist Randy Weston recorded his own version for Riverside under the title "Fire Down There." Weston performed the song as a calypso, like Rollins, but composer credits were listed as "traditional." Since the tune was in the public domain, Rollins was legally within his rights to retitle it and call it his own. Technically Rollins's "ownership" applies only to his rendition of the song. But since his version became so popular, his title stuck to subsequent recordings of the tune, and he continues to receive composer credit and royalties.

Within the Charlie Parker canon, "Ornithology" is typically credited to Parker, but was in fact written by trumpeter "Little" Benny Harris, who is sometimes listed as cocomposer. The tune does, however, begin with a quote from the opening lick of Bird's solo on "Jumpin' Blues."

Producer Teddy Reig explained how he "transformed" Charlie Parker's blues head "Now's the Time" into the R&B hit, "The Hucklebuck": "Of course it's almost the same as Bird's 'Now's the Time' but we were careful to change one note to make it different enough so we could get away with it."[51] Reig saw to it that the composition was registered under his own name. The tune took off and was quickly covered by Frank Sinatra, Pearl Bailey, and even Tommy Dorsey, earning much more than Parker's original piece. In actuality, Parker probably borrowed the original lick from a Lucky Millinder recording of "D Natural Blues," though again, this riff may have been around well before then.

There is a long history of record producers receiving copyright ownership in lieu of salary. Producers were originally known as Artists and Repertoire (A&R) men, indicating that record companies considered choosing the material as important as hiring the artists. A&R men were typically remunerated from a variety of legal and semi-legal sources, including direct payoffs from publishers and their song-pluggers. But often the A&R men simply demanded ownership of publishing and composer's rights as well. One of the first to perfect this technique was Mayo "Ink" Williams, whom we met in the previous chapter. He became manager of Paramount's publishing arm, Chicago Music, reputedly the first such company created by a record label.[52] Williams's many duties included securing artists, registering songs with the Library of Congress, and commissioning arrangements for sheet music and published stocks. He drew no salary but personally bought every song he published outright, paying independent songwriters $50 or $60 for each piece, and Paramount artists between $5 and $20. According to Stephen Calt, author of a fascinating profile on Williams, "The musicians and songwriters he worked with had no objection to selling their songs outright in this fashion; their credo, he said, was 'Give me mine now Mister Williams; whatever you make beyond that, that's yours.' On occasion he would give himself partial composer credit for a song he retouched, which usually amounted to no more than correcting the grammar."[53]

It would be a mistake to assume that all African-American artists parted with their royalties in exchange for the "privilege" of recording. Pianist, composer, and record producer Perry Bradford, who also ran his own publishing company, told of receiving an initial $10,000 royalty check for the 1920 Mamie Smith recording of his tunes "Crazy Blues" and "That Thing Called Love."[54] The worldwide success of "St. Louis Blues" has kept W. C. Handy's publishing company in business to this very day. In his autobiography, Handy tells of receiving a $1,857 check for just one recording of "Beale Street Blues," and as much as $7,000 in one year for "Yellow Dog Blues."[55]

The master of raking in profits by recording folk and mainstream artists and acquiring rights to their music was Ralph Peer. Peer created both the term and concept of "race" records in 1920, when he supervised the "Crazy Blues" session featuring Mamie Smith for OKeh Records. He later worked for Victor where, like Mayo Williams, he agreed to produce records for no salary, instead acquiring titles for his publishing company, Southern Music. Peer was a pioneer of location recordings and discovered many artists who otherwise would be lost to posterity. But in the process he enriched himself through ownership of publishing rights to the work of such well-known figures as Fats Waller, Jelly Roll Morton, Louis Armstrong, and Count Basie, plus scores of blues and hillbilly artists. Southern Music grew to be one of the most powerful concerns in the business, holding the publishing rights to such evergreens as "You Are My Sunshine" and Hoagy Carmichael's "Georgia on My Mind." In the 1950s Peer even branched into rock 'n' roll, holding the rights to the music of Buddy Holly and Little Richard.[56]

Richard Carpenter, who obtained his wealth from managing jazz musicians and gaining the rights to their music, was something of a legend in the jazz world. He earned enough to become perhaps the first African-American to have a home in the upscale suburb of Scarsdale, New York. He specialized in handling musicians with drug problems, such as Sonny Stitt and Chet Baker. His name is famously attached to Miles Davis's blues theme, "Walkin'," which was first recorded as "Gravy" and attributed to saxophonist Gene Ammons (though pianist Junior Mance swears he was present when Jimmy Mundy originally came up with the melody line). Carpenter for a brief period managed Dizzy Gillespie, who, in an odd turn of events, used Carpenter's strong-arm tactics to regain copyright ownership of tunes he had previously lost, such as "Con Alma."[57]

More than any other well-known musician, Miles Davis might have managed to put his name on a plethora of tunes he didn't in fact write. Davis did contribute to "Donna Lee," but more in the form of expanding on "Tiny's Con" by drummer Tiny Kahn from 1946. (Sometimes Charlie Parker is given composer credit for this tune as well.) But other compositions the trumpeter blatantly stole: Jackie McLean wrote "Dig"; "Chance It" was actually "Something for You" by Oscar Pettiford; "Serpent's Tooth" was by Jimmy Heath; "Tune Up" and "Four" were by Eddie "Cleanhead" Vinson; and "Solar," which is even inscribed on Davis's tombstone, was written by guitarist Chuck Wayne.

Miles Davis's bestselling album—and probably the bestselling jazz album of all time—is *Kind of Blue*.[58] According to the drummer on the album, Jimmy Cobb, "Actually, a lot of that stuff was composed in conjunction with Bill Evans."[59] Davis admits in his autobiography that some of the music was indeed collaborative. Evans always maintained that he was the sole writer of "Blue in Green," and said, "It's a small matter to me, but when someone asks me about it I tell the truth."[60] Likewise, arranger Gil Evans cowrote the tunes "Mademoiselle Mabry" and "Petit Machins" (which began life as Evans's tune "Eleven") for Davis's *Filles de Kilimanjaro* album without receiving credit.[61]

Guitarist John Scofield and Gil Evans both created material for Davis's 1983 album *Decoy* and didn't receive any rights to the music. Scofield recalled a conversation with Evans on the subject: "I asked Gil, 'How come Miles does that—takes the tunes and puts his own name to them, when you or I were involved in it?' See, I knew Gil had a history of that happening to him. And Gil said, 'Well, it's just fame, Miles wants the fame.' And I said, 'Well that's funny, because he's so famous already,' and Gil said, 'Yeah, but he really likes that fame.' And the way he said it, he wasn't judgmental at all—'Well you know, some people like spinach, some people really like this or that, that's what Miles likes.'"[62] In many other ways Davis showed generosity to Gil Evans, his lifelong friend and advisor. Their relationship was hugely beneficial to both, and now that they're gone, perhaps it's best to savor their music and let the publishing companies fight over who owns what.

Those who feel that African-Americans have overwhelmingly been victims of abuse at the hands of the music industry should take a hard look at the conflicting evidence. Exploitative behavior was often color-blind, with both whites and African-Americans as perpetrators and victims. Once again, the issue is not as simple as black and white.

NOTES

1. I thank Don Sickler, Dean Pratt, Phil Schaap, John Gill, Orange Kellin, Bill Kirchner, Michael Fitzgerald, Richard M. Sudhalter, and Frank Büchmann-Møller for providing much of the information contained in this section.

2. Those who question the government's role in subsidizing the arts through the NEA should note that promoting "the useful arts" appears in the Constitution even before the power to declare war and the formation of an army and navy.

3. In 1999, along with George Avakian, I supervised *The Re-Discovered Louis and Bix* (Nagel-Heyer CD 058), a recording that included nine Armstrong tunes that were duly registered but never recorded.

4. Southern, *The Music of Black Americans*, 311.

5. Sanjek and Sanjek, *American Popular Music Business in the 20th Century*, 36.

6. Russell, ed., *Oh, Mister Jelly*, 224.

7. Sanjek and Sanjek, 92; I do not mean to imply that all of BMI's policies are fair to jazz composers. In many ways, pop and classical writers are still favored by their accounting practices.

8. Interviews with Orange Kellin and John Gill, 2003.

9. Hogan Jazz Archive. DeDroit interview conducted December 4, 1969.

10. Handy, *Father of the Blues*, 99.

11. Brunn, *The Story of the Original Dixieland Jazz Band*, 86.

12. Brunn, 44–45.

13. Brunn, 75–86.

14. Brunn, 85.

15. Brian Rust, "The Original Dixieland Jazz Band: Creator of Jazz," *Jazz Journal International* 54, no. 12 (December 2001): 13.

16. Alan Lomax Library of Congress recordings, *Jelly Roll Morton: The Saga of Mr. Jelly Lord*, vol. 1, Circle LP L 14001.

17. Hogan Jazz Archive. Laine interview conducted May 23, 1960.

18. Charters, *Jazz New Orleans, 1885–1963*, 24.

19. Bergreen, *Louis Armstrong*, 128–129.

20. Wright, *"King" Oliver*, 258.

21. Brothers, ed., *Louis Armstrong, in His Own Words*, 132.

22. Berrett, ed., *The Louis Armstrong Companion*, 44.

23. Brothers, ed., 131, 136.

24. Pastras, *Dead Man Blues*, 144.

25. Collins and Collins, *Oh, Didn't He Ramble*, 38.

26. Harrison Smith, "The 'Fabelous' Jelly Roll," *Record Research* 2, no. 5, issue 11 (January–February 1957): 9, and "Debunking Jelly Roll," *Record Research* 3, no. 1, issue 13 (June–July 1957): 5.

27. Interviews with Orange Kellin and John Gill, 2003.

28. Brothers, ed., 136.

29. Russell, ed., 312.

30. Russell, ed., 179.

31. Taped interviews with Dean Pratt and Don Sickler, and Phil Schapp, 2003

32. Singer, *Black and Blue*, 209–212.

33. Taped interview with Dean Pratt and Don Sickler, 2003.

34. Manone and Vandervoort, *Trumpet on the Wing*, 79.

35. This information on Eltee Loving is taken from Barbara Brown Meyer, "The Melody Haunts My Reverie: The 'True' Story of Stardust," *IAJRC Journal* 34, no. 1 (Winter 2001): 39–41. Carmichael never mentioned Loving by name in either of his two autobiographies, but did mention that during his student days in Bloomington, Indiana, he and "a young black musician with a soul for jazz" would sit "far into the night, exchanging ideas and doodling on the piano."

36. Eric Townley, "Reminiscing with Cootie," *Storyville* 71 (June–July 1977): 170–174.

37. Mercer Ellington, *Duke Ellington in Person*, 42.

38. Mercer Ellington, 109–110.

39. Mingus, *Beneath the Underdog*, 324.

40. David Sager, liner notes to *King Oliver: The Complete 1923 Jazz Band Recordings*, Archeophone CD OTR-MM6-C2.

41. Dodge, *Hot Jazz and Jazz Dance*, 86.

42. Bigard, *With Louis and the Duke*, 64.

43. Taped interviews with Dean Pratt and Don Sickler, and Phil Schapp, 2003. Confirmation for "Sophisticated Lady" comes in a Rutgers/NEA Oral History Project interview with Lawrence Brown done in 1976. Brown says, "Mainly I had the theme, which I played all the time, which is the first eight bars, and Otto Hardwick played the release."

44. Wright, 26.

45. Wright, 27.

46. Nicholson, *Reminiscing the Tempo*, 322

47. *Tempo Music v. Famous Music*, 838 Supp. 162 (S.D.N.Y. 1993).

48. The personal and business relationship between Ellington and Strayhorn is well documented in David Hajdu's Strayhorn biography, *Lush Life* (New York: Farrar Straus Giroux, 1996).

49. Taped interviews with Dean Pratt and Don Sickler, and Phil Schapp, 2003.

50. Gitler, *Jazz Masters of the Forties*, 177.

51. Reig and Berger, *Reminiscing in Tempo*, 32.

52. Stephen Calt, "The Anatomy of a 'Race' Music Label: May Williams and Paramount Records," *78 Quarterly* 1, nos. 3–4 (1989). Reprinted in *Rhythm and Business*, ed. Norman Kelley, 86–111.

53. Calt, "The Anatomy of a 'Race' Music Label."

54. Bradford, *Born with the Blues*, 138.

55. Handy, 132, 198.

56. Sanjek and Sanjek, 22–23.

57. Taped interview with Dean Pratt and Don Sickler, 2003.

58. Kahn, *Kind of Blue*, 16.

59. Kahn, 98.

60. Pettinger, *Bill Evans*, 82.

61. Hicock, *Castles Made of Sound*, 161–162, 198.

62. Hicock, 224.

10

_~_

Show Me the Money

"How warm is the bread?"

—Lester Young

How much have pay scales really differed across racial lines? Is it true that white musicians have more often than not been the beneficiaries of higher paying work?

For jazz researchers, written contracts and payroll sheets are almost nonexistent. The musicians' unions, such as New York's Local 802, tend to throw away old paperwork, especially in the course of changing locations. As Alfred Appel Jr. rightly notes, "Potential jazz historians and biographers are deprived of what serious scholars take for granted—a paper trail of letters, diaries, and so forth."[1] Especially in regard to money, all we have to rely on are the often faulty memories of the musicians themselves. Sometimes two musicians will give different figures for the same job, even when band members were paid equally. There are inevitable gaps, and when amounts are recalled the time frame is often unclear. Some people like to discuss financial matters and others don't. Bandleaders almost never do, while sidemen can be quite garrulous, but at times unreliable. So we should take the figures I list as a guide; they are not meant to be definitive.

Going back to New Orleans in the first decades of the twentieth century, it appears that black and white musicians earned pretty much the same amount of money for the same kind of work. According to Samuel Charters, "For a night's work, from 8 to 4, they [black musicians] got $1.50 or $2.00 and free wine, but tips ran as high as $15 a piece."[2] Peter Bocage confirms that he received $2 a night working at the Tuxedo.[3] Given the long hours, these figures seem absurdly low until we realize that a beer in the same places cost a nickel.

Whereas the average "tonk" paid in the range of $7 to $10 a week, King Oliver reportedly made $25 at Pete Lala's.[4] Jelly Roll Morton, who was given to exaggeration, claimed his tips at Lulu White's Mahogany Hall, an upscale brothel, ran as high as $100 a night.

Jazz historian Lawrence Gushee writes, "Certainly the saloon keepers were not indulging in affirmative action." Gushee also wonders if black bands were favored in Storyville partly because they were "substantially less expensive than those of white musicians."[5] But evidence suggests this was not the case. Tony Sbarbaro, former drummer with the ODJB, said that when he worked at Tom Anderson's, "You got a buck and a half to play. I don't think anybody got over $2."[6] Pay for parades was better, according to both black and white musicians; Roy Palmer recalled getting $2 per hour.[7]

So it would seem that musicians, regardless of color, made roughly the same money working the same kinds of jobs. Kid Ory was doing so well that when he decided to leave New Orleans for California in 1919, he had to return $500 in deposits for work he cancelled.[8]

As black bands became favored in white society circles, their earnings often outpaced white bands. In Boston, James Reese Europe's brother John led the band in the Copley Plaza, the largest and most luxurious hotel in the city. In 1915 a white musician wrote a letter to the *Boston Globe* complaining of losing lucrative work to black bands. This letter was reprinted in the black-circulation *New York Age*, and James Weldon Johnson fired off a reply: "It might be thought that black musicians are simply cheaper to hire, but the white musician does not make this claim because he knows it is not so. The fact is that black musicians charge more, and are still preferred."[9]

It is frequently lamented in the jazz literature that the Original Creole Band, whose personnel was African-American, didn't get the distinction of being the first jazz band to record. They were offered the opportunity in 1916 by the prestigious Victor Company, the same label that signed the Original Dixieland Jazz Band a year later. There are various accounts as to why this invitation was rebuffed. Most claim that the band's cornetist, Freddie Keppard, was afraid that other cornetists would steal his ideas, or that mass-producing the band's music would limit its commercial viability. Others simply maintain that financial terms couldn't be worked out to the satisfaction of the band.

Were the Creoles offered less money to record than the white ODJB? In his book *Buddy Bolden and the Last Days of Storyville*, guitarist Danny Barker cites a conversation he had with George Baquet, the clarinetist with the Creole Band. Baquet described how, during an intermission at an engagement at the Winter Garden Theater in New York, "The Victor official approached Keppard for the fifth time and handed him a contract to sign. The contract specified that Freddie would receive $25 and the sidemen would be paid $15 to record four songs. Freddie yelled at the official: 'Take this piece of paper and shove it up your rear. Do I look like a goddam fool? Why, I buy that much whiskey a day.'"[10] This contract failed to provide for royalties, and both Baquet and Keppard felt that Victor was in a position to offer substantially better terms.

I have been unable to locate a copy of the original Victor contract for the ODJB, but I did find one for the series of recordings they did for the same company in 1921. This contract, dated December 1, 1920, stipulates a payment of $416.67 for the satisfactory completion of twelve selections, with no further obligations (meaning no royalties paid) by the record company.[11] If we do the math, the ODJB was paid $34.66 per title. For these sessions the band had six members, having added a saxophone. If we assume the money was divided equally, each band member would have received $5.77 per selection, or $23.11 for four selections. This is better than the $15 offered the sidemen in the Creole Band, but less than Keppard's take of $25. However, the ODJB contract came on the heels of their proven success with Victor, and it was tendered four years after the one offered the Creoles, who had no preexisting track record. In this light the differences are not very significant.

With some reservations, we can also compare the income of King Oliver's Creole Jazz Band at the Lincoln Gardens with that of the New Orleans Rhythm Kings, a white band, at the Friar's Inn. These were the two most important and influential jazz bands of the early twenties. Their engagements were roughly contemporaneous, and the two Chicago venues were only some thirty blocks apart. The Lincoln Gardens accommodated larger crowds, but the Friar's Inn was more expensive, catering to gangsters and "big money men."

Oliver's band eventually broke up because of financial disagreements concerning both the Lincoln Gardens and their recording work. Lil Hardin, along with Johnny and Baby Dodds, discovered that the management of the Gardens intended for each musician to receive $95 a week, but Oliver was only paying them $75. In addition, Oliver refused to divulge how much money he was making from the band's recordings, though as leader he had no formal obligation to do so.[12] Al Monroe, a manager at the Lincoln Gardens, recalled paying the Oliver band "under $1,000 weekly."[13] If we accept Hardin's figure of $95, then the club paid $665 weekly for the seven sidemen. Oliver's fee as leader is unknown, but it was probably in the neighborhood of $200, at least double the figure for the sidemen. This would mean a total weekly outlay of around $865 for the band. Oliver's wife, Stella, stated that her husband was the highest paid bandleader in Chicago at the time, and his take may even have been higher.

The New Orleans Rhythm Kings were a cooperative band, so the money was divided evenly. Joe Mares, brother of the NORK's cornetist Paul Mares, said that individual band members received $90 a week.[14] Trombonist George Brunis, whose memory for facts and figures could be faulty, recalled being paid $125 per week.[15] Drummer Ben Pollack thought he got $50. If the $90 figure is correct, then both bands received roughly the same amounts, with Oliver's leader's fee possibly tipping the scales in his favor.

Up until the mid-twenties, pay for black and white musicians appears to be roughly equivalent. White groups working in Chicago hotels—including bands booked by Edgar Benson, Ben Bernie and Isham Jones—paid in the neighborhood of $50 a man per week, a respectable but hardly spectacular figure.[16] Similar numbers are cited for black bands playing in the black-and-tans. Cab Calloway started out making $50 a week as a singer at the Dreamland Café in Chicago, and $65 at the Sunset.[17] Sonny Greer's starting salary with Duke Ellington at the Cotton Club in 1927 was reportedly $45, though apparently it nearly doubled in just a few years.

Some black musicians did better, some worse. In 1923 banjoist Elmer Snowden received $40 a week as leader of the band at the Hollywood Club in New York; his sidemen, including a young Duke Ellington, got $35.[18] A few years later, Milt Hinton took a job with violinist Eddie South in a white hotel in downtown Chicago for $75 a week.[19] Jelly Roll Morton, relying on freelance bookings from white clients, was able to pay his sidemen between $80 and $90 weekly in the mid-twenties.[20]

Louis Armstrong and Baby Dodds earned $50 a week on the riverboats, in addition to room and board. They also received an end-of-the-week $5 bonus as an incentive to stay on the job.[21] Fletcher Henderson hired Louis at a salary of $55, and Lil Hardin lured him back to Chicago with an offer of $75 to work at the Dreamland Café.[22] Riding the popularity of his Hot Five and Hot Seven recordings, Armstrong became a bandleader in his own right and appeared at the Sunset from April 1926 to November 1927. His salary there remains a mystery, but he reportedly earned $200 a week for himself at Chicago's Savoy Ballroom.[23]

The second half of the 1920s witnessed a dramatic increase in the salaries of successful commercial white bands. A 1927 salary sheet from Jean Goldkette's orchestra shows Bix Beiderbecke earning $123.50 per week. A similar payroll sheet from Paul Whiteman's orchestra, dated January 20, 1928, lists Beiderbecke at $200. Other Whiteman sidemen made as much as $350, but of course Whiteman led the highest earning and paying band in the country at that time.[24]

In the late twenties, some white musicians made extraordinary incomes from a steady round of recordings, radio broadcasts, and live performances. Two of the most successful white musicians of the era were Benny Goodman and Jack Teagarden. By any measure they did quite well, even in the depths of the Depression. Both worked for Ben Pollack from the late 1920s to 1931; their exact salary is not known, and it probably fluctuated depending on the band's engagements. But it was reported that in 1928 Teagarden made as much as $250 a week, a figure that included both his sideman work and his many freelance record dates. By adding pit band work to his already busy schedule he was able to pull in as much as $500 a week.[25]

Goodman worked for a time with Isham Jones in 1927 and reportedly earned $175 per week. This is the same figure he made in 1930 as a member of the pit band at the Paramount Theater in New York.[26] By 1931 he was making $350 to $450 a week from radio staff work, Broadway shows, single engagements, and recordings (of which very few were jazz-related).[27] By 1933 Goodman found his freelance work disappearing, as radio leaned toward hiring name bandleaders.

The most successful black bandleaders of the era, such as Duke Ellington, Cab Calloway, and Fletcher Henderson, were able to pay salaries of around $100 by the end of the 1920s, though individual figures differed according to seniority. Reportedly Coleman Hawkins was making an average of $150 per week with Henderson in 1930.[28] But musicians working in black-and-tans were also paid in tips. "It didn't really matter what the salary was," Ellington said. "A big bookmaker like Meyer Boston would come in late and the first thing he'd do was change $20 into half dollars. Then he'd throw the whole thing at the feet of whoever was singing or playing or dancing."[29] Barney Bigard recalled customers tipping as much as $100.[30] White musicians playing in dance halls, hotels, or theaters were probably rarely tipped.

Duke Ellington was typically tight-lipped about his business affairs, but Cab Calloway left a wealth of financial information in his autobiography, which provides insight into Ellington's finances as well. In 1930 Calloway began his run at the Cotton Club as a paid employee making $200 a week. After a successful year his salary was raised to $500, and as already stated, his sidemen earned in the neighborhood of $100. By the end of 1931 Calloway was making an additional $26,000 a year by virtue of being made a partner in Cab Calloway, Inc., a corporation formed by Irving Mills. A few years later, in the depths of the Depression, Calloway's share reached $50,000 a year. Undoubtedly Ellington was making more than that, and his salaries kept pace with Calloway's. By the end of the thirties, Calloway's musicians were earning $200 a week, with two-week paid vacations at Christmas time.[31]

Ellington and Calloway were at the top of the food chain, and other black bands didn't fare nearly as well. In Chicago, Al Capone "chained Earl Hines to a $150 a week contract that was constructed to last forever," according to Chicago jazz historian Dempsey Travis. "Capone, through his Grand Terrace manager [Ed Fox], had a contract with Hines that literally would not permit Hines to use his own name if he attempted to leave the Grand Terrace plantation."[32] Hines's Grand Terrace engagement lasted all the way from December 1928 until 1939. As noted, his sidemen made between $70 and $90 per week.

Louis Armstrong also had problems extricating himself from a gangland contract at Connie's Inn, and eventually relocated to Europe to avoid trouble. During the years 1931 to 1933, before leaving for Europe, he was mostly on the road doing one-nighters with a ten-piece band. A young Teddy Wilson played piano with the band and recalled getting $40 a week. At the same time, said Wilson, "Armstrong had made a deal with his manager under which he was earning 1500 dollars a week."[33] It's more than likely that this figure covered expenses for the entire band.

Black musicians also freelanced at private parties, which at times could be extremely lucrative. Claude Hopkins told of playing at a party for the daughter of industrialist Andrew Mellon, and earning $250 plus a $200 tip. The family was so pleased with his performance that they gave Hopkins six bottles of imported champagne and sent him home in their chauffeur-driven Rolls Royce.[34]

Garvin Bushell told of a time he and Fats Waller played a private concert for an audience of one: Mr. W. K. Vanderbilt. According to Bushell, Vanderbilt told them, "I'd give anything in the world just to be free to do like you guys. I don't know how to have fun." Waller stood up and replied, "Mr. W. K., you give me some of your money and I'll show you how to have some fun!"[35]

Many musicians amassed small fortunes during the twenties only to be wiped out by the crash of October 1929. Bix Beiderbecke's biographer Jean Pierre Lion estimates the cornetist made as much as $25,000 during his two-year tenure with Paul Whiteman.[36] He dutifully sent much of his earnings to his sister for her to invest in the stock market, but the money disappeared almost overnight, just when he was without steady employment. Red Nichols made untold sums working in radio and recording studios, in addition to directing pit bands for Broadway shows. But in 1931, with much of his accumulated wealth gone, he suffered a breakdown due to overwork and landed in the hospital with pleurisy.

The Depression was hard on black and white musicians alike. "In 1933 I didn't get a single gig the entire summer," recalled trumpeter Max Kaminsky.[37] A few months later Kaminsky managed to find a job in Joe Venuti's band. "I had my own private bread line outside Delmonico's every night that spring of 1934," the trumpeter wrote. "Promptly at nine o'clock, during intermission, I'd be at the side door with a pocket of fifty-cent pieces for the out-of-work musicians waiting in the cold: Pee Wee Russell, Eddie Condon, Bud Freeman and his brother Arnie, Buzzy Drootin's brother Al, Freddy Goodman, Benny Goodman's brother—sometimes it seemed like everybody and his brother."

Throughout the thirties, any misgivings white middle-class parents may have had about their sons or daughters becoming professional musicians were overridden by the need for hard cash. "I never had to ask my parents for money, even in the Depression," related bassist Bob Haggart. "There was work for musicians so my parents didn't look down on it."[38] The lucky ones received a steady salary; Muggsy Spanier and George Brunis earned as much as $250 a week from Ted Lewis, the "High-Hatted Tragedian" of vaudeville fame. But to earn it they had to dispense the most banal brand of corn.

By contrast, Ellington sailed through the hard times. "The money kept getting better and better," related his clarinetist Barney Bigard. "We worked clean through the Depression without ever knowing there was one. I guess we were one of the best-paid, best-known bands in the USA."[39] In 1933 Ellington's manager, Irving Mills, also secured work for the band in Europe, where economic conditions were markedly better.

But for legions of musicians, both white and black, steady work was a thing of the past. Many sought other forms of employment and never worked professionally in music again. Others took what they could find for much less money than they were getting only a few years before. Black musicians were especially hard hit during the Depression. In 1933 Garvin Bushell worked at the Rosemont Ballroom in Brooklyn for $38 a week, and the Arcadia Ballroom in midtown for $47. The following year he took a job with Fletcher Henderson at Roseland, where salaries had remained fixed at $50 a week.[40]

One source of resentment among black musicians was the fact that Roseland paid a higher scale than the Savoy. The Savoy was the larger venue, but its entrance fees were lower: Roseland charged over a dollar, whereas the Savoy could be as low as thirty-five cents. Sideman scale at Roseland was around $50 a week, while the Savoy offered only $35 to $40. It was widely suspected that the difference resulted from the clientele: Roseland catered to whites, the Savoy to blacks. It wasn't until late 1943 that scale at the Savoy was upped to the $50 mark, achieving parity with the downtown ballrooms. (However low the scale at the Savoy or on 52nd Street, the trio at Monroe's in Harlem—consisting of Al Tinney, Leonard Gaskin and Max Roach—was paid only $2 per man per night in 1940.)[41]

Another source of resentment was the growing field of live radio work, for which salaried staff positions were available only to whites. But there was yet another economic wedge that drove white and black musicians apart in the thirties. The "swing era" was a time when all bands, regardless of race, had to appeal to a broad range of popular tastes. Black bands lost business to white bands that weren't expected to stick strictly to jazz. But how did this play out in terms of dollars and cents?

When Benny Goodman achieved his initial success as a bandleader in the mid-thirties, he was able to offer his sidemen $100 a week, in the neighborhood of what Cab Calloway and Duke Ellington were paying. Over the next few years Goodman kept this figure as a base but offered his stars considerably more: Harry James, who had been making $75 with Ben Pollack a few years before,[42] reached $250 per week; Gene Krupa topped out at $500; and Lionel Hampton beat them both by earning $750.[43]

Many big bands that went on to commercial success started out paying low salaries. When Max Kaminsky began working for Artie Shaw he received only $65 a week, while the other men were making as little as $45.[44] A few years later, with some hit records to his credit, Shaw was able to offer his men in the neighborhood of $185.

Harry James, having established a reputation from his work with Goodman, initially offered his sidemen $85.[45] Frank Sinatra's first paycheck was for $75 at a time when band singers typically earned less than musicians. But circumstances for James got worse before they got better. The band began losing money in its first year at an astounding rate of $15,000 per week, and all salaries were reduced to $75. Only income from record royalties prevented James from filing for bankruptcy. By September, 1941, after nearly three years of hard work, he was still $42,000 in debt. Tommy Dorsey lured Sinatra away with a better offer of $125 a week. James's luck finally turned around in 1941, when he scored a hit with the pop ballad "You Made Me Love You." For that year James paid only $25 in income taxes; success came so fast that for 1943 he owed $620,000, having grossed over a million dollars.[46]

As noted, Fats Waller thrived from a combination of live appearances, movies, recordings, and radio broadcasts. When he died in 1943, he was reportedly earning $5,000 a week. Of course very few other black performers generated anything near that figure. Chick Webb paid his musicians $75 a week at the Savoy until his premature death in 1939. Second-tier bands, like those of Lucky Millinder, Erskine Hawkins, and Cootie Williams, gave their sidemen only around $40 per week.[47]

A few territory bands did better than New York bands, but most didn't. Alphonso Trent, working primarily in the society field around Dallas, was able to pay his musicians $150 a week and sometimes as much as $300. But Count Basie's musicians were earning between $18 to $22 at the Reno in Kansas City.[48] That figure rose to $75 a week in 1936 after Basie came to New York and signed with MCA. Drummer Gus Johnson remembered making only $16 a week with Jay McShann's band around Kansas City; Johnson's bandmate, the young Charlie Parker, probably got the same amount.

Lionel Hampton was notorious for underpaying his musicians. He often denied them a steady salary, paying them on a per-job basis instead. In 1940 Hampton paid $11 per job; by 1951 this figure had only risen to $17.[49] By contrast, in 1953 pianist Marty Napoleon was earning $300 a week as a sideman with Louis Armstrong's All Stars, reputedly the highest paying band fronted by an African-American at that time.[50]

Yearly income figures for the leading big bands of the early forties, as reported in the trade papers, broke down as follows. Kay Kyser's sweet and novelty band led the pack by grossing over $1,000,000. (I haven't located the figures, but I suspect others in the sweet category, such as Guy Lombardo and Wayne King, neared or even exceeded that figure.) Glenn Miller, Goodman, and Shaw each came in around $700,000, while Bob Crosby was about $300,000. In 1944 Cab Calloway grossed $750,000; Ellington $600,000; Basie $400,000; and Lionel Hampton $350,000.[51] What's remarkable about these figures is that the income gap between black and white bands was not as severe as one might expect, given the lack of commercial radio sponsorship available to African-American groups.

The clubs along 52nd Street tended to pay only union scale, which for most of the mid-thirties was around $40 weekly for sidemen and $60 for the leader. Musicians who developed significant drawing power were able to negotiate much better salaries. Reportedly, Art Tatum was the highest paid instrumentalist ever to work on the street, earning as much as $1,150 per week for his trio. Coleman Hawkins and his group received $900 per week at the Downbeat Club in 1945. Billie Holiday's fee at Kelly's Stable shot up from $175 to $1,250 over the course of only a few years.[52]

By the end of the war, salaries in general seemed to increase dramatically. As drummer Johnny Blowers recalled, "On 52nd Street you could almost name your price. The money was very good—a couple of hundred a week [for a sideman]."[53] At Café Society, owner Barney Josephson paid his musicians well: Red Allen received $150 a week, and trombonist J. C. Higginbotham earned $200.[54] When Charlie Parker was booked into Billy Berg's club in Los Angeles in 1945, he also reportedly earned $200 a week.[55]

George Wein's average weekly budget for his Boston club, Storyville, was $1,000 in the early fifties, but many artists were paid significantly more. Johnny Hodges asked for and received $1,750. George Shearing, on the strength of his hit recording of "September in the Rain," got $2,500. This same figure was paid to Ella Fitzgerald, but Sarah Vaughan earned even more: $2,750. Dave Brubeck, who had yet to score his first hit, accepted an offer of $800 for the week, out of which he had to pay for his band's transportation, hotel, and agency commission. Ellington topped the list at $4,000, which included working a six-night week plus a Sunday matinee.[56]

In 1961 Nat Hentoff reported salaries for the New York jazz clubs of the time: "In some of the Greenwich Village jazz clubs, scale is as low as $76 for a six-day week (Local 802 is seldom militant for its jazz constituents). Birdland in midtown pays about $130 for a six-day week, as does the Roundtable with hours from 8:15 to 2:30 or 9:45 to 3:45. A sideman can get all of $154 for a six-night week."[57] Of course the most successful leaders were able to negotiate considerably more.

Hentoff also offered a fascinating glimpse into the economic life of a working band, in this case a struggling unit formed by Cannonball Adderley in 1956:

> "Cannonball," during his first expeditions as a leader, was getting $1,000 a week for five men. As he recalls, 'Out of that came $150 commission for my manager and booking office, $75 in union taxes (a third of which we eventually got back), and about $125 in Federal withholding taxes, and maybe another $15 is social security taxes. Now we should have deposited the money due the government in a separate account every week. But after a while, we began spending that money because we also had gasoline bills, hotel bills (for my brother and myself). We were paying the sidemen $125 out of which they had to pay their hotel bills. By September of the next year, 1957, although we had been working steadily, we were about $9,000 in debt. We had no royalties from our recordings and had only made scale for making them. Besides, a lot of recording costs were charged against us, which shouldn't have been. The band had not been particularly successful in that we had done about the same amount of business all the time. Very few clubs lost money on us, but they didn't make a hell of a lot either. We finally broke up that first band. After twenty months, we still couldn't get more than $1,000 a week.
>
> Adderley then spent two years as a featured sideman with Miles Davis, became better known, and started a band again in 1959. His quintet now gets a minimum of $1,000 for a one-nighter, averages $1,500 to $2,000 a week, and is gradually moving into the $2,500-a-week category.[58]

As Adderley scored more hits his income rose dramatically.

The figure of $1,250 a week seems to have been something of an industry standard for many of the better-known jazz groups in the early and mid-fifties. That's the sum Lester Young earned for a week at Birdland, and also what Charlie Parker was paid for a week at the Showboat Club in Philadelphia. Parker's contract, dated June 25, 1954, specified that the $1,250 was for himself as leader plus four other musicians, working a six-day week from Monday through Saturday.[59] George Wein also paid Miles Davis and his group $1,250 for a week at Storyville in 1955.[60] "The economics of jazz were such that it was difficult for *anyone* to keep a band," noted Wein.[61] In 1956 Davis, with John Coltrane in his quintet, was still earning $1,250 a week for clubs and $1,000 a night for individual concerts. "I was taking $400 a week for myself out of that and dividing the rest with the group," said Davis. He told his manager, Jack Whittemore, to up his price to $2,500 per week for nightclub appearances: "A lot of club owners got mad at me for that but they gave me what I wanted."[62]

By 1961 the Miles Davis quintet got as much as $3,500 for one set at a major festival, $2,500 to $3,500 for most concerts, and $3,500 to $4,000 for a week in a club.[63] (In the same year, the *New Yorker* reported that Dave Brubeck's quartet was "the world's best-paid" jazz group, grossing "a couple of hundred thousand dollars a year.")[64] In 1971 Davis earned $130,000 for a summer tour involving twenty-six dates. In 1981 (as Brubeck's popularity and earnings were waning) George Wein paid Davis $70,000 for a single concert at Avery Fisher Hall in New York.[65] With a town house in Manhattan and property in Malibu, Miles Davis became one of the few millionaire jazz musicians, but he wasn't the only one.

The director of a major international festival, who asked to remain anonymous, supplied me with figures for some of the foremost jazz artists as of the early 2000s. This money generally pays for the entire band for one performance only, with the festival picking up travel and accommodation expenses. Bear in mind that these prices are often negotiable, and can fluctuate in accordance with the artist's popularity.

The breakdown was as follows. Dave Douglas received around $5,000, with the Bad Plus and Regina Carter in the $5,000 to $7,000 range. James Carter got $7,000, and Nicholas Payton and Joe Lovano up to $10,000. Roy Hargrove received $10,000 to $12,000; Joshua Redman $12,000 to $15,000; Branford Marsalis $15,000 to $20,000; and Maria Schneider's big band $17,500 and up. McCoy Tyner and his group went for $12,000, and Chick Corea received $15,000.

In the very upper reaches of the jazz business, Pat Metheny and Dave Brubeck both went for $30,000; Wynton Marsalis got $30,000 to $40,000, with the Lincoln Center Jazz Orchestra upping the price tag to $50,000 or $60,000; Herbie Hancock, Sonny Rollins, and Ornette Coleman were in the $50,000 to $70,000 range; and Keith Jarrett and the late Oscar Peterson topped the list with an asking price of $100,000.

These figures make clear that a good number of African-American musicians continue to be well-rewarded, both critically and financially, for their work; and that within the jazz world, they make up the majority of top-tier artists, certainly as far as income is concerned.

To be sure, some white jazz musicians, such as Benny Goodman, Dave Brubeck, and Chick Corea, have done extremely well financially, but they have been the exceptions. More representative of the rank and file would be the clarinetist Pee Wee Russell, who died in 1969. Russell took in only $1,500 over the last two years of his life, despite consistently placing at the top of jazz polls.[66] Eddie Edwards, the trailblazing trombonist of the ODJB, ended up working at a newsstand on West 57th Street, across from Carnegie Hall. The once hugely influential Miff Mole reportedly was reduced to selling pencils on the street.[67] Surely it's time to give the old canard that white jazz musicians have consistently out-earned blacks a rest (if not a Viking funeral).

I, for one, think the sums cited above for festivals are generally well deserved, and would welcome seeing many other artists break through to these esteemed and well-paid ranks. But my point here is that once again, the old cliché of African-American artists invariably suffering at the hands of white businessmen is not borne out by the evidence. A great many black musicians have done just fine by any standard.

NOTES

1. Appel, *Jazz Modernism*, 60.
2. Charters, *Jazz New Orleans*, 18.
3. Hogan Jazz Archive. Bocage interview conducted January 29, 1959.
4. Wright, *"King" Oliver*, 3.
5. Gushee, *Pioneers of Jazz*, 32.
6. Hogan Jazz Archive. Sbarbaro and Emile Christian interview conducted February 11, 1959.
7. Hogan Jazz Archive. Palmer interview conducted September 22, 1955.
8. Hogan Jazz Archive. Ory interview conducted April 20, 1957.
9. Badger, *A Life in Ragtime*, 122.
10. Barker, *Buddy Bolden and the Last Days of Storyville*, 136.
11. This contract is from the Vince Giordano collection.
12. Wright, 37.
13. Wright, 12.
14. Sudhalter, *Lost Chords*, 30.
15. Dan Havens and Thomas B. Gilmore, "Conversations with George Brunis," *Mississippi Rag*, September 1998, 4.
16. Kenney, *Chicago Jazz*, 84.
17. Calloway and Rollins, *Of Minnie the Moocher & Me*, 58–59.
18. Dance, *The World of Swing*, 53.
19. Hinton and Berger, *Bass Line*, 45.
20. Lomax, *Mister Jelly Roll*, 211.
21. Dodds and Gara, *The Baby Dodds Story*, 22.
22. Berrett, ed., *The Louis Armstrong Companion*, 40–41.
23. Bergreen, *Louis Armstrong*, 307.
24. Evans and Evans, *Bix*, 277, 321.
25. Smith and Guttridge, *Jack Teagarden*, 59.
26. Goodman and Kolodin, *The Kingdom of Swing*, 64, 102.
27. Firestone, *Swing, Swing, Swing*, 65.

28. DeVeaux, *The Birth of Bebop*, 86.

29. Haskins, *The Cotton Club*, 58.

30. Bigard, *With Louis and the Duke*, 51.

31. Calloway and Rollins, 78, 110.

32. Travis, *An Autobiography of Black Jazz*, 45.

33. Teddy Wilson, *Teddy Wilson Talks Jazz*, 15.

34. Vaché, *Crazy Fingers*, 29.

35. Bushell, *Jazz from the Beginning*, 80.

36. Lion, *Bix*, 234.

37. Kaminsky, *My Life in Jazz*, 57.

38. Taped interview with Bob Haggart, 1995.

39. Bigard, 52.

40. Bushell, 84–89.

41. DeVeaux, 232.

42. Levinson, *Trumpet Blues*, 55.

43. Hampton, *Hamp*, 54, 68.

44. Kaminsky, 97.

45. Levinson, 61, 68.

46. Levinson, 89, 142.

47. Dance, *The World of Swing*, 88.

48. Basie and Murray, *Good Morning Blues*, 202.

49. Bryant et al., eds., *Central Avenue Sounds*, 41, 72.

50. Taped interview with Marty Napoleon, 2000.

51. Berger, Berger, and Patrick, *Benny Carter*, 239. This information was derived from *Billboard*, February 3, 1945, 13–15.

52. DeVeaux, 286, 385, 388.

53. Taped interview with Johnny Blowers, 2000.

54. Chilton, *Ride Red Ride*, 110.

55. Colette, *Jazz Generations*, 106.

56. Wein, *Myself Among Others*, 82, 93, 159.

57. Hentoff, *The Jazz Life*, 51.

58. Hentoff, 57.

59. A copy of this contract is reproduced (in very small print) in Saks and Vail, *The Norman R. Saks Collection*, 25.

60. Dance, *The World of Earl Hines*, 158.

61. Wein, 458.

62. Davis, *Miles*, 201–213.

63. Hentoff, 54.

64. Robert Rice, "The Cleanup Man: Profile of Dave Brubeck," *New Yorker*, June 3, 1961.

65. Wein, 464–468.

66. John McDonough, liner notes to *Giants of Jazz: Pee Wee Russell*, Time-Life Records, TL-J17.

67. Sudhalter, *Lost Chords*, 129.

11

*

Is Everything About Race?

"Relations between Negroes and whites, like any other province of human experience, demand honesty and insight; they must be based on the assumption that there is one race and that we are all part of it."

—James Baldwin

A guitarist friend of mine named Joel Perry once traveled to Africa as the only white member of the Johnny Copeland Blues Band. Or so he thought. An African guest at a diplomatic get-together asked why there were so many whites in the group. Apparently this perfectly well-intentioned individual was not aware of America's Byzantine racial traditions, which stipulate that anyone with a single drop of black blood is considered black. This African gentleman had just the opposite viewpoint: anyone with white blood was white. This unexpected racial reclassification was certainly news to my friend, and even more so to the African-Americans in his band.

The "one-drop" rule became a legally sanctioned means of classifying people by race as a result of the 1896 *Plessy v. Ferguson* Supreme Court ruling and other rulings. The fact that this court case originated in the racially hybrid city of New Orleans is only one of its many ironies. Louisiana historian John Blassingame wrote that before the turn of the twentieth century, "More people of both the 'black' and 'white' populations in New Orleans and Louisiana had ancestors in the other race than did residents of any other city or state in America."[1]

This mixed ancestry could lead to unfortunate consequences for people on both sides of the racial divide. "Whites often grew up afraid to know their own genealogies," writes Virginia R. Domînguez in her book *White By Definition*. "Many admit that as children they often stared at the skin below their fingernails and through a mirror at the white of their eyes to see if there was any 'touch of the tarbrush.'"[2] Louis Armstrong biographer Laurence Bergreen noted, "When racial differences were too close to call, particularly in the upper strata of New Orleans society, doctors were willing to alter birth certificates for a price."[3]

In 1917, as a seven-year-old child living in Vicksburg, Mississippi, Milt Hinton witnessed the aftermath of a lynching. The murdered man, whose skin reminded Hinton of burnt bacon, had been accused of making an untoward advance on a white woman. Hinton pointed out that despite these hysterical fears over miscegenation, "Every worthwhile white man in the South had some black woman that he was screwing on the side. He had children and raised them, had separate families. Nobody said a damn word about it."[4] Black concubinage and the one-drop rule were just two of the many manifestations of racial hypocrisy openly practiced in the United States.

Scientists tell us that racial variance is a relatively recent phenomenon in human evolution, and furthermore that classifying people according to a few fixed categories is meaningless and arbitrary. In determining differences between people, race is much more a historical and political factor than a biological one. But our racial history is a heavy burden.

The purpose of racial classification is generally to uphold power relationships or to benefit one group at the expense of another. Throughout most of American history, political power stood squarely on the side of whites and against people of color. After *Plessy*, any appeals to white ancestry on the part of African-Americans were considered irrelevant and simply ignored. Homer Plessy himself was light-skinned enough to pass for white, as his great-grandmother was his closest purely African-American relative. Though many blacks practiced a form of self-discrimination, prizing lightness of skin color, this intra-group prejudice had nowhere near the destructive power of legally mandated racial classifications.

In my opinion the majority of jazz writers impale themselves on the spiky contradictions of America's quirky racial views. They position themselves on the side of racial equality, yet end up adhering to strict notions of racial classification. This was true in the 1930s and it's true now. Many jazz books continue to divide and classify musicians according to race as if segregation were still the law of the land.

Once again, early New Orleans jazz history shows us the folly of observing simple racial classifications. Jelly Roll Morton always spoke proudly of his French ancestors, and Milt Hinton would refer to him as "half white." In fact, all New Orleans Creoles by definition have European ancestry. Drummer Paul Barbarin believed his great-grandfather had been a white Frenchman. Louis Keppard, Freddie's brother, said that their father had a French mother and looked so European that "he never had any trouble on the streets." As for mixed ancestry generally in New Orleans, Keppard noted, "It was all jubileed up."[5]

Bassist George "Pops" Foster said that his mother was a full-blooded Indian, and from the same tribe that "white" clarinetist Pee Wee Russell was descended from![6] For some inexplicable reason, many bass players in addition to Foster have had Native American bloodlines, including Jimmy Blanton, Oscar Pettiford, John Simmons, and Bob Cranshaw. Edmond Hall, who went on to play clarinet with Louis Armstrong's All Stars, thought that legendary cornetist Buddy Petit was "kinda mixed with Indian. It had to be, his complexion and his hair, he had hair kinda like a horse mane. I never see a guy with the hair with such coarse grain. So many mixtures here in New Orleans."[7]

Louisiana historian Jerah Johnson tells us: "Because most African slaves brought to Louisiana were males, great numbers married Indian women, whom the French colonials had early begun enslaving as food growers, cooks, bedfellows, and translators. Consequently, as the decades passed, there developed an unusually high degree of intermixing of the two groups and their cultures, an intermixing that, by the end of the nineteenth century, had resulted in the absorption of the local Indian populations into the New Orleans black community."[8]

As noted, Buddy Bolden, the supposedly prototypical "uptown black," had a light complexion and reddish hair. And anyone who has seen the only known photograph of Charlie Patton, a kind of Bolden-like figure in early blues, cannot fail to be intrigued and mystified by the dark face with the Caucasian features.[9] Yet out of this jumbled mélange, jazz historians are apt to draw hard and fast conclusions based upon one's supposed race.

Nowhere is the capriciousness of racial classification more evident than in the case of Latin Americans. People from Spain, Cuba, Saint-Domingue (now Haiti), and South America emigrated to New Orleans in successive waves beginning well before the founding of the United States. They contributed vast amounts of music to that city, some of which filtered into jazz and produced what Jelly Roll Morton referred to as the "Spanish tinge." Latin music would, like the blues, reassert itself time and time again in many guises throughout the history of jazz.

Several musicians with Hispanic names figure prominently in histories of early jazz. A short list would include the three clarinetists of the Tio family, Manuel Manetta, Manuel Perez, Jimmy Palao, Willie Santiago, Lawrence Marrero, Ray Lopez, Martin Abraham, and Alcide Nunez. Whatever the differences or commonalities of their cultural heritage, once in this country they were divided up according to the "one drop rule," which could have huge consequences in both their personal and professional lives. Ray Lopez was reckoned "white" while Manuel Perez was considered "colored," so they could never perform together in public.

In the U.S., the entire Latin American spectrum of nationalities and colors has been divided on the artificial basis of the "one drop rule" and thrust into two stark categories. "I came from a culture that doesn't have the same racial barriers as the United States," says the contemporary trumpeter Claudio Roditi, originally from Brazil. "Not to say that there isn't racism there, but Brazilian culture and Latin American cultures are much more integrated. So when I came here and saw such huge distinctions it's something that made me uncomfortable and it still makes me uncomfortable."[10]

The "one drop rule" itself has undergone a curious transformation: it was introduced by racist whites after emancipation and reinvigorated by African-Americans a hundred years later. What was once intended as a mark of shame has become instead a badge of honor. In the recent PBS special *African American Lives*, the host and producer Henry Louis Gates Jr., a Harvard black studies professor, is visibly disappointed when a DNA test confirms that as much as fifty percent of his genetic makeup is European.

"For today's black leaders, black solidarity remains a central organizing principle for the battles to come," writes Dinesh D'Souza in his book *The End of Racism*. "How can an African-American community so divided between a middle class and an underclass expect to preserve a cohesive political identity? Part of the answer comes as a surprise: the one-drop rule." D'Souza adds, "Liberal antiracism now sanctions state-sponsored discrimination and embraces the ideological premise of the one-drop rule."[11]

As Stephan and Abigail Thernstrom point out in their book *America in Black and White*:

> Ironically, the main guardians of the traditional and blatantly racist one-drop rule are the mainline civil rights organizations. They have much to lose by the institution of a multiracial category [in the U.S. census]. If the number of Americans who check 'black' drops off as a result, African-American claims to X number of executive jobs at Texaco and Y number of places at the University of Michigan Medical School will have to be modified . . . The stakes are very high, and the rhetoric is correspondingly ugly. The civil rights groups, in fact, are generally opposed to any and all moves (for example, trans-racial adoption) that blur racial lines and thus potentially diminish the black head count. And so they hold fast to a system of racial classifications that sharply distinguishes blacks from whites.
>
> Although almost every national black organization opposes any modification of our current system of racial classifications, 48 percent of African

Americans and 47 percent of whites believe that the census "should stop" collecting information on race and ethnicity.[12]

The balance of power has shifted so that now, in an age of racial redress, black skin can entitle its bearer to preferential treatment in many areas of education and employment. The liberal notion of equality has been supplanted by race-based initiatives that seek to tip the balance in favor of minorities who have been historically disadvantaged. Many argue that such remedies have not gone far enough, so now is not the time to complacently abandon racial classifications. For these activists the one-drop rule is viewed as a ticket to salvation, a shield against endemic racism.

Yet what would jazz history look like if we gave up this antiquated notion of discrete racial boundaries? If we choose, at least momentarily, to disassociate ourselves from the one-drop rule, then many rigid distinctions and assumptions begin to melt away. Let me revisit one famous example. Much has been made of the fact that the Original Dixieland Jazz Band, a white group, made the first jazz records, while the Original Creole Band, typically identified as "black," were offered the honors earlier but declined.

If we look at the racial makeup of the Creole band we find George Baquet, whose brother Achille passed for white and whose father was listed in the 1870 census as white.[13] As noted, Freddie Keppard's brother Louis said their father had a French mother and "looked white." Louis Armstrong described Bill Johnson, the band's leader and bassist, as follows: "He had the features and even the voice of a white boy—an ofay, or Southern, white boy at that."[14] The assumption has always been that the difference in race between these two bands produced starkly different music. But perhaps these supposed musical differences were as spectral as the supposed racial disparities between them. In the end, is it really any more or less meaningful to classify one group as basically French and the other as Italian (with a few other ethnicities thrown in)?

Many black leaders were extremely conscious of their white ancestry, which may well have fueled their lifelong outrage over discriminatory laws and treatment. Frederick Douglass's father was white. Historian Alan Pomerance wrote that Walter White, for many years executive secretary of the NAACP, "seemed totally Caucasian. He was blond, blue-eyed, with a mother one-sixteenth black and a father one-quarter black."[15] His appearance was so white that he was able to infiltrate meetings of the Ku Klux Klan.

W. E. B. Du Bois was descended from a Dr. James Du Bois, a wealthy physician of French Huguenot origins.[16] Adam Clayton Powell Jr.'s mother was a German woman whose maiden name was Schaefer. According to Isabel Powell, the congressman's wife for twelve years, "Adam used to say, 'I'm neither fish nor fowl.' He said when he grew up in Harlem the Irish boys would beat him up because he wouldn't admit being white, and the blacks would beat him because he wasn't black enough to be black."[17] Powell may have bonded with boyhood friend Fats Waller because Waller's maternal grandfather was an Irishman named Thomas Dunn.[18] Even that firebrand of black nationalism, Malcolm X, told of how his mother "looked like a white woman. Her father *was* white." Malcolm claimed that this man raped his grandmother, and says his mother was "glad that she had never seen him. It was, of course, because of him that I got my reddish-brown 'mariny' color of skin, and my hair of the same color."[19] The African-American writer Ishmael Reed once commented that if Alex Haley, author of *Roots*, had traced his father's lineage back instead of his mother's, he would have ended up in Ireland![20]

In today's jazz world, the saxophonist Joshua Redman is reckoned as African-American despite being raised by his white, Jewish mother. Altoist Jackie McLean may have had as many as seven white great-grandparents.[21] Similarly, Barack Obama and Academy Award winner Halle Berry had black fathers and white mothers, yet both are deemed black in American society.

Of course, we can't turn a blind eye to a tangled and dishonorable history that cast entire groups of people into a prison of racial divisions with no hope of escape. As Harlem Renaissance writer Claude McKay put it, "The Negro in America is not permitted for one minute to forget his color, his skin, his race."[22] Nor can we fail to recognize cultural differences that became magnified through a forced separation of the races (however much these cultural differences have been exaggerated and distorted in the jazz literature). Yet still I can't fail to observe how this imposing and sometimes all-consuming edifice of racial classification in the United States is built on the flimsiest and most fanciful of foundations. Thus it was at the beginning of the twentieth century, and so it is now.

As Henry Louis Gates Jr. said, "It's important to remember that 'race' is *only* a sociopolitical category, nothing more. At the same time—in terms of its practical performative force—that doesn't help me when I'm trying to get a taxi on the corner of 125th and Lenox Avenue."[23]

NOTES

1. Blassingame, *Black New Orleans*, 201.

2. Domînguez, *White By Definiton*, 159. Huey P. Long, the infamous governor of Louisiana, once remarked that all the pure whites in his home state could be fed from a single rice bowl.

3. Bergreen, *Louis Armstrong*, 180.

4. Taped interview with Milt Hinton, 1990.

5. Hogan Jazz Archive. Louis Keppard interview conducted August 4, 1957.

6. Hogan Jazz Archive. Pops Foster interview conducted April 21, 1957.

7. Hogan Jazz Archive. Edmond Hall interview conducted April 11, 1957.

8. Jerah Johnson, *Congo Square in New Orleans*, 11.

9. Interestingly enough, Samuel Charters said that Patton "sang for everybody in the delta, white and colored, and he had songs for every kind of audience. . . . He could almost be thought of as a songster, rather than a blues singer." According to his last wife, Bertha Lee, Patton developed bronchitis and died from overexerting himself at a winter dance for a white audience. "You have to work so much harder at a white dance in the South," she said. "They don't want to stop dancing." Charters, *The Bluesmen*, 38, 56.

10. Taped interview with Claudio Roditi, 2000.

11. D'Souza, *The End of Racism*, 204, 242.

12. Thernstrom and Thernstrom, *America in Black and White*, 422.

13. Gushee, *Pioneers of Jazz*, 38.

14. Armstrong, *Satchmo*, 238.

15. Pomerance, *Repeal of the Blues*, 72.

16. Du Bois, *The Autobiography of W. E. B. Du Bois*, 65.

17. Kisseloff, *You Must Remember This*, 296.

18. Kisseloff, 268.

19. Malcolm X, *The Autobiography of Malcolm X*, 2.

20. Schlesinger, *The Disuniting of America*, 90.

21. Feather, *The New Edition of the Encyclopedia of Jazz*, 84.

22. Robin D. G. Kelley, *Freedom Dreams*, 48.

23. Gates, *Loose Canons*, 37.

12

~~~~

Tomorrow Is the Question

"We may have come in separate ships but we're all in the same boat now."

—Martin Luther King Jr.

Jesse Jackson was appearing on the *Today* show, railing against the government's failure to send a high-level representative to the U.N. conference on racism in Durban, South Africa, when the first plane hit the World Trade Center. If the nineteen hijackers, who received so much goodwill in America as they went about their diabolical business, didn't spell the doom of political correctness, Sacha Baron Cohen's film *Borat* may just do the trick.

At the time of the attacks, Amiri Baraka (formerly known as LeRoi Jones) was the poet laureate of New Jersey, a title conferred by the New Jersey Council for the Humanities and the New Jersey State Council on the Arts. He tried to stir up old racial animosities by composing a poem perpetuating the conspiracy myth that Jewish workers were warned to stay home on 9/11. The poem provoked a chorus of criticism from blacks, including an op-ed piece in the *New York Post* by John McWhorter: "Visceral ejaculation does not make one a serious poet, regardless of race. . . . [Baraka] has spent a lifetime being lauded for mediocre work by whites with their hearts supposedly in the right place. The last thing young blacks need today is more of the message that idle rebellion is the essence of their race. . . . Elevating him to represent the soul of an American state was an insult to Gwendolyn Brooks, Langston Hughes and other serious black poets, and to black people in general."[1]

The invasions of Afghanistan and Iraq in the wake of the 9/11 attacks led many to openly question why the U.S. government was spending billions upon billions of dollars to defeat sectarian tribalism abroad while ethnic sectarianism was being widely promoted and encouraged at home. As the theologian Reinhold Niebuhr once observed, "The chief source of man's inhumanity to man seems to be the tribal limits of his sense of obligation to other men."

Within the jazz world, hopes that the Ken Burns television series would stimulate jazz record sales quickly faded. For a time the companion CDs sold reasonably well, but signs of imminent doom for the recording industry were everywhere. In every category sales were down, but in jazz—whose market share always hovered in the low single figures—business was particularly disheartening.[2] The Internet spelled the end of the vice-grip that major labels had on the distribution of music. The mega-chain retail outlet Tower Records suffered an agonized and prolonged death, filing for bankruptcy three times before finally shutting its doors in 2006.

The "young lions" were approaching middle age and had failed to leave a significant mark on the music. Reissue sales far outsold new releases. As jazz writer and producer Jeff Levenson noted, "They've gotten supplanted by dead people."[3] Jazz departments at major labels were hanging on by a thread or being summarily dismissed. Those that remained never seemed to attribute their troubles to having produced such bland and unadventurous recordings over the past twenty years. Blue Note was kept alive by the surprise success of singer Norah Jones, whose anodyne style can barely be considered jazz at all. Blue Note was careful not to label her a "jazz" singer, but the fact that she was signed to the premier jazz label was almost enough to vindicate Stanley Crouch and Albert Murray's narrow definition of jazz.

The Federal Telecommunications Act of 1996 deregulated radio and allowed media conglomerates such as Clear Channel Communications to buy up unlimited numbers of independent stations. Radio became more corporate and homogenous, with fewer outlets for new jazz releases. The limitless variety promised by satellite radio never materialized, as both XM and Sirius relegated jazz (not counting "smooth jazz" and its offshoots) to only one channel, characterized by a bland uniformity.

At the same time, the misfortunes of the major labels (now down to four after the giant merger between RCA/Bertelsmann and CBS/Sony) have proven to be a boon for independent jazz artists. Through the Internet, musicians have been able to distribute their own products and publicity for the first time in the history of the music. In this arena at least, they can compete on an equal footing with the giant conglomerates. The majors, at least for the time being, have largely abandoned making payoffs to clubs and festivals, promising to democratize that facet of the business as well.

And the success of trumpeter and composer Dave Douglas has shown that a hunger for new musical approaches is still alive and well in the jazz world.

Yet in many ways we are still left with the distorted and artificial environment the major labels created in the 1980s and 1990s. That is, the jazz stars they fabricated are still jazz stars today, in terms of press coverage and high-profile bookings. Almost no new stars have risen in the meantime. Will this situation go on indefinitely? Time will tell.

One depressing trend, at least for musicians, is the increased influence of critics. "The musicians aren't playing the music anymore, the critics are," lamented ex-Ellington saxophonist Harold Ashby.[4] There are no musical literacy standards for critics, and many are paid $40 or less for reviews in major jazz publications. Many seem to feel they are not getting paid enough to think, and their first impulse is to consign artists to predesignated stylistic boxes. Music that challenges them is usually too much work, and the musical clichés of old are much easier for them to digest. The vast majority of critics seem more interested in tracing influences than recognizing individual creativity, another reason for a paucity of new and authentic jazz stars today.

What is the current state of race relations in America? That depends on how you interpret what you see around you, what you read, and what you allow yourself to believe. Black studies professor Cornel West writes of a country still "chronically racist, sexist, and homophobic,"[5] and a "profoundly decadent American civilization at the end of the twentieth century . . . [a] twilight civilization—an American Empire adrift on a turbulent sea in a dark fog."[6] For conservative social critic Ann Coulter, however, "The gravest danger facing most black Americans today is the risk of being patronized to death."[7]

In 1999 *Newsweek* ran a cover story entitled "The Good News about Black America (and why many blacks aren't celebrating)." Author Ellis Cose outlined the many areas in which African-Americans had achieved unprecedented gains: employment and home ownership were up, the middle class was booming, incomes for comparable work were achieving parity with whites, test scores were improving, more blacks were attending college, fewer were on welfare, the percentage of blacks living below the poverty line was the lowest on record, murder and violent crime were way down, out-of-wedlock births were at their lowest rate in four decades, and even job opportunities were opening up for young, unskilled blacks.

However, Cose warns, "It would be a mistake to assume that today's good times have brought good tidings to all blacks. They have not. More black men than ever languish in prisons. Black academic achievement still lags behind that of whites. And suicides among young black men have risen sharply. . . . And fear is pervasive that an economic downturn—or the legal-political assault on affirmative action—would wipe out blacks' tenuous strengths."[8] Cose also notes that segregation still defines American living patterns, though of course every major city has its share of integrated neighborhoods.

According to statistics compiled by the U.S. Census Bureau, 24.2 percent of blacks were living below the poverty line in 2006, as compared to 10.3 percent of whites. Improving the economic and spiritual prospects of the black urban poor has defied efforts by local and federal politicians (meager as those efforts may have been) as well as black leaders. The tragic spectacle of Hurricane Katrina in New Orleans showed the ineptitude and indifference of governmental agencies in coming to the aid of this segment of American society. Sociologist William Julius Wilson believes that an entrenched underclass was formed in the 1970s when the black middle class largely abandoned urban ghettos. He argues that the social pathologies found in the ghetto result not from contemporary racism but from the residual effects of historical racism, as well as an economy largely unable to accommodate unskilled workers.[9]

On a more positive note, African-Americans seem increasingly comfortable with celebrating the full range of their past cultural achievements. Until the 1980s, whites had been virtually alone in keeping earlier jazz traditions alive. Wynton Marsalis's Lincoln Center Jazz Orchestra rightly deserves credit for being the first major effort by a younger generation of African-Americans to reclaim their musical heritage. Jazz at Lincoln Center programs have always attracted a certain number of black audience members. There is an even greater black presence at the large outdoor jazz festivals presented free to the public in Chicago and Detroit. As many successful African-American professionals reach retirement age, jazz cruises have become a highly popular leisure activity.

Yet in many ways, the African-American community still holds jazz at arm's length. In the place where I vote, a public school in Brooklyn with a majority black student population, there was a display of student drawings of "Great African-Americans." Of the twenty figures, some were known and unknown to me, but only one was a musician: the venerable Duke Ellington. I find this remarkable, since jazz and other musical genres are *the* preeminent contributions of African-Americans to world culture. When I step into a cab in Dublin, Osaka, Rio, or St. Petersburg, Russia, the music issuing from the car speakers is almost always of African-American origin.

I noticed a similar disregard for African-American music at Chicago's DuSable Museum of African American History. Housed in a magnificent structure are exhibits commemorating the glories of African kingdoms, the civil rights crusade, artists Augusta Savage and Henry O. Tanner, and Annie Malone, described as a "black beauty culture pioneer and mil-lionaire." But there was nothing about the glories of "The Stroll" on South 35th Street where one could hear King Oliver, Louis Armstrong, Earl Hines, and Jimmie Noone on any given night; nothing about the flourish-ing club and festival circuit in which I, as a young teenager, was able to hear Miles Davis, John Coltrane, Duke Ellington, Count Basie, Cannon-ball Adderley, Wes Montgomery, and so many others; nothing about the AACM or the entire Chicago avant-garde movement that shone brightly in the sixties and seventies and revived again in the nineties; nothing even on the legendary Chicago blues scene that continues to draw tourists from all over the world.

Even school textbooks reflect a bias against showing blacks as mu-sicians. In 1981, the major educational publisher Houghton Mifflin established guidelines calling for the "elimination of stereotypes." For approved multicultural literature, editors were told to avoid stories or essays that "depict African Americans as athletes, musicians, or entertain-ers."[10] Other publishers have adopted similar measures.

Musically and socially, America is undergoing a period of transition. It's too early to tell just where we're headed, but I remain guardedly opti-mistic. As a musician I travel across the U.S., and I see more and more Af-rican-Americans everywhere welcomed and treated with friendship and respect, enjoying the fruits of their labor. I see African-Americans flying all over the world, carrying out the nation's business. And I see a relax-ing of the stranglehold of racial consciousness. Notions of black cultural or intellectual inferiority seem to have gone the way of the divine right of kings as relics of a bygone, and much less enlightened, era.

How will jazz fare in this brave new world? For one thing I think there will be a tendency for artists and musicians to abandon big overpriced cities. New York may very well cease to be a home for the next genera-tion of jazz players. The more persistent ones may resort to a gypsy-like existence, traveling from one regional arts center to another. More and more it's up to individual artists to create their own careers from scratch. If they're lucky enough to build a strong fan base, they may go on to na-tional or international recognition. (This is essentially what Dave Douglas did; he also largely bypassed the traditional jazz scene and arose instead from within the much more color-blind "new music" community.)

The artist will have to develop a wide range of skills, and we'll see more of the creator as self-promoter, the musician as publicity-focused politi-cian. I can't help wondering how well Bird or Bix, not to mention Bach or Beethoven, would have succeeded in this type of environment. American art, like American politics, may end up mostly in the hands of those with independent means. At the same time, the Internet promises to further democratize art. One thing is certain: human beings will always create art, even in the most adverse circumstances. And sometimes the most adverse circumstances produce the best art.

The real question for the future of jazz is: will people accustomed to the kind of interactive recreation provided by the Internet be willing to sit still long enough to take in and appreciate the intricacies of jazz? Will jazz go the route of the epic novel or poem, cultural remnants of a slower-paced era that prized contemplative solitude? Today, most people experience music while multitasking: working, taking care of children, exercising, or driving. What does this portend for the future of a music that demands serious engagement? Are people today as equipped to internalize further developments as they once were?

For the future of the arts, I can only hope that racial debates take a backseat to aesthetic concerns; that common sense prevails over radical ideologies; that society can once again reach a consensus about standards that apply to both art and human conduct; that full equality can be granted to everyone regardless of race or gender; and that people stop mistrusting each other across the various social divides. One very encouraging development is the return of groups with racially mixed leadership, such as the Clayton-Hamilton Jazz Orchestra, or the duos of Russell Malone/Benny Green and Jay Leonhart/Wycliffe Gordon. Whether this becomes a trend remains to be seen, but I suspect it might.

What new role will jazz take within American society if its race-specific iconography should ever recede in the public mind? Will jazz again fulfill its potential to become a dominant art form of the twenty-first century, or will it wither away towards institutionalized marginality? Will it evolve into something else entirely? Could jazz, even more than in its heydey, become music qua music, free of ideology? That is my hope.

What can we conclude from our investigations into this meeting of dark and light folks within the sphere of American music? Clearly, racial interaction has been a huge and almost invariably positive factor in the creation and spread of jazz, and jazz has been a vital and positive influence on race relations in general. As I said at the outset, jazz unquestionably sprang from a black milieu but attained much of its richness and sophistication through a combination of musical traditions and attitudes contributed from a variety of sources. White influences were reinterpreted by African-Americans and vice versa in an ever-simmering musical stew. In the process, to paraphrase black social critic and author John McWhorter, blacks have gotten whiter and whites have become blacker, not just within the jazz world but throughout society as a whole. This view is not likely to please the politically correct, but it points the way to the hard-won racial harmony I believe we are on the threshold of achieving in this country. I strongly feel that an understanding of jazz unburdened by its most erroneous sociopolitical baggage can only result in greater empathy between the races. And that African-American artists, as well as jazz musicians in general, deserve to be restored to their rightful place: not in some isolated corner, but squarely within the framework of American culture.

NOTES

1. John H. McWhorter, "N.J.'s Insult to Blacks," *New York Post*, October 7, 2002.

2. I've long felt that official sales figures are not good indicators of general interest in jazz, because they don't include most independent labels, foreign labels, or bootlegs, not to mention the thriving business in second-hand jazz CDs, LPs, and even 78s.

3. Nicholson, *Is Jazz Dead?*, 15.

4. Taped interview with Harold Ashby, 2000.

5. D'Souza, *The End of Racism*, 247.

6. West, *Race Matters*, 56, 78.

7. Coulter, *Slander*, 1.

8. Ellis Cose, "The Good News about Black America (and why many blacks aren't celebrating)," *Newsweek*, June 7, 1999, 28–40.

9. See William Julius Wilson, *The Declining Significance of Race* and *The Truly Disadvantaged*.

10. Ravitch, *The Language Police*, 46.

Books and Interviews Cited

Albertson, Chris. *Bessie*. New York: Stein and Day, 1974.

Allen, Walter C. *Hendersonia: The Music of Fletcher Henderson and His Musicians*. Highland Park, NJ: Walter C. Allen Jazz Monographs, 1973.

Anderson, Jervis. *This Was Harlem: A Cultural Portrait, 1900–1950*. New York: Farrar, Straus and Giroux, 1982.

Appel, Alfred Jr. *Jazz Modernism: From Ellington and Armstrong to Matisse and Joyce*. New York: Alfred A. Knopf, 2002.

Armstrong, Louis. *Satchmo: My Life in New Orleans*. New York: Prentice-Hall, 1954.

Backus, Rob. *Fire Music: A Political History of Jazz*. Chicago: Vanguard Books, 1976.

Badger, Reid. *A Life in Ragtime: A Biography of James Reese Europe*. New York: Oxford University Press, 1995.

Barker, Danny. *Buddy Bolden and the Last Days of Storyville*. New York: Continuum, 2001.

———. *A Life in Jazz*. New York: Macmillan, 1986.

Barnet, Charlie, with Stanley Dance. *Those Swinging Years: The Autobiography of Charlie Barnet*. New York: Da Capo Press, 1992.

Basie, Count, with Albert Murray. *Good Morning Blues: The Autobiography of Count Basie*. New York: Da Capo Press, 2002.

Beckwith, Francis J., and Michael E. Bauman, eds. *Are You Politically Correct? Debating America's Cultural Standards*. Buffalo, NY: Prometheus Books, 1993.

Berger, Morroe, Edward Berger, and James Patrick. *Benny Carter: A Life in American Music*. Metuchen, NJ: Scarecrow Press, 1982.

Bergreen, Laurence. *Louis Armstrong: An Extravagant Life*. New York: Broadway Books, 1997.

Berrett, Joshua, ed. *The Louis Armstrong Companion*. New York: Schirmer Books, 1999.

Bigard, Barney, edited by Barry Martyn. *With Louis and the Duke*. London: Macmillan, 1985.

Blassingame, John W. *Black New Orleans, 1860–1880*. Chicago: University of Chicago Press, 2006.

Blassingame, John W., ed. *Frederick Douglass Papers: Volume 3, 1855–1863*. New Haven, CT: Yale University Press, 1985.

Blesh, Rudi. *Shining Trumpets: A History of Jazz*. New York: Alfed A. Knopf, 1946. Citations from later edition (New York: Da Capo Press, 1976).

Bradford, Perry. *Born with the Blues: Perry Bradford's Own Story*. New York: Oak Publications, 1965.

Brothers, Thomas, ed. *Louis Armstrong, in His Own Words: Selected Writings*. New York: Oxford University Press, 1999.

Brunn, H. O. *The Story of the Original Dixieland Jazz Band*. New York: Da Capo Press, 1977.

Bryant, Clora, et al., eds. *Central Avenue Sounds*. Berkeley, CA: University of California Press, 1998.

Bushell, Garvin, with Mark Tucker. *Jazz from the Beginning*. Ann Arbor, MI: University of Michigan Press, 1988.

Calloway, Cab, and Bryant Rollins. *Of Minnie the Moocher & Me*. New York: Thomas Y. Crowell, 1976.

Charters, Samuel B. *The Bluesmen*. New York: Oak Publications, 1967.

———. *Jazz New Orleans, 1885–1963*. New York: Oak Publications, 1963.

———. *The Roots of the Blues*. New York: Da Capo Press, 1981.

Charters, Samuel B., and Leonard Kunstadt. *Jazz: A History of the New York Scene*. New York: Da Capo Press, 1981.

Chernoff, John Miller. *African Rhythm and African Sensibility*. Chicago: The University of Chicago Press, 1979.

Chilton, John. *Ride Red Ride: The Life of Henry "Red" Allen*. London: Cassell, 1999.

———. *Roy Eldridge: Little Jazz Giant*. London: Continuum, 2002.

———. *Sidney Bechet: The Wizard of Jazz*. New York: Oxford University Press, 1987.

———. *Song of the Hawk: The Life and Recordings of Coleman Hawkins*. Ann Arbor, MI: The University of Michigan Press, 1990.

Clayton, Buck, and Nancy Miller Elliott. *Buck Clayton's Jazz World*. New York: Oxford University Press, 1986.

Cockrell, D. *Demons of Disorder: Early Blackface Minstrels and their World*. Cambridge, UK: Cambridge University Press, 1997.

Collette, Buddy, with Steven Isoardi. *Jazz Generations: A Life in American Music and Society*. London: Continuum, 2000.

Collins, Lee, with Mary Collins. *Oh, Didn't He Ramble: The Life Story of Lee Collins*. Urbana, IL: University of Illinois Press, 1989.

Cook, Richard. *Blue Note Records: The Biography*. Boston: Justin, Charles & Co., 2001.

Coulter, Ann. *Slander: Liberal Lies about the American Right*. New York: Crown Publishers, 2002.

Crouch, Stanley. *Always In Pursuit: Fresh American Perspectives, 1995–1997*. New York: Pantheon, 1998.

Cruse, Harold. *The Crisis of the Negro Intellectual*. New York: William Morrow, 1967.

Dahl, Linda. *Morning Glory: A Biography of Mary Lou Williams*. New York: Random House, 1999.

Dance, Stanley. *The World of Count Basie*. New York: Charles Scribner's Sons, 1980.

———. *The World of Duke Ellington*. New York: Da Capo Press, 1970.

———. *The World of Earl Hines*. New York: Charles Scribner's Sons, 1977.

———. *The World of Swing*. New York: Charles Scribner's Sons, 1974.

Davis, Miles, with Quincy Troupe. *Miles: The Autobiography*. New York: Simon and Schuster, 1989.

Denning, Michael. *The Cultural Front*. London: Verso, 1997.

DeVeaux, Scott. *The Birth of Bebop: A Social and Musical History*. Berkeley, CA: University of California Press, 1997.

Dodds, Warren "Baby," and Larry Gara. *The Baby Dodds Story*. Los Angeles, CA: Contemporary Press, 1959.

Dodge, Roger Pryor. *Hot Jazz and Jazz Dance*. New York: Oxford University Press, 1995.

Domînguez, Virginia R. *White By Definition: Social Classification in Creole Louisiana*. New Brunswick, NJ: Rutgers University Press, 1986.

Douglas, Ann. *Terrible Honesty: Mongrel Manhattan in the 1920s*. New York: Farrar, Straus and Giroux, 1995.

Driggs, Frank, and Chuck Haddix. *Kansas City Jazz: From Ragtime to Bebop—A History*. New York: Oxford University Press, 2005.

D'Souza, Dinesh. *The End of Racism*. New York: Free Press, 1995.

Du Bois, W. E. B. *The Autobiography of W. E. B. Du Bois*. New York: International Publishers, 1968.

DuPuis, Robert. *Bunny Berigan: Elusive Legend of Jazz*. Baton Rouge, LA: Louisiana State University Press, 1993.

Eberly, Philip K. *Music in the Air: America's Changing Tastes in Popular Music, 1920–1980*. New York: Hastings House, 1982.

Ellington, Duke. *Music Is My Mistress*. New York: Da Capo Press, 1973.

Ellington, Mercer, with Stanley Dance. *Duke Ellington in Person: An Intimate Memoir*. Boston: Houghton Mifflin, 1978.

Evans, Philip R., and Linda K. Evans. *Bix: The Leon Bix Beiderbecke Story*. Bakersfield, CA: Prelike Press, 1998.

Faulkner, Robert R. *Hollywood Studio Musicians: Their Work and Careers in the Recording Industry*. Chicago: Aldine-Atherton, 1971.

Feagin, Joe R., Hernán Vera, and Pinar Batur. *White Racism*. New York: Routledge, 2001.

Feather, Leonard. *The New Edition of the Encyclopedia of Jazz*. New York: Bonanza Books, 1960.

———. *The Passion for Jazz*. New York: Da Capo Press, 1980.

Ferguson, Otis, edited by Dorothy Chamberlain and Robert Wilson. *The Otis Ferguson Reader*. New York: Da Capo Press, 1997.

Firestone, Ross. *Swing, Swing, Swing: The Life & Times of Benny Goodman*. New York: W. W. Norton, 1993.

Floyd, Samuel A. Jr. *The Power of Black Music: Interpreting Its History from Africa to the United States*. New York: Oxford University Press, 1995.

Foster, George "Pops," and Tom Stoddard. *Pops Foster: The Autobiography of a New Orleans Jazzman*. Berkeley, CA: University of California Press, 1971.

Gammond, Peter. *Scott Joplin and the Ragtime Era*. London: Sphere Books, 1975.

Gates, Henry Louis Jr. *Loose Canons: Notes on the Culture Wars*. New York: Oxford University Press, 1992.

Gennari, John. *Blowin' Hot and Cool: Jazz and Its Critics*. Chicago: The University of Chicago Press, 2006.

Giddins, Gary. *Riding on a Blue Note*. New York: Oxford University Press, 1981.

———. *Rhythm-A-Ning*. New York: Oxford University Press, 1986.

Gillespie, Dizzy, and Al Fraser. *To Be or Not To Bop*. London: Quartet Books, 1982.

Gitler, Ira. *Jazz Masters of the Forties*. New York: Da Capo Press, 1983.

———. *Swing to Bop: An Oral History of the Transition in Jazz in the 1940s*. New York: Oxford University Press, 1985.

Gleason, Ralph J. *Celebrating the Duke*. Boston: Little Brown, 1975. Citations from later edition (New York: Da Capo Press, 1995).

Goffin, Robert. *Jazz: From the Congo to the Metropolitan*. Garden City, NY: Doubleday, Doran & Co., 1944.

Goodman, Benny, and Irving Kolodin. *The Kingdom of Swing*. New York: Frederick Ungar, 1961.

Gourse, Leslie. *Wynton Marsalis: Skain's Domain*. New York: Schirmer Books, 1999.

Groves, Alan, and Alyn Shipton. *The Glass Enclosure: The Life of Bud Powell*. London: Bayou Press, 1993. Citations from later edition (London: Continuum, 2001).

Gushee, Lawrence. *Pioneers of Jazz: The Story of the Creole Band*. New York: Oxford University Press, 2005.

Hadlock, Richard. *Jazz Masters of the 20s*. New York: Macmillan, 1972. Citations from later edition (New York: Da Capo Press, 1995).

Hajdu, David. *Lush Life: A Biography of Billy Strayhorn*. New York: North Point Press, 1996.

Hammond, John, with Irving Townsend. *John Hammond On Record*. New York: Ridge Press/Summit Books, 1977.

Hampton, Lionel, with James Haskins. *Hamp: An Autobiography*. New York: Warner Books, 1989.

Handy, W. C. *Father of the Blues: An Autobiography*. New York: Macmillan, 1941. Citations from later edition (New York: Da Capo Press, 1991).

Haskins, Jim. *The Cotton Club*. New York: Random House, 1977.

Hasse, John Edward. *Beyond Category: The Life and Genius of Duke Ellington*. New York: Simon and Schuster, 1993.

Hentoff, Nat. *The Jazz Life*. New York: Da Capo Press, 1961.

Hentoff, Nat, and Albert J. McCarthy, eds. *Jazz*. New York: Rinehart, 1959.

Herskovits, Melville J. *The Myth of the Negro Past*. New York: Harper & Brothers, 1941. Citations from later edition (Boston: Beacon Press, 1958).

Hicock, Larry. *Castles Made of Sound: The Story of Gil Evans*. New York: Da Capo Press, 2002.

Hilbert, Robert. *Pee Wee Russell: The Life of a Jazzman*. New York: Oxford University Press, 1993.

Hinton, Milt, and David G. Berger. *Bass Line: The Stories and Photographs of Milt Hinton*. Philadelphia: Temple University Press, 1988.

Hodes, Art, and Chadwick Hansen. *Hot Man: The Life of Art Hodes*. Urbana, IL: University of Illinois Press, 1992.

Hoffman, Franz. *The Henry "Red" Allen & J. C. Higginbotham Collection: A Bio-Disco-Documentation: Part 1a, 1906–1934*. Berlin: self-published, 2000.

——. *Jazz Advertised 1910-1967, Volume 7: Out of the New York Times*. Berlin: self-published, 1989.

——. *Jazz Advertised in the Negro Press, Vol. 4: The Chicago Defender 1910–1934*. Brilon, Germany: self-published, 1980.

Horricks, Raymond. *Count Basie and his Orchestra*. London: Victor Gollancz, 1958.

——. *The Importance of Being Eric Dolphy*. Tunbridge Wells, UK: D. J. Costello, 1989.

Hughes, Robert. *Culture of Complaint: The Fraying of America*. New York: Warner Books, 1994.

Jacoby, Tamar. *Someone Else's House: America's Unfinished Struggle for Integration*. New York: Free Press, 1998.

James, Burnett. *Coleman Hawkins*. Tunbridge Wells, UK: Spellmount, 1984.

Johnson, James Weldon. *The Autobiography of an Ex-Colored Man*. Boston: Sherman, French & Company, 1912. Citations from later edition (New York: Hill and Wang, 1960).

——. *Black Manhattan*. New York: Alfred A. Knopf, 1930. Citations from later edition (New York: Atheneum, 1977).

Johnson, Jerah. *Congo Square in New Orleans*. New Orleans, LA: Louisiana Landmarks Society, 1995.

Johnson, Paul. *Art: A New History*. New York: HarperCollins, 2003.

——. *A History of the American People*. New York: HarperCollins, 1997.

Jones, LeRoi. *Black Music*. New York: Quill, 1967. Citations from later edition (New York: William Morrow, 1971).

——. *Blues People: The Negro Experience in White America and the Music That Developed From It*. New York: William Morrow, 1963.

——. *Dutchman and the Slave*. New York: William Morrow, 1964.

——. *Home: Social Essays by LeRoi Jones*. New York: William Morrow, 1966.

Jones, Max. *Jazz Talking: Profiles, Interviews, and Other Riffs on Jazz Musicians*. London: Macmillan, 1987. Citations from later edition (New York: Da Capo Press, 2000).

Jones, Max, and John Chilton. *Louis: The Louis Armstrong Story 1900–1971*. London: Studio Vista, 1971.

Jost, Ekkehard. *Free Jazz*. New York: Da Capo Press, 1994.

Kahn, Ashley. *Kind of Blue: The Making of the Miles Davis Masterpiece*. New York: Da Capo Press, 2000.

Kaminsky, Max, with V. E. Hughes. *My Life in Jazz*. New York: Harper and Row, 1963.

Kelley, Norman, ed. *Rhythm and Business: The Political Economy of Black Music.* New York: Akashic Books, 2002.

Kelley, Robin D. G. *Freedom Dreams: The Black Radical Imagination.* Boston: Beacon Press, 2002.

Kenney, William Howland. *Chicago Jazz: A Cultural History, 1904–1930.* New York: Oxford University Press, 1993.

Kirk, Andy, as told to Amy Lee. *Twenty Years on Wheels.* Ann Arbor, MI: University of Michigan Press, 1989.

Kirkeby, Ed. *Ain't Misbehavin': The Story of Fats Waller.* New York: Dodd, Mead and Company, 1966. Citations from later edition (New York: Da Capo Press, 1975).

Kisseloff, Jeff. *You Must Remember This: An Oral History of Manhattan from the 1890s to World War II.* New York: Harcourt Brace Jovanovich, 1989.

Kmen, Henry. *Music in New Orleans: The Formative Years 1791–1841.* Baton Rouge, LA: Louisiana State University Press, 1966.

Kofsky, Frank. *Black Music, White Business.* New York: Pathfinder Press, 1998.

———. *Black Nationalism and the Revolution in Music.* New York: Pathfinder Press, 1970.

Kramer, Hilton. *The Twilight of the Intellectuals: Culture and Politics in the Era of the Cold War.* Chicago: Ivan R. Dee, 1999.

Lees, Gene. *Cats of Any Color: Jazz, Black and White.* New York: Oxford University Press, 1994.

———. *Leader of the Band: The Life of Woody Herman.* New York: Oxford University Press, 1995.

Lester, James. *Too Marvelous for Words: The Life and Genius of Art Tatum.* New York: Oxford University Press, 1994.

Levine, Lawrence W. *Black Culture and Black Consciousness: Afro-American Folk Thought from Slavery to Freedom.* New York: Oxford University Press, 1977.

Levinson, Peter J. *Tommy Dorsey: Livin' in a Great Big Way.* New York: Da Capo Press, 2005.

———. *Trumpet Blues: The Life of Harry James.* New York: Oxford University Press, 1999.

Lewis, David Levering. *When Harlem Was in Vogue.* New York: Oxford University Press, 1979.

———. *W. E. B. Du Bois, 1868–1919: Biography of a Race.* New York: Owl Books, 1994.

Lion, Jean Pierre. *Bix: The Definitive Biography of a Jazz Legend.* New York: Continuum, 2005.

Litweiler, John. *The Freedom Principle: Jazz After 1958.* New York: Quill, 1984.

———. *Ornette Coleman: A Harmolodic Life.* New York: William Morrow, 1992.

Lomax, Alan. *Mister Jelly Roll.* New York: Grosset and Dunlap, 1950.

Lyons, Len. *The Great Jazz Pianists.* New York: William Morrow, 1983. Citations from later edition (New York: Da Capo Press, 1989).

Magee, Jeffrey. *The Uncrowned King of Swing: Fletcher Henderson and Big Band Jazz.* New York: Oxford University Press, 2005.

Magro, Anthony. *Contemporary Cat: Terence Blanchard with Special Guests.* Lanham, MD: Scarecrow Press, 2002.

Malcomson, Scott L. *One Drop of Blood: The American Misadventure of Race*. New York: Farrar, Straus and Giroux, 2002.

Manone, Wingy, and Paul Vandervoort II. *Trumpet on the Wing*. New York: Doubleday, 1964.

Marks, Carole, and Diana Edkins. *The Power of Pride: Stylemakers and Rulebreakers of the Harlem Renaissance*. New York: Crown, 1999.

Marquis, Donald M. *In Search of Buddy Bolden*. New York: Da Capo Press, 1978.

McCarthy, Albert. *The Dance Band Era*. London: Spring Books, 1974.

Mezzrow, Milton "Mezz," and Bernard Wolfe. *Really the Blues*. New York: Random House, 1946.

Miller, Paul Eduard, ed. *Esquire's 1946 Jazz Book*. New York: A. S. Barnes, 1946.

Mingus, Charles. *Beneath the Underdog: His World as Composed by Mingus*. New York: Vintage Books, 1991. Originally published by Alfred A. Knopf, 1971.

Minstrel Songs: Old and New. Boston: Oliver Ditson, 1882. Editor unknown.

Monson, Ingrid, ed. *The African Diaspora: A Musical Perspective*. London: Routledge, 2003.

Morgenstern, Dan. *Living with Jazz*. New York: Pantheon, 2004.

Murray, Albert. *The Hero and the Blues*. Columbia, MO: University of Missouri Press, 1973. Citations from later edition (New York: Vintage, 1995).

———. *The Omni-Americans: Black Experience and American Culture*. New York: Da Capo Press, 1970.

———. *Stomping the Blues*. New York: Da Capo Press, 1978.

Newton, Francis (Eric Hobsbawm). *The Jazz Scene*. London: MacGibbon and Kee, 1959. Citations from later edition (London: Penguin, 1961).

Nicholson, Stuart. *Is Jazz Dead? (Or Has It Moved to A New Address)*. New York: Routledge, 2005.

———. *Reminiscing in Tempo: A Portrait of Duke Ellington*. Boston: Northeastern University Press, 1999.

Nisenson, Eric. *Blue: The Murder of Jazz*. New York: St. Martin's Press, 1997.

Oliver, Paul. *Savannah Syncopators: African Retentions in the Blues*. London: Studio Vista, 1970.

Osofsky, Gilbert. *Harlem: The Making of a Ghetto: Negro New York, 1890–1930*. New York: Harper & Row, 1963.

Panassié, Hugues. *The Real Jazz*. New York: Smith & Durell, 1943.

Panish, Jon. *The Color of Jazz*. Jackson, MS: University Press of Mississippi, 1997.

Pastras, Phil. *Dead Man Blues: Jelly Roll Morton Way Out West*. Berkeley: University of California Press, 2003.

Pearson, Nathan W., Jr. *Goin' to Kansas City*. Urbana, IL: University of Illinois Press, 1994.

Peress, Maurice. *Dvořák to Duke Ellington*. New York: Oxford University Press, 2004.

Peretti, Burton W. *The Creation of Jazz*. Chicago: University of Illinois Press, 1994.

Pettinger, Peter. *Bill Evans: How My Heart Sings*. New Haven, CT: Yale University Press, 1998.

Piazza, Tom. *Blues Up and Down: Jazz In Our Time*. New York: St. Martin's Press, 1997.

Podhoretz, Norman. *Breaking Ranks: A Political Memoir*. New York: Harper & Row, 1979.

Pomerance, Alan. *Repeal of the Blues: How Black Entertainers Influenced Civil Rights*. Secaucus, NJ: Citadel Press, 1988.

Porter, Eric. *What Is This Thing Called Jazz? African American Musicians as Artists, Critics, and Activists*. Berkeley, CA: University of California Press, 2002.

Porter, Lewis. *Jazz: A Century of Change*. New York: Schirmer Books, 1997.

———. *John Coltrane: His Life and Music*. Ann Arbor, MI: The University of Michigan Press, 1999.

Post, Robert, and Michael Rogin, eds. *Race and Representation: Affirmative Action*. New York: Zone Books, 1998.

Priestley, Brian. *Chasin' the Bird*. New York: Oxford University Press, 2006.

Raeburn, Bruce Boyd. "New Orleans Style: The Awakening of American Jazz Scholarship and its Cultural Implications." PhD diss., Tulane University, 1991.

Ramsey, Frederic, Jr., and Charles Edward Smith, eds. *Jazzmen*. New York: Harcourt Brace Jovanovich, 1939.

Ravitch, Diane. *The Language Police: How Pressure Groups Restrict What Students Learn*. New York: Knopf, 2003.

Reich, Howard, and William Gaines. *Jelly's Blues: The Life, Music, and Redemption of Jelly Roll Morton*. New York: Da Capo, 2003.

Reig, Teddy, with Edward Berger. *Reminiscing in Tempo: The Life and Times of a Jazz Hustler*. Metuchen, NJ: Scarecrow Press, 1990.

Reisner, Robert George. *Bird: The Legend of Charlie Parker*. New York: Bonanza Books, 1962.

Royal, Marshal, with Claire R. Gordon. *Marshal Royal: Jazz Survivor*. London: Cassell, 1996.

Russell, William, ed. *"Oh, Mister Jelly": A Jelly Roll Morton Scrapbook*. Copenhagen, Denmark: JazzMedia, 1999.

Rust, Brian. *Jazz Records 1897–1942*. Chigwell, Essex, UK: Storyville Publications, 1961.

Saks, Norman R., and Ken Vail. *The Norman R. Saks Collection: Charlie Parker & Jazz Club Memorabilia*. New York: Lincoln Center Library Editions, 2007.

Sanford, Herb. *Tommy and Jimmy: The Dorsey Years*. New York: Arlington House, 1972.

Sanjek, Russell, and David Sanjek. *American Popular Music Business in the 20th Century*. New York: Oxford University Press, 1991.

Sante, Luc. *Low Life: Lures and Snares of Old New York*. New York: Vintage, 1992.

Schiffman, Jack. *Harlem Heyday*. Buffalo, NY: Prometheus Books, 1984.

———. *Uptown: The Story of Harlem's Apollo Theater*. New York: Cowles, 1971.

Schlesinger, Arthur M., Jr. *The Disuniting of America: Reflections on a Multicultural Society*. New York: W. W. Norton, 1998.

Schuller, Gunther. *Early Jazz: Its Roots and Musical Development*. New York: Oxford University Press, 1968.

Scott, William B., and Peter M. Rutkoff. *New York Modern: The Arts and the City*. Baltimore, MD: The Johns Hopkins University Press, 1999.

Shapiro, Nat, and Nat Hentoff. *Hear Me Talkin' to Ya*. New York: Rinehart & Company, 1955.

Shaw, Arnold. *52nd St.: The Street of Jazz*. New York: Da Capo Press, 1977.

Sidran, Ben. *Black Talk*. Edinburgh, Scotland: Payback Press, 1971.

Simon, George T. *The Big Bands*. New York: Macmillan, 1967.

Singer, Barry. *Black and Blue: The Life and Lyrics of Andy Razaf*. New York: Schirmer Books, 1992.

Sleeper, Jim. *Liberal Racism: How Fixating on Race Subverts the American Dream*. New York: Penguin Books, 1997.

Smith, J. D., and Len Guttridge. *Jack Teagarden: The Story of a Jazz Maverick*. London: Cassell, 1960. Citations from later edition (New York: Da Capo Press, 1976).

Smith, Willie "The Lion," with George Hoefer. *Music on My Mind: The Memoirs of an American Pianist*. London: MacGibbon & Kee, 1965.

Southern, Eileen. *The Music of Black Americans: A History*. 3rd ed. New York: W. W. Norton, 1997.

Sowell, Thomas. *Black Rednecks and White Liberals*. San Francisco: Encounter Books, 2005.

Starr, S. Frederick. *Louis Moreau Gottschalk*. New York: Oxford University Press, 1995. Citations from later edition (Urbana, IL: University of Illinois Press, 2000).

———. *Red & Hot: The Fate of Jazz in the Soviet Union*. New York: Oxford University Press, 1983.

Stearns, Marshall W. *The Story of Jazz*. New York: Oxford University Press, 1956.

Stewart, Rex. *Jazz Masters of the 30s*. New York: Da Capo Press, 1972.

Stoddard, Tom. *Jazz on the Barbary Coast*. Berkeley, CA: Heyday Books, 1998.

Stowe, David W. *Swing Changes: Big Band Jazz in New Deal America*. Cambridge, MA: Harvard University Press, 1994.

Sudhalter, Richard M. *Lost Chords: White Musicians and Their Contribution to Jazz*. New York: Oxford University Press, 1999.

Sudhalter, Richard M., and Philip R. Evans. *Bix: Man & Legend*. New York: Arlington House, 1974.

Szwed, John F. *Space Is the Place: The Lives and Times of Sun Ra*. New York: Da Capo Press, 1998.

Taylor, Arthur. *Notes and Tones*. New York: Da Capo Press, 1993.

Taylor, Yuval, ed. *The Future of Jazz*. Chicago: A Cappella Books, 2002.

Thernstrom, Stephan, and Abigail Thernstrom. *America in Black and White: One Nation, Indivisible*. New York: Simon and Schuster, 1997.

Travis, Dempsey J. *An Autobiography of Black Jazz*. Chicago: Urban Research Institute, 1983.

Tucker, Mark. *Ellington: The Early Years*. Urbana, IL: University of Illinois Press, 1991.

Tucker, Mark, ed. *The Duke Ellington Reader*. New York: Oxford University Press, 1993.

Ulanov, Barry. *Duke Ellington*. New York: Creative Age Press, 1946.

Vaché, Warren W. Sr. *Crazy Fingers: Claude Hopkins' Life in Jazz*. Washington, DC: Smithsonian Institution Press, 1992.

Vail, Ken. *Duke's Diary, Part One: The Life of Duke Ellington 1927–1950*. Cambridge, UK: Vail Publishing, 1999.

Walser, Robert, ed. *Keeping Time: Readings in Jazz History*. New York: Oxford University Press, 1999.

Ward, Geoffrey C., and Ken Burns. *Jazz: A History of America's Music*. New York: Alfred A. Knopf, 2000.

Webster, Yehudi O. *The Racialization of America*. New York: St. Martin's Press, 1992.

Wein, George, with Nate Chinen. *Myself Among Others: A Life in Music*. New York: Da Capo Press, 2003.

West, Cornel. *Race Matters*. Boston: Beacon Press, 1993.

White, John. *Artie Shaw: His Life and Music*. New York: Continuum, 2006.

Williams, Martin. *The Jazz Tradition*. New York: Oxford University Press, 1970.

Wilmer, Valerie. *Jazz People*. Indianapolis, IN: Bobbs-Merrill Company, 1970.

Wilson, Teddy, with Arie Ligthart and Humphrey van Loo. *Teddy Wilson Talks Jazz*. London: Cassell, 1996.

Wilson, William Julius. *The Declining Significance of Race*. Chicago: The University of Chicago Press, 1978.

———. *The Truly Disadvantaged: The Inner City, the Underclass, and Public Policy*. Chicago: The University of Chicago Press, 1987.

Wolfenstein, Eugene Victor. *The Victims of Democracy: Malcolm X and the Black Revolution*. London: Free Association Books, 1989.

Wright, Laurie. *"King" Oliver*. Chigwell, Essex, UK: Storyville Publications, 1987.

X, Malcolm, with Alex Haley. *The Autobiography of Malcolm X*. New York: Grove Press, 1966.

Yetnikoff, Walter, with David Ritz. *Howling at the Moon: The Odyssey of a Monstrous Music Mogul in an Age of Excess*. New York: Broadway Books, 2004.

Taped interviews conducted by the author:

Richard B. Allen, Harold Ashby, George Avakian, Johnny Blowers, Conte Candoli, Doc Cheatham, Buck Clayton, Dave Douglas, Art Farmer, John Gill, Chris Griffin, Bob Haggart, Milt Hinton, Plas Johnson, Dick Katz, Orange Kellin, Jay McShann, Marty Napoleon, Flip Phillips, Bucky Pizzarelli, Dean Pratt, Claudio Roditi, Phil Schaap, Ed Shaughnessy, Arvell Shaw, Don Sickler, Clark Terry, and Joe Wilder.

Interviews from the Hogan Jazz Archive at Tulane University:

Danny Barker, Peter Bocage, George Brunies, Emile Christian, Johnny DeDroit, Lawrence Duhé, Edmond Hall, Monk Hazel, Louis Keppard, Jack Laine, Johnny Lala, Ray Lopez, Manuel Manetta, Joe Mares, Kid Ory, Roy Palmer, Tony Sbarbaro, and Alice Zeno.

Index

108–9, 111–15, 124, 157–58, 159–60, 172–73, 175, 179, 180–81, 189–90, 195, 228–30, 245; in the 1970s, 5, 30–31, 33, 63, 66–67, 93, 109–10, 122, 151, 160, 169, 173, 174–75, 177, 179, 244; in the 1980s, ix, 5, 6, 11, 28, 33, 110, 117, 123, 126, 131–35, 160–61, 162, 169, 173, 195, 215–16, 229, 243, 244; in the 1990s, 5, 28, 98, 123–29, 132–36, 161–63, 173–74, 195, 242, 243–45; and academia, 1, 6, 30, 34, 66–67, 69n55, 93, 114–16, 125; African music and culture, relation to, 4, 26, 30, 39–48, 57–58, 62, 63, 71, 87, 99, 104n73, 124, 233; agents and managers, 8, 15, 20, 131–32, 181–97, 210, 224, 228; as art music, 108; audience for, 3, 4, 7–8, 66, 76, 95–97, 136, 139–63, 173, 197, 239n9, 244–45; avant-garde jazz, 9, 29–30, 33, 63–67, 109, 160, 172–73, 245; bebop, 4, 9, 22, 23, 24, 37n62, 57–62, 63, 88–89, 157, 158, 212–13; black-and-tans, 9–10, 144, 146–48, 151–52, 154, 222, 223; and black theater, 76, 77, 92, 95, 144–45, 150–51; the business side of, 3, 5, 8, 15, 19–20, 37n62, 96, 98, 127, 131–34, 140–44, 159–60, 167–97, 201–16, 219–30, 242, 247n2; and classical music, 18, 40, 41, 87–93, 134, 175; cool jazz, 9, 109; and copyrights, 201–16; creative stagnation in, 5, 6, 125–27, 131–34, 242–43; as entertainment, 95, 107–8, 109; as folk music, 3, 17, 18, 60, 203–4; fusion, 9, 109–10; the future of, 245–46; hard bop, 9, 109; income of jazz musicians, 49, 154–57, 170–72, 178, 190, 219–30, 245; and the Internet, 174, 242, 245, 246; and Jews, 189, 196–97; metatonal music, ix, 10; and middle-class morality, 93–97; and musical theater, 144–45; and musicians unions, 8, 50, 82, 152, 175, 177, 191, 219, 227, 228; origins of, 2–3, 18, 25–26, 41–44, 54, 128, 141; and the Popular Front,

15–17; and radio, 15, 59, 135, 153, 154–55, 174, 175, 176, 178, 180, 187, 188, 190, 203, 223, 225, 227, 242; and record companies, 5, 8, 16, 18, 19, 20, 80, 92, 96, 97, 107, 109, 110, 122, 123, 131–34, 153, 154, 157, 159–60, 161, 167–74, 181, 182–83, 184, 196, 202, 205, 206, 211–12, 214, 220–21, 228, 242–43, 247n2; and rhythm and blues, 157, 160, 177, 198n27; and rock music, 71, 97, 109, 158, 172, 203, 215; and studio work, 3, 18, 122, 160, 174–81, 198n27; "swing era," 25, 108, 153–56, 176, 202, 208–9, 226–27; as a tool to promote social change, 2–6, 15–35, 118–19; West Coast jazz, 26–27; "young lions," 5, 110, 130–33, 173, 242. *See also* blues; brass bands; Chicago; gospel; Kansas City; New Orleans; New York; race; ragtime; spirituals

Jazz at Lincoln Center. *See* New York
Jefferson, Blind Lemon, 31
Jeffries, James, 169
Jenkins, Freddie, 186
John, Dr., 196
Johnson, Arnold, 207
Johnson, Bill, 237
Johnson, Billy, 144, 145
Johnson, Bunk, 23, 31, 54, 80, 81, 85, 86, 108
Johnson, George W., 169
Johnson, Gus, 226–27
Johnson, J.J., 109, 178
Johnson, Jack, 169
Johnson, James P., 87, 91, 100, 145
Johnson, James Weldon, 76, 80, 140–41, 145, 149, 203, 220
Johnson, Jerah, 46, 51–52, 54, 235
Johnson, Lonnie, 101
Johnson, Lyndon, 112, 115
Johnson, Paul, 126, 134–35
Johnson, Plas, 177–78, 181
Johnson, Rich, 128
Johnson, Robert, 31
Johnson, Tillie, 56
Jolson, Al, 144

About the Author

Randall Sandke has been a working professional jazz musician for the past thirty years, performing extensively throughout the United States, Europe, and Japan. He has recorded over thirty albums as a leader, many featuring his own compositions. Throughout the 1990s he was a frequent arranger and guest conductor for the Carnegie Hall Jazz Orchestra. Mr. Sandke is the author of *Harmony for a New Millennium: An Introduction to Metatonal Music* (Second Floor Music, 2001), outlining a new approach to composition and improvisation based on the use of non-tonal chords. He has also contributed articles and reviews to *The Oxford Companion to Jazz* and the *Annual Review of Jazz Studies*.

Breinigsville, PA USA
12 April 2011
259644BV00002B/2/P